CRCT TEST PREP

8TH GRADE GEORGIA STUDIES
Teaching the Georgia Performance Standards

Glen Blankenship, Ph.D.
Vicki Wood

Clairmont Press
Atlanta, Georgia

AUTHORS

Dr. Glen Blankenship, Ph.D., Senior Development Consultant, is the Associate Director and Chief Program Officer at the Georgia Council on Economic Education in Atlanta, Georgia. He taught 8th grade Georgia Studies at Renfroe Middle School in Decatur, Georgia. Dr. Blankenship is a frequent presenter at state, regional, and national conferences and consults with school districts across the nation to develop curriculum and improve student learning. He is also a past president of the Georgia Council for the Social Studies and currently serves as the GCSS Historian. Dr. Blankenship earned his B.A. and M.Ed. in Political Science from Georgia State University, and a Ph.D. in Educational Leadership from Emory University.

Vicki Wood earned a B.A. degree in Social Studies and an M.A. degree in history from Marshall University. She has completed post-graduate work in history, curriculum, and administration. She is the author of two United States history textbooks and a West Virginia history textbook and has published numerous articles and teaching materials. She has conducted teacher workshops on integrated strategies, thinking skills, and GEMS. She is a retired curriculum specialist from Kanawha County Schools, West Virginia.

Editor: Kathy Conway
Design: Cherry Bishop
Design Cover: New Diameter Creative Services, Inc.
Maps: Spatial Graphics

ISBN: 978-1-56733-097-7

Printed in the U.S.A.
Second Printing

CONTENTS

TO THE STUDENT

You are beginning a study of the story of our home . . . the State of Georgia. Since the founding of the original colony of Savannah, Georgia has grown into one of the largest states in our nation both in geographic size and number of citizens. This year you will learn about the important people, places and events that shaped our state as we know it today.

This workbook will guide you and help you focus on the most important parts of our state's geography, history, government, and economy. You will be given specific information about the information that will be tested on the Georgia CRCT next spring. The CRCT helps you, your teacher, and our state leaders know that you learned the information that will help our state continue to grow and prosper in the future.

So get ready to learn about our state! You will be given short readings to show you what is important. Then you will be given some multiple choice questions to answer about that reading so that you can check your learning.

If you complete the workbook and take the practice tests, you should have a very good score on the CRCT next spring.

Good luck!

INTRODUCTION

All of us want to do well on tests. This book will teach you some techniques to better prepare for tests. After you learn these techniques, you will have the opportunity to practice them as you get ready for the Georgia CRCT.

To become a better test taker, you need to

- Become familiar with the content of the test,
- Become familiar with the format of the test questions,
- Determine if the test is timed, and
- Know if there is a penalty for wrong answers.

CONTENT

Tests are given to find out what you know. To be successful on any test, it is necessary you know what will be tested. Suggestions for preparing for the content of the test include:

- Predict what questions will be asked. Look over your notes or assignments or talk with classmates. Think about the information that the teacher emphasized or wrote on the chalkboard or overhead projector. The questions, people, concepts, and so on that are covered in class assignments generally are the things that are tested. Make a list of the important facts and concepts that might be tested.

- Take notes carefully if there is a test review. Note any comments by your teacher such as "This will be on the test," "These are the important people you should know," or "Remember these two points."

- Complete any test review sheet that the teacher might provide. You can use the review sheet as a practice test, or you can make a practice test using the review sheet as a guide.

- Devise methods to study for the test. For example,

  - Make a set of flashcards. Do this by writing a name, date, event, place, vocabulary word, or question on one side of the card. On the other side, write the answer or some information to describe what is listed on the front side of the card.

  - Make an outline of the information. Include major headings, people, events, dates, and so on.

  - Use memory strategies such as mnemonics or graphic organizers (such as concept diagrams, cause and effect charts, Venn diagrams, maps, or timelines) to organize information.

  - Recite the information. Some students are auditory learners and hearing the content helps them to remember.

  - Find a study buddy. Study with a friend or group of friends. Make practice tests for each other or orally ask one another questions.

PACING

It is important to know if a test is timed. Two considerations associated with timed tests are (1) using the allotted time effectively and (2) avoiding text anxiety. There are a number of strategies to help you budget time and, as a result, lessen your anxiety and increase your performance.

One of the biggest problems with timed tests is using the allotted time efficiently. Some students move numerically — from the first question to the last question — on a test. However, the progression of questions often does not move from easy questions at the beginning of the test to more difficult ones at the end. Rather, the degree of difficulty of questions may be random. When you encounter a difficult question, you may spend too much time trying to determine the answer. As a result, the allocated time for the test may elapse before you have completed all the questions.

Through ongoing testing, you can learn to answer the easier questions first. You should skip the harder ones and go back to them at the end of your time. When beginning a test, it is wise to look at the number of items on the test and then figure out how much time you have to answer each one. Following this model ensures that you will answer all the questions you believe you know before time runs out. Try to increase the total number of questions you can complete in a given amount of time.

If the test is not timed, you should work carefully and deliberately. Do not spend an inordinate amount of time on difficult questions, but rather return to those questions later. Do not make random guesses, unless there is no penalty for wrong answers. If there is no penalty, then try to answer all the questions, even if you have not read all of them. When there is a penalty for a wrong answer, answer those questions you know as well as those you can narrow down to two choices. If you have no idea of the answer, do not attempt to answer the question. Later you will learn methods to help you eliminate obviously wrong answers.

Many students have test anxiety, which can increase when the test is timed. The more experience you have with taking tests, the more the anxiety level will decrease. As you feel more comfortable with the content, pacing, and format, you will feel less anxious about the unknown.

COMPLETING ANSWER SHEETS

Many tests require students to bubble in an answer sheet to record their responses. Sometimes, however, students do not clearly understand how to do this simple mechanical process. This lack of understanding can have a bearing on test performance.

Bubbling in an answer sheet requires students to darken a space for their selected response. Many students believe they must fill in the entire space, making it as dark as possible. They spend lots of time, sometimes too much time, darkening in these spaces. In reality, the entire space does not need to be darkened, and it also does not need to be as dark as students sometimes make it.

Ask your teacher for a sample bubble answer sheet and practice filling it in. You may also want to time yourself to see how long it takes to bubble in the answers to a set number of questions. Practice will help you increase the number of bubbles you can darken in a given amount of time.

Another problem with completing answer sheets is that sometimes students skip a question, but they do not skip the corresponding space for its answer. When this happens, the answers to questions are coded incorrectly. Through practice, you can overcome this problem as well. In practice sessions, your teacher may ask you to complete every third or fourth question so you become familiar with skipping answer spaces as well as questions. When you have completed the test, you can go back and check to be sure your answers correctly align with the questions.

You may also want to check the alignment often instead of waiting until you have finished the test. If you only check your answers at the end of the test, you may not have time to make changes, especially if the misalignment began near the beginning.

FORMAT

The test questions on the Georgia CRCT Test are in multiple choice format. Questions that have a multiple choice format are also referred to as selected response questions. These questions, the most common format found on standardized tests, provide a set of choices — one of which is the correct answer. CRCT multiple choice questions contain a phrase or stem followed by 4 choices (selections). Multiple choice formats will ask a student to either answer a question or complete a statement.

When answering multiple choice questions, consider the following suggestions:

- Read the question before looking at the answers.
- If you have an answer, check to see if it is one of the choices. If it is, mark the answer sheet and go on to the next question. If your answer is not one of the choices, discard it and look carefully at the selected responses from which you can choose. Put a mark through choices that are clearly incorrect.
- Identity key words in the stem and selected responses. Check the relationship of the words.

- Locate the verb in the stem. Determine what the verb is asking you to do.
- Note words like *always*, *none*, and *never*. If a choice includes one of these words, it is probably not the correct answer.
- Note words like *often*, *frequently*, and *usually*. If a choice includes one of these words, it is likely to be the correct selection.
- Examine each answer to see how precisely it is written. A precise answer is often the correct one.
- Don't second guess yourself. Generally, your first choice is best.
- Note the use of "All of the above" as a selection. If you know that at least two of the choices are correct, then "All of the above" is probably the correct choice.
- Watch for negative words in the stem. Negative words generally ask you to choose an answer that is not true. When examining a question that contains a negative word, try to find three answers that are correct. This process helps you to narrow down your choices.
- Note similar choices. If two choices are similar, one of them is probably the correct answer. However, if there are two choices that essentially mean the same thing, neither answer is likely to be the correct choice.
- Note selected responses that are complete opposites. Generally, one of the responses is the correct answer.
- Note complex questions. If a question has complex choices, mark each item true or false. This will help you narrow your choices before deciding on the correct answer.

Use the following graphic organizer to analyze a selected response (multiple choice) question. Remember, you should read the sample question and, without looking at the selected responses, answer the question. Check to see if your answer if one of the choices. If it is one of the choices, you would normally mark the answer and move on to the next. For this practice, assume that your answer is not one of the choices. Refer to the list of clues to help you complete the analysis.

| Read the stem or question. |
| The first Europeans to settle in what is now the United States were the |
| A.   French. |
| B.   English. |
| C.   Germans. |
| D.   Chinese. |
| **Identify key words.** |
| **Locate the verb.** |
| **Decide what action the verb requires.** |
| **Eliminate any choices you know are incorrect.** |
| **List the remaining choices.** |
| **Make your choice.** |
| **Why did you choose that option?** |

INTRODUCTION

Because multiple choice is the most common test format, especially on standardized tests, it is important to examine a variety of types of questions that test social studies content. Sometimes, before answering questions, you will need to

- Read a long or short passage,
- Analyze a political cartoon,
- Use a variety of maps, or
- Interpret data on a graph, table, or chart.

To help you analyze these types of questions, examine the test-taking tips that follow.

Reading a Long Passage

When you are reading a long passage,

- Look at the selected responses (choices) before you read the passage. Knowing what the possible answers are will direct your thinking while you read.
- Read the paragraph and note any key words. Some of the key words might also be found in the selected responses.
- Use the skills you learned for examining multiple choice (selected response) questions.

Read the following paragraph and answer the questions that follow.

By the end of 1863, with the South divided and the purpose of the Civil War reaffirmed, the Union was ready to begin its final assault. President Abraham Lincoln changed commanders one last time, putting Ulysses Grant in charge of Union forces on March 9, 1864. Although Grant was considered rather brutal, Lincoln was convinced he was a man who would not shy away from Confederate leader Robert E. Lee. Lincoln needed a leader who would continue to pursue the enemy, not attack and stop or withdraw as his predecessors had done. Grant brought a new type of war to the East. He was not as cautious as his predecessors had been. His strategy was simply to wear the enemy down with repeated attacks. He was not concerned about the number of lives that were lost; his philosophy was to replace fallen men with new recruits. Although this attitude was perceived by some as inhumane and uncaring, Grant believed in the long run it would save lives by bringing the war to an end instead of having it drag on for another year or longer.

1. **The man put in charge of the Union troops in 1864 was**
   A. Ulysses Grant.
   B. Robert E. Lee.
   C. Abraham Lincoln.
   D. William Sherman.

2. **Ulysses Grant's military strategy was to**
   A. divide the South.
   B. be cautious when fighting the enemy.
   C. attack and retreat to regroup and attack again.
   D. continue fighting no matter how many men were killed.

3. **The paragraph implies that**
   A. Grant was a great general.
   B. Lincoln was a friend of Grant.
   C. Union forces had been commanded by several people.
   D. Grant's style of fighting was similar to other northern generals.

Analyzing a Political Cartoon

When you are analyzing a political cartoon,

- Look at any titles or captions. This will help you identify what the cartoon is about.
- Identify people, places, or events that are shown. Knowing who or what is depicted in the cartoon will help you to place it in a historical or political setting.
- Examine the date when the cartoon was published. Knowing this will help you to know if the cartoon was published at the time an event was taking place or at a different period of time.
- Determine the point of view of the cartoonist. Note the size and mannerisms of the figures as well as their interaction with one another. Note the use of exaggeration or facial expression to convey a point.

Look at the cartoon below and answer the three questions that follow.

A Job for the New Cabinetmaker

This cartoon appeared in Frank Leslie's Illustrated Newspaper, February 2, 1861.

1. What is Lincoln doing in the cartoon?

   A. He is demonstrating his building skills.

   B. He is giving the North power over the South.

   C. He is repairing a crack between the North and the South.

   D. He is building a wall to separate the North and the South.

2. The title of the cartoon suggests that is was published

    A. on Lincoln's birthday.

    B. during Lincoln's election campaign.

    C. before the Lincoln-Douglas debates.

    D. after Lincoln's election to the presidency.

3. What is the point of view of the cartoonist?

    A. He shows a problem that Lincoln must fix.

    B. He shows that glue can be used to repair a crack.

    C. He shows Lincoln's skills as a construction worker.

    D. He shows Lincoln allowing the North and the South to separate.

Using a Map

A map provides information in a graphic way. Types of maps include topographic, political, raised relief, weather, and natural resource. When reading information on a map,

- Read its title to determine the subject and purpose,
- Look to see if it has a scale to help you find distances between two or more points,
- Examine its key or legend to see what symbols are used and what each represents, and
- Look at any other information that is included.

Use the map below to answer the three questions that follow.

2000 Election Results

1. How many states did Al Gore carry in the 2000 election?

    A. 15

    B. 18

    C. 20

    D. 22

2. **How many states did George Bush carry in the 2000 election?**
   A. 25
   B. 27
   C. 30
   D. 32

3. **Which of the following is an accurate statement about the data represented on this map?**
   A. Al Gore carried the largest states.
   B. George Bush carried all of the southern states.
   C. The person who carried the largest number of states won a large majority of the electoral vote.
   D. Both candidates carried states in the four regions (North, South, East, and West) of the United States.

Interpreting a Graph

There are many types of graphs, including line, bar, and circle. Different types of graphs are used to illustrate different types of data. For example, a *line graph* is most often used to show how something has changed over a period of time. A *bar graph* often is used to make comparisons. A circle graph is used to illustrate parts of something to the whole. A *circle graph*, which usually contains percentages, is also called a *pie graph* since the parts illustrated might symbolically represent pieces of a pie. The whole circle represents 100 percent.

When you are answering questions about graphs, you should
- Read the title to determine its content,
- Examine the key to see what specific things are included, and
- Look at the specific parts; that is, the pieces of the pie.

Look at the following line graph and answer the three questions that follow.

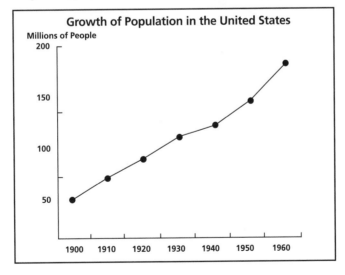

1. **In 1905, the population of the United States was about**
   A. 60 million.
   B. 80 million.
   C. 84 million.
   D. 86 million.

2. In what year were there approximately 100 million people in the United States?
   A. 1905
   B. 1925
   C. 1945
   D. 1965

3. The smallest growth in population occurred between
   A. 1900 and 1910.
   B. 1910 and 1920.
   C. 1920 and 1930.
   D. 1930 and 1940.

Look at the bar graph below and answer the three questions that follow.

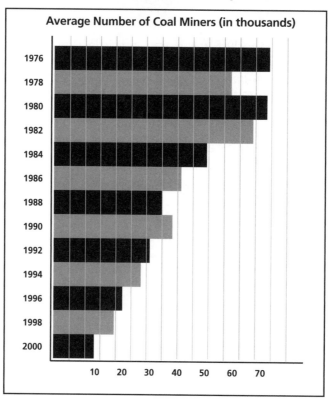

Average Number of Coal Miners (in thousands)

1. Which year had the highest number of miners?
   A. 1976
   B. 1978
   C. 1980
   D. 1982

2. Which statement best describes employment in the coal mines between 1976 and 1980?
   A. The number of miners increased steadily.
   B. The number of miners decreased steadily.
   C. The number of miners remained about the same.
   D. The number of miners dropped off and then increased.

3. Which statement best describes employment in the coal mines between 1976 and 2000?

A. The number of miners peaked in 1982.

B. The number of miners mostly increased.

C. The number of miners decreased every year.

D. The number of miners decreased by around 55,000.

Look at the circle graph below and answer the four questions that follow.

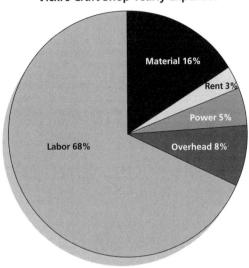

Vicki's Craft Shop Yearly Expenses

Material 16%

Rent 3%

Power 5%

Overhead 8%

Labor 68%

1. The second largest expense for Vicki's Craft Shop was for

A. rent.

B. power.

C. material.

D. overhead.

2. Vicki spends the same amount on Rent and Power as she spends on

A. labor.

B. materials.

C. expenses.

D. overhead.

3. Vicki's largest expense goes to

A. paying workers.

B. purchasing supplies.

C. paying the land owner.

D. powering her craft shop.

4. What percentage of Vicki's expenses are NOT labor?

A. 25 percent

B. 32 percent

C. 38 percent

D. 42 percent

Reading a Chart or Table

A chart or table is a good way to place text into a visual format. Charts are used to categorize data so it is easy to read and understand. Information that would take many pages to put in a text format can be summarized on a chart that may be one page or less.

When you are examining a chart or table, you should

- Read the title to determine what the subject is,
- Read the column headings and labels,
- Draw conclusions from the data, and
- Try to identify trends.

Look at the chart below and answer the three questions that follow.

George W. Bush		Al Gore	
State Carried	**Electoral Vote**	**State Carried**	**Electoral Vote**
Alaska	3	California	54
Alabama	9	Connecticut	8
Arkansas	6	District of Columbia	2
Arizona	8	Delaware	3
Colorado	8	Hawaii	4
Florida	25	Iowa	7
Georgia	13	Illinois	22
Idaho	4	Massachusetts	12
Indiana	12	Maryland	10
Kansas	6	Maine	4
Kentucky	8	Michigan	18
Louisiana	9	Minnesota	10
Missouri	11	New Jersey	15
Mississippi	7	New Mexico	5
Montana	3	New York	33
North Carolina	14	Oregon	7
North Dakota	3	Pennsylvania	23
Nebraska	5	Rhode Island	4
New Hampshire	4	Vermont	3
Nevada	4	Washington	11
Ohio	21	Wisconsin	11
Oklahoma	8		
South Carolina	8		
South Dakota	3		
Tennessee	11		
Texas	32		
Utah	5		
Virginia	13		
West Virginia	5		
Wyoming	3		
Total	**271**	**Total**	**266**

1. **Which state has the largest number of electoral votes?**
   A. Texas
   B. Florida
   C. California
   D. New York

2. **How many states, plus the District of Columbia, have fewer than five electors?**
   A. 10
   B. 14
   C. 18
   D. 22

3. **Which statement best explains why George Bush carried 10 more states than Al Gore, but only received 5 more electoral votes?**
   A. Bush carried only small states.
   B. Gore carried all the large states.
   C. Bush carried a large number of small states.
   D. More people voted in the states that Bush carried.

Content

In addition to all the specific test-taking strategies that you have learned, the following are general suggestions to help you feel confident and ready when time for the test comes.

The Night Before the Test:

- Review major concepts/objectives.
- Take a break from studying if you get tired.
- Get a good night's sleep

The Day of the Test:

- Get up early enough to exercise lightly.
- Eat a good, healthy breakfast (avoid sugar and caffeine).
- Wear comfortable clothing to school.
- Arrive at school on time.
- Take any needed materials to the testing site, such as pencils, scrap paper, and a calculator.
- Choose a seat that is free from distractions, for example, in the front of the room or away from the door.
- Take deep breaths if you feel yourself tensing up.
- Listen carefully to any directions. Then, before starting the test, quickly re-read the directions to check for understanding.
- Quickly preview the whole test. Devise a plan to budget your time if the test is timed.
- Be serious. Don't think that any test is unimportant.
- Apply test-taking clues when answering the questions.
- Don't second guess yourself; your first thought is generally best.
- Keep a positive and confident attitude.
- Check your answer sheet periodically to be sure the questions and your answers align properly.
- Reward yourself after the test for a job well done!

PREPARING FOR THE GEORGIA CRCT TEST

HISTORICAL UNDERSTANDINGS

> **SS8H1** **The student will evaluate the development of Native American cultures and the impact of European exploration and settlement on the Native American cultures in Georgia.**
>
> a. Describe the evolution of Native American cultures (Paleo, Archaic, Woodland, and Mississippian) prior to European contact.

PALEO PERIOD

The earliest known culture is that of the Paleo Indians, whose culture lasted until about 10,000 years ago. The word Paleo comes from the Greek and means "very old" or "long ago." Early people sometimes can be identified by the material they used to make knives, scrapers, and points for spears. Because most tools and spear points used by the people of this culture were made of stone, this period is referred to as the paleolithic (old stone) age. The Paleo culture also used an amazing invention called an atlatl. This smooth stone sling-like implement threw darts far more accurately than if they were thrown by hand.

The Paleo people were nomadic (roaming) hunters who wandered from place to place following herds of large animals. The hunters used long wooden spears to kill the large animals, which they then used for food. The hunters may also have chased the animals over the cliffs to kill them.

Remains of their dwelling places indicate that Paleo people lived in groups of 25 to 50 people. Because these people moved around, however, they did not leave many artifacts in any one place. Only a few Paleo sites have been found in Georgia.

_____ 1. **Of what material were MOST of the tools of the Paleo people made?**
   A. flint
   B. wood
   C. stone
   D. copper

_____ 2. **The oldest known Native American culture in North America was the**
   A. Paleo culture.
   B. Archaic culture.
   C. Woodland culture.
   D. Mississippian culture.

_____ 3. **Why are there so few Paleo sites in Georgia?**
   A. Paleo Indians lived primarily in western states, not in Georgia.
   B. Paleo sites were often looted by cultural groups that came after them.
   C. Remains from the Paleo period have been destroyed by natural forces.
   D. The nomadic Paleo Indians did not leave many artifacts in any one place.

_____ 4. **Why have few Paleo artifacts been found in any one place?**
   A. People moved frequently.
   B. Artifacts disappeared over time.
   C. People did not leave any artifacts.
   D. Few people lived during that time.

_____ **5. Which people were the FIRST to use the atlatl?**
   A. Paleo
   B. Archaic
   C. Woodland
   D. Mississippian

ARCHAIC PERIOD

The Archaic period (from the word archaic, meaning "old") included three distinct time spans: early, middle, and late.

Early Archaic Period

During the early Archaic period, from about 8000 B.C. to about 5000 B.C., the people still hunted large game. Those animals, however, slowly became extinct. Archaic Indians then began hunting smaller game, such as deer, bear, turkey, and rabbit. The people also began to eat reptiles, game birds, and fish.

The early Archaic people invented useful items, such as choppers, drills, and chipping tools made from deer antlers. Archaeological evidence indicates that the early Archaic people moved each season. During the fall, they lived where berries, nuts, and fruits were plentiful. In summer, they moved to good fishing locations. They also migrated during spring and winter to find food.

Middle Archaic Period

Geographers tell us that by 5000 B.C., when the middle Archaic period began, the area grew warm and dry. Water levels along rivers and the coastal areas receded (moved back), and the people began to eat shellfish. Scientists have found hooks made from animal bones that came from this period. These hooks were sometimes on the ends of long spears that were weighted in the middle with polished stones. Because hunters could throw the weighted spears long distances, food became easier to get. Finding more food meant the people did not need to move as often as they once had. Evidence also suggests that several small groups joined together to establish camps.

Late Archaic Period

A common artifact from the late Archaic period (4000 B.C. to 1000 B.C.) is the grooved axe. Indians made this tool by putting a stone axe head on a wooden handle. Excavations (archaeological diggings) of late Archaic settlements indicate that axes were used to clear trees and bushes around the camp. The late Archaic people also saved seeds to plant in the next growing season. It is thought that **horticulture**, the science of cultivating plants and trees, began in the late Archaic period.

By 2500 B.C., the climate had become cooler and wetter. The Archaic people of this period depended on shellfish for most of their food. On Stallings Island, a few miles north of Augusta on the Savannah River, archaeologists discovered a mound of mussel and clam shells that was 512 feet long and 300 feet wide. Also at the Stallings site were remains of burial grounds, fire hearths, pipes, axes, shell beads, bone pins and needles, bone hooks, and many different spear points. Because of these discoveries, historians think late Archaic villages were more permanent than those of any group before them.

The way food was prepared also changed. Pottery shards dating from the Archaic period indicate that clay containers were used for storing, cooking, and serving food. Archaeologists think learning to make and use pottery may be one of the greatest contributions the Archaic people made to Native American culture.

_____ 6. **During which prehistoric period did large game become extinct?**
   A. Paleo
   B. Archaic
   C. Woodland
   D. Mississippian

_____ 7. **Why did the Archaic people move frequently?**
   A. to locate farmland
   B. to trade with others
   C. to find enough food
   D. to find secure shelter

_____ 8. **During which prehistoric period did horticulture begin?**
   A. Paleo
   B. Archaic
   C. Woodland
   D. Mississippian

_____ 9. **Which people were the FIRST to make and use pottery?**
   A. Paleo
   B. Archaic
   C. Woodland
   D. Mississippian

_____ 10. **Which factor resulted in prehistoric Indians making permanent settlements?**
   A. The Indians began to cultivate plants.
   B. The Indians had abundant large game.
   C. The Indians followed herds of large animals.
   D. The Indians wanted to band together for protection.

WOODLAND PERIOD

The Woodland culture developed about 1000 B.C. and lasted until about 1000 A.D. Evidence suggests that, during that period, several hundred families began banding together to form tribes. A **tribe** is a group of people who share a common ancestry, name, and way of living. The tribes lived in villages and built huts as houses. The Woodland people used small trees and bark to build dome-shaped huts.

Hunting became easier when the Woodland people developed the bow and arrow. Arrow points were made out of stone, shark teeth, or deer antlers. Fishing, hunting, and gathering nuts and berries remained important ways of getting food. The people also grew such things as squash, wild greens, and sunflowers.

The Woodland people learned how to make pottery last longer by mixing clay with sand. They used wooden paddles to make designs on the pottery. After the clay containers dried in the sun, they were baked in a hot fire to make them hard enough to use for cooking.

Elaborate religious ceremonies were introduced during the Woodland period. The Woodland people also built cone-shaped burial mounds for the dead. They adorned bodies with necklaces, bracelets, rings, and copper or bone combs. When Woodland people were buried, their families and friends put special funeral pottery, tools, tobacco pipes, and weapons in the graves with them. These artifacts cause archaeologists and anthropologists to think this group of people believed in some type of life after death.

_____11. **The prehistoric culture that developed the bow and arrow for hunting was the**
   A. Paleo culture.
   B. Archaic culture.
   C. Woodland culture
   D. Mississippian culture.

_____12. **Which people were the FIRST to live in tribes?**
   A. Paleo
   B. Archaic
   C. Woodland
   D. Mississippian

_____13. **Who were the FIRST people to use burial mounds?**
   A. Paleo
   B. Archaic
   C. Woodland
   D. Mississippian

_____14. **Archaeologists think that prehistoric Indians believed in some form of life after death because**
   A. tribal centers had churches and other symbols of worship.
   B. pictographs and cave drawings depicted a spiritual afterlife.
   C. legends of an afterlife were passed down from generation to generation.
   D. burial mounds contained items such as tools, tobacco pipes, and weapons.

MISSISSIPPIAN PERIOD

The Mississippian culture is considered to be the highest prehistoric civilization in Georgia. The culture, which started about 700 A.D., is so called because the first things learned about it were from villages excavated along the Mississippi River.

From archaeological sites, we know that the people grew most of their food. Maize (corn), beans, pumpkins, and squash were all planted together in hills. They grew tobacco to use in ceremonies. The Mississippians planted in different fields each year so the soil would stay fertile.

The Mississippians began to dress and fix their hair differently. Their clothes were less simple, and they wore beads and ear ornaments. Sometimes they painted or tattooed their bodies. They also began wearing feather headdresses.

Villages grew, and several thousand families might live in a single settlement. They built centers for religious ceremonies. Moats and **palisades** (wooden fences) often protected the villages. In some Georgia villages, guard towers have been found along the palisades, indicating that they needed to defend themselves against tribal enemies.

About 1600 A.D., the people left the villages, and there is nothing to tell us where they went. Because this was in the prehistoric period (before written history), we may never learn what happened to the Mississippians.

____15. **Which prehistoric people were the FIRST to paint and tattoo their bodies?**
   A. Paleo
   B. Archaic
   C. Woodland
   D. Mississippian

Use the map to answer questions 16-18.

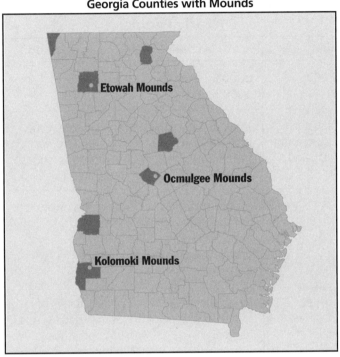

Georgia Counties with Mounds

____16. **Which section of the state has no mounds?**
   A. northeast
   B. southeast
   C. northwest
   D. southwest

____17. **The information on the map indicates that the moundbuilders**
   A. spread across Georgia.
   B. settled along the coast.
   C. believed in an afterlife.
   D. built cone-shaped mounds.

____18. **Mounds are located in how many Georgia counties?**
   A. 5
   B. 6
   C. 7
   D. 8

_____ **19. Which early people grew tobacco to use in ceremonies?**
A. Paleo
B. Archaic
C. Woodland
D. Mississippian

Use the table to answer questions 20-23.

Early People				
	Paleo	**Archaic**	**Woodland**	**Mississippian**
Time Period	before 10,000 years ago	8000 B.C. to 1000 B.C.	1000 B.C. to 1000 A.D.	700 A.D. to 1600 A.D.
Food Sources	large animals such as bison, mammoth, ground sloth, and mastodon	small game, reptiles, fish, shellfish, berries, nuts, fruits	small game, fish, nuts and berries, some crops (squash, sunflowers)	crops (maize, beans, pumpkins, squash)
Weapons, Tools	spears	spears, choppers, drills, chipping tools, bone fish hooks, grooved axes, pipes, pottery	bow and arrow, pottery	similar to Woodland culture, stone hoes, copper headdresses
Shelter	no fixed shelter; followed herds of large animals	crude shelters, stayed in one place longer	small villages of dome-shaped huts with grass roofs, mounds	larger villages with ceremonial buildings

_____ **20. How long did the Woodland Indians live in what is now Georgia?**
A. 1,000 years
B. 2,000 years
C. 8,000 years
D. 10,000 years

_____ **21. During which period was the use of pottery introduced?**
A. Paleo
B. Archaic
C. Woodland
D. Mississippian

_____ **22. Which period saw the building of large villages with impressive ceremonial buildings?**
A. Paleo
B. Archaic
C. Woodland
D. Mississippian

_____ 23. **When were people building small, dome-shaped huts with grass roofs as their shelters?**

    A. between 700 A.D. and 1600 A.D.

    B. between 1000 B.C. and 1000 A.D.

    C. between 1600 A.D. and 1900 A.D.

    D. between 10,000 B.C. and 8,000 B.C.

SS8H1   **The student will evaluate the development of Native American cultures and the impact of European exploration and settlement on the Native American cultures in Georgia.**

    b. Evaluate the impact of European contact on Native American cultures; include Spanish missions along the barrier island, and the explorations of Hernando de Soto.

HERNANDO DE SOTO

In 1539, the Spanish explorer Hernando de Soto left Havana, Cuba, with a huge group of men and animals. They landed in Florida and marched north. In 1540, they entered the southwestern part of Georgia, close to present-day Albany. De Soto and his army wanted one thing as they moved across the state: to find gold.

When de Soto arrived in Georgia, the native tribes saw white men and horses for the first time. De Soto had only a small number of men to face thousands of American Indians, but his weapons were better. The Spanish also wore plated armor, which arrows could not pierce.

During de Soto's search for gold in Georgia, his soldiers killed thousands of American Indians. Many more Indians died from diseases brought to the New World by the Spanish and other explorers. Some historians believe almost half the Native American population died from measles, smallpox, influenza, and whooping cough.

De Soto's expedition into North America was a failure, however. He found no gold or treasure. Most of his army was lost to starvation and disease. De Soto himself died somewhere along the Mississippi River. However, his march through Georgia changed the lives and culture of the American Indians forever.

_____ 24. **Why did Hernando de Soto explore much of Georgia in 1540?**

    A. He wanted to build forts and missions in the state.

    B. He was attracted by rumors of large gold deposits.

    C. He was searching for the magical Fountain of Youth.

    D. He believed that he would find a passage to Asia through Georgia.

_____ 25. **Who was the first explorer to enter present-day Georgia?**

    A. Ponce de Leon

    B. Francisco Pizarro

    C. Hernando de Soto

    D. Ferdinand Magellan

_____ 26. **Why was de Soto's expedition considered a failure?**

    A. De Soto's men died of disease.

    B. De Soto did not find any gold or riches.

    C. De Soto traveled in the wrong direction.

    D. De Soto died before the expedition was finished.

____27. **How did de Soto's march through Georgia change the lives and culture of Native Americans?**

A. The expedition introduced Native Americans to new types of food.

B. The expedition resulted in the death of thousands of Native Americans.

C. The expedition set up new trading opportunities for Native Americans.

D. The expedition was responsible for converting Native Americans to Catholicism.

Use the map to answer questions 28-31.

de Soto's Travels

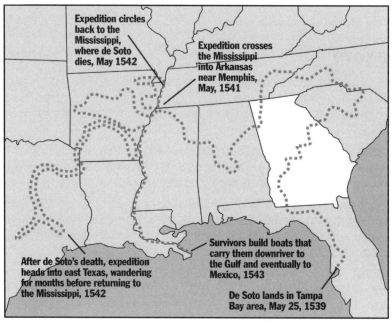

Expedition circles back to the Mississippi, where de Soto dies, May 1542

Expedition crosses the Mississippi into Arkansas near Memphis, May, 1541

After de Soto's death, expedition heads into east Texas, wandering for months before returning to the Mississippi, 1542

Survivors build boats that carry them downriver to the Gulf and eventually to Mexico, 1543

De Soto lands in Tampa Bay area, May 25, 1539

____28. **Hernando de Soto began his travels near present-day**

A. Tampa, Florida.

B. Atlanta, Georgia.

C. Memphis, Tennessee.

D. Vicksburg, Mississippi.

____29. **Hernando de Soto crossed the Mississippi River for the first time near present-day**

A. Natchez, Mississippi.

B. Memphis, Tennessee.

C. Little Rock, Arkansas.

D. Vicksburg, Mississippi.

____30. **After Hernando de Soto's death, where did his men go?**

A. Texas

B. Alabama

C. Arkansas

D. Mississippi

_____31. **What is the correct chronological order of the places de Soto visited on his travels?**
> 1. De Soto died.
> 2. De Soto entered Florida.
> 3. De Soto's men went to Texas.
> 4. De Soto crossed the Mississippi near Memphis.

   A. 2-4-1-3
   B. 2-3-1-4
   C. 4-3-1-2
   D. 3-4-2-1

SPANISH MISSIONS

In 1565, Spain sent Captain General Pedro Menéndez to found a colony in St. Augustine, Florida. A **colony** is a group of people who settle in a new land but who keep their ties to their homeland. In 1566, the Spaniards moved up the coast to St. Catherines and Cumberland islands. That year, the Spanish founded a mission–Santa Catalina–on St. Catherines Island. The Spanish named the region Guale (pronounced "Wallie") for the Indians living in the area. About thirty men were left to establish the first Spanish post on Georgia soil. The Spanish later established missions on St. Simons Island and at Sapelo at the mouth of the Altamaha River.

The main purpose for the missions was to convert the Indians to the Catholic faith. At the same time, just the fact that there were missions and a few soldiers to guard them established a Spanish claim to the land. The missions were also a place where trade took place between the Indians and the Spanish.

For a time, the missions did well. There were tensions between the Spanish and the Indians as the missionaries tried to force the Indians to conform to their ideas of faith and village life. There were occasional uprisings, and some of the Indians moved away from the missions. The Indian population also decreased because of the diseases brought by the Europeans.

Tensions increased further when the British settled in present-day Charleston, South Carolina, around 1670. The British established trade routes with the local tribes and encouraged the disagreements between the missionaries and the Indians. The British also probably encouraged pirates to raid the Spanish missions. All of these problems led the Spanish to gradually withdraw from the missions along the Georgia coast. By 1685, all of the missions had been abandoned.

_____32. **Which of the following nations built missions along Georgia's barrier islands?**
   A. Spain
   B. France
   C. England
   D. Portugal

_____33. **The main purpose of the Spanish missions in the barrier islands was to**
   A. claim land for Spain.
   B. establish trade with Spain.
   C. convert the Indians to Catholicism.
   D. provide protection for the area's European settlers.

_____34. **Which is NOT a reason for the decline of the Spanish missions?**
   A. Pirate raids along the coast destroyed many missions.
   B. Some Indians resettled in areas that were not served by the missions.
   C. Some missions were raided by Indians who were allied with the British.
   D. Once the Indians adopted Catholicism, the missions were no longer needed.

SS8H1 The student will evaluate the development of Native American cultures and the impact of European exploration and settlement on the Native American cultures in Georgia.

c. Explain reasons for European exploration and settlement of North America, with emphasis on the interests of the French, Spanish, and British in the southeastern area.

EUROPEAN EXPLORATION AND SETTLEMENT

De Soto was followed by many other European explorers, most of them from Spain, France, and England. These nations established settlements in Georgia and competed with each other and with the Native American tribes for control of the land.

For most of the 1500s, Spain's hold over the missions and its colonies made it an important player in the race for control of the New World. As a result of the gold it took from the New World, Spain became rich and powerful. As Spain fought to hold onto its gains, the English and the French tried to gain a share of the treasures.

By the end of the 1500s, the conflict between Spain and England had turned into an undeclared war at sea. English sea captains captured Spanish treasure ships filled with gold, silver, and other valuable goods. They also attacked and burned Spanish settlements in the New World.

To counter these attacks, Spanish King Phillip II plotted to invade England, using a huge fleet of ships that the Spanish called the "Invincible Armada." The plot failed as the English destroyed or ran off much of the Armada in 1588.

England then gained control of the seas and was ready to pursue its interest in the New World. Like most Europeans, the English believed there were large amounts of gold, silver, and exotic foods in the New World. They thought the country that claimed this new land would become even more powerful.

In the 1600s, the English began permanent settlements along the coast of the New World. Their first permanent settlement was Jamestown, Virginia, in 1607. By the close of the 1600s, England had established twelve colonies along the Atlantic coastline.

Although Spain had moved out of Guale by 1686, more than one country claimed the land. France was establishing colonies along the Gulf Coast and in northern Alabama. Both the French and the Spanish posed a threat to the British colonies. Settlers in South Carolina asked that a fort be built at the mouth of the Altamaha River to serve as a "warning point" for invaders. In 1721, Fort King George was completed. The fort established the English presence in Georgia.

_____35. **The main reason the Spanish explored North America was to**
  A. fight the British.
  B. spread Christianity.
  C. find gold and riches.
  D. build permanent settlements.

_____36. **Which country was NOT a major colonizer of North America?**
  A. Spain
  B. France
  C. Portugal
  D. Great Britain

_____37. **The first permanent British settlement in the New World was built at**
   A. Jamestown.
   B. St. Augustine.
   C. Roanoke Island.
   D. Massachusetts Bay.

_____38. **The first permanent Spanish settlement in the New World was established at**
   A. Jamestown.
   B. Los Angeles.
   C. St. Augustine.
   D. Yamacraw Bluff.

_____39. **What was the name of the first British fort constructed in Georgia?**
   A. Fort Guale
   B. Fort Frederica
   C. Fort King George
   D. Fort Santa Catalina

SS8H2   The student will analyze the colonial period of Georgia's history.

a. Explain the importance of James Oglethorpe, the Charter of 1732, reasons for settlement (charity, economics, and defense), Tomochichi, Mary Musgrove, and the city of Savannah.

JAMES OGLETHORPE

James Edward Oglethorpe, born in London in 1696, was well educated and wealthy. He cared greatly about people in trouble and tried to find ways to help them. In 1722, he became a member of Parliament's House of Commons.

During that time, Great Britain was faced with many problems. Many citizens could not pay their debts. Laws concerning debtors were strict and harsh, and those who could not pay went to jail. Among those jailed was Oglethorpe's friend, architect Robert Castell.

Oglethorpe was on a committee studying prison reform when he learned that Castell had died of smallpox. Oglethorpe was angry because he believed debtors should not have to go to jail. He believed that his friend had died needlessly in a dirty prison. Oglethorpe worked to get laws passed that both improved prison conditions and let thousands of prisoners go free.

Unfortunately, just letting people out of prison did not help them. There were no jobs for them, and, without work, they still could not pay their debts. Dr. Thomas Bray, a clergyman, proposed that a colony be founded to help these people. Bray died, but James Oglethorpe and twenty other men developed a plan that promised a fresh start in the New World to "unfortunate but worthy individuals."

In the summer of 1730, Oglethorpe's group asked King George II for a tract of land "southwest of Carolina for settling poor persons of London." The group knew Great Britain's two main reasons for beginning new colonies were (1) a balanced trading policy to make Great Britain self-sufficient and (2) defensive buffers to protect British colonies from the French, Spanish, and Native Americans. They proposed ways for their new colony to carry out those goals.

The new settlement could defend the southern Carolinas from Spanish Florida. It could also provide protection from the French, who were pushing east from the Mississippi River valley.

Oglethorpe's group also listed economic reasons for the settlement. France and Spain made money trading with the Native Americans who lived between the Atlantic Ocean and the Mississippi River. Great Britain could share in this. Oglethorpe and his supporters also said the new colony could produce silk, cotton dyes, and wine–three items Great Britain was importing from France, Russia, and Spain. They promised to send spices and semitropical fruit to Great Britain. British merchants were pleased with the idea of getting a good supply of raw materials while having a new market for their manufactured goods. Georgia, like other American colonies, would also offer religious freedom to Protestants who were being mistreated by the Catholic Church in Europe. The king also liked the idea of more land and greater power for Great Britain.

_____ 40. **One of the reasons given for the colonization of Georgia was to serve as a buffer colony. This meant that Georgia was**
   A. a colony for settlement by the poor.
   B. an outpost for pirates attacking Spanish galleons.
   C. a military protective zone between English and Spanish settlements.
   D. an agricultural station experimenting with new strains of cotton plant.

_____ 41. **What was one of the major reasons for the king wanting to create the colony of Georgia?**
   A. to help pay royal debts
   B. to civilize the native Indians
   C. to release debtors from prison
   D. to create a balanced trade policy

_____ 42. **Why did James Oglethorpe suggest forming a colony for the poor?**
   A. England wanted to get rid of debtors permanently.
   B. The homeless would readily come to the New World.
   C. Oglethorpe had a friend who died in a debtors' prison.
   D. The poor were mostly well-educated people who had fallen on hard times.

_____ 43. **What items, which Great Britain had to import from France, Russia, and Spain, did Oglethorpe promise to produce in Georgia?**
   a. cotton dyes and silk
   B. wheat and rice
   C. tropical fruit and spices
   d. white potatoes, yams, and corn

_____ 44. **Which term BEST describes the kind of people Oglethorpe and his associates wanted to bring to Georgia?**
   A. well educated
   B. former convicts
   C. deeply religious
   D. poor but worthy

CHARTER OF 1732

On June 7, 1732, King George II granted a **charter** to Oglethorpe's group as trustees for establishing the colony of Georgia and for managing it for twenty-one years. A **charter** is a legal document that grants special rights and privileges. **Trustees** are people who hold responsibility on behalf of others. The Georgia charter granted an area of "all those lands, Countries, and Territories" between the Savannah and the Altamaha rivers extending westward "to the South Seas" (the Pacific Ocean).

In the charter, the king stated that the trustees could not own land, hold political office, or be given money for their work. "Papists" (Catholics), blacks, liquor dealers, and lawyers could not become colonists. Catholics were excluded because of a longstanding division between the Catholic Church and the Church of England. Blacks were not admitted so as not to introduce slavery to the colony. The trustees feared settlers would not work if liquor was permitted. They wanted colonists to settle their differences out of court and did not think lawyers would allow them to do this.

The colony belonged to the Crown, so the trustees were to get instructions from King George II. They could pass no laws unless the king agreed. The trustees worked around some of the rules by not having a governor and by using regulations, or government orders, instead of laws.

____45. **Georgia's Charter of 1732 did NOT include a provision that**
  A. banned liquor in the colony.
  B. prohibited Catholics from becoming colonists.
  C. gave the king of England control of the colony.
  D. guaranteed every settler his day in court to settle differences.

____46. **When did King George II grant Oglethorpe and his group a charter for the colony of Georgia?**
  A. 1492
  B. 1607
  C. 1732
  D. 1776

____47. **According to the charter, what religious group was not allowed to settle in Georgia?**
  A. Jewish
  B. Baptist
  C. Catholic
  D. Methodist

____48. **According to Georgia's Charter of 1732, which group of people was forbidden to enter Georgia?**
  A. blacks
  B. women
  C. soldiers
  D. preachers

____49. **What policy did the king make to ensure that the trustees did not take personal advantage of their position?**
  A. The trustees could not hold office.
  B. The trustees could not serve more than one year.
  C. The trustees had to break off all ties with Great Britain.
  D. The trustees had to donate their own money to provide food for the colonists.

REASONS FOR SETTLEMENT

A search began to find settlers for the newest colony. Newspapers told of a land with mild temperatures and rich soil and the promise of a new start in life. Sir Robert Montgomery's description of it as the "most delightful Country of the Universe" was widely accepted as fact. Clergymen preached sermons, wrote religious books, and raised a great deal of money by talking about the goodness of the proposed colony.

The trustees talked with applicants and planned for the voyage and settlement. Unfortunately, debtors and former prisoners did not get to go. This meant the humanitarian reasons for the colony were all but forgotten. The applicants chosen were promised fifty acres of land, tools, and enough food for one year. Potential colonists who could pay their own way received five hundred acres of land and permission to take ten indentured servants.

In exchange, colonists had to agree to the following: (1) Each man was to defend the new colony against all enemies. (2) Land given to colonists could not be sold, and no money could be borrowed on it. It could, however, be passed on to a male heir. (3) Each colonist was to receive seeds and agricultural tools and was to use them in cultivating the lands of the new settlement. (4) Colonists were to use a portion of their land to grow mulberry trees so that silkworms would eat the leaves and make cocoons for the production of silk. (5) Each colonist was to obey all regulations established by the trustees.

When the chosen settlers gathered on the London docks, they were both excited and a little afraid of the adventure ahead. Historians do not agree on the exact number of men, women, and children who traveled from Gravesend, England, to Georgia. But between 114 and 125 people left London on November 17, 1732. Their voyage to the New World took 88 days.

Besides its passengers and crew, the Ann carried sheep, hogs, ducks, geese, and several dogs. There is no record of the ship being uncomfortable, but it was probably crowded with all the people and their belongings. Only two deaths were reported among the colonists on the trip, both of them infants. Finally, land was sighted, and the Ann docked at Charleston, South Carolina. The ship stayed in Charleston one day, then put in at Port Royal (Beaufort), South Carolina, on January 14, 1733.

_____50. **Which original reason for settling the new colony was forgotten about?**
   A. settling debtors
   B. searching for gold
   C. establishing schools for orphans
   D. growing vegetables and fruits to ship back to England

_____51. **Those who were selected to settle the colony of Georgia were required to**
   A. have served time in a debtors' prison.
   B. bring their own farm tools with them.
   C. only sell their land to another Englishman.
   D. use a portion of their land to grow mulberry trees.

_____52. **The trustees gave the first settlers in Georgia the right to**
   A. vote.
   B. own land.
   C. collect taxes.
   D. hold elections.

TOMOCHICHI AND MARY MUSGROVE

Before the Ann could set anchor, Oglethorpe had to make friends with the Yamacraw Indians through their chief, Tomochichi. Oglethorpe went to the trading post in the Yamacraw village to find an interpreter. The trading post was operated by John Musgrove and his wife Mary, who was part Native American and part British. John agreed to act as interpreter, but Mary soon took over for him. With Mary's help, Oglethorpe and Chief Tomochichi established a close friendship that lasted until the chief's death in 1739.

The passengers waited on board while Oglethorpe and his staff searched for a permanent settlement site. The place decided on was about eighteen miles from the mouth of the Savannah River.

On February 12, 1733, Chief Tomochichi allowed the Ann's passengers to land on sandy Yamacraw Bluff overlooking the Savannah River. The settlement they established was the thirteenth British colony in the New World. Georgia's citizens were added to over 650,000 other colonists spread from Massachusetts through the Carolinas.

Oglethorpe and Tomochichi

_____ 53. **Which statement BEST describes the subject of the illustration?**

A. The Indians and the British exchanged gifts.

B. The British took control over the Indians' land.

C. The Indians showed distrust for the invading Englishmen.

D. The British and the Indians had a disappointing first meeting.

_____ 54. **What Indians were led by Tomochichi?**

A. Creek

B. Oconee

C. Cherokee

D. Yamacraw

_____**55. Who served as the translator for Oglethorpe in his discussions with Tomochichi?**
   A. Sequoyah
   B. William Bull
   C. Mary Musgrove
   D. Robert Montgomery

_____**56. Tomochichi allowed James Oglethorpe to settle on a bluff overlooking which river?**
   A. Flint River
   B. Altamaha River
   C. Savannah River
   D. St. Marys River

THE CITY OF SAVANNAH

When the colonists landed at Yamacraw Bluff, they put up four large tents for shelter. Then they began getting the land ready for planting and preparing timber to build permanent homes. Within two weeks, they began building the first permanent homes.

Oglethorpe had no title and only limited power, but he was accepted as the leader of the colony. During the early months, he got grants of land and made treaties with the Native Americans. He had a small fort built on the bank of the river and trained a **militia**, or citizen army, to defend the settlement. Oglethorpe also worked with Colonel William Bull and surveyor Noble Jones to design the future city of Savannah. The basic pattern of this first planned city in the colonies was after a design by Robert Castell, Oglethorpe's friend who had died in a British debtors' prison.

The plan was for Savannah to have four squares. On the north and south sides of each square were twenty lots. On the east and west sides, four larger lots were set aside for such buildings as churches or stores. The center of each square was for social, political, and religious gatherings. The squares were divided into blocks (called tythings) and wards. There were ten houses in each block and four blocks in each ward.

Each settler was expected to care for his house in Savannah, his five-acre garden plot on the edge of town, and his forty-five farm acres in the country. During the first months, the colonists cultivated mulberry trees to feed silkworms. They also built a sundial for telling time, a gristmill for grinding corn into meal, a courthouse, a water well, and a bakery.

Work was done in spite of growing medical problems likely caused by a lack of fresh vegetables, changes in the climate, poor sanitation, and hard physical labor. Forty settlers died in the first year.

_____**57. Who surveyed and helped design the city of Savannah?**
   A. Noble Jones
   B. Samuel Nunes
   C. James Oglethorpe
   D. Robert Montgomery

_____**58. Where did James Oglethorpe and the first Georgia colonists land when they arrived in Georgia?**
   A. Fort Pulaski on the Savannah River
   B. Ossabaw Island on Ossabaw Sound
   C. Fort Frederica on St. Simons Island
   D. Yamacraw Bluff on the Savannah River

_____ 59. Oglethorpe's plan for the establishment of Savannah could BEST be described as a

    A. heavily defended fort.

    B. decaying neighborhood.

    C. city planned around open squares.

    D. series of circular roads making travel easy.

_____ 60. The basic pattern of Savannah was fashioned after a design by

    A. Noble Jones.

    B. William Bull.

    C. Robert Castell.

    D. James Oglethorpe.

Use the map of present-day Savannah to answer questions 61-62.

Present-Day Savannah

_____ 61. **What historic site is located at the intersection of Oglethorpe Street and Bull Street?**

    A. Cotton Exchange

    B. U.S. Customs House

    C. Tomochichi's gravesite

    D. Juliette Gordon Low's birthplace

_____ 62. **Which location is located furthest to the north on the map?**

    A. Forsyth Park

    B. Factors Walk

    C. Johnson Square

    D. Colonial Cemetery

SS8H2   The student will analyze the colonial period of Georgia's history.

b. Evaluate the Trustee Period of Georgia's colonial history, emphasizing the role of the Salzburgers, Highland Scots, malcontents, and the Spanish threat from Florida.

THE ROLE OF THE SALZBURGERS

In March 1734, Oglethorpe was planning to leave for Great Britain to report to the colony's trustees when new settlers arrived. A group of German Protestants had been forced to leave Salzburg, Germany which was then controlled by Catholics. They were led by John Martin Bolzius, and they asked to live in Georgia. Oglethorpe took the Salzburgers to a place twenty-five miles from Savannah. There they began a town called Ebenezer, which means "the Rock of Help." However, because the land was marshy with poor soil for crops, the Salzburgers asked Oglethorpe for a better site. In 1736, they moved to Red Bluff on the Savannah River. There they built another town, which they called New Ebenezer.

Oglethorpe made a trip to Great Britain. When he returned to Savannah in early February 1736, he brought three hundred new colonists with him. Included were another group of Salzburgers, some Moravians (Protestants who banded together in Saxony, Germany, in 1722), and two religious leaders, John and Charles Wesley. Upon his return, Oglethorpe helped the Salzburgers move to Frederica on St. Simons Island.

_____63. **Why did German Salzburgers come to Georgia?**

A. to escape religious persecution

B. to serve out terms for misconduct

C. to discover new financial opportunities

D. to lead the armed forces for Oglethorpe

_____64. **Who was the leader of the Germans from Salzburg?**

A. John Reynolds

B. Lachlan McIntosh

C. James Oglethorpe

D. John Martin Bolzius

_____65. **Where did the Salzburgers first settle?**

A. Darien

B. Albany

C. Ebenezer

D. Savannah

_____66. **The Salzburgers moved from their original settlement because**

A. they were attacked frequently by the Indians.

B. they had problems with the Spanish who lived nearby.

C. the land on which they settled was marshy and not very productive.

D. the area was plagued by harsh storms that caused extensive damage.

_____67. **On which barrier island did the Salzburgers settle?**

    A. Jekyll Island

    B. St. Simons Island

    C. St. Catherines Island

    D. Cumberland Island

HIGHLAND SCOTS

James Oglethorpe wanted to protect the Georgia colony from possible attacks from Spanish Florida. The men of Scotland had the reputation of being good soldiers, and so Oglethorpe recruited a group of about 175 Highland Scots to settle in the area south of Savannah. The group arrived at the Altamaha River in 1736 and established a settlement they originally called New Inverness. Later, they changed the name to Darien.

Darien was the only Gaelic speaking settlement in Georgia. The Highland Scots kept many of their culture's traditions, including the family clans and the wearing of kilts rather than pants. The Highland Scots were hard workers. When they found that the soil was not good for agriculture, they changed to raising cattle and harvesting timber. Their successful economy encouraged other Highland Scots to emigrate to Georgia.

In 1739, a number of the Darien leaders signed a petition asking that slavery not be introduced into the colony. This was the earliest antislavery petition in the South, and it was successful for a time. The ban against slavery was not lifted until 1749.

_____68. **Where did the Highland Scots settle in Georgia?**

    A. Darien

    B. Augusta

    C. Savannah

    D. New Ebenezer

_____69. **The Highland Scots opposed which policy?**

    A. permitting slavery

    B. trading with the Spanish

    C. giving women the right to vote

    D. keeping close ties with Great Britain

MALCONTENTS

Upon his return from Great Britain in 1736, Oglethorpe introduced several new regulations with the approval of the trustees: Buying rum was to be against the law, and alcohol could not be used in trading with the Native Americans. Slavery was not allowed because Oglethorpe thought it caused landowners to be idle while, at the same time, made them want more land.

Oglethorpe's new regulations were not popular. The regulations, plus the earlier one about passing on land only to male heirs, began to divide the colonists. They were already facing economic hardships. Their mulberry trees were the wrong kind for producing large amounts of silk. The colonists were not able to grow hemp, flax, indigo (a plant used to make blue dyes), or grapes for wine. To make matters worse, their South Carolina neighbors, who had large amounts of land, slaves, and rum, were doing well. They were growing rice, cotton, and tobacco, and their success was due, in part, to the use of slave labor. However, growing numbers of Georgia settlers wanted slaves.

There was less and less support for the trustees' regulations. Many of the malcontent settlers moved to places where they could live more nearly as they wished. When Oglethorpe returned to Georgia after one of his trips to Great Britain, he found upset people all over the colony.

_____ **70. Who were the malcontents of the early Georgia colony?**

    A. the trustees and their families

    B. foreigners from Germany and Scotland

    C. officials who examined the contents of cargo ships

    D. people who were unhappy and constantly complaining

_____ **71. Which was NOT an area of discontent in Georgia?**

    A. slavery

    B. voting rights

    C. the sale of rum

    D. ownership of land

_____ **72. With which trustee policy did the colonists disagree?**

    A. hard work

    B. military training

    C. religious practices

    D. prohibition of slavery

_____ **73. What term was used to describe those who complained about the policies of the trustees?**

    A. rebels

    B. objectors

    C. dissidents

    D. malcontents

THE SPANISH THREAT FROM FLORIDA

Great Britain controlled Georgia's borders, and Spain controlled Florida's. There seemed to be no way to keep the two groups from fighting. In the fall of 1739, a war broke out between Great Britain and Spain. It was called the "War of Jenkins's Ear." Several years earlier, Spanish sailors were said to have cut off the ear of Robert Jenkins, a British seaman, to serve as a warning to British ship captains smuggling goods off the Florida coast.

Oglethorpe welcomed the war. It gave him a good reason to invade neighboring Florida. A force of about two thousand men, mostly Native Americans and settlers from Georgia and South Carolina, was quickly organized. They tried to take major Spanish forts in Florida, particularly St. Augustine. However, a well-organized Spanish militia met Oglethorpe and his soldiers with a surprise attack on June 15, 1740. The Spanish won, and Oglethorpe's forces had to retreat to St. Simons Island.

During the next two years, there were numerous attacks and counterattacks between the Spanish and British settlers, with neither side gaining much ground. In July 1742, Oglethorpe got the opportunity he needed. His forces, assisted by the Highland Scots, waited in the dense woods along the marshes on St. Simons Island. Spanish troops who came that way were caught completely by surprise and forced back across the Florida border. Even though the action was known as the Battle of Bloody Marsh, it was neither big nor very bloody. It did, however, mark the beginning of a safe southern frontier for the British.

_____ **74. The European nation that dominated early exploration in the New World was**

    A. Spain.

    B. France.

    C. Portugal.

    D. Great Britain.

_____ 75. **The greatest threat to the Georgia colony came from**

    A. new diseases.

    B. the area's harsh climate.

    C. Spanish soldiers in Florida.

    D. Indians who lived in the area.

_____ 76. **What was the importance of the Battle of Bloody Marsh?**

    A. It demonstrated the strength of the British militia.

    B. It ended the threat of war from Native Americans.

    C. It resulted in Georgia's gaining new lands on which to settle.

    D. It was the beginning of a safe southern frontier for the British.

_____ 77. **What group came to the aid of James Oglethorpe in the Battle of Bloody Marsh?**

    A. Catholics

    B. Spaniards

    C. Salzburgers

    D. Highland Scots

AN EVALUATION OF THE TRUSTEE PERIOD

In 1743, Oglethorpe was called to Great Britain to answer charges that he had not acted correctly when he failed to capture Spanish-held St. Augustine. Oglethorpe was cleared of the charges, but he did not return to Georgia. Instead, he remained in Great Britain.

William Stephens, the trustees' secretary, was named president of a colony filled with disagreement. The effort to keep rum from being sold stopped in 1742. The people still wanted to own more land and to have slaves. By 1750, this was allowed. The regulation against slavery was repealed, along with the one that allowed a colonist to own only five hundred acres of land. When President Stephens retired in 1751, he was replaced by his assistant, Henry Parker. President Parker died a year later. Over the next three years (1752-1754), Georgia was led by President Patrick Graham. During his tenure, many settlers who had left under the rule of the trustees returned to the colony. In 1752, one year before the charter's end, the trustees returned Georgia to King George II.

During the twenty years of the original charter, 5,500 people had settled in Georgia. They had built new homes and started new lives. Although some left the colony to go elsewhere, they still made an imprint on the society and culture.

A large number of settlers were European Protestants who came to the colony to escape religious persecution. In Georgia, they were able to practice their beliefs without fear of punishment.

Treaties with the American Indians and the elimination of the threat of Spanish invasion ended the need for British military protection. Georgia was a safe haven on the southern frontier.

The colony also had noteworthy religious, social, and political accomplishments. Evangelist George Whitfield established the Bethesda Orphans Home in Ebenezer. Later, it was expanded into a school and renamed Bethesda House. The school provided a basic education for many of Georgia's future leaders. In Savannah, John and Charles Wesley established the first Sunday school in America. They also founded the Methodist Church.

The court system, established during the early days of the settlement, still functioned. By 1750, when the colonists gained outright ownership of the land, women were able to inherit property.

Perhaps the trustees' greatest accomplishment was their ability to enable the Georgia colony to survive the many hardships encountered during the first twenty years. The survival set the stage for Georgia to become a successful and profitable royal colony.

As we look back on the Georgia colony, it is important to remember the state motto, Non Sibi Sed

Allis, which is Latin for "Not for themselves but for others." From that standpoint, we have only to look around us and know they were very successful.

____78. **The Latin motto of the trustees, Non Sibi Sed Allis, meant "Not for themselves but for others." What does this mean?**

    A. The king felt the colony had been a failure and the trustees had to be punished as an example.

    B. The Highland Scots and the Salzburgers were foreigners and couldn't be trusted to defend the British.

    C. Religious leaders could not protect themselves as Catholics because of the members of the new Methodist church.

    D. The trustees established Georgia for the purpose of helping the poor, not for the purpose of making themselves rich.

____79. **What impact did the departure of Oglethorpe to England have on the colony?**

    A. No impact; he was cleared of the charges against him and returned within the year.

    B. No impact; after he married, he quickly returned to the colony to help the poor.

    C. Great impact; under the new leader most of the restrictive laws were changed.

    D. Great impact; the new leaders quickly turned control over to the king.

> **SS8H2 The student will analyze the colonial period of Georgia's history.**
>
>   c. Explain the development of Georgia as a royal colony with regard to land ownership, slavery, government, and the impact of the royal governors.

IMPACT OF THE ROYAL GOVERNORS

The period after Georgia returned its charter and became a British royal colony until the end of the American Revolution was a time of unrest and turmoil in Georgia and in the other colonies. In 1752, Georgia ceased to be a proprietary colony and became a royal colony. A **proprietary colony** was one that was governed by a board of trustees. A **royal colony** was one directly governed by the king.

During the two years before the first royal governor was appointed, some of the people who had left Georgia while it was a proprietary colony began to return. In 1752, Puritans from South Carolina bought 32,000 acres of land at Midway in present-day Liberty County. They moved there, bringing their slaves with them. Soon they began growing rice and indigo. A port was built nearby at Sunbury so the planters could ship their crops.

____80. **In 1752, Georgia became a**

    A. royal colony.

    B. debtor colony.

    C. proprietary colony.

    D. self-governing colony.

____81. **Who controlled Georgia after it became a royal colony?**

    A. James Oglethorpe

    B. the people of Georgia

    C. a bicameral legislature

    D. the king of Great Britain

DEVELOPMENT OF GEORGIA AS A ROYAL COLONY

Governor John Reynolds

On October 1, 1754, Georgians cheered when John Reynolds, their first royal governor, arrived. Because the trustees had believed that the first Georgia settlers were not able to govern themselves, they had not given them the right to vote, hold elections, or collect taxes. Reynolds, a navy captain, introduced the idea of self-government. Unlike the trustees, Governor Reynolds wanted the colonists to help run the government.

A bicameral, or two-chamber, legislature was set up to represent the eight parishes of the colony. (A parish was both a church and a British government district.) The lower house of the legislature was called the Commons House of Assembly; the upper house was called the Governor's Council. Those wishing to become a member of the Assembly had to own at least 500 acres of land. The king of England appointed the members of the Governor's Council.

Governor Reynolds also set up a court system. When the colonists had differences with each other, they went before the Court of Conscience, over which presided a local justice of the peace. Cases that could not be settled in the Court of Conscience could be carried to the Governor's Council.

Georgia's new government met for the first time in 1755 in Savannah, the colony's capital and largest city. The delegates reorganized the state militia and passed bills so roads could be built and repaired. The colonial assembly also drew up codes that restricted the rights of slaves.

For a while, Governor Reynolds and the colonial assembly worked well together. However, during one legislative session, members of the Governor's Council could not agree on how much was needed to improve the military defenses of the colony. Governor Reynolds became so angry at their failure to agree that he stopped the meeting and sent the legislators home.

During the months that followed, Reynolds tried to govern Georgia by himself, leaving the colonists angry. There were arguments between those who thought he should leave and those who wanted him to remain. Many Georgians did not like having their right to self-government taken away and wrote to King George to complain. However, when Reynolds recommended moving Savannah to the Ogeechee River (close to today's Richmond Hill in Bryan County), we can guess that most of his limited support evaporated. Finally, after two years, the group who wanted self-government won. Georgia's first royal governor was replaced.

_____ 82. **What city served as Georgia's capital during its period as a royal colony?**
   A. Macon
   B. Atlanta
   C. Augusta
   D. Savannah

_____ 83. **Who was the first royal governor of Georgia?**
   A. Robert Castell
   B. John Reynolds
   C. James Oglethorpe
   D. Robert Montgomery

_____ 84. **When Georgia was a royal colony, how were members of the upper house of the legislature, the Governor's Council, chosen?**
   A. They were elected by the voters.
   B. They were appointed by the king.
   C. They were appointed by the royal governor.
   D. They were chosen by members of the legislature.

_____ 85. **While John Reynolds was its royal governor, Georgia established**

    A. a court system.

    B. land ownership rights.

    C. local governing bodies.

    D. a unicameral legislature.

_____ 86. **Governor Reynolds disbanded the legislature because**

    A. he believed the governor should have sole power.

    B. there was a conflict between the two houses in the legislature.

    C. some members of the lawmaking body were elected illegally.

    D. there was a disagreement over how to improve military defenses.

Governor Henry Ellis

In February 1757, the king chose Captain Henry Ellis as the next royal governor. Governor Ellis was a naturalist and a scientist who had led voyages to many different parts of the world. Ellis learned quickly from Reynolds's mistakes. During his three years as governor, Ellis brought together people of many different political groups. He sought the advice of the governor of the colony of South Carolina. He also depended on well-known and wealthy citizens to lead the colony.

While Ellis was governor, new colonists came to Georgia from South Carolina and the West Indies. Many of these new settlers brought slaves with them, and the governor granted the newcomers large amounts of land. By 1759, the population of the colony had grown to about 10,000, including 3,600 slaves.

Ellis was a popular governor, under whose direction the colony made economic gains. There were more and profitable farms. There were more merchants with a greater variety of items to sell. As a result, the colonists could buy the things they could not grow or manufacture, such as cloth, sugar, farming tools, and seeds for planting.

In 1759, Governor Ellis became ill, perhaps from heat-related problems, and asked to return to Great Britain. However, he was re-assigned to Nova Scotia as its royal governor in 1761.

_____ 87. **Who was the second royal governor of Georgia?**

    A. Henry Ellis

    B. James Wright

    C. John Reynolds

    D. Henry Musgrove

_____ 88. **What change was NOT brought about during the term of royal governor Henry Ellis?**

    A. More merchants started businesses.

    B. Newcomers brought slaves to Georgia.

    C. The number of profitable farms increased.

    D. The first newspaper in Georgia was published.

_____ 89. **Which royal governor permitted slavery in Georgia, made farms more profitable, and increased the number of merchants selling goods?**

    A. James Wright

    B. Henry Ellis

    C. John Reynolds

    D. William Stephens

Governor James Wright

After Henry Ellis left, the Honorable James Wright became governor. Wright was born in Charleston but educated in Great Britain. He had arrived in Georgia on October 11, 1760, to serve as lieutenant governor. Before coming to Georgia, he had been attorney general of South Carolina for twenty-one years. He was loyal to the king, but he also wanted the colonies to do well. He believed that Georgia would continue to grow if large farms were even bigger, if trading expanded, and if the western lands of the colony were opened to settlers. Wright agreed with the self-government program Governor Reynolds had started, and the colonists were pleased with him at first.

During his early years as governor, Wright completed the defenses around Savannah. Savannah was surrounded with palisades, and the area forts were made stronger. The town of Sunbury grew and became the colony's official port of entry for ships arriving from other countries and colonies. Both houses of the colonial legislature worked together to promote Georgia's economic growth. Farmers were allowed to borrow more money, so they bought more land. The amount of owned land grew from 1 million acres to 7 million acres.

Rice and indigo became profitable crops. Enough silk was being produced so that, by 1767, almost a ton of it was exported to Great Britain each year. There were more schools, and more and more people were reading. Many books were sold, and, in 1763, the colony's first newspaper, The Georgia Gazette, was started. Many of the small frame houses were taken down. In their place, two-story houses were built of wood or tabby (a mixture of lime, crushed shells, sand, and water).

There was, however, another side to Georgia during these early years. Many mothers died in childbirth. School was mostly for children in the upper economic class. A group of what plantation owners called "undesirable people" moved from Virginia and the Carolinas to settle in the middle and western parts of the colony. These people became known as **crackers**. The term may have come from the cracking sounds of whips used on oxen or horses as these new settlers went to market to sell their goods. It may have come from the cracking of corn as they prepared corn meal. Some say the term came from a Scottish word that mean "boasters." No matter how it started, the term was meant as an insult for the lower classes. The crackers were thought of as people who did not obey the law and were not welcome in the colony.

_____90. **The term "crackers" refers to people from Virginia and the Carolinas who settled in Georgia in the 1760s and were?**
   A. considered royalty
   B. a great addition to Georgia society
   C. teachers and lawyers
   D. not welcome and did not obey the law

_____91. **Who was governor of Georgia when the last of the palisades were built around Savannah, Sunbury became Georgia's main port of entry, and the term crackers was used to refer to undesirables?**
   A. Henry Ellis
   B. James Wright
   C. John Reynolds
   D. James Oglethorpe

SS8H3   The student will analyze the role of Georgia in the American Revolution.

a. Explain the immediate and long-term causes of the American Revolution and their impact on Georgia; include the French and Indian War (i.e., Seven Years War), Proclamation of 1763, Stamp Act, Intolerable Acts, and the Declaration of Independence.

THE FRENCH AND INDIAN WAR (SEVEN YEARS' WAR)

The French and Indian War was the result of disputes between France and Great Britain that had been going on for almost sixty-five years. The causes of the nine-year war that began in 1754 were greed and fear. The greed was a hope to capture the most land in the New World and control the treasures of the territory. The fear was that one country would gain more power than the other. With the exception of population differences in America, France and Great Britain were well matched. The British navy was the most powerful in the world, but France had the stronger army. Great Britain had a strong alliance with the six tribes of the Iroquois Confederacy, but the French were trading partners with many of the western tribes. The French had more experienced military leadership and, unlike the British colonists, the French settlers did not argue among themselves.

The tension between the two countries increased because both claimed the area of the Ohio River Valley. This frontier region was a huge area of about 200,000 square miles, which was about the size of France. British traders had formed profitable agreements with many tribes that had formerly traded only with the French.

In 1753, Virginia's governor sent a young George Washington to warn the French that the Ohio River Valley did not belong to them and to stop building forts there. Those demands were ignored. The following year, Governor Dinwiddie again sent Washington to the French with a message. This time, however, Washington did not go alone.

The 22-year-old Washington led 150 Virginia militia troops to Fort Duquesne near present-day Pittsburgh. Washington's men set up a crude, round stockade of wooden stakes, which they named Fort Necessity. After a scout reported about 30 French soldiers in a nearby camp, Washington's men attacked, killing 10 and forcing the rest to surrender. As expected, the French attacked Fort Necessity a short time later. On July 3, 1754, severely outnumbered and having lost about one-third of his troops, Washington had no choice but to surrender to the French. The war had begun. It soon spread to Europe, where it was known as the Seven Years' War.

The first few years of the war in America consisted of a series of disappointing losses for the British and their colonies. As the war progressed, Great Britain continued to suffer losses both in the colonies and on the continent of Europe. In 1757, William Pitt was put in charge of the war effort. He used the strength of the British navy and was able to capture the key French Canadian cities of Quebec and Montreal. A year later, Washington again led troops to Fort Duquesne; this time he was victorious. The frontier was made safe and came under British control.

Georgia did not take part in the war, but it was helped by the war. The Treaty of Paris of 1763, which formally ended the war, set Georgia's western boundary at the Mississippi River.

Results of the French and Indian War

- The British gained control of Canada, which today continues to be a friend and trading partner of the United States.
- The western frontier – the Ohio River Valley and all lands east of the Mississippi River – was opened for settlement by the other colonies.
- Great Britain obtained Florida from Spain, which had been an ally of the French during the war.
- For its help, France gave the Louisiana Territory to Spain.
- After 150 years of colonization, France lost all of its land in the area.
- Perhaps most importantly, the French and Indian War led to the American Revolution. After the war, Great Britain found itself left with a huge war debt. To the British, it seemed only logical to tax the colonists to cover those expenses.

_____92. **Which statement about Georgia regarding the French and Indian War is correct?**

A. Georgia gained new territory as a result of the war.

B. Georgia colonists suffered great losses of lives and property.

C. Georgia was a buffer zone in the fighting between the French and the Indians.

D. Georgia was the only colony to support the French against the British in the war.

_____93. **How did the French and the British compare as the French and Indian War began?**

A. The French had the strongest navy and army but lacked Indian alliances to fight the British.

B. The French had the strongest navy and army but their settlers fought bitterly among themselves.

C. The French forces had more experienced military leaders but lacked a strong army to fight the British.

D. The French had a number of alliances with the Indians, but the British had a larger number of troops.

_____94. **What effect did the French and Indian War have on Georgia's growth and development?**

A. Georgia prospered in a stable and peaceful environment once the French and Indian tribes were defeated.

B. Georgia gained new lands, new water access for shipping, ample farmland, and rich forests with timber and naval stores.

C. Georgia gained many new settlers who were living in the lands that were added to Georgia's colonial boundaries.

D. Georgia took possession of several key French forests, which added to Georgia's defenses against the Spanish.

_____95. **During the French and Indian War, why did most of the Native American tribes side with the French?**

A. The Indians had become Catholic.

B. The Indians worked for the French as guides.

C. The Indians negotiated treaties with the French.

D. The Indians were trading partners with the French.

_____96. **Which statement BEST describes how the French and Indian War led to America's Revolutionary War?**

A. Great Britain gained control of Canada and tried to use Canada's tax structure on the thirteen colonies.

B To get revenge, France incited rebellion in the colonies and enticed Spain to move into the territories of the British colonies.

C. France lost the Louisiana territory, and the southern colonies argued with Great Britain over claims to the newly acquired land.

D. To get money to repay war debts, Great Britain taxed the colonies on the premise that the war had been necessary to protect the colonies from the French.

PROCLAMATION OF 1763

King George III issued the Proclamation of 1763 shortly after the end of the French and Indian War. The proclamation forbade the colonists to settle west of the Appalachian Mountains. This proclamation also moved Georgia's southern boundary to the St. Marys River. At the same time, the Cherokee and the Creek gave up all lands between the Ogeechee and Savannah rivers north to Augusta, which was Georgia's second oldest city. They also gave up the coastal land south of the Altamaha River.

When the land came under Georgia's control, settlers began to migrate to the colony. The new boundaries were important to Georgia's growth. Not only did they provide water access for future shipping, but they also provided good farmland and dense forests with timber and naval stores resources.

_____ 97. **What law forbade colonists to move west of the Appalachian Mountains?**
   A. Intolerable Acts
   B. Missouri Compromise
   C. Proclamation of 1763
   D. Emancipation Proclamation

_____ 98. **The Proclamation of 1763 moved Georgia's southern boundary to the**
   A. Flint River.
   B. St. Marys River.
   C. Altamaha River.
   D. Suwannee River.

_____ 99. **What natural feature did the Proclamation Line of 1763 follow?**
   A. Ohio River
   B. Atlantic Ocean
   C. Mississippi River
   D. Appalachian Mountains

STAMP ACT

In 1765, the British Parliament passed the Stamp Act in an attempt to raise money to pay for the French and Indian War. This act placed a tax on newspapers, legal documents, and licenses. Throughout the colonies, the reaction to the Stamp Act was swift and sometimes violent.

A Stamp Act Congress met in Boston, Massachusetts, to speak against the tax. The Georgia colonial assembly was not in session at the time, so it did not send a representative to the Stamp Act Congress. Nevertheless, on the day before it went into effect, a few Georgia citizens showed their dislike of the Stamp Act by burning an effigy (a likeness) of the stamp master in the streets of Savannah.

On November 6, a group of Georgians came together to oppose the Stamp Act. They called themselves the Liberty Boys. The Liberty Boys were part of a larger group, the Sons of Liberty, whose daring acts came to represent the spirit of the Revolution.

Although the taxes did not bother the average Georgian very much, the colony felt their effect. Georgia was the only colony that ever sold the stamps. Only a few were sold, but Georgia's neighbors in South Carolina, who were more directly affected, spoke out with anger against it. Also, Georgia's only newspaper, The Georgia Gazette, had to stop printing until the Stamp Act was repealed a year later.

_____**100.**What was the first direct tax by Parliament on the American colonies, which caused the colonies to unite against King George?

    A. Sugar Act

    B. Stamp Act

    C. Currency Act

    D. Quartering Act

_____**101.**Georgians who came together to oppose the Stamp Act called themselves the

    A. Liberty Boys.

    B. Sons of Liberty.

    C. Revolutionary Guards.

    D. Stamp Act Opposition.

THE INTOLERABLE ACTS

To punish the colonists of Massachusetts for the Boston Tea Party, Parliament enacted four laws, which because of their harshness became known as the Intolerable Acts. One law closed the port of Boston until the citizens of Massachusetts paid for the tea. Under another law, Massachusetts colonists could not have a town meeting without the agreement of their governor, who was also the commander of the British troops. The operation of the court system was changed so that any British officials who committed capital crimes would be tried in Great Britain rather than by a colonial court. Finally, the Quartering Act required that the citizens of all colonies house and feed British soldiers at their own expense.

Although the laws were aimed at Massachusetts, representatives of all the colonies except Georgia gathered in Philadelphia to protest them. On September 5, 1774, the delegates organized a Continental Congress. That Congress agreed to stop all trade with Great Britain and urged each colony to set up committees of safety. These committees would enforce the boycott.

Anti-British sentiment was growing in Georgia, but the people still seemed to care more about which parish would have the most power in the Georgia assembly. Because the colony still depended on Great Britain, the assembly chose not to send a delegate to the Continental Congress. However, in August 1774, a group of Georgians met to discuss their reaction to the Intolerable Acts. After talking for a long time, they decided to send a resolution to Parliament demanding that citizens of the thirteen colonies have the same rights as British citizens living in Great Britain. They insisted that the Intolerable Acts did not agree with the "Rights and Privileges of an Englishman."

The assembly also decided to have a meeting in Georgia to talk about the growing unhappiness over their ties with Great Britain. This meeting, called the Provincial Congress, was held in Savannah in January 1775. Less than one-half of Georgia's parishes were represented, and the meeting ended without much being done.

_____**102.**Actions taken by the British to punish the colonists for the Boston Tea Party became known as the

    A. Tea Act.

    B. Stamp Act.

    C. Intolerable Acts.

    D. Navigation Acts.

____103. **Which was NOT a provision of the Intolerable Acts?**
    A. The British required colonists to possess identifiation at all times.
    B. The British required colonists to possess identification at all times.
    C. The British required citizens in all the colonies to house and feed British soldiers.
    D. The British closed the port of Boston until the colonists paid for the tea that was destroyed in the Boston Tea Party.

Use the facts to answer questions 104 and 105.

> - Many colonists had relatives in Great Britain and did not want to put them in danger.
> - The British king was still paying money to support the colonists.

104.   **Like many colonists, Georgians were divided on the issues of the Revolutionary War. The colony was reluctant to join the revolution at first because Georgia**
    A. was self-sufficient.
    B. had no objections to the Intolerable Acts.
    C. was financially dependent on Great Britain.
    D. had a long, successful history of self-government.

____105. **What was the behavior of most Georgians during the Revolution?**
    A. They moved to Virginia.
    B. They rioted in the streets.
    C. They attacked British troops.
    D. They were loyal to King George.

____106. **All of the following are reasons for Georgia to stay loyal to England EXCEPT**
    A. Georgia had more British settlers than the other colonies and they were more loyal to Great Britain.
    B. Georgia was not as successful as the other colonies, and it could not afford to raise funds to fight the British.
    C. Georgia was far younger as a colony than the other colonies, and it still needed much support from Great Britain.
    D. Georgia had a much smaller population than the other colonies, and it did not have enough men for an army to fight the British.

THE DECLARATION OF INDEPENDENCE

In January 1776, Thomas Paine's pamphlet Common Sense appeared. In it, Paine urged the colonists to separate from Great Britain in language all people could understand. The pamphlet was a sensation and sold 120,000 copies in less than three months. By the end of the year, it had sold 500,000 copies. Paine quickly followed Common Sense with a series of pamphlets. Paine had a great deal of influence on the actions of the Second Continental Congress. John Adams said, "Without the pen of Paine, the sword of Washington would have been wielded in vain."

On July 4, 1776, over a year after the battles of Lexington and Concord, the Second Continental Congress approved the Declaration of Independence. The 1,458-word document, written primarily by Thomas Jefferson, can be divided into three parts. The Preamble, or introduction, stated how the colonists felt about democracy. The second part, or body, listed twenty-seven grievances (complaints) against King George III and his government that led the colonists to seek independence from Great Britain. The third part, the conclusion, declared the colonies to be an independent nation for all future times.

The Declaration meant that the colonies were one nation, still not in total agreement, but one nation nevertheless. When the Declaration of Independence was read in Georgia, it produced great excitement, although some colonists decided to return to Great Britain. Georgians began to prepare for war. They sent food and ammunition to the Continental Army and began to strengthen the home militia.

_____107. **What is the opening part of the Declaration of Independence called?**
- A. Preface
- B. Preamble
- C. Objective
- D. Introduction

_____108. **Who was the primary author of the Declaration of Independence?**
- A. John Adams
- B. Thomas Paine
- C. Thomas Jefferson
- D. Benjamin Franklin

_____109. **What is included in the middle part of the Declaration of Independence?**
- A. a declaration of war
- B. a list of grievances against the king
- C. a rationale for supporting the royal family
- D. signatures of the participants at the Continental Congress

_____110. **What is included in the third part of the Declaration of Independence?**
- A. a declaration of war on Great Britain
- B. a warning to King George to change his ways
- C. a statement about separation from Great Britain
- D. a call for a meeting to establish a new government

SS8H3   The student will analyze the role of Georgia in the American Revolution.
b. Analyze the significance of people and events in Georgia on the Revolutionary War; include loyalists, patriots, Elijah Clarke, Austin Dabney, Nancy Hart, Button Gwinnett, Lyman Hall, George Walton, Battle of Kettle Creek, and siege of Savannah.

LOYALISTS AND PATRIOTS

Loyalists, also called Tories, British Royalists, or "King's friends," were those who were loyal to the king of England, George III.

Patriots, also referred to as Whigs, Liberty Boys, Colonials, or Sons and Daughters of Liberty, were those citizens ready to cut ties with Great Britain.

_____111. **Most of the fighting in Georgia during the American Revolution was between**

    A. Spanish and British soldiers.

    B. British and French soldiers.

    C. Georgia Loyalists and Indians.

    D. Georgia Patriots and Loyalists.

Use these items to answer question 112.

- Committees of Correspondence
- Boston Tea Party
- Continental Congress

_____112. **These activities were supported by most of the**

    A. Patriots.

    B. Loyalists.

    C. Colonists.

    D. Royalists.

ELIJAH CLARKE AND THE BATTLE OF KETTLE CREEK

Morale throughout the colonies was at an all-time low. Finally, in February 1779, Georgia had a victory. A rebel militia group led by Colonel Elijah Clarke (after whom Clarke County is named) defeated a force of more than 800 British troops at the Battle of Kettle Creek, about eight miles from Washington, Georgia.

The Battle of Kettle Creek was minor when compared to those fought in other parts of the country. It was, however, important to Georgia. The militia was able to take badly needed weapons and horses from the British soldiers, and the spirits of the Georgia militia were lifted by their victory.

_____113. **Where did the first colonial victory in Georgia during the American Revolution occur?**

    A. Sunbury

    B. Savannah

    C. Louisville

    D. Kettle Creek

_____114. **Who was the leader of the militia who led the forces at the Battle of Kettle Creek?**

    A. Elijah Clarke

    B. Nathaniel Greene

    C. Benjamin Lincoln

    D. George Washington

_____115. **What was the importance of the Battle of Kettle Creek?**

    A. The Indians joined with the colonists to defeat the British.

    B. The colonists took needed weapons and horses from the British.

    C. The British were driven into Florida and were unable to regroup.

    D. It was the last battle fought in Georgia during the Revolutionary War.

AUSTIN DABNEY

One of the men who followed Colonel Clarke at Kettle Creek was a Revolutionary War hero named Austin Dabney. Dabney was a freeborn mulatto, a child of mixed parentage. He arrived in Georgia just before the war with a man named Richard Aycock. Aycock, a white North Carolinian, was not known for his bravery. Instead of joining the Georgia militia himself, Aycock proposed that Austin Dabney take his place. After much discussion, some of which centered on whether he was freeborn or a slave, Dabney was accepted. He proved to be a good soldier at Kettle Creek and was wounded in action. A family named Harris cared for him while his wounds healed.

After the Revolutionary War, veterans were given plots of land as partial payment for their military service. Many did not want Dabney to get his veteran's share of land. However, Governor George Gilmer and some members of the Georgia legislature praised Dabney as a patriot. After months of debate, Dabney received a valuable piece of land in Madison County. When he moved to his new home, he took the Harris family with him. Together, they made the property profitable. Austin Dabney died in 1834, fifty-five years after the Battle of Kettle Creek.

_____116. **Who was the black soldier who was seriously wounded at the Battle of Kettle Creek?**
   A. Crispus Attucks
   B. Austin Dabney
   C. Frederick Douglass
   D. Alonzo Herndon

_____117. **Austin Dabney received a plot of land in Madison County**
   A. from the Harris family.
   B. right after the Battle at Kettle Creek.
   C. because he had recently moved into Georgia.
   D. as payment for his service in the Revolutionary War.

NANCY HART

Around 1771, Benjamin and Nancy Hart and their eight children settled twelve miles outside of what we now call Elberton. Several legends surround Nancy Hart. Probably the most repeated one concerns Colonel John Dooley, a neighbor of the Harts who was killed by Tories. A few days after Dooley's murder, five of those Tories stopped by Nancy's home and demanded that she cook dinner for them. As the men talked, Nancy overheard them bragging about the murder.

Thinking quickly, Nancy brought out a jug of whiskey and offered it to the men. As they drank, they did not notice Nancy motioning to her daughters to go to the woods and sound the alarm for help. Enjoying their drink and food, they also did not realize that Nancy was quietly taking their rifles as she served them.

When Nancy pulled the third rifle away, one of the men finally noticed. As the men rushed her, Nancy calmly pulled the trigger and killed one of them. She grabbed a second rifle and held the other soldiers at gunpoint until help arrived. Some reports say she may have killed two of the soldiers. In any event, the rest were soon put on trial and hanged.

We may never know if the stories of Nancy Hart's courage are true. However, the legend of Nancy Hart remains as an example of the revolutionary spirit of Georgia. Hart County and its county seat, Hartwell, located in northeast Georgia, are named for her. Hart is the only county in Georgia named for a woman.

____ 118. **Who was the female Georgia patriot famous for capturing and killing a group of Tories during the revolution?**

    A. Nancy Hart

    B. Molly Pitcher

    C. Rebecca Felton

    D. Mary Musgrove

____ 119. **Which BEST describes how Nancy Hart captured the group of Tories?**

    A. She gave them food and drink.

    B. She sent her daughters for help.

    C. She took their guns away from them.

    D. She heard them bragging while cooking.

BUTTON GWINNETT, LYMAN HALL, GEORGE WALTON

The Declaration of Independence was officially signed on August 2, 1776. The names of three Georgians – Lyman Hall, George Walton, and Button Gwinnett – appeared on the left side of the document, right below the signature of John Hancock. But it was over a month before Georgians found out how their representatives had voted or even what the Declaration said.

George Walton, at age twenty-six, was the youngest signer of the Declaration of Independence. An autograph of Button Gwinnett is one of the most sought-after collector's autographs in the world. Today, it is valued at over $250,000.

____ 120. **Who were the three Georgians who signed the Declaration of Independence?**

    A. Lyman Hall, Button Gwinnett, and James Wright

    B. Thomas Jefferson, Henry Ellis, and James Wright

    C. George Walton, Lyman Hall, and Button Gwinnett

    D. Lyman Hall, George Walton, and Noble Wimberly Jones

____ 121. **Who was the youngest person to sign the Declaration of Independence?**

    A. Henry Ellis

    B. James Wright

    C. George Walton

    D. Button Gwinnett

____ 122. **Independence from Great Britain came for Georgia and the other colonies in**

    A. 1607.

    B. 1733.

    C. 1776.

    D. 1779.

SIEGE OF SAVANNAH

In December 1778, British forces attacked and took control of Savannah. In early September 1779, twenty-two French ships and 4,000 soldiers under the command of Charles Henri Comte d'Estaing arrived off Tybee Island. Those troops joined about 15,000 Americans under the command of General Benjamin Lincoln. The combined armies laid siege to Savannah. A **siege** occurs when forces try to capture a fortified fort or town by surrounding it and preventing any supplies from reaching it.

Finally, at daybreak on October 9, the American and French troops attacked British positions. The attack, which lasted only 45 minutes, failed. By the time it was over, more than 1,000 men with the American forces (821 of whom were French) and 40 British lay dead. Over 600 men were wounded. One of America's best foreign patriots, Polish Count Casimir Pulaski, had given his life for a country not his own. And, Savannah was set to remain in British hands for the next 3½ years.

_____ **123. How could Georgia's support of the Revolutionary War effort best be described?**
   A. never strong in any area
   B. strong in every area except Savannah
   C. complete in all areas from the beginning
   D. led by Savannah and the upcountry revolutionary leaders

_____ **124. Who was the foreign patriot who died during the siege of Savannah?**
   A. Casimir Pulaski
   B. Bernardo de Galvez
   C. Marquis de Lafayette
   D. Jean Baptist Rochambeau

_____ **125. What was the MOST significant result of the siege of Savannah?**
   A. The British were pushed out of Georgia.
   B. The city of Savannah remained in British hands.
   C. It was the deadliest battle of the Revolutionary War.
   D. It was the last major conflict of the Revolutionary War.

Use this map to answer question 126.

Revolutionary War Battles in Georgia

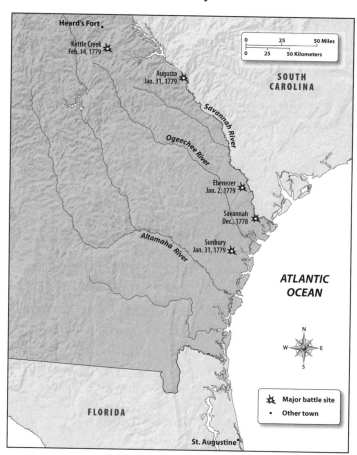

_____ **126. Where was one of the major battle sites of the Revolution in Georgia?**

  A. Atlanta
  B. Ebenezer
  C. Savannah
  D. St. Augustine

SS8H4   The student will describe the impact of events that led to the ratification of the United States Constitution and the Bill of Rights.

  a. Analyze the strengths and weaknesses of both the Georgia Constitution of 1777 and the Articles of Confederation and explain how weaknesses in the Articles of Confederation led to a need to revise the Articles.

GEORGIA CONSTITUTION OF 1777

Georgia joined the other colonies in celebrating the decision to become independent of Great Britain. The former colonies were tired of being governed and living under laws made by Great Britain, which they believed was both out of touch and too far away to understand their needs. The new goal for each colony was statehood. Each new state was to develop its own method of governance and pass laws that met its needs.

Work was begun on a state constitution to replace the earlier "Rules and Regulations," which had been used to govern the state. Writing the new constitution was not easy. Some citizens wanted a government like the one already in place, with most of the power in the hands of a few wealthy landowners and merchants. The Whigs, a more extreme group, wanted to give all the people of Georgia a chance to govern themselves. The Whigs won, and Georgia decided on a government based on the separation of powers and the rights of citizens to agree with how they were governed.

By May 1777, Georgia adopted its first state constitution at a constitutional convention held in Savannah. The parish system was done away with, and eight counties were formed. However well meaning the lawmakers were in developing the 1777 constitution, there were problems. Rather than a bicameral legislature, the Constitution of 1777 provided for a unicameral, or one-house, legislature. This single legislative body had very broad powers, including the ability to make appointments for the judicial branch (the courts) and the executive branch (the governor).

Stung by the loyalty of former governors to the king, the members of the constitutional convention wanted to limit severely the influence and power of the governor. They proposed a one-year term for the governor. The governor was to be selected by the legislature rather than voted on by the people. The actual power, therefore, was in the hands of twelve lawmakers from the legislature who served as an executive council. The executive council could accept or reject any proposals initiated by the governor. The constitutional convention selected John Treutlen, a Salzburger.

_____ **127. What was the main weakness of the Georgia Constitution of 1777?**

  A. It created an independent executive branch.
  B. It established two parts in the legislative branch.
  C. It gave too much power to the legislative branch.
  D. It placed too much importance on checks and balances.

____ 128. **Under Georgia's Constitution of 1777, governors were selected by**
   A. the legislature.
   B. the citizens' vote.
   C. the chairman of each parish.
   D. the executive council of Georgia.

____ 129. **All of the following were reasons Georgia's first constitution limited the power of the governor except**
   A. there were no good candidates for governor.
   B. they feared the governor would become a dictator.
   C. in the past the governor showed too much loyalty to the king.
   D. they believed the legislature, which was closer to the people, should have more power.

____ 130. **Who was chosen Georgia's first governor under the Constitution of 1777?**
   A. Lyman Hall
   B. John Treutlen
   C. George Walton
   D. Button Gwinnett

THE ARTICLES OF CONFEDERATION

The founding fathers wanted to make sure that their new government would be very different from the government of Great Britain. The **Articles of Confederation**, ratified in 1781, intentionally established a weak national government. The new U.S. government consisted of a unicameral legislature–Congress–in which each state had one vote. There was no chief executive, and there was no national court system.

The weaknesses in the Articles of Confederation caused major problems for the new country. Under the Articles, the Confederation Congress that could not pay the colonial soldiers during the Revolutionary War found that it also could not pay them after the war. The Confederation Congress asked the states for help, but many states rejected or ignored the request.

The new government did not have the power to regulate trade between the states or between the United States and foreign countries. Each state had its own money system, which also created problems with trade. The British reoccupied some of the forts in the Northwest Territory (the area north of the Ohio River), and the national government was powerless to do anything to stop them. As a result, foreign countries had little respect for the new country.

George Washington and others were alarmed at what they saw happening to the states under the Articles of Confederation. A movement began to examine and revise the Articles of Confederation. An opportunity arose in 1786 when Virginia asked for a meeting in Annapolis, Maryland, to discuss the continuing trade problems among the states. Representatives from only five states attended, and nothing was accomplished. The delegates at Annapolis did ask that a second convention meet in Philadelphia the next year. They broadened the goals for the Philadelphia meeting and asked to discuss all the problems of the Articles of Confederation. It was hoped that some changes could be made that would make the national government stronger.

____ 131. **The first written plan for the government of the United States was called the**
   A. American Constitution.
   B. Colonial Confederation.
   C. Articles of Confederation.
   D. Constitution of the United States.

____ **132.** **Under the Articles of Confederation, there was no**

    A. governor.

    B. law-making body.

    C. equality among the states.

    D. legislature or court system.

____ **133.** **Why did the authors of the Articles of Confederation want a federal government with little power?**

    A. They did not favor a government that gave power to the southern states.

    B. They considered themselves thirteen separate states rather than one nation.

    C. They wanted to grow the power of the federal government slowly over time.

    D. They had just freed themselves from the domination of a strong, powerful government in Great Britain.

____ **134.** **The initial purpose in calling the Constitutional Convention of 1787 was to**

    A. establish a national court system.

    B. regulate trade between the states.

    C. declare independence from Britain.

    D. gain consent of the states in order to confront the British.

SS8H4 **The student will describe the impact of events that led to the ratification of the United States Constitution and the Bill of Rights.**

    b. Describe the role of Georgia at the Constitutional Convention of 1787; include the role of Abraham Baldwin and William Few, and reasons why Georgia ratified the new constitution.

ROLE OF GEORGIA AT THE CONSTITUTIONAL CONVENTION

In the summer of 1787, the Georgia Assembly appointed William Pierce, William Few, Abraham Baldwin, and William Houstoun as its delegates to the Constitutional Convention to be held in Philadelphia. Only Few and Baldwin stayed until the end and signed the new U.S. Constitution.

There were many debates and disagreements during the convention. Perhaps the most difficult was over representation in the national legislature. The larger states wanted representation based on population; the smaller states wanted equal representation. William Houstoun voted for the large state position. Abraham Baldwin's vote for the small state position forced the convention to work on a compromise position. Baldwin served on the committee to work out that compromise, which has since become known as the Great Compromise.

____ **135.** **The purpose of the Constitutional Convention, which was held in Philadelphia in 1787, was to**

    A. sign the Treaty of Paris.

    B. select the nation's new president.

    C. revise the Articles of Confederation.

    D. draft a Declaration of Independence.

_____ **136. The U.S. Constitution was actually signed by only two of Georgia's four delegates. The two signers were William Few and**

A. George Walton.
B. Button Gwinnett.
C. Thomas Jefferson.
D. Abraham Baldwin.

REASONS WHY GEORGIA RATIFIED THE NEW CONSTITUTION

Georgia supported the new U.S. Constitution. As more and more people moved into the state, they began to push westward into the land occupied by Indians. The Indians were determined to hold onto their lands. As the youngest state, Georgia needed a strong national government to help protect it from the Indian threat and to acquire land from the Indians in order to expand.

A special convention was called to consider ratification of the U.S. Constitution. Delegates began gathering in December 1787. On January 2, 1788, Georgia became the fourth state to ratify the U.S. Constitution, by a vote of 26-0.

_____ **137. How many states ratified the U.S. Constitution before Georgia?**

A. 2
B. 3
C. 4
D. 5

_____ **138. After the U.S. Constitution was written and signed, it had to be ratified, or approved, by the states. How did Georgia respond to ratification?**

A. slow to approve the new Constitution
B. refused to ratify until the Bill of Rights was added
C. never approved and later had to apply for admission
D. called a special convention and quickly approved the Constitution

---

SS8H5   The student will explain significant factors that affected the development of Georgia as part of the growth of the United States between 1789 and 1840.

a. Explain the establishment of the University of Georgia, Louisville, and the spread of Baptist and Methodist churches.

ESTABLISHMENT OF THE UNIVERSITY OF GEORGIA

Educational growth was slow during the post-Revolutionary War period. Some people received only a few years of elementary education. Often even the best farmers knew little, if anything, about reading or mathematics. Most of Georgia's citizens had not been to school at all. Governor Lyman Hall recommended that the state set aside land for schools, but few were built.

Even though the building of schools was slow, people believed in the value of education. In 1784, the government set aside twenty thousand acres of land for a state college. In 1785, the University of Georgia was chartered as a land grant university (a school for which the federal government donated the land). It is the oldest school of its kind in the nation. The university, which was to oversee all public schools in the state, opened for classes in 1801. The first building for the all-male, all-white student body was Franklin College, and for many years, the University of Georgia was frequently called Franklin College. Women were not admitted to the University of Georgia until 1918, 117 years after the college was opened to men.

_____ 139. Which statement BEST describes a "land grant university," such as the University of Georgia?

    A. The land for the college was donated by the federal government.

    B. The land could not be used for any purpose other than a college.

    C. The college was a public university with free tuition to state residents.

    D. The college was established as an agricultural college to improve farming.

_____ 140. What was the first building constructed at what is now the University of Georgia?

    A. Allen Hall

    B. Wesleyan Hall

    C. Franklin College

    D. The School of Commerce

_____ 141. Who gave the tract of land that became the University of Georgia?

    A. Governor Hall

    B. Native Americans

    C. General Assembly

    D. Federal Government

LOUISVILLE

Georgia has had several different capital cities. For much of the state's early history, the capital rotated between Savannah and Augusta. Savannah was a coastal city. When most of Georgia's population moved inland, it became difficult for the state's citizens to travel to Savannah for state business. Augusta was too far east for many of the state's citizens. In 1786, the legislature appointed a commission to find a site for a permanent, centrally located capital.

The commission was given funds to purchase 1,000 acres of land for a new city that was to be modeled from the then-U.S. capital of Philadelphia. The legislature required that the new location be 20 miles from an Indian trading post on the Ogeechee River in what is now Jefferson County. The legislature also insisted that the new capital be called "Louisville" to honor King Louis XVI of France for his help in America's Revolutionary War. While finding the site was relatively easy, it was 1796 before a new Capitol was constructed in Louisville. Louisville served as the capital for ten years.

Little is known about the Louisville Capitol other than it was a brick, two-story building. One important event did take place on the grounds of the Capitol. On February 21, 1796, all the records of the Yazoo land sales were collected and burned in front of the Capitol. The "Holy Fire from Heaven" was started with the aid of a magnifying glass.

As more Indian lands opened to the settlers, Georgia's citizens continued to move west and wanted a capital that was more convenient for the western part of the state. In 1804, the legislature voted to build a new capital city in Baldwin County. It set aside funds to purchase 3,240 acres of land and agreed to name the newest capital "Milledgeville" in honor of Governor John Milledge.

_____ 142. From the colonial era until Reconstruction, the capital of Georgia was moved many times in response to what factor?

    A. changing political influences in the state

    B. the changing population center of the state

    C. the changing geographic center of the state

    D. changing transportation patterns in the state

____ 143. **All the records from the Yazoo land fraud were burned in public in Georgia's capital city of**
   A. Athens.
   B. Atlanta.
   C. Savannah.
   D. Louisville.

____ 144. **Why was Louisville chosen as Georgia's capital in 1786?**
   A. Louisville was the state's largest city.
   B. Louisville was more centrally located.
   C. Louisville was the most important center for trade.
   D. Louisville played an important role in the American Revolution.

____ 145. **The city of Louisville was modeled after**
   A. Atlanta.
   B. New York.
   C. Philadelphia.
   D. Washington, D.C.

THE SPREAD OF BAPTIST AND METHODIST CHURCHES

After the Revolutionary War, many ministers left America for Great Britain. Still, churches in Georgia grew, both in size and in importance to their communities. In addition to the Anglicans, Quakers, and Baptists, Methodist circuit riders (ministers who went from district to district) founded churches in the frontier region. Sometimes these ministers could have only one service a month for each church. However, they stayed in touch with their members and visited them as often as possible.

In 1787, free blacks founded the Springfield Baptist Church in Augusta. The First African Baptist Church in Savannah was founded in 1788 under the leadership of Andrew Bryan. In Savannah, a Jewish synagogue had a small but committed membership. In 1796, Georgia's first Roman Catholic Church was established in Wilkes County. In 1801, a second parish was formed in Savannah.

Like many others in the South, Georgians were caught up in the Great Revival movement of the early 1800s. Religious revivals, often in the form of camp meetings, were popular, especially among Methodists. Sometimes people came from miles away and camped while attending a two- or three-day meeting. Often, the camp meetings lasted for a week or longer.

During the 1850s, church membership grew in Georgia; by 1860, there were 2,393 churches in the state. In the South, Georgia was second only to Virginia in the number of churches. Methodist and Baptist were the two largest denominations, but the Episcopal, Catholic, and Presbyterian churches also grew during this period. Jews, one of colonial Georgia's earliest religious groups, were few in number, but they added to the state's religious diversity. There were a few segregated churches, but slaves usually attended the same churches as their masters.

Slavery caused great divisiveness among some denominations. Methodists in the South pulled out of their national organization and formed the Methodist Episcopal Church. In 1845, southern Baptists met in Augusta to form the Southern Baptist Convention. Baptists in the South left the American Baptist Union when its foreign mission board would not accept slave owners as missionaries.

146. **The First African Baptist Church in Georgia was established in 1788 under the leadership of Andrew Bryan in**
    A. Albany.
    B. Augusta.
    C. Savannah.
    D. Brunswick.

147. **By 1860, the two largest church denominations in Georgia were**
    A. Baptist and Jewish.
    B. Methodist and Baptist.
    C. Episcopal and Catholic.
    D. Episcopal and Methodist.

148. **Which church sent circuit riders to frontier settlements to provide monthly services?**
    A. Baptist
    B. Catholic
    C. Episcopal
    D. Methodist

149. **The Methodist and Baptist churches split over permitting**
    A. slavery.
    B. divorce.
    C. communion for children.
    D. ordained women ministers.

> **SS8H5   The student will explain significant factors that affected the development of Georgia as part of the growth of the United States between 1789 and 1840.**
>   b. Evaluate the impact of land policies pursued by Georgia; include the headright system, land lotteries, and the Yazoo land fraud.

HEADRIGHT SYSTEM

Along with their hunger for independence from Great Britain, many Georgians of the late 1700s and early 1800s developed a huge appetite for land. During the settlement of the colony, much of the land east of the Oconee River belonging to the Indians was given to settlers by means of the **headright system**. Under this system, each white male counted as a "head" of a family and had the "right" to receive up to 1,000 acres. Although parts of this system lasted until the early twentieth century, it was largely replaced by a land lottery in 1803.

150. **What was the purpose of the headright system in Georgia?**
    A. It distributed Indian lands to new settlers.
    B. It administered voting and election districts.
    C. It established a method of counting population.
    D. It provided an organized system of collecting taxes.

____ **151. How many acres of land could the head of a family receive under the headright system?**

A. 1,000 acres

B. 2,000 acres

C. 2,500 acres

D. 5,000 acres

____ **152. What system replaced the headright system as a way of allocating land?**

A. land rush

B. surveying

C. feudalism

D. land lottery

LAND LOTTERIES

When public domain lands (lands owned by the state or federal government) were opened for settlement, Georgia surveyed land lots of different sizes. This so-called lottery land was located west of the Oconee River. For a small fee, any white male twenty-one years of age or older could buy a chance and, on the spin of a wheel, win land. Heads of households with children, war veterans, and widows were given extra chances in the land lotteries. Other states also had lotteries, and about 30 million acres of land were given away through them.

____ **153. In the early 1800s, Georgia's policy of giving land to citizens through lotteries was meant to**

A. open the land to yeoman farmers.

B. encourage the development of large cities.

C. introduce new crops and farming methods.

D. ensure peaceful relations with Native Americans.

____ **154. Which was NOT a provision of the land lotteries?**

A. Only men could participate.

B. War veterans were given extra chances.

C. A person had to pay a fee to participate.

D. A person had to be over 21 to participate.

YAZOO LAND FRAUD

Georgians' growing hunger for land reached a peak in 1795. At that time, Georgia's western borders were the Mississippi River and one of its tributaries (branches), the Yazoo River. Included in this territory were the present states of Mississippi and Alabama. Both South Carolina and Spain also claimed some of the same land, and the matter went to court for settlement.

Before any settlement was made, however, four land companies approached Governor George Mathews and members of the General Assembly and bribed them to pass a bill allowing the land companies to buy the western lands. When the Assembly enacted the bill, the land companies bought between 35 and 50 million acres of land for $500,000—about 1-1/2 cents an acre.

The public quickly learned of this bargain basement sale, and there were protests all over the state. Many citizens called for the resignations of the legislators involved in what became known as the Yazoo land fraud.

As a result of public anger and pressure, the legislators involved were voted out of office. The new legislature repealed the law that had allowed the land to be sold. All records of these land sales were burned in public.

The state offered to refund the money from the land sales. However, there were many people who had bought land from the land companies and wanted to keep it. These people went to court. Finally, the federal government resolved the matter by paying over $4 million to settle the Yazoo land claims.

Contrary to its initial hopes, Georgia lost rather than gained from the Yazoo land scheme. The state lost a large part of its land and a lot of money because of the failed plan. Also, after Spain renounced its claims to the area, the federal government contested Georgia's right to it. The long aftermath of the Yazoo affair created bad feelings among many of the state's citizens, and they appealed to the legislature to give in to the federal government. Therefore, in 1802, Georgia ceded (gave up) its land west of the Chattahoochee River to the federal government for $1.25 million, making the river Georgia's western boundary.

_____ 155. **With which topic was the Yazoo fraud concerned?**
    A. Indian lands in north Georgia
    B. sale of land in western Georgia territory
    C. ratification of the Constitution in Georgia
    D. creation of a national park on state property

_____ 156. **What scandal took place when Georgia's governor and some legislators were bribed to sell public land to private developers at below-market prices?**
    A. Yazoo land fraud
    B. Trail of Tears fraud
    C. Georgia's land lottery
    D. Mississippi land fraud

_____ 157. **Why did Georgia give up land claims in what is now Mississippi and Alabama?**
    A. The federal government wanted to set that land aside for the Indian population.
    B. The state did not have the millions of dollars required to purchase the land from Spain.
    C. The state could not claim the land because the General Assembly illegally sold it to private companies.
    D. The federal government paid millions to settle the Yazoo land fraud and disputed Georgia's right to the land.

_____ 158. **The Yazoo land fraud occurred because land companies**
    A. claimed land that had been acquired illegally.
    B. took land from the Native Americans by force.
    C. made illegal treaties with the Native Americans.
    D. bribed legislators so they could buy land cheaply.

_____ 159. **To whom did Georgia's governor and members of its General Assembly sell the land between the Mississippi and Yazoo rivers, resulting in the Yazoo land fraud?**
    A. land companies
    B. state government
    C. federal government
    D. private land owners

SS8H5 **The student will explain significant factors that affected the development of Georgia as part of the growth of the United States between 1789 and 1840.**

c. Explain how technological developments, including the cotton gin and railroads, had an impact on Georgia's growth.

COTTON GIN

In 1793, Eli Whitney visited the home of Mrs. Catherine Greene Miller at Mulberry Grove Plantation near Savannah. Whitney, a friend of the family, was a schoolteacher and an inventor from Westborough, Massachusetts.

As the story goes, Mrs. Miller asked Whitney to repair a broken watch, which he agreed to do. Not long afterward, a visitor to the Miller home wished aloud for a machine to separate cotton fiber from its seed. Mrs. Miller, remembering the watch repair, asked Whitney if he could make a machine that would speed up the work done so slowly by hand.

After working several weeks, Whitney developed a model for a cotton machine. He made the machine with wire teeth on a turning cylinder. It did separate the cotton from the seeds, but the lint got caught in the wire teeth and stopped up the machine. Several legends say that Mrs. Miller saw the machine's problem, took a clothes brush, and brushed the lint off the teeth. Before long, Whitney built a factory near Augusta and had a working cotton engine, later shortened to just "gin."

Cotton growers welcomed Whitney's gin. Before its invention, a worker might have been able to separate six or seven pounds of cotton seed a day by hand. After the cotton gin's introduction, workers were able to separate about fifty pounds a day.

Eli Whitney earned virtually nothing from his invention. Because they planted so much cotton, the planters "pirated" the gin before Whitney could register his patent. He had to appeal to Congress to save him from financial ruin.

_____ **160. How did Eli Whitney's invention influence the growth of slavery in the South?**

A. It made it easier for slaves to pick cotton.

B. It increased the profits from growing cotton.

C. It made it easier to produce cloth from cotton.

D. It replenished the soil so that more cotton could be grown.

_____ **161. What was invented in Georgia during the 1790s that quickly changed the state's agricultural landscape and led Georgia to develop an economy based on farming?**

A. the combine

B. the cotton gin

C. the steam engine

D. the spinning jenny

_____ **162. The chief cash crop in Georgia before the Civil War was**

A. apples.

B. cotton.

C. grapes.

D. pecans.

____ 163. **The cotton gin was used to**

    A. pick cotton.

    B. plant cotton.

    C. turn cotton fiber into thread.

    D. separate the seeds from the cotton fiber.

RAILROADS

A major economic development during the early 1800s was the building of railroads. Before the railroads were built, people traveled on horses, boats, or stagecoaches. Freight was sent to market by riverboats, ferries, or wagon trains.

At first, rail travel was, perhaps, the least favored means of transportation. In 1830, there were only 13 miles of laid track in the United States, and those belonged to the Baltimore & Ohio Railroad. But just ten years later, there were 3,300 miles of track. Most of the track in Georgia belonged to the Western and Atlantic Railroad, which was chartered in 1836. The Western and Atlantic ran from a point near present-day Chattanooga, Tennessee, to a point on the southeastern bank of the Chattahoochee River. That point was called Terminus, which literally means the end of a railroad line. Today it is known as Atlanta. The railroads dramatically shortened travel time for both passengers and freight, reducing to hours trips that had previously taken days.

____ 164. **Which mode of transportation was developing in Georgia just before the Civil War and was very important to Georgia's war effort and post-war economic development?**

    A. canals

    B. railroads

    C. highways

    D. riverboats

____ 165. **Atlanta at one time was called Terminus because**

    A. all the railroads ended there.

    B. no major railroad went through the city.

    C. the railroad line ended there at one time.

    D. a majority of the railroads went through the city.

____ 166. **Which of the following was NOT a major source of transportation prior to the railroad?**

    A. car

    B. ferry

    C. riverboat

    D. stagecoach

Use the map to answer questions 167-169.

Georgia's Railroads

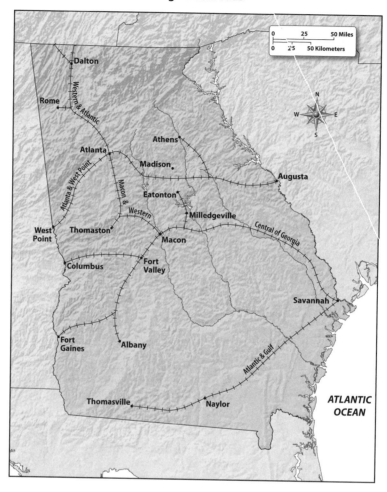

_____ 167. **Which cities were connected to Atlanta by rail?**
   A. Athens and Madison
   B. Madison and Augusta
   C. West Point and Augusta
   D. Augusta and Thomasville

_____ 168. **Which railroad was used to travel from Dalton to Atlanta?**
   A. Atlantic and Gulf
   B. Macon and Western
   C. Western and Atlantic
   D. Atlantic and West Point

_____ 169. **The Atlantic and Gulf Railroad connected Savannah and what city?**
   A. Macon
   B. Atlanta
   C. Augusta
   D. Thomasville

SS8H5 **The student will explain significant factors that affected the development of Georgia as part of the growth of the United States between 1789 and 1840.**

d. Analyze the events that led to the removal of Creeks and Cherokees; include the roles of Alexander McGillivray, William McIntosh, Sequoyah, John Ross, Dahlonega Gold Rush, Worcester v. Georgia, Andrew Jackson, John Marshall, and the Trail of Tears.

ALEXANDER MCGILLIVRAY

Tensions between the Creek and the settlers had grown during the late 1700s as pioneers pushed into Creek lands along the Oconee River. Tribes led by Chief Alexander McGillivray sent warriors against some of the pioneer settlements. The Indians burned houses, stole horses and cattle, and killed or captured over two hundred settlers. Georgia settlers got some men together and told them to kill on sight any Creek who were not members of friendly tribes. Although it was not quite a full-scale conflict, these skirmishes and attacks became known as the Oconee War.

Fighting between the settlers and the Creek went on for several years. In 1790, President Washington called Chief McGillivray to New York. President Washington and the chief talked and exchanged presents. McGillivray then signed the Treaty of New York, by which the Creek gave up all their land east of the Oconee River. They also promised to honor an earlier treaty in which they gave up lands through the Currahee Mountains to Tugaloo. In return, the United States government promised that no whites would go into land west of the boundary. The government also agreed to help the Creek start farms by giving them tools and animals.

When word of the treaty reached Georgians, they were very angry because it appeared to them that the federal government had taken the side of the Creek. Over the next few years, neither the Creek nor the Georgians paid any attention to the treaty. There were bad feelings between the tribes and the whites until both groups accepted other treaties. This "peace" lasted from 1797 until 1812.

It was during this time that the Yazoo land fraud took place. When the federal government stepped in and had Georgia give up all land west of the Chattahoochee River, it also promised to move the Native Americans out of the state. The federal government did little to carry out this promise.

_____ 170. **Who was the Creek leader in the Oconee War between the Creek and the Georgia pioneers?**
A. John Ross
B. Elias Boudinot
C. William McIntosh
D. Alexander McGillivray

_____ 171. **Which treaty required the Creek to give up all their land east of the Oconee River?**
A. Treaty of Paris
B. Treaty of Ghent
C. Treaty of New York
D. Treaty of Indian Springs

WILLIAM MCINTOSH

As more and more of their land was ceded to the government, Creek tribes became separated from each other. There was little chance for them to talk or to trade with each other. The strong Creek confederacy, which had united the tribes before the arrival of the settlers, was no more. Groups of Creek sometimes signed treaties without asking the tribes to agree. This practice led to the death of one well-known Creek leader.

By February 12, 1825, Creek Chief William McIntosh and his first cousin, Georgia Governor George Troup, had worked out the terms of the Treaty of Indian Springs. The United States paid McIntosh and a large group of Lower Creek chiefs $200,000 to cede the last Creek lands in Georgia to the federal government. The government, in turn, gave the use of that land to Georgia.

Groups of Creek who disagreed with the treaty met secretly to decide how to punish McIntosh. They agreed that, in accordance with Creek law, he should die. They sent a rival chief, Menawa, to execute him. According to reports, somewhere between 170 and 400 Creek marched to McIntosh's home in Butts County. After two days, they were a mile from McIntosh's house. McIntosh did not know they were there.

At daybreak, the Creek set fire to the McIntosh home. They allowed the women and children to leave before they exchanged gunfire with the chief they had come to kill. Smoke and his wounds stopped McIntosh from fighting. The Creek dragged him from the house and stabbed him in the chest. McIntosh's scalp was taken as a warning to others who might want to give Creek land to white men.

_____ **172. Why was William McIntosh, a Creek chief, murdered by his own people?**
   A. He fell to defeat in a fight with the Georgia militia.
   B. He was the cousin of Georgia's Governor George Troup.
   C. He signed a peace treaty with the Cherokee Indians without permission.
   D. He signed a treaty giving up the last Creek lands in Georgia to the federal government.

_____ **173. Who worked out the Treaty of Indian Springs, which ceded the last Creek lands in Georgia?**
   A. Andrew Jackson and Chief Menawa
   B. Andrew Jackson and William McIntosh
   C. Governor George Troup and Chief Menawa
   D. Governor George Troup and William McIntosh

SEQUOYAH

One of the most important contributions to the advancement of Cherokee culture was made by George Gist, who was born around 1760. Gist's father was a Virginia scout and soldier, and his mother was a Cherokee princess. Gist's Indian name was Sequoyah, which meant "lonely lame one." Sequoyah was crippled, from either a childhood illness or a hunting accident, so he could no longer hunt or farm. Instead, he learned to work with silver. He also became a blacksmith.

Sequoyah was very interested in the white man's "talking leaves," pieces of paper with marks on them. He noticed that the papers could be carried many miles, and the people who used them could understand the meaning of the various marks. In 1809, Sequoyah began to make a syllabary. Unlike an alphabet of letters, a **syllabary** is a group of symbols that stand for whole syllables.

It took twelve years for Sequoyah to decide on the eighty-five symbols. According to legend, Sequoyah's wife, fearing that the white government would not like what he was doing, once burned all his work. Sequoyah spent more than a year reconstructing the syllabary.

When he completed it, members of the tribal council at first made fun of the syllabary. However, after Sequoyah was able to teach his daughter and some young chiefs to write and understand the symbols within a few days, the council members changed their minds. They sent Sequoyah all over the territory to teach his method to other Cherokee. In about six months, most of the tribes could write and read the new symbols. By 1830, over 90 percent of the Cherokee could read and write. As a result, the Cherokee were the first Indians to have their language in written form. Equally important, it demonstrated that Indians could communicate with each other without using the language of the white settlers.

____ **174. What was George Gist's (Sequoyah's) major contribution to the Cherokee culture?**

      A. He gained fame as a proud Cherokee hunter and trapper.

      B. He signed a treaty giving Cherokee lands to the United States.

      C. He signed a treaty moving the Cherokee to the Indian Territory.

      D. He developed a syllabary so the Cherokee could have a written language.

____ **175. Sequoyah developed a syllabary for which Native Anerican group?**

      A. Creek

      B. Seminole

      C. Cherokee.

      D. Yamacraw

DAHLONEGA GOLD RUSH

Gold was discovered in Dahlonega in the summer of 1829. In a matter of months, gold fever swept through the North Georgia mountains. Although the Cherokee knew there was gold in the hills, the person given credit for the discovery was a farmer named Benjamin Parks. Parks found the valuable yellow metal while deer hunting in what was then Habersham (now White) County. Auraria, in nearby Lumpkin County, became the first gold mining center in the United States. Over ten thousand miners with gold pans, picks, and shovels moved onto Cherokee land.

The Georgia legislature passed a law that placed part of the Cherokee land under state control. It declared Cherokee laws null and void and would not let the Cherokee speak against white men in a court of law. This meant any white person could hurt or even kill a Cherokee without much fear of punishment. A second law, passed on December 19, 1829, refused the Cherokee any right to gold mined in the Dahlonega area. While the miners searched the mountains and streams for "a spot that showed good color," the Cherokee were losing their homes, lands, and legal rights.

____ **176. What discovery led to the Cherokee losing their land in Georgia?**

      A. oil in Columbus

      B. zinc in Madison

      C. gold in Dahlonega

      D. silver on Creek lands

____ **177. Which provision was NOT included in the laws that were passed after gold was discovered on Cherokee land?**

      A. Cherokee laws were declared null and void.

      B. Cherokee land was placed under state control.

      C. The Cherokee could not speak against white men in courts of law.

      D. The Cherokee were given a small percentage of the gold that was mined.

Use this illustration to answer question 178.

____ **178. What event is shown in this drawing?**
   A. picking cotton on Coastal Plain plantations
   B. building the railroad from Macon to Atlanta
   C. farming the rich soil of the Piedmont region
   D. mining for gold in the North Georgia mountains

Use the diagram to answer questions 179-180.

Panning for Gold

> Choose a gravelly stream that is at least 6 inches deep.

> Fill the bottom of a shallow pan about 3/4 full with gravel.

> Submerge the pan in water and shake it so the heavier gold settles to the bottom. Remove all rocks larger than a pea.

> Still holding the pan under water, add more water and tilt the pan away from you. Swirl it around to wash out lighter materials. Continue this step until only the heavier materials remain.

> Look for gold particles among the heavier, darker minerals left in the pan.

> Put any gold particles in a vial or other container.

____ **179. In what part of a stream is gold found?**
    A. shallow end
    B. along the bank
    C. gravelly bottom
    D. swift moving water

____ **180. Which tool is needed to pan for gold?**
    A. shovel
    B. pick axe
    C. shallow pan
    D. wheelbarrow

WORCESTER V. GEORGIA, JOHN MARSHALL, AND JOHN ROSS

Most Georgians did not care what happened to the Indians, but a group of white missionaries living in Cherokee territory did. To remove the missionaries, the Georgia legislature passed a law on December 22, 1830, that said a white person could not live on Cherokee land without taking an oath of allegiance to the governor. Eleven people, including the Reverend Samuel Worchester, postmaster at the Cherokee capital of New Echota, refused to sign the oath. They were jailed in March, 1831. They were set free but arrested again in July. This time, they were chained and made to walk from the North Georgia mountains to Lawrenceville. At their trial in September, the jury took only fifteen minutes to return a verdict of guilty. Gwinnett County Judge Augustin Clayton sentenced the group to four years at the state penitentiary in Milledgeville. Governor George Gilmer agreed to pardon anyone who would take an oath of loyalty to the state, and all but two agreed. Missionaries Worchester and Elizur Butler took their cases to the U.S. Supreme Court. Chief Justice John Marshall ruled in Worchester v. Georgia that the decision of the Lawrenceville court could not stand because Cherokee territory was not subject to state law.

The Cherokee thought the ruling meant they could keep their land and government. Chief Justice Marshall ordered Butler and Worchester set free, but Judge Clayton refused. Georgia's newly elected governor, Wilson Lumpkin, would not take a stand against the judge. Even the president refused to honor the Supreme Court order.

Cherokee lands were divided into lots of 40 and 160 acres. In 1832, the government held a state lottery to give the Cherokee lands to white men. Even then, the Cherokee refused to leave their home.

On January 9, 1833, Worchester and Butler gave up and told Governor Lumpkin that they would "abandon litigation." (**Litigation** is a legal court action.) The governor pardoned them and then said the two missionaries must leave the state and never return.

More and more, the Cherokee were run off their lands, whipped, and even killed. Chief John Ross made several trips to Washington to ask Congress for help. He wanted the Cherokee protected and the terms of past treaties honored. No help was given. Time was running out for the Cherokee Nation.

____ **181. Who was the Chief Justice of the U.S. Supreme Court who ruled that Cherokee territory was not subject to state law?**
    A. John Marshall
    B. John C. Calhoun
    C. Andrew Jackson
    D. Augustin Clayton

_____ **182.** **Who was the chief of the Cherokee who took a petition to Congress protesting the Cherokee removal from their land?**
    A. Sequoyah
    B. John Ross
    C. Chief Menawa
    D. William McIntosh

_____ **183.** **Who disagreed with the governor of Georgia about his removal policy for the Cherokee?**
    A. the military
    B. the president
    C. the gold miners
    D. the judicial branch

ANDREW JACKSON

In 1828, Andrew Jackson was elected president of the United States. Jackson had been friendly to the Native Americans, especially the Cherokee, when he needed their help to fight the Red Stick Creek. However, he was wise enough politically to know that white voters wanted the Native Americans removed from the southern states.

In 1830, Congress passed a bill, the Indian Removal Act, that called for all Native Americans to be moved to the western territories. There were strong feelings on both sides, and the bill passed by only fourteen votes. After Jackson signed the bill into law, however, there was no question about what would happen to the Southeast tribes. Congress allocated $500,000 to enforce the provisions of the Indian Removal Act.

When the Supreme Court issued its order protecting the rights of the Cherokee, President Andrew Jackson refused to honor the Supreme Court order. Jackson thought that state governments should be in charge of Indian territories. He reportedly said, "John Marshall has rendered his decision, now let him enforce it!"

_____ **184.** **When Andrew Jackson said "John Marshall has rendered his decision, now let him enforce it," he meant that the**
    A. Congress would see that troops were sent to enforce the decision.
    B. Congress and the president agreed with and supported the decision.
    C. Supreme Court could not enforce the decision without the support of the president.
    D. Supreme Court was the supreme law of the land and could do whatever it wanted.

_____ **185.** **The intent of the Indian Removal Act was to**
    A. destroy the Native American way of life.
    B. remove the Native Americans to reservations in the East.
    C. remove the Native Americans from the eastern United States.
    D. help the Native Americans buy land east of the Mississippi River.

REMOVAL OF THE CREEK AND CHEROKEE

Removal of the Creek

After the passage of the Indian Removal Act, the Creek refused to leave the lands of their fathers. When they refused, Alabama took away all their legal rights. The Creek could not defend themselves against whites who moved in and took their lands.

The Creek in Georgia, who no longer had hunting lands, were hungry. Some reports say they stood in the streets of Columbus and begged for food. In 1832, the Creek signed the Treaty of Washington, by which they ceded to the federal government the 5 million acres of land they still owned. In return, the government agreed to set aside 2 million acres on which the Creek would live and farm. Creek could own land, but only after living on it for five years. Then they could choose to sell the land and move west. The decision to stay on reserved land or to move to the western territory was up to each individual.

Once signed, the treaty was broken almost at once. Creek homes were burned, items were stolen from their farms, and Indians were killed. By 1835, some Creek gave up and began the trip west. However, in 1836, bands of Lower Creek attacked whites between Tuskegee, Alabama, and Columbus, Georgia. Afraid of another Indian war, the U.S. Army captured over one thousand Creek and took them to the Indian Territory (present-day Oklahoma). During the next two years, a few Creek escaped and a few were made slaves, but the federal government forced thousands of them to move west.

Toward the end of the Creek removal in Georgia and Alabama, the United States became involved in another Indian war in Florida. They asked seven hundred Creek to help them fight the Seminole. After winning the war, the Creek returned to their families, who had been gathered in camps. Then the whole group, including those who had just fought with the army, was moved to the west.

____ 186. **In addition to the Cherokee, what Southeastern Native American tribe was removed from Georgia in the 1830s?**
   A. Creek
   B. Sioux
   C. Seminole
   D. Yamacraw

____ 187. **Which treaty required the Creek to give up all their land east of the Oconee River?**
   A. Treaty of Paris
   B. Treaty of Ghent
   C. Treaty of New York
   D. Treaty of Washington

Removal of the Cherokee

At the same time that the Creek were being moved, Georgia was also making plans to remove the Cherokee. Georgians wanted to homestead Cherokee land and to mine the gold that had been found on Cherokee land.

The Cherokee had made great efforts to become acclimated to the lifestyle of their European neighbors. The Cherokee established a representative government with executive, legislative, and judicial branches outlined in a written constitution. They established a capital city, New Echota, with government buildings and homes. They lived in log cabins, published a newspaper, the Cherokee Phoenix, in both English and Cherokee. In the end, however, they were removed from the North Georgia mountains forcibly because of the desire for land and the discovery of gold in the area.

____ **188. Which of the following led to the removal of the Cherokee from North Georgia?**
  A. Gold was discovered on the Cherokee's land.
  B. The Cherokee had sided with the French in an earlier war.
  C. The Cherokee were found to have obtained the land illegally.
  D. William McIntosh signed a treaty giving up all Cherokee land.

Use the map to answer questions 189-191.

Indian Land Cessions

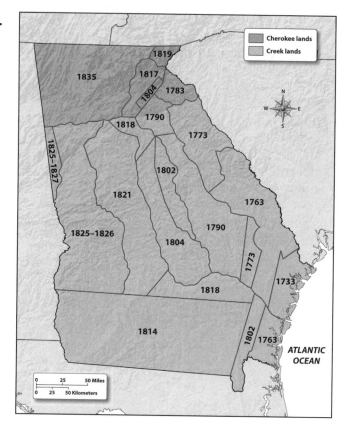

____ **189. In what year did the Creeks first cede land to the Europeans?**
  A. 1733
  B. 1793
  C. 1827
  D. 1835

____ **190. By what year had Europeans competed the removal of the Creeks from Georgia?**
  A. 1763
  B. 1814
  C. 1827
  D. 1835

____ **191. The largest land cession from the Cherokee was in what year?**
  A. 1763
  B. 1814
  C. 1821
  D. 1835

Trail of Tears

In December 1835, the Cherokee were told to come to New Echota. There they were to sign a treaty giving up all Cherokee land that remained in the Southeast. Any member of the tribe who did not come was considered to have agreed with the treaty. Three to five hundred Cherokee out of about seventeen thousand were at the meeting.

Cherokee trader Major Ridge, his son John, and a small number of others agreed to sign the government's treaty. The treaty said the Cherokee would move west, and Georgia would give them a little money and food for the trip.

By May 1838, about two thousand Cherokee had gone. General Winfield Scott was ordered to remove the fifteen thousand or more Cherokee who refused to leave their home. In May 1838, Scott and nearly seven thousand troops arrived in New Echota. The troops first built stockades to house the Cherokee. Then they went into homes and community buildings and forcibly moved the Cherokee to the stockades. Hundreds of men, women, and children died of cholera, dysentery, and fever while in the stockades. During the summer of 1838, the army loaded several thousand Cherokee onto crowded boats and sent them on the Tennessee, Mississippi, and Arkansas rivers to their new homes. The boats were dirty, and the food the government gave them was often not fit to eat. By the time these Indians arrived in Indian Territory, nearly one-third of the group had died.

A few Cherokee escaped and hid in the North Carolina mountains. The rest began a 700-800 mile walk to Indian Territory. Winter winds, snow, and too little food led to the deaths of thousands of Cherokee. The exact number of how many were moved is not known, but about four thousand of this group died while they were in prison before they left or during the march west.

President Martin Van Buren, in his December 1838 address to Congress, said, "the measures of the Removal have had the happiest effect . . . the Cherokees have emigrated (moved out) without apparent reluctance." Today, we can only imagine the fear, despair, and hurt felt by those who had to leave the land of the "principal people." The Cherokee called the move to Indian Territory "ANuna-da-ut- sun'y," which means "the trail where they cried." To this day, the move is sadly remembered as the Trail of Tears.

____ 192. **The removal of the Cherokee from Georgia is remembered as the**
   A. Trail of Tears.
   B. Overland Trail.
   C. Trail to Nowhere.
   D. Long Journey Home.

____ 193. **All the trails along which the Indians were taken ended in the Indian Territory, which is mainly in the present-day state of**
   A. Texas.
   B. Kansas.
   C. Arkansas.
   D. Oklahoma.

____ 194. **What group of north Georgia Indians was forcibly removed from its land after gold was discovered there?**
   A. Seminole
   B. Cherokee
   C. Upper Creek
   D. Lower Creek

Use the map to answer questions 195-197.

Cherokee Removal

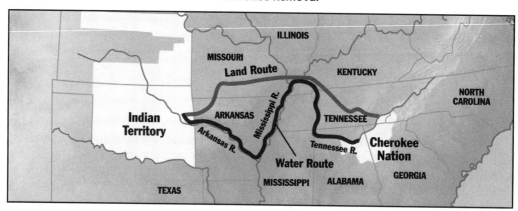

_____ 195. **The Cherokee Nation was primarily located in what is today the state of**
   A. Georgia.
   B. Alabama.
   C. Oklahoma.
   D. Tennessee.

_____ 196. **Which river was NOT part of the water route taken by the Cherokee?**
   A. Missouri
   B. Arkansas
   C. Tennessee
   D. Mississippi

_____ 197. **How many routes led from the Cherokee Nation to the Indian Territory?**
   A. 1
   B. 2
   C. 3
   D. 4

SS8H6   The student will analyze the impact of the Civil War and Reconstruction on Georgia.

a. Explain the importance of key issues and events that led to the Civil War; include slavery, states' rights, nullification, Missouri Compromise, Compromise of 1850, the Georgia Platform, Kansas-Nebraska Act, Dred Scott case, election of 1860, the debate over secession in Georgia, and the role of Alexander Stephens.

SLAVERY

The most divisive issue that led to the Civil War was the question of slavery. Did one man have the right to own another? In order to answer that question, let us first look back in history.

Much of the **antebellum** period (the period before the Civil War) was about "cause and effect," the concept that for each event or thing that happens, there is a cause. In turn, each cause leads to a result, or effect. Then, that result can cause another event, resulting in a chain reaction of cause-and-effect relationships. Several events from the past directly impacted the antebellum period. By 1800, the South was stagnant (not growing or changing) both in terms of population growth and agriculture.

Tobacco had depleted the soil in Virginia and North Carolina. Rice could only be grown in the coastal areas of South Carolina and Georgia. And cotton was not cost effective. But Eli Whitney's cotton gin greatly increased the profits of growing cotton in the South. In turn, that led to a dramatic increase in the numbers of slaves needed to cultivate "King Cotton." By 1860, the lower South, which became known as the "Cotton Kingdom," produced most of the world's supply of cotton and accounted for over 50 percent of America's exports.

According to the 1860 census, there were 118,000 white families in Georgia. Of these, 41,084 families, or 35 percent, owned slaves. In 1860, there were 3,500 free blacks living in Georgia. Slaves were about 4 million of the total black population in the country in the 1860s. By far, the majority lived in the South, and by 1860, about 11.5 percent of the slaves lived in Georgia.

There were classes of slaves, which, on some plantations, were as rigid as the class structure among whites. Skin color made a difference in the slave social structure. Slaves with lighter complexions often had positions inside the plantation house, which meant better clothes or hand-me-downs, food, and huts. It was illegal for slaves to learn to read and write.

Use the graph to answer questions 198-200.

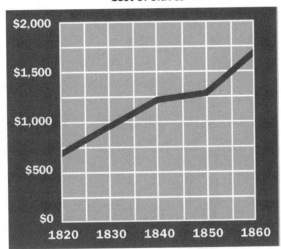

Cost of Slaves

_____ **198. How much did a slave cost in 1840?**
  A. $750
  B. $1,000
  C. $1,250
  D. $1,500

_____ **199. In what year did slaves cost the least?**
  A. 1820
  B. 1830
  C. 1840
  D. 1850

_____ **200. During what ten-year period did the cost of slaves change the least?**
  A. 1820-1830
  B. 1830-1840
  C. 1840-1850
  D. 1850-1860

_____ **201. Why were people from Africa brought to Georgia?**
   A. to help produce silk
   B. to be forced into labor
   C. to settle the backcountry
   D. to help fight Georgia's enemies

_____ **202. Which statement BEST explains why there are so few accounts written by slaves about their lives during the antebellum era?**
   A. It was illegal for slaves to learn to read and write.
   B. Only abolitionist leaders wrote books about slavery.
   C. Books about slavery were not as popular as other books.
   D. Slaves were not willing to write about the horrors of slavery.

_____ **203. What was the major type of labor used on Georgia's plantations before the Civil War?**
   A. slavery
   B. sharecropping
   C. hourly wage labor
   D. indentured servitude

Use the graph to answer questions 204-205.

Cotton Production/Slave Population

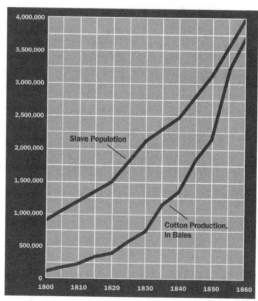

_____ **204. How many bales of cotton were produced in 1830?**
   A. 500,000
   B. 750,000
   C. 1,000,000
   D. 1,250,000

_____ **205. What is the main idea presented in this graph?**
   A. Bales of cotton went up in price as the Civil War approached.
   B. The slave population increased sharply between 1800 and 1860.
   C. As the number of slaves increased, so did U. S. cotton production.
   D. Slavery decreased as a result of abolitionists refusing to buy cotton.

STATES' RIGHTS

Probably the simplest, or at least the clearest, difference between the North and South involved the concept of states' rights. **States' rights** is the belief that the state's interests should take precedence over the interests of the national government.

Northern states believed that, in order for the United States to function as one Union, political decisions should be made that would benefit the entire country. They believed that all states should abide by laws made by Congress, signed by the president, or decreed by the courts.

Southern states, on the other hand, believed deeply in the idea of states' rights. They thought that states had the right to govern themselves and to decide what would be best for their own needs and situation. They believed that politicians from a state like Maine or New York could not possibly understand or care about Georgia or South Carolina.

____ 206. **Which region of the United States believed that the states should be able to govern themselves without interference from the national government?**
   A. Southern states
   B. Northern states
   C. Great Lakes states
   D. Pacific Coast states

____ 207. *States' rights* **can BEST be defined as the belief that states**
   A. could leave the Union at any time if they chose to.
   B. could maintain slavery if their population wished to.
   C. could ignore national laws if they were harmful to the state.
   D. could force the national government to turn over all national government property to the states.

____ 208. **Someone who believed in states' rights would probably support which statement?**
   A. National laws always take precedence over state laws.
   B. The national government has no right to tell states how to operate.
   C. States could only pass legislation on issues set out in the U.S. Constitution.
   D. Disputes between states should always be settled by the national government.

NULLIFICATION

In the early 1800s, Congress passed several protective tariffs. A tariff is a tax on imported goods designed to keep out competition. The tariffs raised the price of goods sold in the United States. Because the South had so few factories and had to import most products, southerners were particularly hard hit by the tariffs and blamed the tariffs for their poor economy. John C. Calhoun, then vice president of the United States, had written in The *South Carolina Exposition* that a state could nullify (prevent the enforcement of) a federal law. Recognizing that the slave states would lose their power as time passed, Calhoun believed nullification provided a way for the South to protect slavery.

South Carolina challenged the enforcement of the tariff of 1832 and called for a special convention. The convention nullified the tariff and refused to collect any tariff taxes. The state also threatened to set up a separate government outside the Union–effectively seceding–if the federal government resorted to force. South Carolina found little support among the other southern states. A compromise settled the crisis. Congress passed a new tariff that gradually reduced the tariff duties to earlier rates. South Carolina repealed its nullification of the earlier tariff.

_____ **209. The early 1800s belief of some people that a state could vote down a federal law was known as**
   A. absolution.
   B. ratification.
   C. justification.
   D. nullification.

_____ **210. In 1832, the state of South Carolina attempted to exert its state's rights by nullifying a Congressional tariff. What U. S. vice presiden had said that this action was permitted?**
   A. Henry Clay
   B. Zachary Taylor
   C. Millard Fillmore
   D. John C. Calhoun

MISSOURI COMPROMISE

In 1819, the United States had twenty-two states. Eleven were **slave states** (states that did allow slavery), and eleven were **free states** (states that did not allow slavery). This meant that, in the Senate, there was an equal number of senators from slave states and senators from free states. In the House of Representatives, the free states had more representatives than the slave states.

In 1819, the territory of Missouri applied for statehood as a slave state. After a great deal of debate, Congress adopted the **Missouri Compromise** in 1820. Maine entered the Union as a free state, and Missouri entered as a slave state. The measure also prohibited slavery north of 36°20' latitude, which was Missouri's southern border. This included the Louisiana Territory lands west of Missouri. This compromise kept a balance of power between the free states and slave states in the Senate and provided a temporary solution to the slavery question.

_____ **211. The purpose of the Missouri Compromise was to**
   A. let Missouri have slavery until 1850.
   B. allow slavery in Maine but not in Missouri.
   C. maintain a balance of slave and free states.
   D. return slaves captured in free states to slave states.

_____ **212. As a result of the Missouri Compromise**
   A. slavery was allowed in all states east of the Missouri.
   B. slavery was banned in all territories west of the Missouri.
   C. slavery was banned north of Missouri's southern border.
   D. slavery was allowed north of Missouri's southern border..

COMPROMISE OF 1850 AND THE GEORGIA PLATFORM

By late 1849, the population of California was over 100,000, enough to ask for statehood. In 1850, there were fifteen slave states and fifteen free states. California's constitution did not allow slavery. If California became a state, the balance in the Senate between slave states and free states would change. For eight months, what was later called "The Great Debate" raged as Congress tried to agree on what to do about California.

Senator Henry Clay of Kentucky proposed a compromise bill in early 1850. Although there was strong opposition on both sides, Clay's **Compromise of 1850** was passed by Congress. The compromise offered something to please both North and South.

Benefits for the North
- California came into the Union as a free state.
- Slave trading was ended in the District of Columbia.
- Texas gave up its idea of annexing New Mexico, thus taking that territory away from a slave state.

Benefits for the South
- The territories of New Mexico and Utah would determine whether they wanted to be slave or free.
- The residents of the District of Columbia could keep the slaves they already had.
- Congress would pass a law (the Fugitive Slave Act) stating that slaves who ran away to free states would be returned to their owners.

Many Georgians did not like the Compromise of 1850. However, Democrat Howell Cobb and Whigs Alexander Stephens and Robert Toombs asked the citizens of Georgia to accept it. In part because of the persuasiveness of these congressmen, the "Georgia Platform" supporting the compromise was adopted at a convention held in the state capital of Milledgeville. It was clear even to those Georgians who did not approve of it that the Compromise was necessary if the state were to stay in the Union.

Not long after the platform was adopted, some Georgians formed the Constitutional Union party. Howell Cobb, who had been a Democrat, joined the new party along with former Whigs Stephens and Toombs. Cobb was elected governor in 1851.

The Constitutional Union party broke up in August 1852. It had done what it set out to do: get Georgians to accept the Compromise of 1850. Toombs and Stephens joined the Democrats, while other Whigs joined the Know Nothing party, which did not want immigrants to become citizens or anyone not born in the United States to hold political office. It was a secret group whose members answered questions with, "I don't know," thus the name Know-Nothing.

After all the changes, the Democrats became the leading party. In 1856, James Buchanan, the Democratic presidential candidate, carried Georgia with no trouble. The next year, Democrat Joseph E. Brown became governor. Brown was re-elected in 1859, and he served two more terms during the Civil War.

___ **213. Which was a result of the Compromise of 1850?**
    A. Owning slaves was forbidden in Washington, D.C.
    B. Slavery was permitted in the new state of California.
    C. Importation of slaves from Africa was declared illegal.
    D. Runaway slaves had to be returned to southern owners.

___ **214. Which outcome resulted from the Compromise of 1850?**
    A. Slavery was eliminated in the District of Columbia.
    B. California was allowed to enter the Union as a free state.
    C. Texas was allowed to annex New Mexico extending slavery into that territory.
    D. Popular sovereignty was established, allowing states to vote on whether or not to have slavery.

____ **215. The "Georgia Platform" was a statement supporting**
   A. states' rights.
   B. popular sovereignty.
   C. the Compromise of 1850.
   D. slavery throughout the United States.

____ **216. The purpose of the Constitutional Union party in Georgia was to**
   A. preserve the Constitution.
   B. replace the Republican party in the South.
   C. get acceptance of the Compromise of 1850.
   D. illustrate the differences between the North and South.

____ **217. The purpose of the Fugitive Slave Act was to**
   A. prevent slaves from having group gatherings or meetings.
   B. prevent slaves from testifying against whites in court trials.
   C. require slaves that had run away to go back to their owners.
   D. require slaves to have citizenship papers in order to obtain jobs.

Use the map to answer questions 218-219.

The Underground Railroad

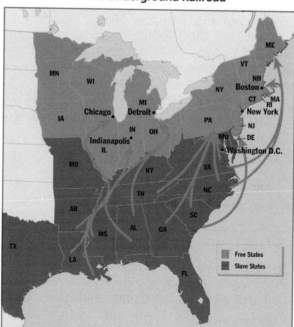

____ **218. The Underground Railroad was a network of people helping escaped slaves leave the south for freedom in northern cities. To which city did most slaves from Georgia flee?**
   A. Chicago, Illinois
   B. Indianapolis, Indiana
   C. Boston, Massachusetts
   D. Philadelphia, Pennsylvania

____ 219. **Through which free states did most of the routes run?**
    A. Missouri and Illinois
    B. Illinois, Indiana, and Ohio
    C. New York and Pennsylvania
    D. South Carolina, North Carolina, and Virginia

KANSAS-NEBRASKA ACT

The slavery issue would not die. As more people moved into the grassy plains west of Missouri and Iowa, there was a need for a territorial government. In 1854, Stephen Douglas of Illinois brought about passage of the Kansas-Nebraska Act, which created the territories of Kansas and Nebraska and which contained a clause on popular sovereignty. **Popular sovereignty** meant that when a territory asked for statehood, the people of that territory could vote on whether they wanted to be a free state or a slave state. Northerners were angry because this law changed the Missouri Compromise, which did not permit slavery north of Missouri's southern boundary.

Most people in the new territories belonged to one of two groups: proslavery or free soil. Free soilers were against slavery and also wanted land to be given to western settlers for farming. After Congress passed the Kansas-Nebraska Act, bloody fights broke out between proslavery and free soil groups. Abolitionists in other states promised to send antislavery settlers with guns into Kansas. Missouri proslavery people promised to send men across the border to fight for slavery. When Congress rejected Kansas's bid for statehood, southerners again realized that northern votes alone could keep slave states from the Union. There was so much violence in Kansas between the proslavery people and the free soilers that the territory was called "Bleeding Kansas."

____ 220. **Who was responsible for the passage of the Kansas-Nebraska Act?**
    A. Henry Clay
    B. Daniel Webster
    C. Abraham Lincoln
    D. Stephen A. Douglas

____ 221. **How did the Kansas-Nebraska Act change the Missouri Compromise?**
    A. It admitted Missouri to the Union as a free state.
    B. It created the territories of Kansas and Nebraska.
    C. It permitted slavery north of Missouri's southern boundary.
    D. It changed the requirements necessary for a territory to become a state.

THE DRED SCOTT CASE

In 1834, Dred Scott, a slave, was taken by his owner from the slave state of Missouri to the free state of Illinois. Later they went to Wisconsin, another free state. When Scott and his master returned to Missouri, Scott filed a lawsuit claiming he was free since he had lived in a free state. Abolitionists from the North raised enough money to take the case to the U.S. Supreme Court. In March 1857, the Supreme Court ruled that Scott could not sue because he was a slave, and slaves were not citizens. The Court also said Congress had no right to stop slavery in territories. The Dred Scott decision further divided the North and South and pushed them closer to war.

____ 222. **Why did the U.S. Supreme Court rule against Dred Scott?**
    A. because he returned to a slave state and he could not be freed
    B. because he was a slave and he was not eligible to sue in court
    C. because he did not live long enough in a free territory to be free
    D. because he was the property of his owner and could be taken anywhere

223. **Which statement explains how the *Dred Scott* decision pushed the nation closer to war?**
   A. The Supreme Court ruled that, while slaves were citizens, they could not sue.
   B. The Supreme Court ruled that slavery was not a legal right of the southern states.
   C. The Supreme Court ruled that the federal government could not stop slavery in the territories.
   D. The Supreme Court ruled that slave owners had to be reimbursed for slaves who escaped on the Underground Railroad.

ELECTION OF 1860

When the Democrats met in Charleston, South Carolina, for their national convention in 1860, there was a fight over the party platform. The supporters of Stephen A. Douglas of Illinois controlled the platform committee. They wanted to campaign on the issue of popular sovereignty. Southern Democrats did not agree and believed slavery should be allowed in all the territories. The two groups split over the issue. Northern Democrats nominated Douglas for president. Southern Democrats met separately in Baltimore and nominated Vice President John Breckinridge of Kentucky for president. Whigs from the border states also met in Baltimore to form the Constitutional Union party. They supported the Union and named John Bell of Tennessee as their presidential candidate.

At the same time, the Republicans met in Chicago, where they nominated Abraham Lincoln of Illinois. The Republican platform was not just against slavery, although the party said it would not try to end slavery in the slave states. It also supported a protective tariff, proposed a plan to give free western land to settlers, and called for the construction of a transcontinental railroad with one end in the North. None of these measures would benefit the South. The Republican party and its presidential candidate, Abraham Lincoln, appeared to be against everything southerners wanted.

The election amounted to a revolution in politics. For the first time, a party getting votes from only one section of the nation won the election. Abraham Lincoln received 1.9 million votes (a minority of the votes cast) and was elected president. Almost all of Lincoln's electoral votes were from the free states. He won without receiving a single electoral vote from the states in the South. Abraham Lincoln received only 16,388 votes from the slave states.

Use this map and the table to answer questions 224-228.

John Bell
John C. Breckinridge
Stephen A. Douglas
Abraham Lincoln

States shown with number of electoral votes

Candidate	Popular Vote Georgia	Popular Vote National	Electoral Vote
Bell	42,960	592,906	39
Breckinridge	52,176	848,356	72
Douglas	11,581	1,382,713	12
Lincoln	0	1,865,593	180
Total	106,717	4,689,568	303

224. **Which candidate for president of the United States in 1860 won the electoral vote?**
    A. John Bell
    B. Abraham Lincoln
    C. John Breckinridge
    D. Stephen A. Douglas

225. **Which candidate won the majority of the vote in only one state in his bid for the presidency?**
    A. John Bell
    B. Abraham Lincoln
    C. John Breckinridge
    D. Stephen A. Douglas

226. **Which two candidates split the southern vote?**
    A. Bell and Lincoln
    B. Lincoln and Douglas
    C. Breckinridge and Bell
    D. Douglas and Breckinridge

227. **Which candidate for president was the choice of people living in Georgia?**
    A. John Bell
    B. Abraham Lincoln
    C. John Breckinridge
    D. Stephen A. Douglas

228. **Which state had the most electoral votes in 1860?**
    A. Texas
    B. Georgia
    C. New York
    D. California

DEBATE OVER SECESSION IN GEORGIA AND THE ROLE OF ALEXANDER STEPHENS

After Lincoln's election, talk of **secession** (the act of pulling out of the Union) and war swirled around every barbecue, quilting bee, and picnic. Wherever Georgians gathered in a group, passionate debates took place. For eighty-four years, the nation had lived with the concept of a union of all states. Now southerners had to deal with questions over the conflict between states' rights and Union rights. Could they believe in the concept of the Union while maintaining a state's right to pass laws for the good of that state rather than to accept laws forced on it by the federal government? There was no easy answer to the question. Georgians were, for the most part, for the Union; however, they were even more strongly for states' rights. Now they were suddenly forced to make a choice, and many households in Georgia found themselves in the midst of a bitter split.

Immediately after the election of Abraham Lincoln as president, Georgia Governor Joseph E. Brown called a legislative session to determine whether a special convention should be held to decide the question of secession. The special session could also suggest that Georgia bide its time and see what South Carolina did. The legislative chamber was buzzing with activity as arguments resounded off the walls and memos and notes were passed back and forth. Speakers rose in quick succession to argue their views. Alexander Stephens of Crawfordville was especially stirring with his arguments against seceding.

"The first question that presents itself is, shall the people of Georgia secede from the Union in consequence of the election of Mr. Lincoln to the Presidency of the United States. My countrymen, I tell you frankly, candidly, and earnestly, that I do not think they ought. In my judgment, the election of no man, constitutionally chosen to that high office, is sufficient cause to justify any State to separate from the Union. It ought to stand by and aid still in maintaining the Constitution of the country. . . .

Whatever fate is to befall this country, let it never be laid to the charge of the people of the South, and especially the people of Georgia, that we were untrue to our national engagements. Let the fault and the wrong rest upon others. If all our hopes are to be blasted, if the Republic is to go down, let us be found to the last moment standing on the deck with the Constitution of the United States waving over heads."

Stephens's speech was interrupted many times by Robert Toombs, who along with Thomas Cobb, strongly supported immediate secession. Other conservative legislators, however, loudly applauded Stephens's pleas for caution. But his eloquence was no match for the fiery leadership of Toombs, Cobb, and Governor Brown. On November 21, 1860, Governor Brown called for a secession convention. Later, after Georgia joined the Confederacy, Alexander Stephens became its vice president.

_____ **229. Which Confederate official was from Georgia?**
    A. Jefferson Davis, the president
    B. Lyman Hall, the secretary of state
    C. Alexander Stephens, the vice president
    D. William Sherman, the commander-in-chief

_____ **230. After Lincoln's election, which man called for Georgia to remain in the Union?**
    A. Joseph Brown
    B. Thomas Cobb
    C. Robert Toombs
    D. Alexander Stephens

ANTIETAM

Near the town of Sharpsburg, Maryland, is a stream called Antietam Creek. The Northern and Southern armies collided here on September 17, 1862, in what was the bloodiest one-day battle of the Civil War. That day, 23,000 soldiers were killed, wounded or missing after twelve hours of savage combat.

The Battle of Antietam was the Army of Northern Virginia's first invasion into the North. Led by General Robert E. Lee, the Army of Northern Virginia fought Major General George R. McClellan's Army of the Potomac. The Union victory at the Battle of Antietam gave Abraham Lincoln the opportunity to issue the preliminary Emancipation Proclamation.

_____ **231. Where did the bloodiest one-day battle of the Civil War take place?**
   A. Shiloh
   B. Antietam
   C. Vicksburg
   D. Gettysburg

_____ **232. The Battle of Antietam took place in**
   A. Virginia.
   B. Tennessee.
   C. Maryland.
   D. Pennsylvania.

EMANCIPATION PROCLAMATION

On September 22, 1862, five days after the Battle of Antietam, President Lincoln issued the **Emancipation Proclamation**, a document ultimately affecting 4 million slaves in the United States. Lincoln wanted the Confederate states to end the war, return to the Union, and end 244 years of slavery. In this now-famous document, Lincoln stated that unless the South surrendered by January 1, 1863, "all slaves in states or districts in rebellion against the United States will be thenceforth and forever free." For three months and nine days after the Proclamation was issued, the South faced a choice. If it surrendered, slavery would continue in the South. If it did not surrender, the institution of slavery would end. The Confederate leaders chose to continue to fight.

_____ **233. After what battle was the Emancipation Proclamation issued?**
   A. Bull Run
   B. Antietam
   C. Vicksburg
   D. Gettysburg

_____ **234. How was the Emancipation Proclamation a concession to the South?**
   A. All slaves would be freed.
   B. Only male slaves would be freed.
   C. The South could keep their slaves if they stopped fighting.
   D. The slaves could decide if they wanted to remain on the plantations.

GETTYSBURG

The Battle of Gettysburg in Pennsylvania was a turning point in the Civil War. The battle was fought July 1-3, 1863, and resulted in a Union victory that ended General Robert E. Lee's second invasion of the North.

The Army of the Potomac, the Union Army led by General George Gordon Meade, collided with Lee's Army of Northern Virginia at the town of Gettysburg. The Union victory at the Battle of Gettysburg resulted in Lee's retreat to Virginia and ended the hopes of the Confederacy for victory. It was the war's bloodiest battle with 51,000 casualties.

____ 235. **In what state did the Battle of Gettysburg take place?**
  A. Virginia
  B. Maryland
  C. Mississippi
  D. Pennsylvania

____ 236. **Who was the Confederate commander at the Battle of Gettysburg?**
  A. Robert E. Lee
  B. George Meade
  C. Ulysses S. Grant
  D. George McClellan

CHICKAMAUGA

In late 1863, Union forces moved against the major Confederate railroad center in Chattanooga, Tennessee, just across the Georgia line. On September 19-20, Union General William Rosecrans led his troops against Confederate General Braxton Bragg seven miles south of Chattanooga at Chickamauga Creek. Bragg's army defeated the Union forces and forced the Union Army back into Tennessee. But Bragg did not follow up on the Union retreat. By November 1863, General Ulysses Grant had arrived with more troops and recaptured Chattanooga, forcing Bragg to retreat south to Dalton.

____ 237. **Who was the Confederate commander at Chickamauga?**
  A. John Floyd
  B. Robert E. Lee
  C. Braxton Bragg
  D. P. G. T. Beauregard

____ 238. **Who was the Union commander at Chickamauga?**
  A. Ulysses S. Grant
  B. George McClellan
  C. William Rosecrans
  D. William T. Sherman

____ 239. **Near what city is Chickamauga located?**
  A. Atlanta
  B. Savannah
  C. Birmingham
  D. Chattanooga

_____ **240. Why was Chickamauga important to the North and the South?**

    A. It was near a major railroad center.

    B. It was a major recruiting center for the South.

    C. It was located halfway between two state capitals.

    D. It had a number of factories that produced war supplies.

UNION BLOCKADE OF GEORGIA'S COAST

When the Civil War started, the Union strategy was to **blockade**, or obstruct, all Confederate ports. A blockade would prevent the South from selling its cotton abroad and importing needed war equipment and supplies from foreign nations. Early in the war, twenty-six Union ships steamed up and down the Atlantic and Gulf coasts to prevent ships from moving into or out of southern harbors. Later, the North spent millions of dollars to build more ships. However, Union vessels were no match for the blockade runners, mostly private ships that slipped around the blockade and sped into and out of the blocked ports. There were over 650 private blockade runners during 1861. As the war progressed, however, it became more and more difficult for blockade runners to get past federal ships. Before the Confederacy surrendered, it is estimated that 6,000 vessels carrying clothes, medicines, ammunition, and supplies worth $200 million made it through the federal blockade.

The blockade took its toll. In 1863, the South had to import everything from a hairpin to a toothpick, from a cradle to a coffin. Southerners found it difficult to get such farm supplies as seed, horse harnesses, ropes, and water tubs. The cost of feed for the animals and salt to cure, or preserve, meat was high. Household items, such as soap, candles, and matches were hard to come by. People often went without oil or gas for lighting and wood or coal for heating. There were not enough medical supplies for the civilians or the army. Many of the rail lines were inoperable because there were no tracks to replace war-damaged lines. There was a severe lack of replacement parts for manufacturing machinery. The few manufacturing facilities in the South were not functional as the war wore on. Life in Georgia, as in all southern states, became very difficult.

_____ **241. What contributed to the lack of success of the Union blockade?**

    A. The South had a superior navy.

    B. Blockade runners slipped through the blockade.

    C. Great Britain found other ways to trade with the South.

    D. The Union did not have enough ships to enforce the blockade.

_____ **242. The South needed to keep its ports open during the war**

    A. to maintain its navy for attacks on northern seaports.

    B. to maintain the only major transportation resource in the South.

    C. to ship and sell its cotton in Europe in exchange for supplies and arms.

    D. to protect the privateers who were making millions in profits from the war.

SHERMAN'S ATLANTA CAMPAIGN

When General U.S. Grant moved his army east to attack General Robert E. Lee, he left 112,000 men in Chattanooga under the command of General William T. Sherman. Sherman took those men and began a campaign toward Atlanta. Atlanta was important because of its industries and the fact it was a railroad hub. Sherman faced General Joseph E. Johnston, who had replaced General Braxton Bragg. Johnston had 60,000 troops to hold back Sherman's army.

During the late spring and early summer of 1864, the two armies fought time and again with major battles at Dalton, Resaca, Allatoona, Kennesaw Mountain, and New Hope Church. Because of shortages of ammunition and men, Johnston was forced to retreat southward. But he burned bridges and blocked roads as he retreated and slowed Sherman's advance to about two miles a day.

Jefferson Davis, president of the Confederacy, disagreed with Johnston's strategies and wanted Sherman's troops attacked head-on. Davis replaced Johnston with General John Bell Hood. In July, Hood led his troops in an attack on Sherman, losing over 11,000 men in two days. The two armies continued to fight during July until Hood concentrated his troops within the city of Atlanta. The main battle of Atlanta was on July 22.

The two armies fought for the rest of July and August until Hood finally left the city. On September 1, the Union army moved into Atlanta and took over its railroads and factories. The soldiers stayed until November 15 when, about three o'clock in the afternoon, they set fire to the city. On November 16, Sherman's army left Atlanta in flames and began their infamous "March to the Sea."

_____ **243. Atlanta's military importance to the Confederacy was that it was the**
   A. capital city of the Confederacy.
   B. most populated city in the Confederacy.
   C. industrial and transportation center of the Confederacy.
   D. home to the largest number of slaves in the Confederacy.

_____ **244. The fighting of the Civil War in Georgia can be described as**
   A. all in north Georgia.
   B. light and almost nonexistent.
   C. concentrated in the Savannah area.
   D. heavy along a line from Dalton to Atlanta to Savannah.

_____ **245. Who was the Confederate commander during the battle for Atlanta?**
   A. John Floyd
   B. John Hood
   C. Robert E. Lee
   D. William T. Sherman

_____ **246. How long did the Union army occupy Atlanta before burning it to the ground?**
   A. Six weeks
   B. Two weeks
   C. One month
   D. Over two months

_____ **247. Prior to leaving Atlanta, Sherman's army**
   A. burned the city
   B. killed all the inhabitants
   C. allowed the citizens to return
   D. gave the city to Lincoln as a present

SHERMAN'S MARCH TO THE SEA

After leaving Atlanta, Sherman's army moved quickly through the state heading for Savannah, burning everything in a path sixty miles wide. On his way from Atlanta to Savannah, Sherman destroyed all military targets and the civilian economic system (farms, homes, towns, railroads, bridges, roads) that supported the Confederate military. The move took over two months and left a large area of the state totally destroyed. In response to criticism of the destruction, Sherman reportedly said, "If the people [of Georgia] raise a howl against my barbarity and cruelty, I will answer that war is war and not popularity seeking." Estimates of the damage from Sherman's March to the Sea were as high as $100 million.

On December 22, 1864, Sherman sent a wire to President Lincoln: "I beg to present you as a Christmas gift the City of Savannah with one hundred fifty heavy guns, plenty of ammunition, also about twenty-five thousand bales of cotton." The next day, Union troops took over Savannah. Interestingly enough, Sherman did not burn Savannah. He knew that there was a treasure to be saved in Savannah, a treasure the Union Army needed. Since the city had been cut off by the naval blockade, bales of cotton had been accumulating in the warehouses and on the docks. Sherman quickly had it loaded, shipped to the North, and sold for a reported $28 million.

When Savannah surrendered, Sherman had effectively divided the upper and lower Confederacy, cutting Robert E. Lee off from the vital supplies needed to continue the Southern war effort and ending the war in Georgia. The main concern of those who remained in Georgia was finding food and shelter. The factories, rail lines, mills, plantations, and farm fields lay around them in ruins.

Use this map to answer questions 248–249.

Union States and Confederate States

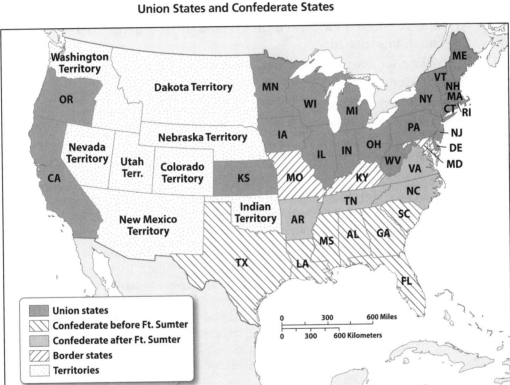

248. **This map shows the United States in what year?**
   A. 1776
   B. 1863
   C. 1964
   D. 1989

249. **Which statement summarizes the information shown on this map?**
   A. The nation is evenly split, East and West, into slave states and free states.
   B. The nation is divided evenly, North and South, into colonies and territories.
   C. The East is overpopulated, forcing citizens to move to the western territories.
   D. The West is unsettled territory, yet the East is organized into large and small states.

____ **250. What Union general led the northern army on its "March to the Sea" and saw to it that much of Georgia's capital resources were destroyed?**
A. Robert E. Lee
B. Ulysses S. Grant
C. Stonewall Jackson
D. William T. Sherman

____ **251. After the destruction caused by his march through Georgia, why did General Sherman refrain from burning Savannah?**
A. He spared the hometown of his West Point roommate.
B. He gave Savannah to President Lincoln as a Christmas present.
C. He protected over $28 million worth of cotton stored in Savannah.
D. He had divided the upper and lower Confederacy and so did not need to destroy the city.

____ **252. William T. Sherman attacked the civilian infrastructure between Atlanta and Savannah in order to**
A. retaliate for lives lost in the battle for Atlanta.
B. force Georgia troops to return home to defend Georgia.
C. end civilian support for the war effort and shorten the war.
D. punish the South for seceding from the Union and forming the Confederacy.

ANDERSONVILLE

A particularly dark side of the Civil War was the way prisoners of both sides were treated by their captors. At first, each side routinely exchanged prisoners. However, in 1864, General Grant stopped exchanging prisoners with the South. This kept the Confederacy from getting back men needed for the army. It also made military prisons overflow.

One of the Confederate prisons for Union soldiers was in Andersonville, Georgia. The prison was dirty. The only shelter was whatever the prisoners could put together. There was not enough food, water, or medical supplies. Much of the available water was contaminated. The prison was always crowded. During the fifteen months Andersonville operated, almost 13,000 Union prisoners died. Stories of the conditions at Andersonville were so bad that the Confederate War Department had a medical team look at the prison. The team recommended moving the soldiers to better places. Although records indicate Andersonville's commander, Captain Henry Wirz, tried to improve conditions at the prison, he was executed in 1865 for "excessive cruelty." Today, Andersonville is a national cemetery where 13,700 Union dead are buried.

____ **253. Where was a notorious Confederate prison in Georgia?**
A. Fulton
B. Alcatraz
C. Belle Isle
D. Andersonville

____ **254. Who was the commander of the Confederate prison at Andersonville?**
A. John Hood
B. Henry Wirz
C. John Calhoun.
D. George Murphy

> **SS8H6   The student will analyze the impact of the Civil War and Reconstruction on Georgia.**
>
> c. Analyze the impact of Reconstruction on Georgia and other southern states, emphasizing Freedmen's Bureau; sharecropping and tenant farming; Reconstruction plans; 13th, 14th, and 15th amendments to the constitution; Henry McNeal Turner and black legislators; and the Ku Klux Klan.

FREEDMEN'S BUREAU

The thousands of **freedmen** (former slaves) faced great hardships. Homeless, uneducated, and free for first time in their lives, the freedmen had little more than the clothes on their backs. Many went from place to place looking for food, shelter, and work. Some traveled just to demonstrate that they could. Others searched for spouses, children, other family members, or friends who had been sold away from them during slavery.

In an effort to help the struggling freedmen, the United States government established the Bureau of Refugees, Freedmen, and Abandoned Lands in March 1865. Its first commissioner was Union General Oliver O. Howard, who later founded Howard University in Washington, D.C. The original purpose of the agency, which soon became known as the **Freedmen's Bureau**, was to help both former slaves and poor whites cope with their everyday problems by offering them clothing, food, and other necessities. After a while, the bureau's focus changed; it became concerned mainly with helping the freedmen adjust to their new circumstances. An important focus was education. The bureau set up over 4,000 primary schools, 64 industrial schools, and 74 teacher-training institutions for young African Americans in addition to spending over $400,000 to help establish teacher-training centers.

Northerners and missionary societies helped by sending both money and teachers. In 1867, the American Missionary Association sponsored the chartering of Georgia's Atlanta University. The American Baptist Home Mission society organized Morehouse College in Augusta (which moved to Atlanta in 1870). A third Georgia Reconstruction-era school was Clark College in Atlanta, which first opened as a school for children.

____ **255. The purpose of the Freedmen's Bureau was to help**

    A. former slaves.

    B. all free people in the South.

    C. all poor people in the South.

    D. former slaves and poor whites.

____ **256. Who was the first commissioner of the Freedmen's Bureau?**

    A. Alfred Terry

    B. Rufus Bullock

    C. Ulysses S. Grant

    D. Oliver O. Howard

____ **257. The BEST description of the Freedmen's Bureau during Reconstruction was that it**

    A. registered newly freed slaves to vote.

    B. helped the newly freed slaves adjust to their freedom.

    C. provided education, training, and social services for the newly freed slaves.

    D. managed the distribution of farm land and animals to the newly freed slaves.

____ 258. **Which statement BEST describes the contributions of the Freedmen's Bureau in education?**

A. The bureau founded over 10,000 primary schools throughout the South for black and white children.

B. The bureau established six major colleges in the South, all of which are located in the metropolitan Atlanta area.

C. The bureau opened government agencies, including schools, colleges, and universities for poor blacks and whites in the South.

D. The bureau set up thousands of primary schools, industrial or vocational schools, and teacher-training centers for African Americans in the South.

SHARECROPPING

After the war, planters and farmers needed laborers to work on their land. There were many former slaves, as well as some landless whites, who needed jobs. Workers who had nothing but their labor to offer often resorted to **sharecropping**. Under this system, the landowners provided land, a house, farming tools and animals, seed, and fertilizer. The workers agreed to give the owner a share of the harvest. Until the workers sold their crop, the owners often let them have food, medicine, clothing, and other supplies at high prices on credit. **Credit** is the ability to buy something now and pay for it later or over a period of time.

For many, this credit was their undoing. After selling the crop and paying the bills, the typical sharecropper had little, if any, cash left. Because few sharecroppers could not read or count, the planter or the store owner could easily cheat them, and many did. Year after year, sharecroppers were in debt. They had little hope they could ever save enough to buy their own land and equipment.

____ 259. **After the Civil War, what system was developed to provide labor to work the former plantations?**

A. Convict Lease

B. Land Lottery

C. Sharecropping

D. Farmers' Alliance

____ 260. **Sharecroppers paid their landowners by**

A. paying a monthly rental or lease fee.

B. allowing landowners to use their equipment.

C. providing labor and a large percentage of the crop.

D. agreeing to work without pay for five to seven years.

____ 261. **With whom did sharecroppers share their harvest?**

A. the poor

B. creditors

C. neighbors

D. landowners

TENANT FARMING

Tenant farming was similar to sharecropping. The main difference was that tenants usually owned some agricultural equipment and farm animals, such as mules. They also bought their own seed and fertilizer. At the end of the year, tenant farmers either paid the landowner a set amount of cash or an agreed-upon share of the crop. Because tenant farmers owned more than sharecroppers, they usually made a small profit. However, the lives of both groups were very hard. The tenant farming and sharecropping systems allowed landowners to keep their farms in operation without having to spend money for labor.

On the surface, it would seem that landowners who used tenants and sharecroppers made a profit while taking few risks. However, many landowners who did not have the money to buy the needed seed, fertilizer, and tools borrowed the money and used the crops to back up the loan. Interest on such loans was often more than the crops were worth. Because bankers expected farmers to grow cotton or tobacco year after year, the soil was eventually ruined. In time, many landowners in the South, like the sharecroppers and tenants who worked their land, became poorer each year.

____ **262. How were tenant farmers different from sharecroppers?**
   A. Tenant farmers owned all their equipment.
   B. Tenant farmers usually made a small profit.
   C. Tenant farmers bought their seed from the owner.
   D. Tenant farmers usually didn't pay rent for their houses.

____ **263. Which BEST describes the differences between sharecropping and tenant farming?**
   A. Tenant farmers earned equity or an interest in the land they worked from year to year so that eventually they would own their own property.
   B. Tenant farmers received a cash salary or wage for their farm work, while sharecroppers received only a portion of the crops they raised.
   C. Sharecroppers owned nothing but their labor, while tenant farmers owned farm animals and equipment to use in working other people's lands.
   D. Sharecroppers received a percentage of the crops produced and could set aside cash money to purchase their own land, while tenant farmers had difficulty saving cash.

RECONSTRUCTION PLANS

Lincoln Plan

During the closing days of the Civil War, President Lincoln developed a plan, commonly called the "Ten-Percent Plan," to rebuild the South and restore the southern states to the Union as quickly and easily as possible. The process was known as **Reconstruction.** Lincoln's plan had two simple steps: (1) All southerners, except for high-ranking Confederate civil and military leaders, would be pardoned after taking an oath of allegiance to the United States; and (2) when 10 percent of the voters in each state had taken the oath of loyalty, the state would be permitted to form a legal government and rejoin the Union.

Congressional Plan

Congress and many northerners thought that the South should be punished. They believed that those Confederate states that had seceded should be treated like a conquered country. In 1864, Congress passed the Wade-Davis Bill, which Lincoln saw as an attempt to punish the South for the actions of the secessionists. Lincoln did not sign the bill into law; he let it die quietly. This action signaled that there would be a fight over Reconstruction. Lincoln's assassination took place before his plan for Reconstruction went into effect. Upon Lincoln's death, Vice President Andrew Johnson, a North Carolinian, became the nation's seventeenth president. Soon after taking office, he took on the responsibility for returning the former Confederate states to the Union. In June 1865, President Johnson appointed James Johnson as Georgia's provisional governor because, as a congressman, Johnson had opposed secession.

Johnson's Reconstruction plan was much like Lincoln's plan except that Johnson expanded the groups of southerners not granted a general pardon. Those who had owned property worth more than $20,000 or those who had held high civil or military positions had to apply directly to the president for a pardon. At first, some of the radicals were willing to work with Johnson because they approved of his plan to offer a reward for the arrest of Jefferson Davis. But after Davis was captured and imprisoned, the radicals turned their attention back to the president's plan and began to disagree with it. They were afraid that the freedmen would be **disfranchised** (have their voting rights taken away). They also thought that the South deserved a greater punishment than Johnson's plan provided.

After some pressure, President Johnson added several more requirements. First, the southern states had to approve the Thirteenth Amendment, which made slavery illegal. Second, the southern states had to nullify their ordinances of secession. Third, the southern states had to promise not to repay the individuals and institutions that had helped finance the Confederacy.

_____ **264. What was President Abraham Lincoln's plan for Reconstruction called?**
  A. 10 Percent Plan
  B. 100 Percent Plan
  C. Congressional Plan
  D. Radical Republican Plan

_____ **265. To whom did President Johnson's Reconstruction plan deny a general pardon?**
  A. Southerners who owned more than 25 slaves
  B. Southerners who owned more than 50 slaves
  C. Southerners who owned more than $20,000 worth of land
  D. Southerners who owned more than $50,000 worth of land

_____ **266. Why was President Lincoln's Reconstruction plan NOT enacted?**
  A. The plan was too easy on the South.
  B. The plan did not pass with a majority vote.
  C. The plan did not have the support of the states.
  D. The plan did not become effective before Lincoln was assassinated.

_____ **267. Why did President Johnson appoint James Johnson as provisional governor of Georgia in 1865?**
  A. He had opposed succession as a congressman.
  B. He was extremely popular with the people of Georgia.
  C. He denounced the Congressional Reconstruction plan.
  D. He had supported Johnson when he ran for vice president.

268. **Which statement accurately describes the difference between Lincoln's and Radical Republicans' plan for Reconstruction?**
    A. Lincoln's plan consisted of many complicated steps; the Radical Republicans' plan was simpler.
    B. Lincoln's plan sought to punish the south for the Civil War; the Radical Republicans' plan was aimed at rehabilitation.
    C. Lincoln's plan called for the quick return of Southern states to the Union; the Radical Republicans' plan sought to delay their return.
    D. Lincoln's plan called for the abolition of slavery throughout the South; the Radical Republicans' plan would have allowed slavery to continue.

THIRTEENTH, FOURTEENTH, AND FIFTEENTH AMENDMENTS

After the Civil War, three amendments were passed and ratified to ensure the rights of the former slaves. These three amendments are sometimes called the Reconstruction Amendments.

The **Thirteenth Amendment** to the U.S. Constitution, which continued the work of the Emancipation Proclamation, officially abolished slavery. The amendment was passed by Congress in January 1865 and submitted to the states for ratification. It was ratified in December 1865. President Andrew Johnson made ratification of the amendment a requirement for the southern states to rejoin the Union.

Although the Thirteenth Amendment abolished slavery, it did not abolish **discrimination** (unfair treatment of a person or group because of prejudice). By 1865, most of the southern states, including Georgia, had passed a number of laws known as **Black Codes**, which were designed to restrict the rights of the freedmen. Congressional reaction to the Black Codes was fairly swift. The **Fourteenth Amendment** granted citizenship to the freedmen and forbade any state from denying anyone the "equal protection of the law." Congress passed the amendment in June 1866, and it was ratified in July 1868.

The **Fifteenth Amendment** granted all male citizens the right to vote regardless of "race, color, or previous condition of servitude." The amendment was submitted to the states in February 1869 and ratified in February 1870.

269. **What did the Thirteenth Amendment to the U.S. Constitution do that brought about many changes in Georgia's society and economic structure after the Civil War?**
    A. It freed the slaves.
    B. It changed who owned land.
    C. It gave blacks the right to vote.
    D. It made blacks United States citizens.

270. **Under the terms of the radical Congressional plan of Reconstruction, what amendment did a southern state have to ratify before it could rejoin the Union?**
    A. Fifteenth
    B. Sixteenth
    C. Thirteenth
    D. Fourteenth

271. **What did the Fourteenth Amendment to the U.S. Constitution do?**
    A. It gave blacks citizenship.
    B. It gave blacks their freedom.
    C. It gave blacks the right to vote.
    D. It gave blacks the right to own property.

91

____ **272. What did the Fifteenth Amendment to the U.S. Constitution do?**

    A. It gave blacks citizenship.

    B. It gave blacks their freedom.

    C. It gave blacks the right to vote.

    D. It gave blacks the right to own property.

____ **273. The Fourteenth Amendment to the U.S. Constitution was passed in response to the**

    A. adoption of laws known as Black Codes by the southern states.

    B. rising violence from terrorist organizations such as the Ku Klux Klan.

    C. refusal of white southerners to provide freedmen with land and farm animals.

    D. refusal of some southern states to adopt constitutional provisions calling for an end to slavery.

HENRY MCNEAL TURNER AND BLACK LEGISLATORS

In 1867, African Americans voted for the first time in Georgia. In 1868, they helped elect a Republican governor. They also helped elect twenty-nine African Americans to the Georgia house of representatives and three African Americans to the Georgia senate. Some of those elected were Tunis G. Campbell, Jr., Henry McNeal Turner, and Aaron A. Bradley. However, all of these men were expelled in September 1868 on the grounds that although the constitution had given them the right to vote, it did not specifically give them the right to hold political office.

During Reconstruction, African Americans formed the largest group of southern Republicans, and thousands voted in the new elections to help keep Republicans in power. By the same token, Republican carpetbaggers, along with some agents and many volunteers of the Freedmen's Bureau, worked hard to make African Americans part of the political scene.

Realizing **political empowerment** (the ability to bring about change) for the first time, thousands joined the Union League, which had become the freedmen's political organization. From church meetings to picnics and family gatherings, politics became "the" topic of discussion and debate.

____ **274. Henry McNeal Turner was expelled from his seat in the Georgia state legislature on the grounds that he did not**

    A. win the election fairly and honestly.

    B. have the knowledge to be a legislator.

    C. have the right to vote or hold political office.

    D. live in the district from which he was elected.

____ **275. Which political organization did African Americans join during Reconstruction?**

    A. the Union League

    B. the Ku Klux Klan

    C. the Freedmen's Bureau

    D. the Civil Rights Bureau

KU KLUX KLAN

During Reconstruction, the **Ku Klux Klan** became a force in Georgia. The Klan, as it was called, was one of several secret organizations that tried to keep freedmen from exercising their new civil rights. The group began in Pulaski, Tennessee, in 1865 as a social club for returning soldiers. However, it quickly changed into a force of terror. Its members dressed in robes and hoods so no one would recognize them. They terrorized and intimidated African Americans to keep them from voting and, by doing so, to return control of the state to the Democrats. There were numerous reports of beatings, whippings, and murders.

Freedmen who were not frightened away from the polls were carefully watched. Those voting Republican lay awake at night listening for the sounds of horses, indicating the Klan was nearby. All knew that the price for **suffrage** (voting rights) could be death. Hostilities between whites and African Americans increased, and there were many incidents of racial conflict.

Ku Klux Klan activities increased throughout the state, and there was evidence that the group had prevented many African Americans from voting in the 1868 presidential election. Governor Rufus Bullock appealed to the federal government for help. Congress responded by passing the **Georgia Act** in December 1869. This law returned Georgia to military control for the third time. General Alfred Terry became Georgia's new military commander, and Rufus Bullock became the provisional governor.

276. **Beginning soon after the end of the Civil War, what secret organization used force and violence to influence Georgia's society?**
    A. Ku Klux Klan
    B. Freedmen's Bureau
    C. Free and Accepted Masons
    D. United Confederate Veterans

277. **The Ku Klux Klan began in Tennessee in 1865 as a**
    A. social club.
    B. terrorist group.
    C. college fraternity.
    D. church organization.

278. **The main goal of the Ku Klux Klan was to**
    A. return land to former Confederates.
    B. attract members from all social classes.
    C. force the carpetbaggers to move back north.
    D. to prevent the freedmen from exercising their rights.

279. **What was the Georgia Act of 1869?**
    A. state legislation allowing freedmen the right to vote and the right to hold public office
    B. state legislation ending Reconstruction in Georgia thanks to its demonstrated success
    C. federal legislation returning Georgia to military control because of KKK terrorism against freedmen
    D. federal legislation refusing to admit Georgia to the Union until it ratified the Thirteenth Amendment

BOURBON TRIUMVIRATE

When Reconstruction was finally over and it was time to "redeem" the state from the hardships it had fared, the job fell primarily to three Democrats–Joseph E. Brown, Alfred H. Colquitt, and John B. Gordon. All of these leaders wanted stronger economic ties with the industrial North in order to expand Georgia's economy. They also wanted to keep many old southern traditions including **white supremacy** (the belief that the white race is superior to any other race).

The three Georgia leaders were called the Bourbon Triumvirate. Bourbon was the name of a castle and territory in France, as well as a line of French kings who ruled for over two hundred years. Triumvirate refers to a ruling body of three. Although the background of each man was different, politics and power drew them together.

Joseph E. Brown

Joseph E. Brown was a lawyer from Canton. He was elected to the state senate in 1849 and served there until 1855, when he became a judge for the Blue Ridge Judicial Circuit. In 1857, Brown was elected governor. He became a popular "states' rights" governor.

Governor Brown guided the state through the difficult war years. When Reconstruction began, Brown lost much of his popularity by asking Georgians to go along with radical Reconstruction policies, believing this would shorten Reconstruction. Brown remained in office until June 1865, when federal officials took over Reconstruction. Governor Rufus Bullock appointed Brown chief justice of the Georgia supreme court. He served there two years before resigning to head a company that leased the Western and Atlantic Railroad.

In 1880, Brown re-entered politics. When John Gordon resigned from the U.S. Senate, Governor Colquitt appointed Brown to Gordon's Senate seat. Brown stayed in the Senate until 1891.

Alfred H. Colquitt

Alfred H. Colquitt was the son of U.S. Senator Walter Colquitt, for whom Colquitt County is named. After graduating from Princeton University, he fought in the Mexican War. In 1849, he was elected to the state senate. Before the Civil War, Colquitt served in Congress and at Georgia's secession convention. During the war years, he was an able military leader and rose to the rank of major general.

Colquitt was elected governor in 1876. Around that time, he became involved in a scandal over government jobs. Colquitt himself called for an investigation, and a legislative committee found Colquitt innocent of the charges. Colquitt was re-elected and served until 1882. During his administration, the state's debt was reduced and, in 1877, a new state constitution was approved.

John B. Gordon

John B. Gordon, the third member of the Bourbon Triumvirate, worked for a while as a newspaper correspondent, then as manager of a coal mine in Dade County. When the Civil War broke out, Gordon proved an able leader and was one of three Georgia officers who reached the rank of lieutenant general. After the war, Gordon wrote a book and became a popular speaker across the nation.

In 1872, Gordon defeated Alexander Stephens to become Georgia's U.S. senator. In 1880, he resigned from the Senate and accepted a position with one of the railroads. In 1886, he began the first of his two terms as governor of Georgia. While governor, Gordon reduced the state's debt and brought new industry into the area.

_____ **280. Which of the following men was NOT a member of the Bourbon Triumvirate?**
   A. Henry Grady
   B. John Gordon
   C. Joseph Brown
   D. Alfred Colquitt

_____ **281. Joseph Brown, a member of the Bourbon Triumvirate, did NOT support**
   A. white supremacy.
   B. increased agricultural development
   C. creating stronger economic ties to the North.
   D. increasing the number of industries in the South.

_____ **282. The Bourbon Triumvirate believed in**
   A. improving working conditions.
   B. increased industrial investment.
   C. economic assistance for the poor.
   D. expansion of educational opportunities.

_____ **283. Which of the following best describes the Bourbon Triumvirate's goals during Redemption period?**
   A. A time for black and white southerners to come together and work in harmony to rebuild the state's economic, social, and political systems
   B. A blending of the new and the old, keeping old southern traditions while building new traditions around industries to rival the North
   C. A New South Progressive era when farms had to be replaced by business and industry in order for the South to prosper
   D. A time for social, economic, and political reforms to ease the suffering caused by the war

HENRY GRADY

Known as the "voice of the New South," Henry Woodfin Grady was born in 1850, the son of a prominent Athens family. He graduated from the University of Georgia and attended two years of law school at the University of Virginia. Returning to Georgia, he married and settled in Rome, where Henry began working for the Rome Courier. His writing skills caught the attention of editors at The New York Herald, and he was hired as their southern correspondent headquartered in Atlanta.

In 1880, Grady became managing editor of the Atlanta Constitution. He quickly became known for his insightful, timely, and sometimes controversial editorials. Grady visited northern cities and spoke frequently about the **New South**. In one of his most famous speeches, he spoke about the need for industry in Georgia. In the speech, Grady also said that the southern economy was growing as agriculture was replaced by industry, particularly textile mills, coal and iron ore mining, and tobacco factories. He praised the new practices that made farming more productive. He also pointed out that race relations in the South were changing and that African Americans had become partners in developing this New South.

Grady's ability to sell the concept of a New South helped bring jobs, recognition, and investments to the recovering Georgia economy. He consistently backed up his words with actions. He was one of the principal planners for Atlanta's 1881 International Cotton Exposition, which was designed to show off the South's new industries. As a creative journalist and part-owner of the newspaper, he introduced new technology, used the "interview process" in news stories, and increased circulation from 10,000 to over 140,000, making the Atlanta Constitution one of the most widely read newspapers in the nation.

During a Boston speaking engagement in 1889, the 39-year-old Grady caught pneumonia and later died. Even with his numerous accomplishments, we can only wonder what else this man of journalistic influence might have done.

_____ **284. As the leader of the New South movement, what was Henry Grady supporting?**
   A. northern investment in southern industry
   B. southern investment in northern factories
   C. southerners growing more cotton for export
   D. blacks leaving the South to work in the North

_____ **285. Which Georgian and his achievement are matched correctly?**
   A. Tom Watson—civil rights leader
   B. Hoke Smith—inventor of the steam engine
   C. Henry Grady—editor of The Atlanta Constitution
   D. Robert Toombs—mayor of Atlanta after the Civil War

_____ **286. The New South, envisioned by Henry W. Grady, would**
   A. promote tourism.
   B. rival the North economically.
   C. maintain its southern heritage.
   D. provide separate facilities for different races.

_____ **287. What Georgia leader coined the phrase "New South?"**
   A. Alfred H. Colquitt
   B. Rebecca Latimer Felton
   C. John B. Gordon
   D. Henry W. Grady

INTERNATIONAL COTTON STATES EXPOSITION/COTTON STATES AND INTERNATIONAL EXPOSITION

In 1895, Atlanta was host to 800,000 visitors during the three-month-long Cotton States and International Exposition. This exhibition was a way to showcase the economic recovery of the South (in which cotton played a large role), to highlight the region's natural resources, and to lure northern investors. At the 6,000 exhibits of the Exposition, visitors saw new machinery and learned how cotton was made into marketable products.

John Philip Sousa wrote the "King Cotton March" in 1895 for the Cotton States and International Exposition. Sousa's band played at the exposition for three weeks. The march was one of Sousa's personal favorites, and it has become one of his most popular.

_____ **288. The main purpose of the International Cotton Exposition that was held in Atlanta was to**
   A. showcase the cotton gin.
   B. bring visitors to Georgia.
   C. get ideas from foreign countries.
   D. showcase the industries of the New South.

____ **289. The International Cotton Exposition was held in**

    A. Athens.

    B. Atlanta.

    C. Augusta.

    D. Savannah.

TOM WATSON AND THE POPULISTS

Thomson native Tom Watson was a controversial national leader of the Populist party. In 1882, he was elected to the General Assembly. Even though he became wealthy, Watson was concerned about Georgia's poor and struggling farmers. Early in his career, he was the first native southern politician to be concerned about African American farmers, many of whom were tenant farmers or sharecroppers. He realized that agrarian reform was possible if the two races came together politically. With the backing of the Farmers' Alliance, Watson was elected to Congress in 1890 as a Democrat. A year later, Watson switched political sides and spoke for the causes of the Populist party. Watson represented Georgia in the U.S. House of Representatives for only two years.

He did gain a place in congressional history by introducing the Rural Free Delivery (RFD) bill, which required the U.S. postmaster general to find a way to deliver mail to rural homes free of charge. Because of Watson's bill, farm families no longer had to travel to the nearest post office for their mail. The first official RFD route in Georgia was in Warren County. One byproduct of rural free delivery was the boom in the building of roads, bridges, and other improvements needed to deliver the mail to rural areas.

In 1892, the Democrat-turned-Populist became a candidate for re-election. However, the state's Democratic party wanted Watson out of Georgia politics. Because he had no organized support, Watson lost.

Watson ran for Congress again in 1894 and was again defeated. He returned to his home to influence politics through the power of the press. He began two magazines–The Weekly Jeffersonian and the monthly Watson's Jeffersonian.

In 1896, Watson was the Populist party's nominee for vice president; in 1904, he was the party's nominee for president. He lost both elections. In 1905, Watson returned to the Democratic party, but his stand on civil rights had changed significantly. Fifteen years earlier, Watson had asked for African American votes. Now, he opposed all minority rights, including those for African Americans, Catholics, and Jews. In 1920, Watson ran against Hoke Smith for the U.S. Senate and won. Two years later, he died in Washington, D.C.

____ **290. What Georgia Populist leader called on black and white farmers to unite in an effort to gain fair treatment from the state and national governments?**

    A. Hoke Smith

    B. Tom Watson

    C. Henry Grady

    D. Joseph E. Brown

____ **291. The Populist party in Georgia was the party of the**

    A. wealthy.

    B. abolitionists.

    C. small farmers.

    D. federal bureaucrats.

_____ **292. What group was supported by Tom Watson, a Georgia populist?**
   A. miners
   B. farmers
   C. mill workers
   D. railroad workers

_____ **293. What was Tom Watson's greatest accomplishment?**
   A. a bill allowing women to vote
   B. a bill to provide meat inspections
   C. a bill requiring rural mail delivery
   D. a bill to increase the minimum wage

REBECCA LATIMER FELTON

By the end of Reconstruction, a new group calling itself Independent Democrats was slowly gaining recognition. One of the group's leaders was William Felton, a doctor, farmer, Methodist preacher, and public speaker. His wife Rebecca worked with him to support political causes. The two used their family-owned newspaper, The Cartersville Courant, to attack the Bourbons. They traveled the state arguing that the leaders of the Democratic party in Georgia were ignoring the poor and the lower middle class.

Just like her husband, Rebecca Latimer Felton was a tireless worker for fairness and justice and was deeply involved with many causes. She was a leader in the suffrage and **temperance** (anti-alcohol) movements. She also worked hard to bring about reform in the state's prison system. Long before the early 1900s, when women began to push for equal rights, Rebecca Latimer Felton was publicly active. In 1889, Hoke Smith, publisher of the Atlanta Journal, asked her to be a columnist. She was a popular writer, and she continued to share her ideals and influence through the newspaper for the next forty-one years.

Felton is perhaps best remembered today as the first woman in the U.S. Senate. When Senator Thomas E. Watson died on September 26, 1922, Governor Thomas Hardwick appointed her as his replacement to serve until a special election could be held. Felton's appointment was an acknowledgment of her outstanding reform work and efforts supporting the suffrage movement. Since the Senate was not in session at the time of her appointment, Felton was not officially sworn in to her new office. Nor did she really serve time in Congress; Walter F. George was elected to the Senate seat in a special election. But when the Senate reconvened, the 87-year-old Felton was sworn in for a day, making her the first woman to serve in the U.S. Senate.

_____ **294. When Rebecca Latimer Felton wrote for the Atlanta Journal, she focused on the need for reforms in**
   A. voting laws.
   B. race relations.
   C. the prison system.
   D. working conditions.

_____ **295. Rebecca Latimer Felton did NOT support the**
   A. suffrage movement.
   B. temperance movement.
   C. convict lease movement.
   D. educational reform movement.

Use the political cartoon that follows to answer questions 296-297.

296. **What is the subject of the political cartoon?**

    A. a women meeting with a U. S. senator

    B. Rebecca Latimer Felton serving as a U.S. senator

    C. a recognition ceremony for widows of World War I

    D. Carrie Nation's testimony before the U.S. Congress

297. **Which clue helps to identify the content of the political cartoon?**

    A. the gentleman's greeting

    B. the desk and table in the cartoon

    C. the name of one of the people pictured

    D. the clothing that the two people are wearing

1906 ATLANTA RIOT

The year 1906 was a memorable year in Atlanta's history. While Georgia's politicians worked for political control, Atlanta experienced one of the worst race riots in the nation's history. Some thought the riot came about because men like Tom Watson spread racial fears. Others believed that Hoke Smith had used racial fears to gain votes during the gubernatorial campaign of that year. Still others blamed Atlanta newspapers, which printed story after story of African American violence against whites.

On the afternoon of Saturday, September 22, local newspaper headlines carried false reports of black assaults. By 9 p.m., a crowd of over 5,000 whites and African Americans had gathered on Decatur Street. Some accounts reported that thousands of whites brought guns and began to roam through the downtown area. Fears grew, and the attacks became real.

The riot lasted two days. Martial law was declared before the city once again became calm. (**Martial law** occurs when military forces are used to maintain order because civilian forces will not or cannot maintain order.) The cost in human life was high. At least eighteen African Americans and three whites were killed; hundreds of people were injured. The value of property destroyed was also high, but it could not be accurately estimated.

____ **298. The immediate cause of the riot that occurred in Atlanta in 1906 was**
    A. the killing of a black family.
    B. blacks being denied the right to vote.
    C. the election of Hoke Smith as governor.
    D. articles of black violence against whites.

____ **299. How long did the Atlanta riot of 1906 last?**
    A. 12 hours
    B. 18 hours
    C. 24 hours
    D. 48 hours

____ **300. Which was NOT a result of the Atlanta riot of 1906?**
    A. the mayor resigned
    B. martial law was declared
    C. eighteen blacks were killed
    D. hundreds of people were injured

LEO FRANK CASE

Georgia suffered a civil rights setback with a court case that attracted national attention and that resulted in the rebirth of the Ku Klux Klan. On August 17, 1915, Leo M. Frank was lynched in Marietta.

The 29-year-old Frank was from Brooklyn and had been the superintendent of the National Pencil Company factory in Atlanta for five years. On April 26, 1913, he was charged with the murder of Mary Phagan, a 14-year-old employee. The trial that followed was one of the most debated in Georgia's history. Although there was little evidence, Frank was convicted and sentenced to death, largely because of the testimony of Jim Conley, the factory's African American janitor. Because Conley was also a suspect, his testimony normally would not have been heard. However, these were not normal times. Frank was Jewish, and during that time, many people disliked Jews.

Frank's lawyers appealed the case to the state supreme court. Governor John Slaton was under pressure to pardon Frank. The day before his term of office ended in June 1915, Slaton changed Frank's sentence from death to life imprisonment. In his magazine, The Weekly Jeffersonian, Tom Watson led a public outcry against Slaton's action. He even called on the people to take matters into their own hands. Two months after the sentence change, twenty-five armed men walked into the state penitentiary in Milledgeville and took Frank from his prison cell. They drove to Marietta, the home of Mary Phagan, and hanged Frank from a tree. The next day, about 15,000 curious people filed by Frank's open casket in an Atlanta mortuary. Pictures of Frank's hanging body were sold, and "The Ballad of Mary Phagan" became popular.

In July 1915, amid the anti-Jewish feelings and continuing racial unrest of the Leo Frank case, the Ku Klux Klan received a charter from the Fulton County Superior Court. On Thanksgiving night 1915, Atlanta preacher and salesman William Simmons and thirty-four others climbed to the top of Stone Mountain near Atlanta. There, the group, which called itself the Knights of Mary Phagan, lit torches as they circled a burning cross. The Ku Klux Klan was reborn in Georgia and elsewhere in the country.

____ **301. The murder trial of Leo Frank resulted in a(n)**
    A. mistrial.
    B. acquittal.
    C. hung jury.
    D. death sentence.

302. **Which was the governor who commuted Leo Frank's from death to life in prison?**
    A. Ellis Arnall
    B. John Slaton
    C. Tom Watson
    D. Eugene Talmadge

303. **What happened to Leo Frank after his trial?**
    A. He was sentenced to life in prison.
    B. He was sentenced and put to death.
    C. He was taken from jail and lynched.
    D. He was found guilty, but was later freed.

COUNTY UNIT SYSTEM

The 1917 Neill Primary Act established a **county unit system** for political primaries. At that time, the Democratic party was the only active political party in the state. This meant the outcome of primary elections and general elections were usually the same. Because that was true, the county unit system, in fact, affected both elections.

Under the county unit system, the 8 most populated counties had 6 county unit votes each (total, 48). The next 30 counties had 4 county unit votes each (total, 120), and the remaining 121 counties had 2 county unit votes each (total, 242). The 38 largest counties had two-thirds of Georgia's voters, but the other 121 counties together could decide a state election.

Those who opposed the county unit system pointed out that people were elected to office without a majority of the state's popular vote. Those who supported it said the system allowed small, less-populated counties to have the same power and influence as larger ones. The county unit system was in effect until 1962, when it was declared unconstitutional.

304. **The county unit system affected voting and politics in Georgia by**
    A. giving the rural areas more power.
    B. helping blacks get more voting power.
    C. focusing power inside the Atlanta area.
    D. favoring cities where most people lived.

305. **Who benefited from the county unit system?**
    A. cities
    B. rural areas
    C. urban areas
    D. metro regions

306. **What was a positive aspect of the county unit system?**
    A. It made the administration of elections easier.
    B. It made buying votes easier for elected officials.
    C. It allowed people to be elected without a majority of the popular vote.
    D. It allowed less populated areas to have the same political power as larger populated areas.

_____ **307. Which piece of legislation allowed less populated counties in Georgia to have the same or greater power and influence in the General Assembly as the more populated counties?**

A. Populist Party

B. Watson's RFD

C. Voting Rights Act

D. Neill Primary Act

> **SS8H7 The student will evaluate key political, social, and economic changes that occurred in Georgia between 1877 and 1918.**
>
> b. Analyze how rights were denied to African-Americans through Jim Crow laws, Plessy v. Ferguson, disenfranchisement, and racial violence.

JIM CROW LAWS

Jim Crow laws were passed to establish "separate-but-equal" facilities for whites and for blacks. The laws resulted in separate restrooms, water fountains, railroad cars, waiting rooms, lodging facilities, dining areas, and schools. In 1889, the Georgia General Assembly **segregated** (separated by race) a number of public facilities including theaters, prison camps, water fountains, and restrooms. Although facilities for African Americans were separate, they were rarely equal to those set aside for whites. African Americans protested the Jim Crow laws in public meetings throughout the nation. Georgia's Henry McNeal Turner, a bishop of the African Methodist Episcopal Church, called the new civil rights laws and the segregation that followed as a result of them "barbarous."

_____ **308. What was the purpose of the "Jim Crow" or segregation laws passed by Georgia's government at the turn of the century?**

A. to make alcohol illegal

B. to continue white control

C. to promote industry in Georgia

D. to provide equality for black Georgians

_____ **309. Which of the following was NOT segregated as a result of Jim Crow laws?**

A. theaters

B. churches

C. prison camps

D. water fountains

PLESSY V. FERGUSON

In 1892, Homer Plessy bought a train ticket from New Orleans to Covington, Louisiana. Because he was seven-eighths white and one-eighth black, he took a seat in the "whites only" car. When he refused to move, he was arrested under the "Jim Crow Car Act of 1890," which required separate-but-equal accommodations for whites and blacks on railroad cars.

Plessy staged the incident to test the constitutionality of the 1890 law. In 1896, the U.S. Supreme Court heard the case and, by a 7-1 vote, upheld the law. A southerner, Justice John Marshall Harlan, cast the single dissenting vote. Plessy v. Ferguson gave states the right to control social discrimination and to promote segregation. Throughout the South, numerous laws segregated such facilities as parks and public transportation. Schools soon followed.

Plessy was soon tested by a case originating in Augusta. Until 1899, Richmond County had the only public high school in Georgia for descendants of enslaved Africans. The school board, supposedly for "purely economic reasons," closed the school, which served 60 high school students, and opened it as an elementary school for 300 students. Three parents sued the school board based on the Plessy decision that ensured separate-but-equal facilities. They filed for an **injunction** (a court order stating that something must or must not be done) asking that the white public high school be closed until another high school was opened for African American students. The lower court agreed, but the Georgia supreme court overturned that ruling.

The case reached the U.S. Supreme Court in December 1899. The court ruled that (1) African American students had the right to be educated only until the eighth grade, (2) closing the white high school did not relate to the equal rights granted by the Fourteenth Amendment, and (3) the use of funds to open the elementary school and close the high school was a state issue. It was not until 1954 with the Brown v. Board of Education ruling that segregated schools became unlawful.

_____ **310. What became legal under Plessy v. Ferguson?**
   A. slavery
   B. black codes
   C. integration
   D. segregation

_____ **311. Plessy v. Ferguson gave states the right to promote**
   A. integration.
   B. segregation.
   C. equal rights.
   D. voting rights for blacks.

_____ **312. According to Plessy v. Ferguson, what Constitutional amendment was NOT violated by establishing "separate-but-equal" facilities?**
   A. Fifteenth Amendment
   B. Sixteenth Amendment
   C. Thirteenth Amendment
   D. Fourteenth Amendment

_____ **313. Homer Plessy sat in the "Whites Only" car on a train because he wanted**
   A. the only seat available.
   B. the comfortable seats there.
   C. to sit with his traveling companions.
   D. to test the legality of a law requiring separate-but-equal facilities.

_____ **314. What Georgia case tested the decision in Plessy v. Ferguson?**
   A. Roe v. Wade
   B. Worcester v. Georgia
   C. Brown v. Board of Education
   D. Cummings v. Richmond County Board of Education

DISENFRANCHISEMENT

By 1900, almost 12 percent of the African Americans in the nation lived in Georgia, making up about 47 percent of the state's population. More and more, however, these citizens found themselves pushed aside and without political power. African American leaders began to speak out, but law after law was passed with the sole purpose of keeping them from voting.

In 1908, Georgia followed other southern states and enacted a **grandfather clause.** The clause stated that only those men whose fathers or grandfathers had been eligible to vote in 1867 were eligible to vote. Because few African Americans were able to vote in 1867, the grandfather clause kept most of Georgia's African Americans from voting.

Even those who could pass the standards of the grandfather clause faced problems at the voting booth. The state and local areas passed a series of additional qualifications for voting. Voters had to own property, pay a **poll tax** (a tax to be able to vote), and pass literacy tests. Because the literacy tests were not standard, the questions could–and did–contain almost anything the voting clerk thought would stump the potential voter.

Southern politicians also used gerrymandering to prevent African Americans from voting. To **gerrymander** means to draw up an election district in such a way that it benefits a certain group. A district can be drawn up to benefit racial groups, a political party, or any other special interest. In Georgia and throughout the South, voting districts were drawn specifically to weaken African American voting power.

Blacks were not the only people who could not vote in Georgia. Neither could women. Efforts to extend suffrage to the nation's women had been going on for decades. In 1914, W. G. Raoul, Mary Raoul, and Emily MacDougald formed Georgia's Equal Suffrage party to gain support for the **Nineteenth Amendment** giving women the right to vote. Within one year, the group had grown to over 2,000 members.

Thirty-six states had to ratify the Nineteenth Amendment for it to become law. On Wednesday, August 18, 1920, the Tennessee legislature ratified the amendment, making it the law of the land. Georgia, however, was one of five states that did not ratify the amendment.

_____ **315. The purpose of the Grandfather clause of 1908 was to**
      A. take the right to vote away from blacks.
      B. make everyone trace their family background.
      C. give grandfathers opportunities to get better jobs.
      D. ask every family to guarantee living quarters for the elderly.

_____ **316. Why did Georgia's political leaders adopt such policies as the grandfather clause and white primary during the early 1900s?**
      A. to allow women to vote
      B. to stop blacks from voting
      C. to segregate Georgia's schools
      D. to create the county unit system

_____ **317. Which voting qualification was designed to prevent African Americans from voting?**
      A. literacy test
      B. party affiliation
      C. identification number
      D. residency requirement

_____ **318. In 1920, the Nineteenth Amendment to the U.S. Constitution was ratified. How did this amendment change the make-up of those who could vote in Georgia?**

    A. It allowed blacks to vote.

    B. It allowed women to vote.

    C. It stopped blacks from voting.

    D. It stopped women from voting.

SS8H7 The student will evaluate key political, social, and economic changes that occurred in Georgia between 1877 and 1918.

    c. Explain the roles of Booker T. Washington, W. E. B. DuBois, John and Lugenia Burns Hope, and Alonzo Herndon.

BOOKER T. WASHINGTON

Booker T. Washington was one of the outstanding civil rights leaders of his day. He was the president of Tuskegee Institute in Alabama and had worked hard to establish the school. Washington believed that, for African Americans, economic independence was the only road to social and political equality. He spoke throughout the United States and Europe, but one of his most famous speeches was given in Atlanta at the Cotton States and International Exposition on September 18, 1895.

What Washington said that day shaped race relations and strongly influenced black leadership for the next twenty years. Washington began to speak:

A ship lost at sea for many days suddenly sighted a friendly vessel. From the mast of the unfortunate vessel was seen a signal, "Water, water; we die of thirst!" The answer from the friendly vessel at once came back, "Cast down your bucket where you are." A second time the signal "Water, water; send us water!" ran up from the distressed vessel, and was answered, "Cast down your bucket where you are!" A third and fourth signal for water was answered, "Cast down your bucket where you are."

The captain of the distressed vessel, at last heeding the injunction, cast down his bucket and it came up full of fresh, sparkling water from the mouth of the Amazon River. To those of my race who depend on bettering their condition in a foreign land or who underestimate the importance of cultivating friendly relations with the southern white man, who is their next door neighbor, I would say: "Cast down your bucket where you are. . . ."

To whites, Washington offered the same advice:

Cast down your bucket . . . among the eight millions of Negroes . . . who have, without strikes and labor wars, tilled your fields, cleared your forests, builded your railroads and cities . . . the most patient, faithful, law-abiding, and unresentful people that the world has seen.

Suddenly, Washington flung his hand up, the fingers held apart and said:

In all things that are purely social, we can be as separate as the fingers. . .

He then balled up his fingers into a fist and continued:

yet one as the hand in all things essential to mutual progress.

His speech became known as the Atlanta Compromise speech, because it proposed that blacks and whites should agree to benefit from each other economically.

_____ **319. Where is Tuskegee Institute, founded by Booker T. Washington, located?**

    A. Georgia

    B. Alabama

    C. Arkansas

    D. Mississippi

_____ **320. What belief would Booker T. Washington NOT support?**

  A. Vocational education was essential for African Americans who sought equality.

  B. Truth and knowledge would cause different races to understand and accept each other.

  C. Economic equality was much more important than social equality for African Americans.

  D. Political and social equality for African Americans would come from economic independence.

_____ **321. Booker T. Washington is BEST known for his ideas on**

  A. integration

  B. segregation

  C. social equality

  D. economic independence

W. E. B. DUBOIS

Atlanta University Professor William Edward Burghardt DuBois (pronounced Du Boyce) did not agree with Booker T. Washington. At first, DuBois thought truth and knowledge would help different races understand and accept each other. He wanted social and political integration, as well as higher education for 10 percent—what he called a "Talented Tenth"—of the African American population. He believed this group could become leaders for all other African Americans.

However, the late 1800s were a time of extreme racial unrest. Between 1884 and 1918, there were over 2,500 reported **lynchings** (illegal hangings, usually by mobs) or burnings at the stake of African Americans in the United States. He decided that knowledge and truth alone were not enough. There must also be action if African Americans and whites were to understand and accept each other.

After Booker T. Washington made his famous Atlanta Compromise speech, differences in their approaches to racial problems caused a split between the two men. DuBois thought Washington was making social, political, and economic decisions that affected all blacks. DuBois also disagreed with Washington's idea that blacks who became economically successful and waited long enough would see race relations improve. In his book The Souls of Black Folk, DuBois wrote:

Manly self-respect is worth more than land and houses, and . . . a people who voluntarily surrender such respect, or cease striving for it, are not worth criticizing.

DuBois concluded:

So far as Mr. Washington preaches Thrift, Patience, and Industrial Training for the masses, we must hold up his hands and strive with him. . . . But, as far as Mr. Washington apologizes for injustices, North or South, does not rightly value the privilege and duty of voting, belittles the emasculating effects of caste distinctions, and opposes the higher training and ambition of our brighter minds,—as far as he, the South or the Nation, does this—we must unceasingly and firmly oppose them.

_____ **322. With what racial issue, promoted by Booker T. Washington, did W. E. B. Debois disagree?**

  A. the idea that education was important

  B. the idea that all black Americans should have social equality

  C. the idea that economic independence alone would lead to social change

  D. the idea that a "Talented Tenth" of black Americans would lead social change

____ **323.** Which African American leader believed that a "Talented Tenth" of the African American population could serve as leaders for all other African Americans?

    A. John Hope

    B. W. E. B. DuBois

    C. Frederick Douglass

    D. Booker T. Washington

JOHN AND LUGENIA BURNS HOPE

Another important leader in our state during this time was John Hope. Hope was born in Augusta in 1868 to a white father and a black mother. Hope attended Augusta public schools and, in 1886, went to Worchester Academy in Massachusetts. He graduated from Brown University and taught at Roger Williams University in Nashville. He then joined the faculty of Atlanta Baptist College (which was renamed Morehouse in 1913). Hope became the school's first black president in 1906. In 1929, he was chosen to be president of Atlanta University.

While Hope was at Atlanta Baptist College, he became close friends with W. E. B. DuBois, who was then on the faculty at Atlanta University. He was the only college president at the 1909 protest meeting in New York that resulted in the founding of the **National Association for the Advancement of Colored People** (NAACP). During the Atlanta race riot, Hope was an active civic leader who worked to restore calm to his city.

John Hope was president of the National Association of Teachers of Colored Schools and a leader in the Association for the Study of Negro Life and History. He gained international recognition for his work with the YMCA. Under Hope's leadership, Morehouse, Spelman, Morris Brown, and Clark colleges, Gannon Theological Seminary, and Atlanta University formed the Atlanta University Center.

John Hope's wife, Lugenia, was a "mover and shaker" as well as a well-known civic leader. She organized the Neighborhood Union, which offered vocational classes for children, a health center, and clubs for boys and girls. The Neighborhood Union also provided financial aid for needy families and pressured city leaders to improve roads, lighting, and sanitation in the African American neighborhoods of Atlanta.

____ **324.** Who was the first black president of Atlanta Baptist College?

    A. John Hope

    B. W. E. B. DuBois

    C. Frederick Douglass

    D. Booker T. Washington

____ **325.** To what did Atlanta Baptist College change its name?

    A. Spelman

    B. Morehouse

    C. Morris Brown

    D. Atlanta University

____ **326.** What organization was founded by Lugenia Burns Hope?

    A. Y.W.C.A.

    B. D.E.C.C.A.

    C. Girl Scouts

    D. Neighborhood Union

_____ **327. All of the following services were offered by the organization founded by Lugenia Burns Hope EXCEPT**

    A. vocational classes.

    B. clubs for boys and girls

    C. financial aid for the needy.

    D. remedial education classes.

ALONZO HERNDON

Alonzo Herndon was born a slave on a Walton County plantation. After the Civil War, he worked for his former master for a short time at a salary of $25 a year. Herndon learned to be a barber and moved to Jonesboro to open his own barber shop. Thinking that business would be better in Atlanta, he moved there and worked in a barber shop. Within six months, he owned a half interest in the business. By the early 1900s, he had opened three new shops for white customers. Herndon began buying property, and he soon owned a block of office buildings on Auburn Avenue and a hundred rental houses. In 1905, Herndon bought a small insurance company for $140. He knew little about insurance, so he hired African American college graduates to run the Atlanta Mutual Insurance Company.

Herndon was still president of his insurance company when he died in 1927; his son Norris took over. That company is now the Atlanta Life Insurance Company. One of the largest African American-owned businesses in the United States, Atlanta Life has a net worth of over $200 million and operations in seventeen states. Perhaps the secret of Herndon's success in business was best explained when he said, "Some of us sit and wait for opportunity when it is always with us."

_____ **328. What business made Alonzo Herndon a successful businessman?**

    A. Coca-Cola

    B. Georgia Pacific

    C. Western and Atlantic Railroad

    D. Atlanta Mutual Insurance Company

_____ **329. Alonzo Herndon became a successful businessman by**

    A. hiring college graduates to run his company.

    B. becoming the sole employee of his new business.

    C. moving his company to a larger metropolitan area.

    D. spending hundreds of thousands of dollars on advertising.

> **SS8H7** **The student will evaluate key political, social, and economic changes that occurred in Georgia between 1877 and 1918.**
>
> d. Give reasons for World War I and describe Georgia's contributions.

WORLD WAR I

President Woodrow Wilson hoped to keep the United States in the dispute among European nations. But a series of actions by Germany led him to ask Congress to declare war on Germany in April 1917. When President Wilson spoke to Congress, he asked Americans to fight a war "to make the world safe for democracy."

At the start of World War I, the United States was **neutral**. By international law, this meant the United States could trade with both warring sides. This was called "freedom of the seas." The British tried to stop neutral countries from trading with Germany by mining the North Sea with explosives. Germany used its submarines to sink ships trading with the British.

In May 1915, a German submarine sank the British ocean liner Lusitania off Ireland. Among the hundreds killed were 128 Americans. President Wilson warned Germany not to continue to violate international law. Germany apologized and stopped the submarine warfare for fear that the United States would enter the war.

Meanwhile, the United States became more committed to the Allies, who depended on the United States for food and war supplies. The British bombarded America with anti-German **propaganda** (information that is spread for the purpose of promoting some cause). Congress began preparing for war.

In early 1917, Germany resumed its submarine attacks, and in March 1917 German submarines sank several American ships. Meanwhile, the British intercepted and decoded a secret radio message from Germany to Mexico. In this so-called Zimmermann telegram, Germany urged Mexico to attack the United States in return for regaining the southwestern United States. This was the final blow. President Wilson asked Congress to declare war.

When the United States declared war, between 85,000 and 100,000 of Georgia's citizens joined the armed forces. Soldiers came from other states to be trained at military posts located throughout the state, including Camp Benning, Fort McPherson, and Camp Gordon.

Located near Columbus, Camp Benning was opened in 1917 and trained infantry troops. It became Fort Benning in 1922. During the war, a German submarine crew was imprisoned at Fort McPherson, which was just outside of Atlanta. Camp Gordon (later renamed Fort Gordon) is located outside of Augusta. These and other military installations were a major factor in the state's economy.

Georgians contributed to the war effort in other ways. Textile mills made fabric for military uniforms. Railroads carried arms, ammunition, and soldiers to ports where ships waited to sail for Europe. Farmers grew more food crops, tobacco, and livestock. Many town residents planted "victory gardens" to raise their own vegetables so there would be more food for the military. Women volunteered to work for the Red Cross, to welcome soldiers, to knit, and to help sell bonds. However, Georgia's most important contribution was the three thousand young people from all over the state who died in an effort to "make the world safe for democracy."

The entry of the United States into the war and the vast amounts of personnel, supplies, and equipment it was able to contribute helped to defeat the Central Powers. On November 11, 1918, the war officially ended when both sides signed an **armistice** (an agreement to stop fighting). For years afterward, Georgia and the rest of the nation rang church bells and held ceremonies at the 11th hour on the 11th day of the 11th month to commemorate victory and peace.

____ **330. What countries were allies in World War I?**
     A. Germany, Japan, and Russia
     B. Germany, Russia, and Austria-Hungary
     C. Great Britain, France, United States, and Russia
     D. United States, France, Austria-Hungary, and Great Britain

____ **331. What was the "final blow" that led President Woodrow Wilson to ask Congress to declare war against the Central Powers in World War I?**
     A. Zimmermann telegram
     B. sinking of the Lusitania
     C. attacks on American merchant ships
     D. anti-German propaganda in the United States

332. At which Georgia military installation did infantry train in World War I?
   A. Camp Gordon
   B. Camp Augusta
   C. Camp Benning
   D. Camp McPherson

333. What event is celebrated on the 11th hour of the 11th day of the 11th month of the year?
   A. founding of Georgia
   B. sinking of the *Lusitania*
   C. beginning of the Civil War
   D. armistice that ended World War I

334. The information used by the Allied nations to promote their cause and entice the United States to enter World War I was called
   A. libel.
   B. slander.
   C. propaganda.
   D. yellow journalism.

SS8H8   The student will analyze the important events that occurred after World War I and their impact on Georgia.

a. Describe the impact of the boll weevil and drought on Georgia.

BOLL WEEVIL

For many Georgians, the 1920s were not a time of abundance. A small, grayish, long-snouted beetle, the **boll weevil**, was destroying the primary source of income for many Georgia farmers: cotton. The boll weevil had come from Mexico, moved through Texas, and into the southern states in the 1890s. The beetles hatch in the yellow flower of the cotton plant. As the flower becomes a boll (the place were the fibers are formed), the larvae feeds on the growing white, fluffy cotton, making it useless.

The boll weevil appeared in southwest Georgia in 1915 and quickly spread across the state, destroying thousands of acres of Georgia's major agricultural crop. By 1923, cotton production had dropped to 600,000 bales from a high of 2.8 million bales in 1914. The postwar price was only fifteen to seventeen cents a pound.

335. What two events occurred causing Georgia's and the rest of the South's economies to be weakened long before the beginning of the Great Depression?
   A. prohibition and disenfranchisement
   B. the boll weevil and the drop in cotton prices
   C. adoption of child labor laws and the county unit system
   D. election of Woodrow Wilson and the beginning of World War I

336. The boll weevil originally came from
   A. Texas.
   B. Florida.
   C. Mexico.
   D. Mississippi.

_____ **337. The boll weevil larvae feed on the**

    A. white, fluffy cotton.

    B. leaves of the cotton plant.

    C. insects found on the cotton plant.

    D. yellow flowers on the cotton plant.

DROUGHT

In 1924, Georgia farmers were hit with a major drought. The sun-baked fields slowed down the destruction of the boll weevil, but the drought ruined most of Georgia's other crops. Over 375,000 farm workers left Georgia between 1920 and 1925. The number of working farms fell from 310,132 to 249,095. When farms failed, banks that had loaned the farmers money took huge losses. Many farm-related businesses closed. Georgia was in a deep **depression**.

_____ **338. Besides the boll weevil, Georgia cotton farmers in the 1920s were hurt by**

    A. fires.

    B. frosts.

    C. droughts.

    D. tornadoes.

_____ **339. What positive impact did the 1924 drought make on Georgia?**

    A. It decreased tourism at state parks.

    B. It created a good climate to attract industry.

    C. It contributed to the end of the Great Depression.

    D. It slowed down the destruction by the boll weevil.

SS8H8   The student will analyze the important events that occurred after World War I and their impact on Georgia.

    b. Explain economic factors that resulted in the Great Depression.

ECONOMIC FACTORS CAUSING THE GREAT DEPRESSION

One cause of the Great Depression was that the people of the United States had borrowed more money than they could afford to repay. This hurt the banks that had loaned the money and the businesses waiting for their payments. Businesses that did not get paid had to lay off workers.

Many factories had produced more goods than they could sell. When the demand for the goods fell, the businesses had to slow production until their surpluses were gone. Farmers were also guilty of overproduction. For several seasons, the farmers had produced surplus crops, causing prices to decline steadily. After World War I, European farmers began raising crops again; that added to the worldwide overproduction. The decline in farm income meant farmers could not repay their debts or buy goods.

After World War I, Americans wanted to trade with other nations. But the United States and other nations had enacted tariffs. The high tariffs made it difficult for other countries to sell their goods in the United States to get money with which to repay wartime loans and buy American products.

Speculation in the stock market also helped cause the Great Depression. During the 1920s, most people bought stock and paid only a portion of the cost of the stock at the time of the purchase. Even though the stock was not completely paid for, the investor had the right to sell it. If the stock price had gone up, the investor sold the stock and made enough to finish paying for the stock. This practice forced the price of stocks up, making them higher than what they were really worth.

Many banks had purchased large amounts of stock. When the market crashed, the banks lost a lot of money. When depositors learned this, there were runs on the banksand the banks collapsed.

One final cause was the **laissez-faire** attitude of the American people and of American government and business leaders. Almost every government official believed the economy itself, not the government, would work out any problems. President Hoover did what any other politician of the time would have done--nothing. Hoover kept telling the American people that "prosperity is just around the corner." But prosperity was not just around the corner.

Use these events to answer question 340.

- borrowing more money than could be repaid
- speculating in the stock market
- overproducing farm products

____ **340. These events led to**
   A. World War II
   B. the Great Society
   C. Hoover's re-election
   D. the Great Depression

____ **341. In Franklin D. Roosevelt's 1933 inaugural address, he said,** *"We are stricken by no plague of locust. Compared with the perils which our forefathers conquered because they believed and were not afraid, we have still much to be thankful for. Nature still offers her bounty and human efforts have multiplied it. Plenty is at our doorstep. . . ."* **This statement was meant to give the American people hope to overcome**
   A. World War I.
   B. World War II.
   C. the Great Depression.
   D. the nationwide drought.

____ **342. What United States president's policies are blamed for the Great Depression?**
   A. Harry Truman
   B. Herbert Hoover
   C. Dwight Eisenhower
   D. Franklin D. Roosevelt

____ **343. Laissez-faire policies of the U.S. government helped bring about the depression by**
   A. overextending trade agreements.
   B. giving businesses too many loans.
   C. encouraging people to invest in the stock market.
   D. not doing anything to help solve the country's economic problems.

____ **344. Georgians did not feel the impact of the stock market crash because**
   A. the state was already in a depression.
   B. banks were protected by state insurance.
   C. citizens had little money invested in the stock market.
   D. the state constitution prohibited investing tax dollars in the stock market.

c. Discuss the impact of the political career of Eugene Talmadge.

EUGENE TALMADGE

State government changed greatly when Eugene Talmadge became governor in 1933. Talmadge was a dramatic politician. You may have heard the expression that politicians "stumped the state" giving speeches to voters. Talmadge actually took a stump with him, a sawed off section of an oak that was two feet high and three feet in diameter. He put it in the middle of the crowd, stood on it, and delivered fiery speeches. He often told rural Georgia voters that they had three friends–Sears Roebuck, God Almighty, and Eugene Herman Talmadge.

Talmadge was a conservative white supremacist who did not like federal government intervention or government debts. He especially disliked relief efforts, public welfare, and federal assistance programs. After becoming governor, he tried to rid the state of New Deal programs. He used federal funds to build highways more often than to help the unemployed. He reduced property taxes, utility rates, and some license fees.

Talmadge was elected to a second term in 1934 by a landslide. Officials who disagreed with Talmadge were fired and replaced with his supporters. When Talmadge refused to follow federal New Deal regulations, the federal government took over New Deal programs in Georgia. In 1934, during the state's worst textile strike, the governor declared martial law and used the National Guard to arrest strikers.

However, Talmadge's political power plays did not change the fact that Georgia law would not allow him to serve more than two consecutive terms. Because he could not run for governor, Talmadge ran for the U.S. Senate in 1936 against Richard Russell and was soundly defeated.

In 1940, Eugene Talmadge ran for governor again and was elected. Talmadge had softened his anti-Roosevelt stand and began using modified versions of New Deal legislation. The state's economy grew. Then, a series of events angered the voters and put Georgia in a bad light.

A Talmadge supporter at the University of Georgia told the governor that one of the deans at the university and the president of the Teachers College in Statesboro (now known as Georgia Southern University) had plans to **integrate** the school (open it to members of all races and ethnic groups). Talmadge convinced the board of regents to fire the two individuals. He also got rid of several members of the board of regents who publicly opposed his interference in the university system.

There was a great deal of national publicity, strongly against the governor's stand. The situation so offended the Southern Association of Colleges and Schools that they voted to take away the accreditation of white Georgia colleges.

____ 345. **What Georgia governor served during the Great Depression and spent a great deal of his time speaking out against the New Deal, blacks, and the metropolitan areas?**

    A. Ellis Arnall

    B. Eurith Rivers

    C. Richard Russell

    D. Eugene Talmadge

____ 346. **Which policy did Governor Eugene Talmadge support?**

    A. public welfare

    B. voting rights for blacks

    C. reduced property taxes

    D. federal assistance programs

____ **347. From what group of voters did Talmadge receive his greatest support?**
   A. rural voters
   B. black voters
   C. women voters
   D. wealthy voters

____ **348. Which issue did Eugene Talmadge support?**
   A. integration
   B. higher taxes
   C. states' rights
   D. white supremacy

____ **349. What action by Eugene Talmadge resulted in the loss of accreditation of ten Georgia public colleges and universities, including the University of Georgia?**
   A. He withheld federal funds from Georgia's colleges and universities.
   B. He ordered the Confederate flag to be flown at all colleges in Georgia.
   C. He fired two University System administrators who supported integration.
   D. He approved the admission of several black students at two all-white colleges.

____ **350. Besides himself and God, who did Eugene Talmadge call the friend of rural voters?**
   A. Sears Roebuck
   B. William Hartsfield
   C. Montgomery Ward
   D. Franklin D. Roosevelt

SS8H8   The student will analyze the important events that occurred after World War I and their impact on Georgia.

   d. Discuss the effect of the New Deal in terms of the impact of the Civilian Conservation Corps, Agricultural Adjustment Act, rural electrification, and Social Security.

CIVILIAN CONSERVATION CORPS

In 1932, in the midst of the Great Depression, Franklin D. Roosevelt of New York was elected president. When he took office, Roosevelt took steps to fulfill his promise of "a new deal for the American people." He gathered a group of advisers from all over the country. With their help and at Roosevelt's urging, Congress passed a series of laws that came to be known as the **New Deal**. The purpose of these laws was to bring about economic recovery, relieve the suffering of the unemployed, reform defects in the economy, and improve society.

The Civilian Conservation Corps (CCC) was a New Deal program that provided jobs for young single men building forest trails and roads, planting trees to reforest the land and control flooding, and building parks. The CCC was popular in Georgia in part because of its work at Camp Brumby with the Kennesaw Mountain National Battlefield Park. The CCC also built many of the facilities at Roosevelt State Park in Pine Mountain. Other CCC projects in Georgia included construction of sewer projects in many of the state's cities; flood control and drainage projects such as Tybee Island's seawall; recreational facilities such as ball fields, band stands, and theaters throughout the state; and a host of municipal facilities such as Augusta's Savannah River Levee, Atlanta's Municipal Auditorium, St. Simons' airport, Macon's airport, Stewart County's courthouse and jail, and renovations of Dalton's city hall. The CCC also worked to build, expand, or improve schools and hospitals throughout the state. For example, much of the work on Grady Hospital in Atlanta was done by the CCC.

____ **351. What was NOT a purpose of the New Deal?**

    A. to provide loans to students

    B. to improve lifestyles for Americans

    C. to reform the defects in the economy

    D. to relieve the suffering of the unemployed

____ **352. Which New Deal program was responsible for such projects in Georgia as Roosevelt State Park in Pine Mountain, Tybee Island's seawall, Augusta's Savannah River Levee, and Macon's airport?**

    A. CCC

    B. NYA

    C. TVA

    D. WPA

AGRICULTURAL ADJUSTMENT ACT

The Agricultural Adjustment Administration (AAA) was created in March 1933. The AAA paid farmers not to plant crops on part of their land. The legislation created **price supports** (guaranteed higher prices) to farmers who agreed to cut back their cotton and tobacco crops. The idea was to raise farm prices by limiting production. The plan worked, and farm income improved. In 1929, Georgia was already reeling from low cotton prices. Between 1929 and 1932, cotton prices had fallen to 5 cents a pound. The production limits set by the AAA raised cotton prices to 12 cents a pound; by 1936, cotton prices had reached 15 cents a pound.

One drawback of the AAA was that farm **subsidies** (grants of money from the government) went to landowners rather than to the tenant farmers, who were predominantly black. The tenant farmers who worked the land never saw any of the money. In fact, with decreased production, many tenant farmers were without work. The AAA was eventually declared unconstitutional by the U.S. Supreme Court because it was not voluntary.

____ **353. Why did the Agricultural Adjustment Act fail to benefit African-Americans in Georgia?**

    A. Subsidies were paid to property owners, not the tenant farmers.

    B. Only whites were hired by the Works Progress Administration.

    C. Only whites qualified for Social Security and Medicare benefits.

    D. Young blacks were not hired under the National Youth Administration.

____ **354. Which group of Georgians failed to benefit from the Agricultural Adjustment Act?**

    A. renters

    B. wealthy

    C. tenant farmers

    D. property owners

____ **355. Which group of Georgians benefited most from the Agricultural Adjustment Act?**

    A. blacks

    B. alcoholics

    C. property owners

    D. tenant farmers

RURAL ELECTRIFICATION

Rural electrification was an important New Deal program. In the 1920s, power companies mainly ran lines to towns and cities. Because the rural population was spread out, power lines were expensive to build and maintain.

The Rural Electrification Authority (REA) reportedly was a result of President Roosevelt's first night at Warm Springs, Georgia. He was sitting on the porch of his small cottage, trying to catch a breeze on a hot, sultry summer night. He noticed that no lights were showing from neighboring farms. When he received his electrical bill at the end of the month, he saw that it was many times higher than what he paid at his mansion in Hyde Park, New York.

Roosevelt never forgot that night, and on May 11, 1935, he signed into law the act creating the REA. The REA loaned over $300 million to farmers' cooperatives to help them extend their own power lines and buy power wholesale. This program was one on the most important and far-reaching of the New Deal programs. By 1940, a significant percentage of farmers in Georgia and other parts of the nation had electricity. Electric water pumps, lights, milking machines, and appliances made farm life much easier.

_____ **356. What did the New Deal's rural electrification project (REA) do for Georgia's farmers?**

A. It required power companies to provide power at a lower rate.

B. It enabled farms to double their size as a result of federal loans.

C. It provided funds for power companies to run lines in rural areas.

D. It provided loans to farmers' cooperatives so they could run power lines in rural areas.

_____ **357. What New Deal program resulted from President Franklin Roosevelt's view of rural Georgia without electricity while sitting on his porch in the evening?**

A. REA

B. CCC

C. FDIC

D. WPA

_____ **358. How did Franklin Roosevelt's time spent in Georgia bring about the establishment of the Rural Electrification Authority?**

A. He made a campaign promise to provide electricity to rural Georgia.

B. He wanted to reduce the cost of electricity for the poor.

C. He noticed that his neighbors did not have electricity.

D. He owned rural land and wanted to have electricity.

SOCIAL SECURITY

New Deal relief efforts, however, could not reach those people who could not work--children, the blind, widows with small children, and the elderly. In addition, workers needed some protection against unemployment. In 1935, Congress passed the Social Security Act. The federal government would provide retirement and unemployment insurance from taxes paid by both workers and their employers. Farm workers, however, were not covered by the new program. As President Roosevelt stated at the signing of the legislation into law, _"We can never insure one hundred percent of the population against one hundred percent of the hazards and vicissitudes of life, but we have tried to frame a law which will give some measure of protection to the average citizen and to his family against the loss of a job and against poverty-ridden old age."_

359. The purpose of social security is to

    A. create a system to save the banks from collapse.

    B. protect the financial sovereignty of the federal government.

    C. create a system of retirement and unemployment insurance.

    D. give all workers in the United States a savings plan for the future.

360. What group of workers was NOT covered by Social Security?

    A. store clerks

    B. farm workers

    C. schoolteachers

    D. factory owners

SS8H9   The student will describe the impact of World War II on Georgia's development economically, socially, and politically.

    a. Describe the impact of events leading up to American involvement in World War II; include Lend-Lease and the bombing of Pearl Harbor.

LEND-LEASE

President Roosevelt watched as Japan, Italy, the Soviet Union, and Germany carved up the world. Most Americans felt strongly that we should not get involved, but Great Britain was an ally and Roosevelt wanted to help. He thought that only the British could stop Hitler from crossing the Atlantic Ocean. In the 1930s, Congress had passed neutrality acts to keep the United States out of another war. One of those acts would not allow the president to sell weapons to any warring nation. In 1939, Roosevelt asked for and got a new law that allowed the Allied Powers to buy arms if they paid cash and carried them in their own ships. In 1940, Roosevelt gave Great Britain old weapons and traded fifty destroyers for British bases in the Western Hemisphere.

In early 1941, when the British ran out of cash with which to buy American supplies, Congress authorized Roosevelt to lend or lease arms to them. After Germany turned on and invaded the Soviet Union in June 1941, Roosevelt gave lend-lease aid to the Soviets as well. To make sure the supplies got to them, Roosevelt built air bases in Greenland and Iceland. Planes from these bases tracked German submarines. Roosevelt also ordered the U.S. Navy to convoy (escort) British ships part of the way across the Atlantic.

361. Why did the United States start a lend-lease system of war equipment?

    A. It's allies preferred to lease the equipment.

    B. It could charge interest and make more money.

    C. It would get the materials back at the end of the war.

    D. Its allies ran out of money with which to purchase the equipment.

362. Which describes the involvement of the United States in World War II before the bombing of Pearl Harbor?

    A. The United States provided advisory troops to aid Germany.

    B. The United States secretly sank German submarines en route to Britain.

    C. The United States maintained strict neutrality with no involvement at all.

    D. The United States provided lend-lease aid to Great Britain and the Soviet Union.

PEARL HARBOR

Meanwhile, American-Japanese relations got worse. To protest Japanese expansion, the United States stopped exporting airplanes, metals, aircraft parts, and aviation gasoline to Japan. After Japan invaded French Indochina in 1941, Roosevelt seized all Japanese property in the United States.

Badly needing the oil that Roosevelt had cut off, Japan decided to invade the Dutch East Indies (now Indonesia) in late 1941. The only force that could stop the Japanese was the U.S. Navy stationed at Pearl Harbor, Hawaii.

December 7, 1941, was a peaceful Sunday morning. Many of the sailors stationed on the island were eating breakfast or going about their early morning routines. Suddenly, around 8:00 a.m., the air was filled with the sounds of machine gun fire and low level bombing. The Japanese attack on Pearl Harbor was over by 10:00 a.m., but the damage to the Navy's Pacific fleet was incredible. All eight battleships in port were destroyed or severely damaged; more than 180 planes were destroyed. Over two thousand people were killed, and over one thousand were wounded. President Roosevelt called the attack a "day that will live in infamy." Almost half of the U.S. casualties at Pearl Harbor were aboard the U.S.S. Arizona, which sank with most of her crew aboard. Today the National Park Service manages the site of the Arizona's sinking as a national monument.

On December 8, Congress declared war on Japan, and the United States entered World War II. A few days later, Germany and Italy declared war on the United States. Now it was a full-fledged war between the Allied Powers led by the United States, Great Britain, and the Soviet Union and the Axis Powers of Germany, Japan, and Italy. Joining the Allies meant the United States had to fight on two fronts, facing Germany and Italy in Europe and Africa and Japan in the Pacific.

____ **363. The United States entered World War II when Japan attacked**
   A. China.
   B. Midway.
   C. Manchuria.
   D. Pearl Harbor.

____ **364. What famous statement refers to the attack on Pearl Harbor?**
   A. "the British are coming"
   B. "day that will live in infamy"
   C. "we have only begun to fight"
   D. "shot heard around the world"

SS8H9   The student will describe the impact of World War II on Georgia's development economically, socially, and politically.

b. Evaluate the importance of Bell Aircraft, military bases, the Savannah and Brunswick shipyards, Richard Russell, and Carl Vinson.

BELL AIRCRAFT

After Pearl Harbor, the federal government decided to build additional aircraft plants to manufacture the B-29 bomber. Bell Aircraft Company of Buffalo, New York, won a contract to build the B-29 in a new plant in Marietta. The Marietta facility was the largest aircraft assembly plant in the world, with over 4.2 million square feet.

In spring 1943, Bell Aircraft began assembling the bombers for the U.S. Army Air Force. At first, the plant employed about 1,200 people. By April 1945, there were 27,000 employees and the plant was turning out 60-65 planes a month. The initial contract with the government called for the facility to assemble 400 planes. By the time the plant closed at the end of 1945, Bell Aircraft had built 668 planes.

In 1950, the Air Force convinced Lockheed Aircraft Corporation to reopen the Marietta plant. The plant is still open and is operated by the Lockheed Martin Corporation.

_____ **365. What type of aircraft was built at the Bell Aircraft Marietta plant?**

      A. 727s

      B. fighter jets

      C. jumbo jets

      D. B-29 bombers

_____ **366. What happened to the Bell Aircraft Marietta plant?**

      A. It closed down before World War II ended.

      B. It is part of the Lockheed Martin plant today.

      C. It is part of Hartsfield-Jackson Airport today.

      D. It has continued to operate continuously since the war.

MILITARY BASES

World War II brought prosperity to Georgia. Millions of federal dollars poured into the state, strengthening the economy. Because of its climate and the influence of politicians like Senator Richard Russell, Jr., Senator Walter F. George, and Representative Carl Vinson, the state became the site of several military installations.

Major military bases included Fort Benning in Columbus, Camp Gordon in Augusta, Fort Stewart and Hunter Air Field in Savannah, and Warner Robins Air Field near Macon. Fort Benning was the largest infantry center in the country. In fact, only Texas trained more military than did Georgia. Airmen from Glynco Naval Air Station, near Brunswick, flew blimps along the southern Atlantic coast in search of German submarines.

Fort McPherson, in the Atlanta area, was a major induction center for newly drafted soldiers from all over the country. A military hospital, which had been used in World War I, was reopened in Atlanta. Fort Gillem, an army storage facility and railroad yard, began operation in nearby Clayton County. Prisoners of war were also held at Forts Benning, Gordon, Oglethorpe, and Stewart.

In 1943, the Cobb County Airport became the Marietta Army Airfield. At Fort Oglethorpe, some of the 150,000 women who served in the WAAC (Women's Army Auxiliary Corp, later known as WACs) trained to become postal workers, clerks, typists, switchboard operators, code clerks, and drivers or aides.

In Marietta, 30,000 men and women built B-29 bombers at the Bell Bomber plant. The Atlanta airport became an air base in 1941.

_____ **367. Which was a major contribution of Georgia during World War II?**

      A. Radar technology was developed and tested at Georgia army bases.

      B. Military bases were established that trained large numbers of U.S. troops.

      C. Research sites developed the technology for a prototype of the atomic bomb.

      D. Hospitals trained large numbers of doctors and nurses for the Medical Corps.

_____ **368. The Georgia military base that did NOT also serve as a prisoner of war camp was**

      A. Fort Gordon.

      B. Fort Stewart.

      C. Fort Benning.

      D. Fort Campbell.

369. Fort Oglethorpe supported the war effort by serving as a training center for
A. naval aviators.
B. combat soldiers.
C. military intelligence.
D. women in the WAAC.

370. What role did Fort McPherson play in World War II?
A. It was an induction center for newly drafted soldiers.
B. It was a training center for soldiers fighting in Europe.
C. It was a training center for women in the armed forces.
D. It was a detainment center for American citizens of Japanese descent.

SAVANNAH AND BRUNSWICK SHIPYARDS

A number of industries in Georgia were contributing to the war effort. One effort was the building of Liberty ships at Brunswick and Savannah shipyards. President Roosevelt named the cargo ships "Liberty ships" after Patrick Henry's famous quotation, and the ships were essential to the war effort. The first of Georgia's Liberty ships was launched in November 1942–the U.S.S. James Oglethorpe, which was sunk by a German submarine the next year. In all, eighty-eight Liberty ships were built in Savannah by 15,000 workers, many of whom were women.

In Brunswick, over 16,000 men and women worked around the clock in 1943 and 1944 on six ships at a time. In December 1944, they set a national record by building seven ships in just one month. The crews even worked on Christmas Day and donated their checks for that day to the war effort. In all, Brunswick's shipyards produced ninety-nine Liberty ships. Both of Georgia's port cities can be proud of their tremendous contributions to the war effort.

371. What were Liberty ships?
A. battleships
B. cargo ships
C. submarines
D. landing craft

372. Where in Georgia were Liberty ships built during World War II?
A. Atlanta and Augusta
B. Brunswick and Savannah
C. Brunswick and Jekyll Island
D. St. Simons Island and Augusta

RICHARD B. RUSSELL

On June 27, 1931, Winder resident Richard Russell, Jr., became Georgia's youngest governor in the twentieth century. Administering the oath of office was his father, Georgia Supreme Court Chief Justice Richard B. Russell, Sr.

Richard B. Russell, Jr., used his experience as a former member and speaker of the Georgia house of representatives to make some needed changes. One of his first acts was to combine 102 state offices into 17 agencies. In an equally daring political move, he combined the boards of trustees of state colleges and universities into one governing group–the Board of Regents of the University System of Georgia.

During the creation of the new system, some colleges were closed while others were combined. Russell appointed Hughes Spalding, an Atlanta lawyer, as the first chairman of the board of regents. Russell tried to run the state like a successful business. His approach eased some of the problems brought on by the depression.

In 1932, Governor Russell was elected to the U.S. Senate, where he served for the next thirty-eight years. Russell favored national military preparedness and states' rights. He served on the powerful Senate Appropriations Committee, which was responsible for funding government programs. After the war, he served on the Armed Services Committee and supported a strong national defense. Russell also co-sponsored legislation to provide a school lunch to all children.

He became a respected advisor to six United States presidents and, when he served as president pro tempore of the Senate, he was third in line for the presidency.

____ 373. **What was the impact of Richard Russell's service in the U.S. Senate from 1932 to 1971?**
   A. It declined because he lacked wealth or a strong military record.
   B. It was not significant because Russell had no political opposition.
   C. It showed that a Republican could be repeatedly elected from Georgia.
   D. He gave Georgia leadership in the Senate as a result of his length of service.

____ 374. **Because of Senator Richard Russell's sponsorship of a program for schoolchildren, what nickname did he earn?**
   A. Father of the graded school
   B. Father of the unified curriculum
   C. Father of the county school system
   D. Father of the school lunch program

Use these actions to answer question 375.

> - consolidating state offices
> - running state government like a successful business
> - establishing the Board of Regents of the University System of Georgia

____ 375. **Which Depression-era governor implemented these changes?**
   A. Carl Vinson
   B. Walter George
   C. Richard Russell
   D. Eugene Talmadge

____ 376. **The youngest governor in Georgia history was**
   A. Carl Vinson
   B. Walter George
   C. Richard Russell
   D. Eugene Talmadge

CARL VINSON

It is impossible to review World War II without examining the contributions of one of Georgia's most influential leaders, Carl Vinson. He served twenty-five consecutive terms representing Georgia in the U.S. House of Representatives, from 1914 to 1965. When he retired, he had established a record for longevity in the House. Vinson, a native of Baldwin County, served as chairman of the House Naval Affairs Committee for 16 years and its successor, the House Armed Services Committee for 14 years. Even before World War II, Georgia's economy had grown to depend heavily on the state's military installations, and Vinson represented Georgia's interest in the military through his committee work.

Vinson was a major influence in promoting a strong national defense. Alarmed by rising tensions in Europe, President Roosevelt and Vinson worked to increase the country's military readiness. In 1934, he oversaw the passage of the Vinson-Trammel Act, which authorized the manufacture of ninety-two major warships. Almost two years before Japan's attack on Pearl Harbor, Vinson maneuvered two important bills through Congress. One bill expanded the naval aviation system to 10,000 planes, trained 16,000 pilots, and established 20 air bases. The second piece of legislation eased labor restrictions in the shipbuilding industry and allowed faster construction of navy ships. Vinson is often referred to as the "father of the two-ocean navy."

Even after World War II, Vinson continued his dominance in Congress, pushing for a strong defense throughout the Cold War with the Soviet Union. In 1964, President Lyndon B. Johnson awarded Carl Vinson the Presidential Medal of Freedom. After serving for over 50 years in Congress, Vinson retired to his Milledgeville farm in 1965. In 1972, President Richard M. Nixon honored Vinson by naming the country's third nuclear carrier for him. He died in 1981.

_____ 377. **In referring to his active involvement with military advancements, Carl Vinson once said,** *"I devoutly hope that the casting of every gun and the building of every ship will be done with a prayer for the peace of America. I have at heart no sectional nor political interest, but only the Republic's safety."* **Which statement best describes the meaning of Carl Vinson's statement?**
   A. War may be necessary to protect our country.
   B. War is better than peace when being threatened.
   C. The United States needs a strong military to defend itself.
   D. The United States needs to manufacture guns and build ships to keep up with other nations.

_____ 378. **What Georgian is known as the "father of the two-ocean navy?"**
   A. Ben Epps
   B. Carl Vinson
   C. Walter F. George
   D. Richard B. Russell, Jr.

_____ 379. **Which legislation, supported by Carl Vinson, most directly benefited Georgia?**
   A. law to ease labor restrictions in the shipbuilding industry
   B. law to expand the naval aviation system to 10,000 planes
   C. law to increase the military readiness of the United States
   D. law to provide military supplies to our World War II allies

> **SS8H9** The student will describe the impact of World War II on Georgia's development economically, socially, and politically.
>
> c. Explain the impact of the Holocaust on Georgians.

THE HOLOCAUST

In the spring of 1945, as Allied troops pushed into Poland, Austria, and Germany, nothing could have prepared them for what they found. Auschwitz, Buckenwald, Dachau, Treblinka, Bergen-Belsen, and other concentration camps were set up by the Nazis as the "final solution to the Jewish problem." Those who were left alive in the camps were emaciated skeletons from years of starvation, disease, cruel treatment, and forced labor.

The **Holocaust** was the name given to the systematic extermination (killing) of 6 million Jews. An additional 5-6 million people, labeled as "undesirables," were also killed by the Nazis before and during World War II. In the camps, many died from starvation; others died from disease, mistreatment, and medical experiments. Prisoners, including children, were gassed in chambers they thought were showers. Their bodies were incinerated in huge ovens or thrown into mass graves. The deaths of these Jews, Poles, Czechs, Russians, Gypsies, homosexuals, and the mentally or physically disabled all fit Hitler's plan to rid Europe of what he called "inferior" people.

In 1986, the Georgia Commission on the Holocaust was established "to take lessons from the history of the Holocaust and use them to help lead new generations of Georgians beyond racism and bigotry. Through a variety of programs, the Commission fosters tolerance, good citizenship and character development among the young people of the state." Each year, the Commission sponsors an art and writing contest for Georgia middle and high school students.

____ 380. **The Holocaust was a name given to the tactics used by Hitler and the Nazis for**
  A. eliminating enemy prisoners of war.
  B. frightening those who opposed Adolph Hitler.
  C. exterminating 6 million Jews and other "undesirables."
  D. getting rid of the bodies of those who died or were killed in World War II.

____ 381. **Who was the world leader who instigated the Holocaust?**
  A. Adolf Hitler
  B. Joseph Stalin
  C. Emperor Hirohito
  D. Benito Mussolini

Use these terms to answer question 382.

> - Auschwitz
> - Dachau
> - Treblinka

____ 382. **What do these terms associated with World War II have in common?**
  A. concentration camps
  B. Axis Power capitals
  C. battlefields of Europe
  D. Allied Forces generals

SS8H9 **The student will describe the impact of World War II on Georgia's development economically, socially, and politically.**

d. Discuss President Roosevelt's ties to Georgia including his visits to Warm Springs and his impact on the state.

FDR'S IMPACT ON GEORGIA

One of President Roosevelt's New Deal programs that did not work was the National Industrial Recovery Act (NIRA). The NIRA was designed to help workers by setting minimum wages, permitting them to organize unions, and allowing factories to cut back on production. (A **minimum wage** is the least amount an employer can pay an employee for a certain number of hours worked.) In Georgia, this legislation mainly affected the textile industry. Although labor unions had been active in the North for many years, most manufacturers in the South had forbidden unions.

Roosevelt's NIRA posed a major threat to mill owners. They reacted by using the **stretch out**, a practice requiring workers to tend more machines. Under this practice, workers had to do the same amount of work in an 8-hour shift that they had previously done in a 12-hour shift. It was a brutal, if not impossible, schedule and clearly against the intent of the law.

In August 1934, textile workers all over the South joined in a strike called by the Textile Workers of America union. (A **strike** is a work stoppage in protest over some grievance.) In Macon, for example, 3,500 mill workers walked off their jobs. Across Georgia, some 45,000 union workers took part. The strike caused financial hardships for the workers, and on September 22, the union called off the strike. In 1935, the U.S. Supreme Court declared the NIRA unconstitutional. To replace it, Congress quickly passed several laws to protect workers.

One New Deal program was more popular in Georgia. As a result of the Tennessee Valley Authority (TVA), we now have Blue Ridge Lake (which was actually created in 1925), Lake Chatuge, and Lake Nottely.

In 1924, Franklin D. Roosevelt began visiting Warm Springs as treatment for his polio. He made so many trips to the springs that he built a comfortable but small house there in 1932. When he became president, it became known as the "Little White House." On March 30, 1945, the president returned to the Little White House. He planned to rest and work on a speech for the United Nations. On April 24, Roosevelt was sitting for a portrait. Suddenly, the president put his hand to his head and said, "I have a terrific headache."

At 5:48 p.m., a stunned nation learned of the death of the man who had led the country through recovery from the depression, through the New Deal, and to the brink of victory in World War II. He had suffered a massive stroke.

As Roosevelt's body was carried by train from Warm Springs back to the nation's capital, the tracks were lined by thousands of crying Georgians who had come to think of Roosevelt as one of their own. Whole families stood alongside the railroad tracks to say goodbye to their beloved president.

_____ **383. How did the NIRA affect Georgia?**

A. It outlawed unions in the textile industry.

B. It resulted in a strike in the textile industry.

C. It enabled factory owners to hire more workers.

D. It created better working conditions in the textile industry.

_____ **384. Why did Franklin Roosevelt spend so much time in Georgia?**

A. Roosevelt's wife was a native of Calhoun and visited relatives.

B. Roosevelt had originally been a farmer and he loved farm life

C. Roosevelt was a native of Augusta and traveled widely across the state.

D. Roosevelt used the warm mineral waters of Warm Springs to ease his polio.

SS8H10   The student will evaluate key post-World War II developments of Georgia from 1945 to 1970.

a. Analyze the impact of the transformation of agriculture on Georgia's growth.

AGRICULTURAL TRANSFORMATION AFTER WORLD WAR II

When the approximately 313,000 Georgia soldiers and sailors returned home after the war, they found their state in the midst of rapid change. Agriculture was no longer as dominant an industry as it had been. During the war years, many people had moved away from farms to work in wartime industries. That led to a significant growth of our cities.

After synthetic fabrics such as rayon and nylon were introduced, the demand for cotton fell. Trees and row crops such as peanuts, soybeans, and corn were planted in place of cotton. Poultry became an important source of income for farmers. The use of farm machinery, such as tractors and harvesters, allowed fewer workers to produce higher yields per acre. Improved machinery also allowed farmers to work more acres. The average size of a farm in Georgia in 1940 was 110 acres. In 1950, it was 1,299 acres. This sent even more farm employees to the cities in search of jobs. In 1940, 66 percent of Georgia's population was rural and 34 percent was urban. By 1970, those percentages had almost completely switched. Sixty percent of Georgia's population lived in the cities, and 40 percent of Georgia's population was rural.

____ 385. **What was the most important crop in Georgia before World War II?**

A. cotton

B. peanuts

C. soybeans

D. blueberries

____ 386. **After World War II, one of Georgia's most important agricultural products was**

A. goats.

B. cattle.

C. sheep.

D. poultry.

Use the map to answer questions 387-389.

_____ **387. Which crop is grown only in northwest Georgia?**
A. berries
B. cotton
C. peanuts
D. soybeans

_____ **388. Where is the poultry industry concentrated?**
A. south Georgia
B. north Georgia
C. central Georgia
D. coastal Georgia

_____ **389. What is produced along the Savannah River?**
A. pecans
B. soybeans
C. sugar cane
D. beef cattle

SS8H10 The student will evaluate key post-World War II developments of Georgia from 1945 to 1970.

b. Explain how the development of Atlanta, including the roles of mayors William B. Hartsfield and Ivan Allen, Jr., and major league sports, contributed to the growth of Georgia.

DEVELOPMENT OF ATLANTA

The growth that Georgia experienced during the war continued after the war. Returning veterans were able to attend college on the G.I. Bill or to buy houses. Enrollment in colleges and universities soared, and the **suburbs** (residential areas around cities) sprang up.

Businesses continued to move into the state. Georgia's mild climate lured many northern companies that wanted to escape cold winters, high heating costs, and transportation slowdowns caused by snow and ice. The state also had low business and individual tax rates. In 1949, a typical Georgian paid only $38 in state taxes. Most importantly from a business owner's standpoint, Georgia was a nonunion state. Workers could be hired at lower wages and with fewer labor demands than in states controlled by unions. The growth of aviation created even more expansion during this period. By the close of the 1950s, Lockheed was the state's largest employer.

As the state's economy diversified and as air conditioning made life in the hot South more comfortable, more people moved into the state. The descendants of African American citizens who had fled Georgia after the Civil War also began to return to the state as decades of racial injustice and discrimination were replaced by moderation, by integrated schools, and by improved economic opportunities with a higher standard of living.

Atlanta, in particular, grew. By 1954, some eight hundred new industries had appeared in Atlanta, and almost twelve hundred national corporations had Atlanta offices. To accommodate its growing population, Atlanta **annexed** (added territory to an existing city or town) over one hundred square miles. It went from being the 32nd largest city in the country to the 23rd largest city. In the early 1950s, freeways and interstate highways better linked Atlanta with the region and other areas of the country.

Transportation was also in the Georgia spotlight during the 1970s. Atlanta's William B. Hartsfield International Airport offered its first international flights in 1971. The Metropolitan Atlanta Rapid Transit Authority (MARTA) had been established in 1966. In 1975, groundbreaking ceremonies were held for the first rapid rail line, the East Line. The first rapid rail service began in 1979.

Atlanta's metropolitan population grew from 997,666 in 1950 to 1,763,626 in 1970. Georgia's population grew from 3,444,578 in 1950 to 4,589,575. Today, more than half of the state's population lives in the Atlanta metropolitan area.

_____ **390. What Georgia city is the financial, communication, and transportation center for the Southeastern United States?**

A. Macon

B. Atlanta

C. Augusta

D. Savannah

_____ **391. What is a key reason for the migration of people into Georgia since the 1960s?**

A. abundant airports

B. city infrastructure

C. a diversified economy

D. successful school reform programs

_____ **392. What percentage of Georgia's population today lives in the metropolitan Atlanta area?**

A. just over 20 percent

B. just over 30 percent

C. just over 50 percent

D. just over 75 percent

WILLIAM B. HARTSFIELD

William Hartsfield served as the mayor of Atlanta for an astonishing six terms (1937-1941 and 1942-1961). He is widely acknowledged for his leadership in making Atlanta an aviation hub of the Southeast. He was the one who chose Candler Racetrack as the location for Atlanta's airport. He also used his influence to make Atlanta the Southeast's air travel hub.

Hartsfield also helped lead the city in the area of civil rights. In 1946, after the Georgia white primary was outlawed and elections were opened to African Americans, Hartsfield organized a biracial coalition that included Dr. Martin Luther King, Sr., and Reverend William Holmes Borders. African American leaders worked on voter registration drives.

In 1948, Mayor Hartsfield hired eight African American police officers for restricted duties, a move unheard of throughout most of the South. Slowly but surely, Atlanta became known as a city of racial moderation. In 1955, as the result of a U.S. Supreme Court ruling, the city's golf courses were integrated without incident. In 1957, Reverend Borders and a small group of ministers quietly and without fanfare boarded a segregated city transit bus and sat in front. Their arrest and the resulting court hearings led to the integration of the city's bus system.

In 1958, the mayor asked the state to allow Atlantans to decide whether or not to keep integrated schools open. At that time, the state was refusing to fund integrated schools. A state committee finally visited Atlanta in 1960 in response to Hartsfield's request. They found overwhelming support for keeping the public schools open. To the citizens, that issue was far more important than issues involving school integration.

Also in 1960, Dr. King helped organize sit-ins at eight different Atlanta cafeterias, including the one at City Hall. On August 30, 1961, nine African American students integrated four previously all-white high schools without incident. Within months, the local chamber of commerce joined Mayor Hartsfield and local African American leaders in ending lunch counter segregation.

_____ **393. Under the administration of William Hartsfield, racial moderation in Atlanta included the integration of**
   A. theaters.
   B. the City Hall.
   C. lunch counters.
   D. the fire department.

_____ **394. What was the issue for which William Hartsfield is best remembered?**
   A. aviation
   B. business
   C. education
   D. tax reform

IVAN ALLEN, JR.

Businessman Ivan Allen served as mayor of Atlanta from 1962 to 1970. He continued Mayor Hartsfield's approach to peaceful integration. For example, on the day he took office, Mayor Allen ordered the immediate removal of the "Colored" and "White" signs on all entrances and exits to City Hall. Shortly thereafter, he removed the restrictions on the African American policemen, and integrated the city's fire department and city government.

Allen also oversaw construction of a number of public facilities, including a civil auditorium. With new businesses moving to Atlanta, downtown saw the construction of skyscrapers and office buildings. Peachtree Center, for example, was built in 1965. Atlanta became home to a number of sports teams and sports facilities during Allen's two terms. The Metropolitan Atlanta Rapid Transit Authority (MARTA) had been approved by the legislature in 1966, but voters in Fulton and DeKalb counties voted it down. It was finally approved in 1971, and the first rapid rail service began in 1979.

Use these accomplishments to answer question 395.

- integrating city government and fire departments
- reducing restrictions on African American police officers
- removing "Colored" and "White" signs in Atlanta's City Hall

___ **395. These accomplishments were implemented by which mayor?**
 A. Ivan Allen
 B. Sam Massell
 C. Andrew Young
 D. William Hartsfield

___ **396. Who was the mayor of Atlanta responsible for bringing professional athletic teams to the city?**
 A. Ivan Allen
 B. Maynard Jackson
 C. Lester Maddox
 D. William Hartsfield

___ **397. What major improvement in Atlanta was voted down during the term of Ivan Allen?**
 A. MARTA
 B. Atlanta Civic Center
 C. Memorial Arts Center
 D. Atlanta-Fulton County Stadium

MAJOR LEAGUE SPORTS

In the 1960s, the people of Atlanta dreamed of having a "big league city." But the city lacked the facilities to do so. In 1964, the Milwaukee Braves promised to move to Atlanta if the city built a stadium. In just 51 weeks, a new stadium–Atlanta-Fulton County Stadium–was built on land that had been cleared for urban renewal. In 1966, the Atlanta Braves played their first game in the new stadium. That same year, the new Atlanta Falcons football team also began playing there.

Other professional sports teams soon followed. The Atlanta Hawks of the National Basketball Association have played in Atlanta since 1968. In 2008, Atlanta became home to the Atlanta Dream of the Women's National Basketball Association. From 1972 to 1980, the Atlanta Flames played professional hockey in the city. In 1997, the Atlanta Thrashers became the city's new ice hockey team. Atlanta is also home to the Silverbacks, both men's and women's teams, of the United Soccer Leagues.

Collectively these sports teams have accomplished the goal of city leaders to both raise the prestige of the city and generate millions of dollars each year in revenue. In 1974, a member of one sports team–Hank Aaron of the Atlanta Braves–also brought the city a baseball record. On Monday, April 8, 1974, in Atlanta Fulton County Stadium, Hank Aaron hit home run #715, breaking the career home run record held previously by the great Babe Ruth of the New York Yankees. That record stood until 2007. Both the ball and the bat Aaron hit it with are on display at Turner Field.

____ **398. Why did Atlanta business and civic leaders of the 1960s decide to bring professional sports teams to Atlanta?**

    D. to give the people something to do for entertainment

    C. to improve Atlanta's image as a major American city

    B. to give outstanding athletes opportunities to play sports

    A. to boost the ratings of ESPN and other television sports shows

____ **399. Which member of the Atlanta Braves broke Babe Ruth's career home run record?**

    A. Hank Aaron

    B. Phil Niekro

    C. John Smoltz

    D. Chipper Jones

Use the table to answer questions 400-402.

Sport	Team	Facts
Baseball	**Braves**	Team came to Atlanta from Milwaukee in 1966. Plays at Turner Field.
Football	**Falcons**	Team came to Atlanta in 1966 as a league expansion team. Plays in Georgia Dome.
Basketball	**Hawks**	Team came to Atlanta in 1968 from St. Louis. Plays in Phillips Arena.
Hockey	**Thrashers**	Team came to Atlanta in 1997 as a league expansion team. Plays in Phillips Arena.

____ **400. What was the first expansion team to come to Atlanta?**

    A. hockey

    B. football

    C. baseball

    D. basketball

____ **401. When did the Atlanta Hawks arrive in Atlanta from St. Louis?**

    A. 1966

    B. 1968

    C. 1997

    D. 2001

____ **402. Which team plays at the Georgia Dome?**

    A. Hawks

    B. Braves

    C. Falcons

    D. Thrashers

SS8H10   The student will evaluate key post-World War II developments of Georgia from 1945 to 1970.

c. Discuss the impact of Ellis Arnall.

ELLIS ARNALL

Ellis Gibbs Arnall defeated Eugene Talmadge in the governor's race in 1942. A constitutional amendment passed during Governor Talmadge's third term made Arnall the first Georgia governor to serve a four-year term. When Arnall became governor in 1943, he was the youngest governor in the nation.

Arnall quickly took steps to correct problems with university accreditation that arose during Governor Talmadge's term. The General Assembly passed a constitutional amendment that made the board of regents a separate entity, no longer under the influence of the governor's office. The terms of the regents were staggered so there were always experienced members serving on the board. These actions led the Southern Association of Colleges and Schools to restore accreditation to Georgia's colleges and universities.

Arnall also removed the prison system from the governor's control. He established a board of corrections to oversee state prisons and a pardon and parole board to handle those requests. Arnall abolished the poll tax, and, under his leadership, a new state constitution was adopted in 1945.

Governor Arnall is probably best known for leading Georgia to become the first state in the nation to grant eighteen-year-olds the right to vote. When young men were drafted into the armed forces during World War II, Arnall argued that youths old enough to fight for their country were old enough to vote for their country's leadership. In 1966, Arnall again ran for the governor's office. He was defeated in the primary by Lester Maddox.

_____ 403. **Ellis Arnall was the first governor of Georgia to serve a term of**

A. two years.

B. four years.

C. six years.

D. eight years.

_____ 404. **Which state agency was removed from control of the governor's office under the administration of Ellis Arnall?**

A. Board of Regents

B. Board of Public Safety

C. Department of Revenue

D. Department of Natural Resources

_____ 405. **Which of the following is NOT true of former governor Ellis Arnall?**

A. He established the board of corrections.

B. He was the first to serve a four-year term.

C. He fought to prevent integration of Georgia's schools.

D. He regained the accreditation for Georgia's universities.

> ## SS8H11 The student will evaluate the role of Georgia in the modern civil rights movement.
>
> a. Describe major developments in civil rights and Georgia's role during the 1940s and 1950s; include the roles of Herman Talmadge, Benjamin Mays, the 1946 governor's race and the end of the white primary, Brown v. Board of Education, Martin Luther King, Jr., and the 1956 state flag.

BENJAMIN MAYS

Benjamin Elijah Mays was born in South Carolina in 1895 to parents who were former slaves. Mays did his undergraduate work at Bates College and later received his master's and doctoral degrees from the University of Chicago. During the time he was working on his advanced degrees, Dr. Bates also became an ordained Baptist minister.

Dr. Mays was a lifelong educator. He taught at South Carolina State College and Morehouse College and helped students found the Omega Psi Phi fraternity at Morehouse. He became dean of the Howard University School of Religion in 1934 and remained in that position until 1940, when he was appointed to the presidency of Morehouse College. He remained at Morehouse for twenty-five years. During his tenure at Morehouse, Dr. Mays did much to improve and strengthen the school, such as obtaining a chapter of Phi Beta Kappa and enhancing the quality of the faculty.

He also was active in the surrounding Atlanta community and served as the Atlanta school board's first African American president. Dr. Mays was a mentor to many students and had a particularly significant impact on one student–Martin Luther King, Jr. Dr. Mays became an advisor to the young King during King's freshman year at Morehouse and continued to be a strong influence throughout his life. Dr. King later spoke of Dr. Mays as his "intellectual father" and "spiritual mentor."

Dr. Mays retired from Morehouse in 1967. Upon his retirement, he became chairman of the Atlanta Board of Education. He remained in this position for twelve years and retired in 1981. In recognition of Dr. Mays' outstanding contributions to education, a street and a high school in southwest Atlanta were named in his honor. Dr. Mays died in 1984 at the age of 86.

_____ **406. What office did Benjamin Mays hold?**
- A. mayor of Atlanta
- B. governor of Georgia
- C. state legislator in the General Assembly
- D. chairman of Atlanta Board of Education

_____ **407. Benjamin Mays served as a mentor to**
- A. Rosa Parks
- B. Andrew Young
- C. Maynard Jackson
- D. Martin Luther King, Jr.

END OF THE WHITE PRIMARY

After the Civil War, Democrats tried various ways to keep black people from voting. The "white primary" was one of those ways.

The Fifteenth Amendment to the U.S. Constitution guaranteed blacks the right to vote. The state legislature, however, took this to apply to the general election only. It reasoned that a state could pass laws regarding who could vote in primary elections, which were introduced around 1898.

After Reconstruction, the Democratic Party regained control of state government. For the 1900 primary, Democratic leaders ruled that only white Democrats would be allowed to vote in the primary.

Because Republican and independent candidates got little support from whites and rarely ran for office, Georgia was essentially a one-party state. The candidates for office were selected during the primary, and the winners of the primary elections were certain of victory in the general election. By the time blacks were able to enter the decision-making process (in the general election), the eventual winner had already been selected during the white primary.

In 1946, the U.S. Supreme Court ruled in *King v. Chapman* that white primary systems in Georgia were unconstitutional. In the election of 1946, black voters were able to take part in the primary election for the first time since Reconstruction.

____ **408. The purpose of the white primary was to**

      A. prevent blacks from voting for govenor.

      B. help blacks get elected to statewide public office.

      C. keep blacks from having input into the party nominees.

      D. allow blacks to have more influence in the general election.

____ **409. Under the white primary system, only whites were allowed**

      A. to vote in primary elections.

      B. to vote in statewide elections.

      C. to belong to the Democratic party.

      D. to run for political office in Georgia.

1946 GOVERNOR'S RACE

In 1946, Governor Ellis Arnall's term was drawing to a close. Because he could not succeed himself, Georgians had to elect a new governor. The field of candidates in the Democratic primary included segregationist Eugene Talmadge; former governor Eurith Rivers; and James Carmichael, who had headed the Marietta Bell bomber plant during the war. In the primary, Carmichael won the popular vote due, in large part, to black voters being able to take part in the primary election for the first time since Reconstruction. However, Talmadge won the county unit vote, and he became the Democratic candidate.

The Republicans did not have a candidate, so Talmadge ran unopposed in the November general election. Talmadge was sixty-two years old and in poor health. Because his close advisors were afraid he would not live long enough to begin his term, they made a secret plan. The plan was for a few hundred selected supporters to write the name of Eugene Talmadge's son Herman on the ballot as their second gubernatorial choice. When the general election was over, Eugene Talmadge had been elected governor; Melvin Thompson had been elected lieutenant governor.

Shortly before Christmas, and before he was sworn in, Eugene Talmadge died, and the confusion began. The legislature chose Herman Talmadge as governor, based on the size of the write-in votes for him — a good number of which were suddenly "found" after the election. Governor Arnall declared that Lieutenant Governor Thompson was the rightful successor. However, in the early morning hours of January 15, 1947, a group of Eugene Talmadge's men broke into the governor's office, changed the locks on the doors, and readied themselves to run the state.

Because he was locked out of his own office, Governor Arnall set up a temporary office at the Capitol information counter. Three days later, with news cameras flashing, Arnall officially resigned. In the meantime, Lieutenant Governor Thompson opened an office in downtown Atlanta and began legal proceedings to become governor. The government was in a state of total confusion.

Secretary of State Ben Fortson refused to give the official state seal (used for legalizing documents) to either Talmadge or Thompson. As a result, no one was in a position to run the state. The national news media had a field day reporting Georgia's political chaos.

Finally, in March, the Georgia Supreme Court ruled that Thompson was the rightful head of state until a special election could be held in 1948 to fill the unexpired term of Governor-elect Eugene Talmadge. In that election, Herman Talmadge was legally elected as Georgia's governor.

_____ **410. The famous controversy surrounding the 1946 election for governor came about because**

    A. Ellis Arnall was impeached and removed from office.

    B. Herman Talmadge and Eugene Talmadge were on the same ballot.

    C. Eugene Talmadge died before taking office, and two men claimed the office.

    D. Carmichael got more popular votes, and Talmadge got more county unit votes.

_____ **411. When Eugene Talmadge died in 1946 before taking office for his fourth term as governor, who became governor?**

    A. The previous governor remained governor.

    B. Three people claimed to be Georgia's governor.

    C. Georgia's lieutenant governor became governor.

    D. The speaker of the General Assembly became governor.

_____ **412. In the 1946 Democrat primary for governor, who won the popular vote?**

    A. Ed Rivers

    B. Lester Maddox

    C. James Carmichael

    D. Herman Talmadge

HERMAN TALMADGE

Herman Talmadge was easily re-elected governor in 1950. Talmadge was a strict segregationist and opposed all attempts to integrate Georgia's public schools. He had promised voters that he would bring back the white primary, a promise he was unable to keep.

During his tenure as governor, he restructured the state highway department, created the Georgia Forestry Commission, and provided leadership for improvements in soil conservation programs, county health departments, and the state's prison system.

Most of Talmadge's legacy is in the field of education. He provided leadership for a new state constitution that expanded schools to include grades 1-12. In 1949, the General Assembly passed the Minimum Foundation Program for Education Act. This act lengthened the school year to nine months and raised standards for buildings, equipment, transportation, and school curricula. A 3 percent sales tax was passed in 1951 to pay for these changes.

After leaving office, Talmadge was elected to the U.S. Senate in 1956. He served there until 1981.

_____ **413. What factor enabled Herman Talmadge to be elected governor of Georgia in 1950?**

    A. his campaign style and popularity

    B. his support from wealthy businessmen

    C. his position on segregation and voting rights

    D. his victory in the 1948 special election for governor

_____ **414. In what area did Herman Talmadge make his greatest contributions as governor?**

    A. education

    B. tax reform

    C. voting rights

    D. attracting business

_____ **415. Herman Talmadge's 3 percent sales tax was passed primarily to fund**

    A. the creation of county health departments.

    B. the purchase of Jekyll Island as a state park.

    C. Georgia's part in the Interstate Highway System.

    D. a lengthened school year and school improvements.

BROWN V. BOARD OF EDUCATION

In 1950, seven-year-old Linda Brown, a black student, tried to enroll in an all-white school in Topeka, Kansas. When entry was denied, the NAACP helped Brown's father sue the Topeka Board of Education. The case, referred to as **Brown v. Board of Education**, reached the Supreme Court.

In its 1954 ruling, the Court said separate-but-equal schools were unconstitutional. It ordered racial integration of schools "with all deliberate speed." After nearly sixty years of court-approved segregation, the ruling in the _Plessy_ case was finally overturned. Although the Court had spoken, many states were slow to carry out its orders.

_____ **416. What was the ruling of the U.S. Supreme Court in Brown v. Board of Education?**

    A. Schools would be segregated and kept separate.

    B. The separate-but-equal policy was unconstitutional.

    C. Black schools would get more money for books and teachers.

    D. Blacks could only attend white schools if there was space available.

_____ **417. What earlier U.S. Supreme Court decision did the ruling in Brown v. Board of Education overturn?**

    A. _Plessy v. Ferguson_

    B. _Worchester v. Georgia_

    C. _Dred Scott v. Sanford_ decision

    D. _Cummings v. Richmond County Board of Education_

MARTIN LUTHER KING, JR.

Martin Luther King, Jr., was born on January 15, 1929, in Atlanta. His family was actively involved in the African American Baptist Church. King's grandfather was one of the founders of the Atlanta chapter of the NAACP and was also the pastor of Ebenezer Baptist Church. King's father also later became pastor of Ebenezer Baptist.

Dr. King attended several colleges and universities, including Morehouse College. In 1955, Dr. King obtained his Ph.D. in systematic theology. During this time, he also became the pastor of Dexter Avenue Baptist Church in Montgomery, Alabama, and married Coretta Scott.

During the course of his studies, Dr. King became very interested in Mahatma Gandhi's nonviolent approach to bring about social change. When Rosa Parks's refusal to give up her seat on a Montgomery, Alabama, bus resulted in a bus boycott, black residents appointed Dr. King to lead the brand new Montgomery Improvement Association. He received national attention for his leadership role in the boycott, especially when the Supreme Court ruled in December 1956 that Alabama's segregation laws were unconstitutional and that Montgomery buses had to be desegregated. Dr. King believed in a four-pronged approach for gaining civil rights for all Americans: (1) direct, nonviolent actions, (2) legal remedies, (3) ballots, and (4) economic boycotts.

In 1957, Dr. King and other prominent southern black ministers formed the Southern Christian Leadership Conference (SCLC). In 1959, Dr. King moved back to Atlanta to serve as co-pastor of Ebenezer Baptist Church with his father.

In 1963, racial tensions were high across the country and came to a head in Alabama. Dr. King and the SCLC organized huge protests in Birmingham. The city received worldwide coverage of the violence police used against the unarmed black protesters. Appalled at the violence, President Kennedy urged Congress to pass major civil rights laws. This ultimately resulted in the passage of the Civil Rights Act of 1964. Although the legislation was a key piece of civil rights legislation, it did not solve every problem.

Therefore, in 1967, Dr. King began a Poor People's Campaign to address economic issues left unsolved by earlier legislation. Dr. King was a gifted speaker, and he is perhaps most well known for his "I Have a Dream" speech. He gave this speech on August 28, 1963, during the March on Washington, which over 250,000 people attended. Millions more listened on radio and television. In 1968, Dr. King gave what would be his final speech, "I've Been to the Mountaintop," in Memphis, Tennessee. The next day, on April 4, 1968, Dr. King was assassinated, and the country lost a great civil rights leader.

Dr. King earned numerous awards and recognitions for his civil rights work. Most notably, he was awarded Time's 1963 Man of the Year. He also won the Nobel Peace Prize in 1964, becoming only the second African American to achieve this distinction.

_____ **418. Dr. Martin Luther King, Jr., favored bringing about social change through**

    A. unity.

    B. democracy.

    C. compromise.

    D. nonviolence.

_____ **419. Which approach did Dr. Martin Luther King, Jr., NOT use to gain equality and civil rights for all citizens?**

    A. economic boycotts of businesses that did not treat all citizens fairly

    B. direct and nonviolent actions such as marches, protests, and demonstrations

    C. aggressive pursuit of black power through protests, riots, demonstrations, and political organization

    D. legal actions against individuals and businesses that violated the civil rights of individuals based on race

1956 STATE FLAG

In 1956, Georgia's state flag was changed to incorporate the St. Andrew's cross, a Confederate battle emblem. The flag has long been a subject of controversy and division within the state. African Americans were offended by references to the slavery in the state's past. Many modern leaders were offended by the image of a state caught up in its past instead of its future. The use of the Confederate symbol was damaging Georgia's tourist industry, costing the state millions in lost convention and exhibition dollars, and portraying a negative "old-fashioned southern" impression of Georgia to the world's businesses. Other southern states that had used the battle symbol as a part of their flags found their tourism and resort industries damaged as conventions were cancelled and boycotts scheduled. The state that had hosted Super Bowls and the Olympics wanted to project a more modern image to the world.

Civic leaders, businessmen and developers, leaders of the hospitality industry, the powerful Atlanta Convention and Visitors Bureau, the legislative Black Caucus, and developers called on Governor Roy Barnes to change the flag. Atlanta architect Cecil Alexander designed a new flag that featured the state seal in the center. Below the seal, a banner showed small images of Georgia's first three state flags and the first and the current images of the U.S. flag. The motto "In God We Trust" appeared below the banner.

The new flag was introduced shortly after the 2001 legislative session got underway. With almost no time for discussion and dissent, the flag passed the house on January 24, 2001, and the Senate on January 30. On January 31, Governor Barnes signed the bill authorizing the new flag into law. Most Georgians saw the new flag for the first time in the next day's newspapers and on TV news reports.

Those citizens who saw the 1956 flag as a memorial to the Confederate war dead and the proud heritage of a people and a region were outraged that it had been changed. Others who saw the 1956 flag as a symbol of racism were glad for the change but upset that the 2001 flag still contained any Confederate emblem. The 2001 flag had few supporters. Critics even remarked that it would be too difficult for elementary school children to draw.

In the 2002 election, Barnes's Republican opponent, Sonny Perdue, made the changes in the flag a major campaign issue. Those who were offended that the flag had been changed voted against Barnes, and he was not re-elected. Newly elected Governor Sonny Perdue signed a new state flag into law on May 8, 2003. Georgia was to have its third state flag in under thirty months.

Georgia's 2003 flag was based on the first national flag of the Confederacy. It is a field of three horizontal bars, two red and one white. In the upper left corner is a square blue section containing Georgia's coat of arms and the words "In God We Trust." Surrounding the coat of arms is a circle of thirteen white stars representing the original thirteen states. In March 2004, the people of Georgia voted 3-1 in favor of keeping the 2003 flag as the state flag.

_____ 420. **Which group was instrumental in getting the 1956 Georgia state flag changed?**
   A. Rainbow Coalition
   B. public school students
   C. supporters of Governor Zell Miller
   D. Atlanta Convention and Visitors Bureau

_____ 421. **In what year did the Georgia state flag become an issue in the race for governor?**
   A. 1960
   B. 1968
   C. 1984
   D. 2002

_____ 422. **What was one reason for keeping the Georgia state flag of 1956?**
   A. It was easy for school children to draw.
   B. It was a memorial to the Confederate dead.
   C. It was supported by a majority of Georgians.
   D. It was similar to the flags of other southern states.

SS8H11   The student will evaluate the role of Georgia in the modern civil rights movement.

b. Analyze the role Georgia and prominent Georgians played in the Civil Rights Movement of the 1960s and 1970s; include such events as the founding of the Student Non-Violent Coordinating Committee (SNCC), Sibley Commission, admission of Hamilton Holmes and Charlayne Hunter to the University of Georgia, Albany Movement, March on Washington, Civil Rights Act, the election of Maynard Jackson as mayor of Atlanta, and the role of Lester Maddox.

STUDENT NON-VIOLENT COORDINATING COMMITTEE

In February 1960, black students at North Carolina Agricultural and Technical College started a new era of protest with their lunch counter sit-in at the Greensboro, North Carolina, Woolworth's store. A **sit-in** occurs when people enter a public building and refuse to leave until they are served or their demands are met. The students were refused service, but the idea of the sit-in spread to other parts of the South.

The success of the early student sit-ins led to a new organization. In April 1960, black students at Shaw University in Raleigh, North Carolina, organized the **Student Non-Violent Coordinating Committee**. It was abbreviated SNCC and pronounced "Snick." The first president was Georgian John Lewis.

Members of this group worked in southern states helping blacks register to vote. SNCC also led protests, sit-ins at lunch counters, and boycotts of businesses that would not serve blacks.

_____ **423. What organization was founded two months after the 1960 sit-in at the Woolworth's lunch counter in Greensboro, North Carolina?**

A. CORE

B. SCLC

C. SNCC

D. NAACP

_____ **424. Who was the first president of the Student Non-Violent Coordinating Committee?**

A. John Lewis

B. H. Rap Brown

C. Maynard Jackson

D. Dr. Martin Luther King, Jr.

SIBLEY COMMISSION

In Georgia, most of the state's school systems refused desegregation. The opposition to desegregation was so strong that the General Assembly voted in 1955 to cut off state funds to any system that integrated its schools. Ernest Vandiver, who became governor in 1959, was elected, in part, on his promise to keep Georgia's schools segregated. But in 1960, the Georgia General Assembly recognized change was at hand. It organized a fourteen-member commission, headed by Atlanta attorney and banker John Sibley, to study the problem of integration.

The Sibley Commission held hearings all over the state to learn how the public felt about integration. Reaction was swift and direct. By a three-to-two margin, Georgians said they would rather close the schools than integrate them. The commission recommended that local school systems be allowed to decide if they would abide by a probable court order to integrate public schools or if they would close them. In many communities, private schools were opened to avoid the issue.

____ **425. Which statement does NOT illustrate Georgia's initial reaction to the *Brown v. Board of Education* decision of the U.S. Supreme Court?**

    A. The governor pledged not to integrate the state's schools.

    B. Georgia citizens voted 3 to 2 to close schools rather than integrate them.

    C. The General Assembly voted to cut off state funds to any schools that desegregated.

    D. The Sibley Commission traveled throughout the state encouraging the peaceful desegregation of schools.

____ **426. The purpose of the Sibley Commission was to**

    A. study the problem of school integration.

    B. develop a plan for securing jobs for blacks.

    C. set up a series of meetings to bring blacks and whites together.

    D. make recommendations for desegregation in public transportation.

____ **427. The Sibley Commission recommended**

    A. integrating Georgia's public transportation system.

    B. making proposals to the legislature to address racial issues.

    C. establishing a quota system to ensure the hiring of black workers.

    D. allowing local school systems to decide if they wanted integration.

HAMILTON HOLMES/CHARLAYNE HUNTER

Despite resistance from many states, including Georgia, the Supreme Court and federal district courts held their ground. On January 6, 1961, the University of Georgia, with the backing of Governor Vandiver, allowed its first two black students to be escorted into the school by state patrol officers. One of these students was Charlayne Hunter, who graduated from the Henry W. Grady School of Journalism and later, as Charlayne Hunter-Gault, became a nationally known newspaper and public television reporter. The other was Hamilton Holmes, who was installed in Phi Beta Kappa, graduated with honors from the university, and later practiced medicine as an orthopedic surgeon in Atlanta until his death in 1995.

Many university alumni and Georgia politicians had pleaded with Governor Vandiver to close the university rather than allow the two students to enroll. Refusing to bend to pressure, the governor instructed the president of the university, Dr. O. C. Aderhold, to open the doors. This move by the governor shocked and angered many Georgians who had voted for Vandiver based on his pledge not to integrate the state's schools.

During the heated discussions that followed, Vandiver admitted that he had been wrong in his pre-election speeches. After the two students were enrolled, he went even further. The governor asked the legislature to repeal other segregation laws in Georgia. Vandiver's actions were one of the main reasons that Georgia's subsequent efforts at desegregating schools were calmer and smoother than those in many other school systems in both the South and North.

____ **428. Who was one of the first blacks to be admitted to the University of Georgia?**

    A. Rosa Parks

    B. Andrew Young

    C. Maynard Jackson

    D. Charlayne Hunter

_____ **429. Who was the governor of Georgia when the first black students were admitted to the University of Georgia?**

    A. Ed Rivers

    B. Lester Maddox

    C. Ernest Vandiver

    D. Herman Talmadge

ALBANY MOVEMENT

In 1961, Albany, Georgia, became a center of civil rights activity. Mainly a farming community, Albany had a population that was about 40 percent African American. Six years after _Brown v. Board of Education_, Albany schools were still segregated. Only a small number of African Americans were allowed to register to vote.

In 1955, the Interstate Commerce Commission, following a Supreme Court decision, prohibited segregation in interstate bus and train stations. On November 1, 1961, workers with the NAACP and Student Nonviolent Coordinating Committee (SNCC) decided to test the ruling by sitting in the "whites only" waiting room at the city's bus station. They were quickly arrested. This prompted the African American community to unite and form the Albany Movement, which was led by Dr. William Anderson.

In December, black and white "freedom riders" arrived in Albany to support the Albany Movement. They were arrested at the Central Railway Terminal. The next day, SNCC organizer James Forman led a march of African American high school students to the same train station. The students were arrested and jailed while members of the national press watched. At one point during the months of protest in Albany, five hundred people were either in jail or out on bond. Civil rights leaders arrested included Dr. King and Reverend Ralph Abernathy, who had traveled to Albany to ask city officials for a meeting to resolve the dispute. Before the year's end, a biracial committee was formed to study concerns of the African American community in Albany.

_____ **430. The focus of the Albany Movement in Georgia was to**

    A. end segregation of public schools in Albany.

    B. integrate interstate bus station waiting rooms in Albany.

    C. implement a "first-come, first-served" policy on Albany's schools.

    D. force the hiring of African American bus drivers for Albany's bus station.

_____ **431. Which African American group was involved with the Albany Movement?**

    A. Interstate Commerce Commission

    B. Montgomery Improvement Association

    C. Student Non-Violent Coordinating Committee

    D. National Association for the Advancement of Colored People

MARCH ON WASHINGTON 1963

President John F. Kennedy sent the strongest civil rights bill in history to Congress on June 19, 1963. It called for an end to discrimination in public facilities, assurance of fair employment and voter registration practices, withholding of federal funds from projects where discrimination was practiced, and the authority of the attorney general of the United States to file suit against school districts where desegregation had not been carried out.

Congress took its time with the bill. As a result, on August 28, 1963, over 250,000 people representing all races, creeds, and nationalities gathered before the Washington Monument to demonstrate for its passage. As they stood together, Dr. Martin Luther King, Jr., made one of the most remembered speeches of his career.

. . . I have a dream that one day this nation will rise up, live out the true meaning of its creed: "We hold these truths to be self-evident, that all men are created equal." I have a dream that one day on the red hills of Georgia sons of former slaves and the sons of former slave owners will be able to sit down together at the table of brotherhood. I have a dream that one day even the state of Mississippi, a desert state sweltering with the heat of injustice, sweltering with the heat of oppression, will be transformed into an oasis of freedom and justice. I have a dream that my four little children will one day live in a nation where they will not be judged by the color of their skin, but by the content of their character. . . . Let freedom ring from Stone Mountain of Georgia. . . . Let freedom ring from every hill and molehill . . . from every mountainside. Let freedom ring. When we let freedom ring – when we let it ring from every village and every hamlet, from every state and every city, we will be able to speed up that day when all God's children, black men and white men, Jew and Gentiles, Protestants and Catholics, will be able to join hands and sing in the words of that old Negro spiritual, "Free at last, Free at last! Thank God almighty, we are free at last!"

_____ **432. Dr. Martin Luther King Jr.'s "I Have a Dream" speech is associated with the**

    A. Montgomery bus boycott.

    B. eulogy given at his funeral.

    C. Remembrance of his father.

    D. March on Washington, D.C.

_____ **433. The march on Washington was intended to**

    A. urge the passage of a civil rights bill.

    B. extend the Montgomery bus boycott.

    C. integrate the Washington, D.C. public schools.

    D. honor the memory of slain civil rights workers.

CIVIL RIGHTS ACT

The bravery of the civil rights demonstrators caught the nation by storm. In June 1963, President John F. Kennedy went on national television and described segregation as a moral crisis for the country. He told of his plans to ask Congress to pass a new civil rights law. Later that month, Kennedy sent to Congress the strongest civil rights bill in history.

Unfortunately, President Kennedy did not live to see that civil rights bill become law. President Kennedy was assassinated on November 23, 1963, in Dallas. Vice President Lyndon B. Johnson was sworn in as the thirty-sixth president of the United States.

In a speech to Congress shortly after Kennedy's assassination, President Johnson vowed to continue fighting for the earliest possible passage of President Kennedy's civil rights bill. Under President Johnson's leadership, and with the political pressure of both black and white supporters, the Civil Rights Act of 1964 became law. This was the most far-reaching and important civil rights legislation since Reconstruction. Basically, the equal protection clause of the Fourteenth Amendment was given greater influence. The legislation made segregation of all public facilities illegal. This included restaurants, theaters, hotels, public recreational areas, schools, and libraries. It gave the federal government the power to withhold federal funds from schools that refused to integrate. It also prohibited discrimination in businesses and labor unions.

_____ **434. The Civil Rights Act of 1964 did NOT integrate**

    A. hotels.

    B. churches.

    C. restaurants.

    D. public facilities.

435. What did the Civil Rights Act of 1964 do?
  A. It named black principals at previously all-white schools.
  B. It gave more state tax money to schools that did not integrate.
  C. It withheld federal funds from schools that did not end segregation.
  D. It provided armed escorts for students wanting to attend white schools.

436. Which method of influencing political decision making led to the Civil Rights Act of 1964?
  A. the ballot
  B. freedom fighters
  C. special interest groups
  D. the power of public opinion

MAYNARD JACKSON

To the sounds of the Atlanta Symphony Orchestra and Beethoven's "Ode to Joy" and the voice of famous soprano Mattiwilda Dobbs, Maynard Holbrook Jackson was sworn in as Atlanta's youngest and first African American mayor in January 1974. His swearing-in ceremony had to be held in the Atlanta Civic Center because the traditional site, City Hall, was not large enough for the thousands of Atlantans who were celebrating his election.

Jackson earned a B.A. degree in political science and history from Morehouse College. He graduated from North Carolina Central University Law School in 1964. He worked as an attorney in Atlanta until he entered politics and was elected mayor of Atlanta in 1973.

Called by many the "ultimate mayor," Jackson created "neighborhood planning units" to give local community citizens a voice in city politics. He tackled charges of police brutality and made changes in the organization and administration of the police and fire departments and city government. He led the development and expansion of MARTA. He expanded Hartsfield International Airport into one of the largest, busiest airports in the world, and he used airport construction to develop a minority participation plan that served as a model for governments throughout the nation. He put into action a belief that expanding economic opportunity for more people increased the prosperity of all people.

Jackson was a lifelong supporter of the arts. He established a Bureau of Cultural Affairs in 1975 and provided financial support to arts programs throughout the community. He used community development funds to hire artists and to found the Atlanta Contemporary Art Center, IMAGE, and Art Papers. He also had funds set aside in each construction project for works of art. In this way, MARTA stations, Hartsfield Airport, and City Hall became noted for their arts displays. He pushed for funds to restore the historic Cyclorama because it was such an important artistic representation of the city's history.

As one of his final legacies to Atlanta, Jackson led the efforts to secure Atlanta's selection as the host city for the 1996 Olympic Summer Games. His speech to the Olympic Committee, delivered in large part in fluent French, spoke eloquently of Atlanta's great record for racial diversity and humanitarianism. The committee recognized that record by awarding the games to Atlanta.

Maynard Holbrook Jackson died in 2003. In recognition of his many achievements, Atlanta's airport was renamed Hartsfield-Jackson Atlanta International Airport.

437. Who was the first African American mayor of Atlanta?
  A. Sam Massell
  B. Andrew Young
  C. Maynard Jackson
  D. Hamilton Holmes

Use these actions to answer question 438.

- He increased programs for the arts.
- He addressed the need to expand the airport.
- He led an effort to have the Olympics held in Atlanta.

____ **438. Which mayor of Atlanta promoted these improvements for the city?**

    A. Ivan Allen

    B. Sam Massell

    C. Andrew Young

    D. Maynard Jackson

LESTER MADDOX

In 1967, segregationist and restaurant owner Lester Maddox of Atlanta became governor. Maddox had become famous for closing his restaurant in Atlanta rather than desegregate it. The 1966 gubernatorial election was "another one for the books." When no candidate received a majority in the Democratic primary, there was a runoff. Maddox was a surprise winner over former Governor Ellis Arnall. In the general election, Maddox faced Republican Howard "Bo" Callaway. While Callaway had more votes than Maddox, a write-in campaign for Arnall prevented Callaway from getting a majority of the vote. The election then went to the Democratic legislature, which chose Maddox.

Maddox surprised many Georgians by appointing more African Americans to state boards and commissions than all prior governors combined. He named the first black member of the Board of Pardons and Paroles, reformed state prisons, and integrated the Georgia State Patrol. The governor increased spending on teacher salaries and higher education. Governor Maddox also established "People's Days." Twice a month, any Georgian could visit the governor's mansion to talk about anything they wished.

Since he could not succeed himself, Maddox ran for lieutenant governor in 1970 and was elected overwhelmingly.

____ **439. What did Lester Maddox accomplish as governor?**

    A. started the lottery and HOPE scholarships

    B. decreased funding to public schools and the arts

    C. appointed more African Americans to state boards

    D. changed the state flag to remove the Confederate symbols

____ **440. How did Lester Maddox get input from the voters?**

    A. suggestion boxes

    B. monthly luncheons

    C. statewide caravans

    D. meetings with citizens

____ **441. Which governor won office by being elected by the General Assembly rather than the people?**

    A. Zell Miller

    B. Ellis Arnall

    C. Roy Barnes

    D. Lester Maddox

ANDREW YOUNG

One of Georgia's most prominent sons is Andrew Young. Young was a pastor in a Thomasville church when he became involved in the civil rights movement. Later, he joined the Southern Christian Leadership Conference and eventually became its executive director. While there, he helped establish "citizenship schools," which taught nonviolent organizing strategies to potential black leaders. Young was a trusted aide to Reverend Martin Luther King, Jr., and was with him when he was assassinated in 1968.

In 1972, Young was elected to the U.S. House of Representatives, the first African American elected from Georgia since Reconstruction. He was twice reelected. In 1977, President Jimmy Carter named Young as U.S. ambassador to the United Nations. In 1981, Young returned to Atlanta and was twice elected its mayor. He served as co-chairman of the successful effort to bring the 1996 Olympic Games to Atlanta. Young is currently a professor at Georgia State University.

_____ **442. Andrew Young helped establish "citizenship schools," which taught**
   A. young blacks their rights of citizenship.
   B. nonviolent organizing strategies to potential leaders.
   C. the art of campaigning to potential black political leaders.
   D. the basic principles found in the U.S. Constitution to high school students.

_____ **443. What event was the MOST significant in Andrew Young's political career?**
   A. He was a prominent Aftican American involved in the stock market.
   B. He was the youngest African American governor to be elected in Georgia.
   C. He was the first African American to graduate from the University of Georgia.
   D. He was the first African American since Reconstruction to be elected to the House of Representatives from Georgia.

_____ **444. Which position has NOT been held by Andrew Young?**
   C. mayor of Atlanta
   D. college professor
   B. U.S. congressman
   A. governor of Georgia

END OF THE COUNTY UNIT SYSTEM

In the 1960s, two rulings by the federal district court brought dramatic change to Georgia's political structure. The first ruling involved the county unit system. This system had been in place since 1917. It was designed to maintain the power of the rural areas of the state even though the greatest population growth was in urban areas.

In April 1962, the Georgia federal court ruled that the county unit system violated the Fourteenth Amendment. Once the county unit system was ruled unconstitutional, the majority of representatives in the Georgia house came from the urban areas. Political power shifted from rural to urban areas. This also gave predominantly black population areas an equal opportunity to elect legislative representatives. In a 1962 election, Atlanta attorney Leroy Johnson became the first African American state senator in Georgia since Reconstruction.

____ 445. **What change did NOT occur in Georgia as a result of the end of the county unit system?**
   A. More political power went to the more heavily populated areas.
   B. More women were elected to state office in the executive branch.
   C. More African Americans were elected to office in the state legislature.
   D. More members of the General Assembly were elected from the urban areas.

____ 446. **Which amendment to the U.S. Constitution did the county unit system violate?**
   A. Fifteenth Amendment
   B. Sixteenth Amendment
   C. Thirteenth Amendment
   D. Fourteenth Amendment

____ 447. **From what area did most of the members of Georgia's House of Representatives come after the end of the county unit system?**
   A. rural areas
   B. large areas
   C. urban areas
   D. coastal areas

REAPPORTIONMENT

The federal court decision on the county unit system was appealed to the U.S. Supreme Court in *Gray v. Sanders*. It was in the 1963 decision that the phrase "one person, one vote" was first used. The **one-person, one-vote concept** is that every citizen's vote should be equal to every other citizen's vote no matter where the person lived.

In 1964, the federal court again ruled that Georgia's constitution, which ensured each county in the state at least one seat in the legislature, violated the one-person, one-vote concept. In *Wesberry v. Sanders*, the U.S. Supreme Court stated that legislative districts should depend solely on population rather than on county boundary lines. The General Assembly had to **reapportion** (redraw) its Congressional voting districts to ensure that the districts were of equal population sizes.

These two decisions did more than just shift political power from rural to urban areas. They also influenced the campaign styles and election of the state's governor.

____ 448. **How did the end of the county unit system change the focus of campaigning in Georgia?**
   A. Candidates rallies were held less often.
   B. Candidates used television more often.
   C. Candidates had to appeal to voters statewide.
   D. Candidates concentrated on larger populated areas.

_____ **449.** **When the U.S. Supreme Court ordered Georgia to reapportion its Congressional districts in 1964, it meant that**

    A. Georgia's growing population required more districts.

    B. Georgia had too many districts to satisfy the Constitution.

    C all rural areas needed more Congressional representation.

    D. all Georgia congressional districts should have equal populations.

_____ **450.** **The 1963 court decision calling for the Georgia General Assembly to redraw voting districts to guarantee equal representation was the first time which phrase was used?**

    A. "Equality for all"

    B. "One-person, one-vote"

    C. "I have not yet begun to fight."

    D. "Taxation without representation"

_____ **451.** **The term that means to "redraw the boundaries of election districts" is**

    A. realignment.

    B. redistricting.

    C. reconstruction.

    D. reapportionment.

SS8H12   **The student will explain the importance of significant social, economic, and political developments in Georgia since 1970.**

    b. Describe the role of Jimmy Carter in Georgia as state senator, governor, president, and past president.

JIMMY CARTER

In the history of our nation, only one Georgian has served as president of our country – James Earl "Jimmy" Carter, Jr. Carter was born in Plains on October 1, 1924. Carter graduated from the U.S. Naval Academy at Annapolis and served in the Navy for seven years. In 1954, Carter resigned his Navy commission to return to Plains and take over the family's warehouse and cotton gin businesses and a peanut farm.

In 1962, Carter was elected to the Georgia senate and elected governor in 1970. During his term, Governor Carter reorganized the state's executive branch, cutting the number of government agencies from three hundred to twenty-five. He also influenced Georgia's court system, bringing a unified approach to the courts and changing the selection of judges to a merit process. Governor Carter appointed the first woman as a state judge. He created the Georgia Heritage Trust, which is designed to protect our state's natural and cultural resources. He also worked to equalize funding for public schools across the state and expanded special education, vocational education, and pre-school education. Governor Carter also expanded state mental health services for Georgians. At the end of his term, many Georgians were surprised when he announced that he was a candidate for the 1976 Democratic presidential nomination.

He campaigned tirelessly on a platform of revival and reform in the Democratic party. Carter defeated President Gerald R. Ford in November 1976 and served one term in office.

During Carter's term as president, he established a national energy policy, completed major civil service reforms, expanded the national park system, deregulated the trucking and airline industries, and created the Department of Education. However, domestic economic problems plagued his term. Inflation and interest rates were extremely high, and his efforts to reduce them created a short-term recession.

In foreign policy, Carter will probably be best remembered for negotiating the 1978 Camp David Peace Accords between Israel and Egypt, the first peace treaty between Israel and an Arab neighboring state. He obtained congressional ratification of the Panama Canal treaties and established full diplomatic relations with the People's Republic of China. After Russia invaded Afghanistan in December 1979, he withdrew the United States from the 1980 Summer Olympics in Moscow and increased aid to neighboring Pakistan. He also championed worldwide human rights.

In November 1979, militants took control of the U.S. Embassy in Iran and seized 52 Americans, holding them captive for fourteen months. Iran did not release the hostages until 1981 on the day that Carter left office. This probably led to his defeat in 1980.

After leaving office, the Carters returned to Georgia. President Carter is much admired for his efforts to negotiate peace, to defeat diseases, to ensure fair elections around the world, and to build affordable housing with Habitat for Humanity. He has also written numerous books.

_____ **452. Which Georgian has held the highest political office in the United States?**
- A. Sam Nunn
- B. Jimmy Carter
- C. Newt Gingrich
- D. Andrew Young

Use these accomplishments to answer question 453.

- Camp David Middle East Peace Accords
- ratification of the Panama Canal treaties
- establishment of diplomatic relations with China

_____ **453. These accomplishments occurred under which president?**
- A. Gerald Ford
- B. Jimmy Carter
- C. Richard Nixon
- D. Ronald Reagan

_____ **454. What was the centerpiece of Jimmy Carter's foreign policy?**
- A. isolationism
- B. human rights
- C. international free trade
- D. containing communism

_____ **455. What new cabinet position was created under President Jimmy Carter?**
- A. Department of Education
- B. Department of Urban Affairs
- C. Department of Transportation
- D. Department of Homeland Security

SS8H12   The student will explain the importance of significant social, economic, and political developments in Georgia since 1970.

c. Analyze the impact of the rise of the two-party system in Georgia.

RISE OF THE TWO-PARTY SYSTEM

During the 1980s and 1990s, politics underwent a major shift in many southern states, including Georgia. While most citizens continued to elect Democrats to statewide offices, they were more conservative in national politics and tended to favor Republicans in national elections. This led to the election of more Republicans to the U.S. Congress from Georgia and, eventually, to the establishment of a real two-party system in the state for the first time since the Bourbon Redeemers over one hundred years ago.

In 1980, Mack Mattingly of St. Simons Island was the first Republican elected to the U.S. Senate from Georgia since Reconstruction. In the 1992 elections, Republicans won most of Georgia's congressional elections, although Atlanta Democrat Cynthia McKinney became the first African American woman from Georgia elected to Congress.

In 1994, Republicans gained a majority in the U.S. House of Representatives for the first time in forty years, and Georgia's Newt Gingrich was elected Speaker of the House. By the election of 2002, Republicans ended over 100 years of rule by Democrats with the election of Perry native Sonny Perdue, the first Republican governor since Reconstruction. In that same election, the Democratic party maintained control of the General Assembly, but voters chose Republicans for the U.S. Senate seat and the majority of representatives for the U.S. House.

_____ 456. **How did the "Solid Democratic South" affect local and state political races?**

A. The races were much more expensive than races held before this period.

B. Local political races became more important than state races in most areas.

C. It was highly likely that a Democratic candidate would win any political race.

D. It became more likely that the best and most qualified candidate would be elected.

_____ 457. **Which factor denoted a two-party political system in Georgia in the 2002 elections?**

A. Republican Sonny Perdue was elected governor of Georgia.

B. Democrats controlled the House, and there was a Republican governor.

C. There was a full slate of candidates for statewide offices from both the Democratic and Republican parties.

D. Democrats controlled the Georgia General Assembly, but Republicans were elected to the U.S. Senate and House from Georgia.

_____ 458. **The first Republican elected to the U.S. Senate from Georgia since Reconstruction was**

A. Sam Nunn.

B. John Lewis.

C. Newt Gingrich.

D. Mack Mattingly.

____ 459. **Which statement BEST describes the role of political parties in Georgia over the last hundred years?**

    A. Three political parties have played a major role in Georgia politics.

    B. Georgia has gradually changed from a two-party to a one-party system.

    C. Minority parties have been less important than the two major political parties.

    D. Since the end of Reconstruction, Georgia has been dominated by one political party.

SS8H12   The student will explain the importance of significant social, economic, and political developments in Georgia since 1970.

    d. Evaluate the effect of the 1996 Olympic Games on Georgia.

THE 1996 OLYMPIC GAMES

The games of the XXVI Olympiad were held in Atlanta in 1996. The Olympics brought four long-term benefits to the state. First, millions of dollars were spent to create world-class competition facilities such as the $189 million Olympic Stadium, the 1,400-acre Georgia Horse Park, the $17 million Wolf Creek Shooting Range complex, a Stone Mountain tennis facility, and the $10 million Lake Lanier Rowing Center. In addition, Georgia Tech and Georgia State University received new residence facilities, as well as renovated competition sites.

Second, the Olympics brought international recognition to Atlanta. Millions of visitors came to see the Games, and millions more watched on television. Atlanta and the state of Georgia received tremendous media coverage as one of the world's leading business centers.

Third, the Olympics brought volunteer programs, educational and training programs, and employment opportunities to thousands of Georgia's citizens. Fourth, the economic impact of the Olympic Games brought millions of dollars into Georgia's economy.

There were some moments at the Games when Georgia was not seen at its best. A bombing at Centennial Olympic Park on July 29, 1996, killed Alice Hawthorne of Albany and wounded 117, striking a note of fear into athletes and spectators alike. Severe traffic congestion in the Metropolitan Atlanta area made travel from one venue (event site) to another very difficult, and the world's press criticized the Olympic planners for their lack of **infrastructure** (basic facilities such as roads, bridges, and ports) to make transportation work smoothly. There were criticisms of the street vendors and salespersons who seemed to be on every corner. There was even criticism of the overly commercial advertising, particularly by Coca Cola, one of the major sponsors of the events. Nevertheless, the Olympic Games did show off Georgia like no other event ever has.

Southern hospitality, with volunteers working to make sure things ran correctly, was in full bloom. While transportation around the areas was difficult, once visitors arrived at a venue, the competition was unparalleled and excellent. While Atlanta's streets may have been congested, visitors got to see our state's diversity, our graciousness, and our own version of "southern hospitality."

____ 460. **Which statement does NOT describe a benefit Georgia received from hosting the 1996 Olympics?**

    A. Georgia did not have to pay for the production of the televised Olympic Games.

    B. Georgia received world-class athletic facilities throughout the state for use by its own citizens and visitors to the state.

    C. Georgia's convention and meeting facilities, transportation infrastructure, and southern hospitality were showcased.

    D. Georgia received international media attention and recognition for the state and the host city, Atlanta, which lead to tourism and international business expansion.

_____ 461. **Which facility was NOT created especially for the Olympics?**

    A. The Georgia Dome

    B. The Georgia Horse Park

    C. Lake Lanier Rowing Center

    D. The Stone Mountain tennis facility

_____ 462. **Better infrastructure could have lessened the 1996 Olympics problem of**

    A. safety.

    B. housing.

    C. traffic congestion.

    D. television advertising.

SS8H12   The student will explain the importance of significant social, economic, and political developments in Georgia since 1970.

    e. Evaluate the importance of new immigrant communities to the growth and economy of Georgia.

IMMIGRANTS

Georgia is known throughout the world as a leader in the production of carpet. There are many carpet mills and sales outlets for this thriving industry in northwest Georgia centered around the city of Dalton in Whitfield County. As the industry has grown, many jobs have become available. To fill many of these jobs, people from Mexico and other Latin American countries have come to northwest Georgia to live and work. The number of Hispanic immigrants has been so large in some areas that they constitute a majority in some school districts. Restaurants, churches, and Hispanic businesses have located in the area to serve the many people that now make Georgia their home.

Another area where immigrant populations have greatly affected the economy is near the city of Gainesville in Hall County. Here, the poultry industry is very important. Georgia is a leading producer of broilers (young chickens), and they are shipped across the United States and to other countries. Many immigrants have come to this area of Georgia to assist in the production and processing of millions of chickens for food production. Businesses serving mainly Hispanics are thriving in this area.

In South Georgia, the growing Vidalia onion industry is supported by immigrant populations as well. Because the onion crop is seasonal, and there are not enough permanent residents in the area to harvest the onion crop, migrant workers come to the area. When the onions are ready for harvesting, several South Georgia counties swell in immigrant populations. Schools are impacted as well when many students enroll for a brief time while the onions are harvested.

Immigrant populations impact Georgia's economy in a large way. Tens of thousands of immigrants, primarily from countries south of our border, live and work all over Georgia and assist in many jobs and businesses. Churches and ethnic businesses have sprung up in many towns to serve these people and others. All of Georgia is impacted by the contributions of immigrants, and the economy of the state grows as a result.

_____ 463. **Which of the following is NOT an impact immigrant populations have on Georgia's communities?**

    A. new laws and voting requirements are passed

    B. new restaurants, churches, and businessess are founded

    C. school populatins swell as immigrant families move into new areas

    D. seasonal jobs are filled with immigrant workers seeking employment

_____ **464. Immigrants are important to Georgia's economic growth because they bring**

D. seasonal workers for farmers.

C. job security in many industries.

B. multilingual programs to schools.

A. religious diversity to communities.

GEOGRAPHIC UNDERSTANDINGS

> **SS8G1** **The student will describe Georgia with regard to physical features and location.**
> a. Locate Georgia in relation to region, nation, continent, and hemispheres.

LOCATION

In terms of **relative location**, Georgia is located in the northern hemisphere, on the continent of North America, in the southeastern corner of the United States. Five other states touch Georgia borders—Florida on the south, Alabama on the west, Tennessee and North Carolina on the north, and South Carolina along the Savannah River on the northeast. Georgia is also bordered by the Atlantic Ocean on the east.

If you want to know Georgia's **absolute location**, you would have to say that Georgia is located between 30° 21′ and 35°E latitude and between 80° 50′ and 80° 36′ W longitude.

In terms of land area, Georgia is the largest state east of the Mississippi River. Its greatest length is 315 miles, and its greatest width is 250 miles. There are 58,910 square miles of land and 854 square miles of inland water in Georgia. The state has almost as much land as all of the New England states combined. The geographic center of the state is located at a point 18 miles southeast of Macon in Twiggs County.

_____ 465. **Which statement describes Georgia's relative location?**
   A. Georgia is a northeastern state.
   B. Georgia is located north of Florida.
   C. Georgia is located in the southwestern United States.
   D. Georgia is located between 30°E and 35°E and between 80°W and 85°W.

_____ 466. **In which region of the United States is Georgia located?**
   A. central
   B. western
   C. northeastern
   D. southeastern

_____ 467. **Into which hemisphere does the prime meridian place Georgia?**
   A. eastern hemisphere
   B. western hemisphere
   C. northern hemisphere
   D. southern hemisphere

_____ 468. **On which continent is Georgia located?**
   A. Asia
   B. Europe
   C. North America
   D. South America

_____ **469. Which of the following does NOT boarder Georgia?**

A. Pacific

B. Alabama

C. Tennessee

D. Altantic Ocean

SS8G1   The student will describe Georgia with regard to physical features and location.

b. Describe the five geographic regions of Georgia; include the Blue Ridge Mountains, Valley and Ridge, Appalachian Plateau, Piedmont, and Coastal Plain.

BLUE RIDGE MOUNTAINS

The Blue Ridge region of Georgia is known for its rugged beauty. Located in the northeastern part of the state, it is part of the Appalachian Highlands that stretch from New York to Alabama. The Blue Ridge region is a hundred miles wide and has an area of about two thousand square miles. The highest and largest group of mountains in Georgia is in this region. These mountains are important to the rest of the state because they are the first barrier to warm, moist air rising from the Gulf of Mexico. When that air makes contact with the high mountains, it cools. The **precipitation** (rain, hail, sleet, or snow) that results provides water for the entire state.

The region has a mixture of sandy loam (a blend of clay, sand, and organic matter) and clay. The shallow soil is easily eroded, and the steep slopes add to the erosion problems in the region. The area is well suited for hardwood forests, vegetable farming, and apples.

Brasstown Bald, the highest peak in the state, is located in this region. (In the South, high mountains that are treeless on top are often called "balds.") The peak is almost 5,000 feet high. If you climb to the top of the observation tower there, you can catch a glimpse of three surrounding states: North Carolina, South Carolina, and Tennessee.

Travelers to this region can also visit other well-known Georgia landmarks including beautiful Amicalola Falls, which drops 729 feet; the 1,000-foot-deep Tallulah Gorge in Rabun County; and the alpine community of Helen in White County. In addition, this region is known for its many recreational opportunities.

_____ **470. In which region are Amicalola Falls and Tallulah Gorge located?**

A. Blue Ridge

B. Ridge and Valley

C. Piedmont Plateau

D. Appalachian Plateau

_____ **471. What is the highest peak in Georgia?**

A. Tallulah Gorge

B. Amicalola Falls

C. Brasstown Bald

D. Cloudland Canyon

Use the map to answer question 472.

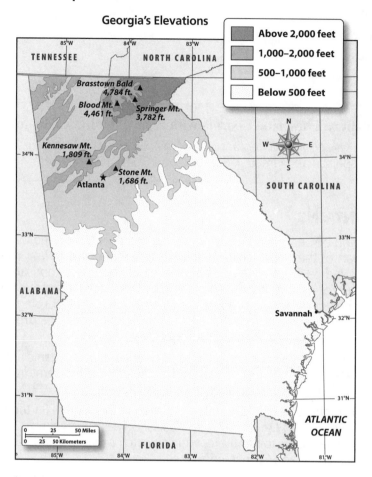

Georgia's Elevations

____ **472. Which mountain rises to the highest elevation?**

    A. Blood Mountain

    B. Stone Mountain

    C. Springer Mountain

    D. Kennesaw Mountain

RIDGE AND VALLEY

Between the Blue Ridge Mountains and the Appalachian Mountains lies the Ridge and Valley region. This area of the state has low open valleys and narrow ridges that run parallel to the valleys. Elevation ranges from 700 to 1,600 feet above sea level. Most of the soil in the region is a mixture of shale and sandstone on the ridges and limestone and clay in the valleys. Forests and pastures dominate the region, but there are flat and fertile farmlands with fields of grain, pastures for cattle, and rows of apple orchards near Ellijay. The valleys are divided by steep and narrow ridges capped with limestone. The rocks that make up the ridges are very resistant to erosion. Ridges include Taylor Ridge and Pigeon Mountain.

The region runs from Polk and Bartow counties northward to Chattanooga, Tennessee. It is known for its industry, particularly textile and carpet manufacturing. Dalton, known as the "carpet capital of the world," leads the way.

A famous story told by the late Bernice McCullar in her *This Is Georgia* explained the northwest Georgia location of Plum Nelly reached over a winding two-lane road. People would refer to it as "plum outa Tennessee and nelly outa Georgia." Today Plum Nelly is the name of a well-known Appalachian folk art center.

Use the map to answer questions 473-475.

Appalachian Trail

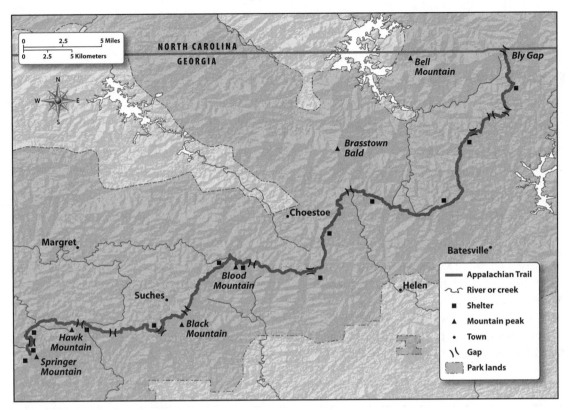

____ **473. How many gaps would a hiker pass through to get from Springer Mountain to Hawk Mountain Shelter?**

    A. 1

    B. 2

    C. 3

    D. 4

____ **474. Where does the Appalachian Trail cross into North Carolina?**

    A. Bly Gap

    B. Blood Shelter

    C. Springer Mountain

    D. Town of Batesville

____ **475. When traveling from Black Mountain to Blood Mountain, which direction is a hiker traveling?**

    A. north

    B. south

    C. northeast

    D. southwest

476. In which region are Taylor Ridge and Pigeon Mountain found?
A. Blue Ridge
B. Ridge and Valley
C. Piedmont Plateau
D. Appalachian Plateau

APPALACHIAN PLATEAU

The smallest of the physiographic areas, the Appalachian Plateau region is a maze of limestone caves, deep canyons, and interesting rock formations. Many people refer to this region in the far northwestern corner of the state as the "TAG Corner" because it is the point at which Tennessee, Alabama, and Georgia meet. Also sometimes called the Cumberland Plateau, the region has the broad, flat-topped, 100-mile-long Lookout Mountain on one side and Sand Mountain on the other, separated by ridges of limestone. In between these two mountains is a long, narrow valley. Soils in this region are a mixture of limestone, shale, and sandstone and are well suited for the region's hardwood forests and pastures. There is also some coal in this region, although there are no active mines.

With an elevation (the height above sea level) of up to 2,000 feet, this region is one of the most scenic but least traveled parts of the state. Civil War buffs frequent the Chickamauga and Chattanooga National Military Park, the site of historic Civil War battles. Cloudland Canyon, located between Trenton and Lafayette, has two beautiful waterfalls that cascade over layers of sandstone, dolomite, and shale millions of years old.

The area between the Appalachian Plateau region and the adjoining Ridge and Valley region marks the beginning of the Appalachian Trail at Springer Mountain, northeast of Dahlonega. Every year, outdoor adventurers begin the 2,144-mile hike, hoping to arrive at its end in Maine.

Use this information to answer question 477.

- smallest region
- source of coal deposits
- location of Lookout Mountain

477. Which Georgia region is described by these phrases?
A. Blue Ridge
B. Ridge and Valley
C. Piedmont Plateau
D. Appalachian Plateau

478. In what area of Georgia is the Appalachian Plateau located?
A. southeast
B. northeast
C. northwest
D. southwest

479. What is the smallest physiographic (geographic) area in Georgia?
A. Blue Ridge
B. Coastal Plain
C. Ridge and Valley
D. Appalachian Plateau

PIEDMONT

The Piedmont Plateau begins in the mountain foothills of northern Georgia and goes to the central part of the state. It has gently sloping hills and valleys in the north and flatlands in the south. The region has well-drained soils, primarily sandy loam and clay, which are suitable for hardwood timber, pine, and agriculture.

Some Georgians refer to the gently rolling hills and southern flatlands as the "heartland" of the state. The term Piedmont means "foot of the mountain," but the plateau is so long that it actually runs from Alabama northward to Delaware. This granite-based landform makes up about one-third of the state's land area. In addition to the granite base, there is another familiar type of soil: our famous Georgia red clay.

About one-half of the state's population lives in the Piedmont region. It was the cotton belt during the period before the Civil War. Today, it is known for the production of wheat, soybeans, corn, poultry, and cattle. Business and industry also flourish throughout the area. The cities of Atlanta, Athens, Madison, and Milledgeville are among some of the densely populated areas crisscrossed by the Chattahoochee, Flint, Ocmulgee, and Oconee rivers.

Use this map to answer questions 480-481.

Geographic Regions with Cities

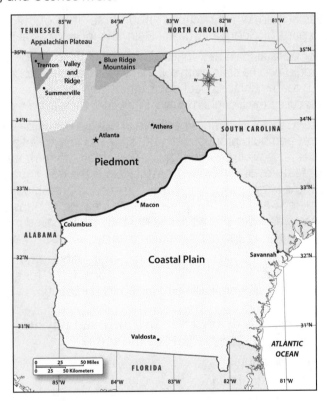

____ **480. Which city is located on the Fall Line?**

    A. Atlanta

    B. Valdosta

    C. Columbus

    D. Summerville

____ **481. Which city is located in the Piedmont?**

    A. Macon

    B. Athens

    C. Trenton

    D. Savannah

_____ **482. In which region is Atlanta located?**
   A. Blue Ridge
   B. Ridge and Valley
   C. Piedmont Plateau
   D. Appalachian Plateau

_____ **483. Which geographical region of Georgia is characterized by its red clay, gently sloping hills, and location near the Fall Line?**
   A. Piedmont
   B. Blue Ridge
   C. Coastal Plain
   D. Appalachian Plateau

COASTAL PLAIN

The Coastal Plain, which occupies about three-fifths of the state, is the largest region. There are actually two parts of Georgia's Coastal Plain: the Inner Coastal Plain and the Outer Coastal Plain.

The Inner Coastal Plain has a mild climate and a good supply of underground water. It is the major agricultural region of the state, with soil that varies from limestone to clay. The Vidalia Upland has become world famous for the unique sweet onions that grow there. The southwestern corner around Bainbridge and Albany is called the Dougherty Plain, in whose rich soil grow peanuts, corn, and pecan trees.

The Outer Coastal Plain does not have drained soil to provide fertile farmlands, but it is the center of naval stores and pulp production in the state. As you travel along the flat coastline area, which in some places is fairly swampy and marshy, you are in the territory first visited by early explorers. One of the major features of the Outer Coastal Plain is the 681-square-mile Okefenokee Swamp. The Okefenokee, the largest swamp in North America, is a freshwater wetland. A wetland is a low-lying land area where water lies close to the surface creating sloughs, swamps, bogs, ponds, and freshwater marshes. A **wetland** can also be a lowland that is influenced by tidal water flows to create salt marshes. Georgia ranks fourth in the nation in the number of acres of wetlands found in the state.

Along the coast, the deep harbors and barrier islands offer recreational facilities, seafood gathering and processing industries, and major shipyard ports. Here, for example, are cities such as Savannah, Darien, and Brunswick with their enduring, genteel beauty.

_____ **484. Georgia is divided into five different physical regions. Which one of these covers the largest part of the state?**
   A. Piedmont
   B. Coastal Plain
   C. Appalachians
   D. Ridge and Valley

_____ **485. What region is known for the production of peanuts, corn, and pecans?**
   A. Piedmont
   B. Blue Ridge
   C. Coastal Plain
   D. Appalachian Plateau

____ **486. Georgia ranks fourth in the nation in the number of wetlands found in the state. Which statement does NOT describe a wetland?**

    A. A wetland is located in an area with heavy annual rainfall.

    B. A wetland contains salt marshes and is found along the coast.

    C. A wetland is a low-lying area where water lies close to the surface.

    D. A wetland contains sloughs, swamps, bogs, ponds, and freshwater marshes.

SS8G1   The student will describe Georgia with regard to physical features and location.

    c. Locate and evaluate the importance of key physical features on the development of Georgia; include the Fall Line, Okefenokee Swamp, Appalachian Mountains, Chattahoochee and Savannah Rivers, and barrier islands.

FALL LINE

The Coastal Plain region is separated from the Piedmont Plateau by a natural boundary known as the Fall Line. The **Fall Line** is the point at which hilly or mountainous lands meet the coastal plain. This line runs from Columbus on the western side of the state, through Macon and into Augusta on the eastern side. Other cities located on the Fall Line are Milledgeville, Roberta, Thomson, and Warrenton. Rivers and creeks flowing from the rocky hill country cut deep channels in the softer soil of the plains. This drops the elevation and creates waterfalls.

As early settlers began to leave the coastal regions and explore inland, many were forced to stop at the Fall Line because they could not travel over the steep and rushing falls. These early settlers, as well as Indians and traders, found the waterfalls an excellent power source and built settlements there.

____ **487. Why have many of Georgia's cities and industries grown up along the Fall Line?**

    A. Railroads were already built there.

    B. Rapid flowing rivers were a source of energy.

    C. Ships can travel northward from there to the northeast.

    D. The land along the Fall Line was fertile and perfect for farming.

____ **488. What two regions are separated by the Fall Line?**

    A. Coastal Plain and Blue Ridge

    B. Blue Ridge and Piedmont Plateau

    C. Coastal Plain and Piedmont Plateau

    D. Appalachian Plateau and Blue Ridge

____ **489. The border between the Georgia Piedmont and the Coast Plain marks the point at which rivers drop in elevation creating waterfalls. This border is known as the**

    A. Fall Line.

    B. Tallulah Gorge.

    C. Savannah River.

    D. Okefenokee Swamp.

____ 490. **Which statement does NOT describe a reason for locating many of Georgia's early settlements on the Fall Line?**
  A. Waterfalls at the Fall Line provided a power source for water mills and developing industries.
  B. The area around the Fall Line, with its clear water and lush vegetation, was a picturesque setting for a settlement.
  C. The rivers and creeks cut deep channels in the softer soils through which they ran, creating fertile land for farming.
  D. Settlers were forced to stop at the waterfalls along the Fall Line because of the difficulty of traveling over the steep, rushing water.

OKEFENOKEE SWAMP

One of the major features of the Outer Coastal Plain is the 681-square-mile Okefenokee Swamp. The Okefenokee, the largest swamp in North America, is a freshwater wetland. Once part of the Atlantic Ocean floor, the Okefenokee received its name from the Indian word o-wa-qua-phenoga, which means "land of the trembling earth." The Okefenokee is filled with a shallow "black water" stained by the tannic acid of decaying vegetation. The swamp covers a half million acres (about seven hundred square miles) and is located in the Outer Coastal Plain near Waycross and Folkston. This primitive wetland is home to hundreds of species of plants, animals, and reptiles, many of whom are endangered. Throughout the area are about seventy "piney woods" islands, once home to Seminole Indians and settled by pioneer Georgians in the 1850s.

If you visit, you will enter a world of giant, 80-foot cypress trees draped with moss overhanging dark, murky waters filled with alligators, herons, egrets, and cranes. The swamp is also home to Georgia's native black bears–and the comic strip character "Pogo."

____ 491. **Which is a characteristic of the Okefenokee Swamp?**
  A. It is located in the Piedmont region.
  B. It has the most precipitation in the state.
  C. It is famous for its hydroelectric potential.
  D. It is the largest freshwater swamp in Georgia.

____ 492. **In which region is the Okefenokee Swamp located?**
  A. Blue Ridge
  B. Coastal Plain
  C. Ridge and Valley
  D. Piedmont Plateau

APPALACHIAN MOUNTAINS

Georgia's three northern regions are all part of the Appalachian Mountains The story of the Appalachians began over 900 million years ago when the continents collided and created one giant continent. This collision also created the Appalachians. Over millions of years, the continents split apart and slowly moved away from each other. The first Appalachian Mountains eroded into what later became the Atlantic Ocean.

About 500 million years ago, the continents once again began to move back together. As the continents moved together, they pushed the sediment from the ocean floor back up and created the second Appalachian Mountains. Once again, the continents collided. The force of the collision caused Earth's crust to fold and more mountains to form. Each time the continents collided and formed more mountains, the existing mountains were pushed further west. That is why the Appalachians have several sets of parallel ridges.

About 200 million years ago, the continents began to drift apart again. Over the past 200 million years, the Appalachian Mountains have eroded from their original height. At times ice glaciers covered the mountain chain. The weight of the glaciers pushed down the mountains underneath. The ice carved valleys and pushed the eroded rock sediments as far south as the southeastern corner of the United States.

____ **493. The mountain chain which reaches into northern Georgia is the**
   A. Ozarks.
   B. Rockies.
   C. Shenandoah.
   D. Appalachians.

____ **494. Through which physiographic (geographic) regions do the Appalachian Mountains run?**
   A. Coastal Plain, Blue Ridge, Ridge and Valley
   B. Blue Ridge, Appalachian Plateau, Coastal Plain
   C. Ridge and Valley, Appalachian Plateau, Piedmont
   D. Blue Ridge, Ridge and Valley, Appalachian Plateau

CHATTAHOOCHEE RIVER

The name of the Chattahoochee comes from the Cherokee and means the "river of the painted rock." It was so named because of the colorful stones that lay across the riverbed. The river itself flows 436 miles from the mountains of North Georgia to the Gulf of Mexico. Part of the southern section forms the natural border between Georgia and Alabama. The chief cities along its banks include Gainesville, Atlanta, and Columbus. Major manmade lakes, including Lake Lanier, West Point Lake, and the Walter F. George Reservoir, are part of the Chattahoochee's winding path. In addition to supplying water to Atlanta and Columbus, the river is a water source for Helen, Buford, LaGrange, and West Point.

____ **495. What river is the primary source of water for Atlanta?**
   A. Flint
   B. Savannah
   C. Altamaha
   D. Chattahoochee

____ **496. What river has its headwaters in the mountains of north Georgia and form part of the boundary between Georgia and Alabama?**
   A. Flint
   B. Savannah
   C. Altamaha
   D. Chattahoochee

SAVANNAH RIVER

By the time the first European explorers reached the Savannah River in 1540, Indians had traveled the 314-mile-long waterway for many years. They called it the Isondega, meaning "blue water."

In 1732, King George II granted to James Oglethorpe "all those lands, Countries, and Territories" between the Savannah and the Altamaha rivers extending westward "to the South Seas." And, of course, Oglethorpe's settlers from the Ann established the first settlement on Yamacraw Bluff overlooking the Savannah River.

Along the border of South Carolina, the river spreads into three lakes: J. Strom Thurmond Lake (formerly called Clark Hill Lake), Lake Russell, and Hartwell Lake. The Savannah is the only river that flows into Georgia from outside its borders. The headwaters of the Savannah River are in South Carolina.

____ **497.** **The earliest settlement of Georgia by the first English colonists was along which Georgia river?**
A. Altamaha
B. Savannah
C. Ocmulgee
D. Chattahoochee

____ **498.** **What is the only river that flows into Georgia from another state?**
A. Coosa
B. Savannah
C. Ogeechee
D. Chattahoochee

Use the map to answer questions 499-501.

Georgia Rivers and Lakes

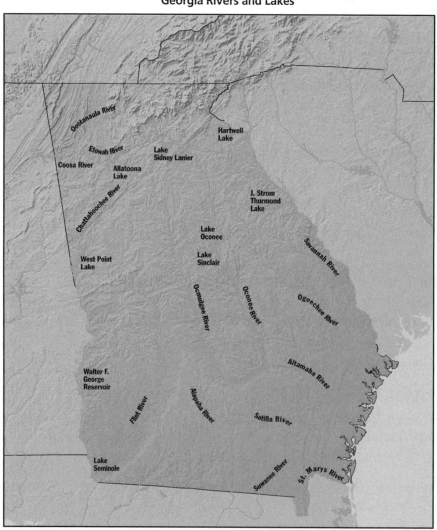

____ **499. Which river forms the boundary between Georgia and South Carolina?**

    A. Altamaha

    B. Savannah

    C. Ogeechee

    D. Chattahoochee

____ **500. Which river does NOT flow into the Atlantic Ocean?**

    A. Flint

    B. Satilla

    C. St. Marys

    D. Ocmulgee

____ **501. Which lake is located along the Oconee River?**

    B. Lanier

    A. Sinclair

    C. Hartwell

    D. Allatoona

BARRIER ISLANDS

The coast is an interlocking chain of marshes, rivers, and tributaries that eventually flow into the Atlantic Ocean. The Spanish explorers called this subtropical region "Islands of Gold." Along the one-hundred mile shoreline is a group of barrier islands, so called because they protect the beaches by blocking much of the wind, sands, and water that could erode the mainland. Even today, this chain of islands offers much in terms of beauty, recreation, and tourism. Jekyll Island is primarily a state park, and Cumberland Island is a national seashore. Perhaps the greatest legacy of the barrier island group is that two-thirds of the land remains wilderness sanctuaries.

____ **502. Today, most of Georgia's sea islands are protected by the state or federal government. What is the main reason they are protected?**

    A. to promote hunting and fishing

    B. to preserve the natural environment

    C. to allow the development of tourism

    D. to prevent the development of desalinization plants

____ **503. What is the primary function of the barrier islands?**

    A. They are frequent targets of hurricanes.

    B. They protect the beaches from erosion.

    C. They protect wild horses from extinction.

    D. They serve as well-stocked hunting preserves.

SS8G1   The student will describe Georgia with regard to physical features and location.

d. Evaluate the impact of climate on Georgia's development.

CLIMATE OF GEORGIA

One of the most distinguishing characteristics of Georgia's geographic regions is the climate of each area. **Climate** refers to the type of weather a region experiences over a long period of time. **Weather** refers to the day-to-day conditions and changes in the atmosphere. While weather varies constantly, a region's climate remains stable. The climate of a region influences the types of homes built, the types of industries that develop, the clothing styles, and even what crops are grown.

As a result of Georgia's latitude and longitude (and our nearness to the equator), the climate in our state overall is mild with a subtropical feel along the coast. We experience four distinct seasons: spring, summer, fall, and winter. In most places, summers are hot and humid while winters are mild. However, there is a narrow band across the north Georgia mountains that has warm summers and moderately cold winters because mountainous terrain also influences temperature. The higher the elevation, the colder the temperature. This phenomenon is sometimes referred to as **vertical climate.**

Generally, temperatures are relatively comfortable through most of the year, which is one of the reasons why so many companies move into our state. Industries tend to favor mild climates because such weather equals lower costs for heating and air conditioning and fewer weather-related absences. Equally important, our mild climate generates longer growing seasons for a variety of crops. Even in today's modern Georgia, one in six Georgia jobs relates to agriculture or agri-business.

Precipitation is vital to Georgia's economy. Snow, which generally falls only in the mountain regions, melts and runs off into streams and lakes. Rainfall aids the growth of crops and forests. In a normal year, Georgia receives an average of 40 to 52 inches of rain in central and southern regions and 65 to 76 inches in the northern mountains, some of which is in the form of snow.

From 1998 through 2002, Georgia, like many other parts of the country, experienced a severe drought, with rainfall far below average. A **drought** is a lack of precipitation over a period of time that results in water shortages. Lack of rainfall for even a short period of time can harm industries, farmers, and homeowners alike. A few weeks without rain and lawns begin to turn brown, plants and shrubs shrivel, fire warnings become common, and water conservation actions run full speed.

_____ **504. How is Georgia's overall climate best described?**

A. wet and hot

B. dry and hot

C. dry and cold

D. humid and mild

_____ **505. Which industry is MOST affected by Georgia's mild climate?**

A. mining

B. chemical

C. agriculture

D. transportation

_____ **506. Georgia's climate attracts business and industry because the state**

A. does not have hurricanes.

B. seldom receives much snow.

C. rarely experiences tornadoes.

D. has a consistently mild climate.

____ 507. In many cases, people have to adjust to a new physical and geographic environment in order to make a living. Which person would have to make the most drastic adjustment?

    A. a Georgia cotton farmer moving to Canada

    B. a computer programmer moving from Boston to Atlanta

    C. a logger moving from the Georgia mountains to northern Maine

    D. a Georgia miner moving from the plateau region to West Virginia

Use the table to answer questions 508-510.

GEORGIA'S CLIMATE				
	January Temperatures	July Temperatures	Annual Precipitation	Length of Growing Season
North Georgia				
Clayton	41°	74°	71 inches	191 days
Blue Ridge	40°	74°	57 inches	184 days
Central Georgia				
Atlanta	44°	79°	48 inches	231 days
Macon	47°	81°	44 inches	240 days
Southern Georgia				
Savannah	53°	81°	45 inches	273 days
Brunswick	54°	82°	50 inches	276 days

____ 508. The warmest areas of Georgia are in which region of the state?

    A. central

    B. northern

    C. southern

    D. cannot determine from data in this table

____ 509. The area of Georgia that receives the most rainfall is

    A. central Georgia.

    B. northern Georgia.

    C. southern Georgia.

    D. cannot determine from data in this table.

____ 510. The area of Georgia best suited for farming is which region of the state?

    A. central

    B. northern

    C. southern

    D. cannot determine from data in this table

SS8G2 The student will explain how the Interstate Highway System, Hartsfield-Jackson International Airport, Georgia's deepwater ports, and the railroads help drive the state's economy.

a. Explain how the four transportation systems interact to provide domestic and international goods to the people of Georgia.

b. Explain how the four transportation systems interact to provide producers and service providers in Georgia with national and international markets.

c. Explain how the four transportation systems provide jobs for Georgians.

TRANSPORTATION SYSTEMS

Georgia has two major deepwater seaports, Savannah and Brunswick, and two inland barge terminals, Bainbridge and Columbus. The economic impact of these ports exceeds $1.8 billion in annual income. They account for over 81,000 jobs and pay over $585 million in state and local taxes. Over 90 steamship lines serve Georgia, which leads the South Atlantic region in foreign cargo handled.

The key to the economic success of Georgia's ports is the transportation infrastructure supporting those ports. The ports of Brunswick and Savannah are located close to two major interstate highways (I-95 and I-16) and to key railroad hubs. From Georgia, goods are two truckload days from 82 percent of the U.S. industrial marketplace and 79 percent of the nation's largest consumer markets. Over 100 motor freight carriers serve the metropolitan areas of Georgia. The state has 35 scheduled carriers, 2,200 intrastate haulers, and 25,000 interstate truckers serving the state. In addition, two major railroad lines operate in the state. Savannah's seaport concentrates on containerized cargo and is the fifth largest container port in the nation, the largest on the East Coast. The Brunswick port concentrates on auto shipping, heavy equipment, farm machinery, and luxury tour buses. In addition, shipping of bulk agricultural products has increased.

A massive amount of imports (goods and supplies shipped into the state) and exports (goods and supplies shipped out of state) flow through Georgia's seaports and inland barge terminals. In fact, the ship on the reverse side of Georgia's state seal represents the state's exports. Georgia has a history of product exporting. In 1788, it was the first state to export cotton to Great Britain. The first cattle exported from America left from Savannah's port. Georgia's marketplace really is the world, and the state's seaports make that marketplace a viable enterprise.

Georgia's outstanding transportation system is one of the main attractions for new businesses and industries locating in Georgia. Atlanta's Hartsfield-Jackson Airport is the busiest in the world. It is the headquarters for Delta Airlines, and over 86 million people a year pass through the airport. There are 26 passenger airlines that operate many direct international flights to 14 countries from Hartsfield-Jackson. There are also 16 cargo airlines that operate from the airport.

Hartsfield-Jackson is considered the largest employment center in the State of Georgia. There are approximately 55,300 airline, ground transportation, concessionaire, security, federal government, City of Atlanta, and Airport tenant employees. In 2005, the total airport payroll was $2.4 billion, resulting in a direct and indirect economic impact of $5.6 billion on the local and regional economy. In addition to Hartsfield-Jackson, there are 121 other public, 142 private, and 6 military airports in the state.

Georgia has 1,200 miles of interstate highways, 17,800 miles of state highways, 87,000 miles of paved city and county road, and 5,400 miles of railroad track. Our cities are connected with one another, enabling workers and materials to be quickly moved to the required location.

Companies looking for a global presence find that Georgia's transportation network can lead to success.

____ **511.** **Which statement BEST describes Georgia's transportation infrastructure today?**

    A. Georgia has been held back because it has less than 1,000 miles of interstate, 12,000 miles of federal and state highways, and only 8 regional airports.

    B. Georgia has a strong transportation infrastructure including over 1,200 miles of interstate highways, over 5,000 miles of railroad track, and over 260 airports.

    C. Georgia has a weak transportation structure because there are limited interstate highways, federal and state highways, and less than 2,500 miles of railroad tracks.

    D. Georgia has an outstanding transportation infrastructure involving over 25,000 miles of state and federal highways, over 1,500 miles of interstate, and over 320 airports.

____ **512.** **Which method of transportation moves the largest amount of freight in Georgia?**

    A. trucks

    B. airlines

    C. railroads

    D. shipping

____ **513.** **Where is the largest single container facility on the East Coast located?**

    A. Savannah

    B. Columbus

    C. Brunswick

    D. Jekyll Island

____ **514.** **Perhaps the MOST IMPORTANT reason to invest in expanding infrastructure is to**

    A. help the economy to grow.

    B. attract new airlines to Georgia.

    C. keep abreast of new developments.

    D. ensure that traffic congestion is minimized.

____ **515.** **Which does NOT describe a reason for the success of Georgia's seaports?**

    A. Georgia's two major railroads

    B. Georgia's network of interstate highways

    C. Georgia's large number of interstate and intrastate truckers

    D. Georgia's lack of state and local taxes on seaports and terminals

GOVERNMENT/CIVIC UNDERSTANDINGS

> **SS8CG1** **The student will describe the role of citizens under Georgia's constitution.**
> a. Explain the basic structure of the Georgia state constitution.

GEORGIA'S CONSTITUTION

Georgia was one of the original thirteen colonies and became a state after the American Revolution. Georgia adopted its first state constitution in 1777. In 1983, Georgians approved the state's tenth constitution. Even though there have been changes in the text of the various constitutions, the purpose of all of them has been the same. The preamble (or introduction) of the state constitution declares:

> *To perpetuate the principles of free government, insure justice to all, preserve peace, promote the interest and happiness of the citizens and of the family, and transmit to posterity the enjoyment of liberty, we the people of Georgia, relying upon the protection and guidance of Almighty God, do ordain and establish this Constitution.*

Georgia's constitution states, "All government, of right, originates with the people, is founded upon their will only, and is instituted for the good of the whole. Public officers are the trustees and servants of the people and are at all times amenable to them." In other words, any power the government has is given to it by the citizens and is for the good of everyone. Persons elected to public office in state government work for the people and are accountable to the voters for their actions.

The constitution further states: "The people of this state have the inherent right of regulating their internal government. Government is instituted for the protection, security and benefit of the people; and at all times they have the right to alter or reform the same whenever the public good may require it." Therefore, Georgia's government is meant to serve the people, and the constitution allows the people to change the government when it fails to serve their needs.

The constitution gives voters the right to control state government by electing state officials. Citizens also may suggest laws that might improve the way the state is governed.

There are eleven articles in the 1983 constitution. The first article consists of a bill of rights, twenty-eight paragraphs that set out the rights of Georgia's citizens. Other articles deal with the three branches of government, various boards and commissions, voting and elections, education, taxes, county and local government, and ways to amend the constitution.

_____ 516. **How many articles are in Georgia's state constitution?**
   A. 8
   B. 11
   C. 13
   D. 15

_____ 517. **Georgia's constitution has articles that deal with all of the following except**
   A. federal government.
   B. voting and elections.
   C. county and local government.
   D. various boards and commissions.

____ 518. **The first article of Geogia's constitution deals with**

    A. a bill of rights.

    B. voting and elections.

    C. county and local government.

    D. ways to amend the constitution.

____ 519. **The purpose of the Georgia constitution is to**

    A. clarify the meaning of vague laws.

    B. protect and benefit all the people of Georgia.

    C. make laws, enforce laws, and collect revenue for Georgia's citizens.

    D. administer those rights assigned to the states by the U.S. Constitution.

SS8CG1   **The student will describe the role of citizens under Georgia's constitution.**

  b. Explain the concepts of separation of powers and checks and balances.

SEPARATION OF POWERS

The Georgia constitution, like the U.S. Constitution, divides the responsibilities of government among the three branches in what is known as a **separation of powers**. Separating government powers creates a "limited government."

____ 520. **The term separation of powers refers to the designation of certain powers to**

    A. the nations citizens.

    B. state and municipal government.

    C. each of the three branches of the government.

    D. the federal government and certain powers to the state government.

____ 521. **What explanation BEST justifies the inclusion of the separation of powers doctrine in the constitution?**

    A. It streamlines government.

    B. It makes government run more smoothly.

    C. It makes a distinction among the branches of government.

    D. It keeps one branch of government from becoming too powerful.

CHECKS AND BALANCES

Each branch of government was given some power to control or prevent some actions of the other two branches. This process is known as a system of **checks and balances**. The checks and balances ensure that no one branch becomes too powerful.

The *executive branch* can veto bills passed by the legislative branch and can call special sessions of the legislature. It also has some appointment powers when officers of the court resign or die.

The *legislative branch* can impeach officials in the executive or judicial branches. It can override a governor's veto of bills to make them into laws. It must also confirm appointments made by the governor. It can propose constitutional changes.

The *judicial branch* determines whether or not laws are constitutional.

In addition, each branch of government is responsive to the citizens of Georgia because most officials in each branch are directly elected by the voters.

____ **522.** According to the system of checks and balances, the judicial branch has the power to

A. appoint state judges.

B. impeach the governor.

C. declare a law unconstitutional.

D. confirm appointments to the judicial branch.

____ **523.** According to the system of checks and balances, the executive branch checks the legislative branch

A. by interpreting laws.

B. through impeachment.

C. through the use of the veto.

D. by proposing constitutional changes.

____ **524.** According to the system of checks and balances, the legislative branch CANNOT check the executive branch by

A. overriding a veto.

B. appointing justices.

C. using impeachment.

D. confirming appointments.

SS8CG1 **The student will describe the role of citizens under Georgia's constitution.**

c. Describe the rights and responsibilities of citizens.

RIGHTS AND RESPONSIBILITIES OF CITIZENS

With the development of the U.S. Constitution at the convention of 1787, one principle of the new government set up by our founding fathers was **sovereignty**, the concept that power and authority rest with the citizens. Another principle was **federalism**, a system where the national, state, and local governments share authority over the same land and the same people. The government gives to us, America's citizens, the status of citizenship. If your parents are U.S. citizens or if you were born in the United States, then you are a U.S. citizen. You are entitled to all of the protections and rights afforded by the federal and state constitutions. These rights include free speech, the right to bear arms, freedom of religion, and the right to a speedy and fair trial.

Naturalized citizens are foreign nationals (those who were born in other countries) who choose to become American citizens and give up their citizenship in those other countries. People who are eighteen years of age, who have lived in this country for at least five years, and who entered the country legally can apply for citizenship. They must meet certain requirements – an ability to read, write, and speak English; a knowledge and understanding of U.S. history and government; good moral character; and a belief in the principles of the U.S. Constitution. Taking an oath of allegiance is the final step in the naturalization process.

Along with the rights that come with being a citizen of the United States, the state of Georgia, and a particular county and town are certain responsibilities. Voting, while certainly a right, is also the most basic responsibility of citizens, enabling them to participate in their government. Unfortunately, voting is suffering in Georgia. In the last presidential election year, Georgia ranked 48th out of the 50 states in the percentage of eligible adults who voted. Never in the state's history have over 50 percent of the state's eligible voters actually gone to the polls. The youngest voters, those between the ages of 18 and 24, have the lowest voter participation.

Another basic responsibility of citizens is to pay federal, state, and local taxes to fund the services those governments provide. Additional responsibilities include participation in government by running for office if you choose, but by voting for candidates for office even if you elect not to serve yourself. Another is upholding the laws of the nation. A third is defending the nation against its enemies. As a citizen, you may be called upon to serve in your community by participating in juries. You may also be called upon to serve in wartime by joining a branch of the military. All young men are required to register with the Selective Service Board when they turn eighteen.

You can fulfill your responsibilities as a citizen by participating at local, state, and even national levels. You can serve on library boards, zoning commissions, and volunteer civic organizations. You can share your talents and your time with your community to make it a better place to live.

____ 525. **Which right is NOT given to United States citizens in the U.S. Constitution?**
   A. freedom of religion
   B. freedom of the press
   C. the right to a fair trial
   D. the right to an education

____ 526. **What is the process by which a person from another country can become an American citizen?**
   A. emigration
   B. immigration
   C. naturalization
   D. nationalization

____ 527. **What financial responsibility does a citizen have toward the government?**
   A. paying taxes
   B. paying debts
   C. buying on credit
   D. political contributions

SS8CG1   The student will describe the role of citizens under Georgia's constitution.
   d. Explain voting qualifications and elections in Georgia.

VOTING QUALIFICATIONS

The major influence on government decision-making is made at the polls on election day by people who vote. Voters in our democratic form of government elect representatives to political office and decide major questions and issues. To register to vote in Georgia, a person must be at least eighteen years old and a citizen of the United States. An individual must also be a legal resident of Georgia and the county in which he or she registers.

____ 528. **How old must a person be to vote in Georgia today?**
   A. 16
   B. 18
   C. 21
   D. 25

_____ **529. Which requirement is NOT necessary to vote in Georgia?**

    A. a citizen of the United States

    B. 18 years of age before the election

    C. a registered member of a political party

    D. a resident of Georgia and the county in which you are voting

ELECTIONS

Voting in national, state, and local elections takes place according to the Georgia Election Code. As the chief election official, the secretary of state makes sure candidates meet the qualifications to run for office. This official also schedules elections, prints ballots, and provides all election materials to Georgia's counties. After an election, the secretary of state checks the results in each county and publishes them.

A general election is held in November in at least every even-numbered year. This is when major federal and state officials are selected. Other elections are held as needed to select public officials at all levels of government: national, state, county, or city.

Voters select the most important state officials. These officials, in turn, appoint others who work for and with them. Therefore, a citizen can, by voting, influence all of government. Voters also have the right and responsibility to decide some issues. Because it requires a vote of the people to change the state constitution, proposed amendments sometimes appear on the ballot.

No matter what the purpose of an election, low voter turnout is a matter of serious concern. Many people fear that democratic government will not last if so few people are concerned enough about the issues and individuals to vote. Some fear that government will be taken over by wealthy, well-organized interests that have only their self-interest at heart. Effective, democratic government needs voters who are interested in the common good of all citizens of the nation, state, or community.

_____ **530. Low voter turnout results in**

    A. less effective government.

    B. more efficient government.

    C. higher costs for government.

    D. influence of special interest groups.

Use the chart on page 173 to answer questions 531-533.

_____ **531. Which age group had the highest voter turnout in the 2000 general election in Georgia?**

    A. age 18-24

    B. age 35-45

    C. age 46-59

    D. age 60-64

_____ **532. Which group by race and gender had the highest participation in the 2000 election in Georgia?**

    A. black males

    B. white males

    C. black females

    D. white females

VOTING STATISTICS FOR GEORGIA GENERAL ELECTIONS		
Voting Category	**1996 Election**	**2000 Election**
Statewide turnout of voters	61.5%	69%
Percent of votes cast by white voters	78.8%	76.8%
Percent of votes cast by African Americans	21.2%	23.2%
Percent of votes cast by 18-24 year olds	5.6%	6.8%
Turnout among registered white voters		71.4%
Turnout among registered African American voters		62.8%
Percent of total ballots cast by women		55.4%
Percent of total ballots cast by men		44.6%
Selected turnout of voters by age		
Age 18-24		44.0%
Age 25-34		59.5%
Age 35-45		70.5%
Age 46-59		75.0%
Age 60-64		81.0%
Selected turnout of voters by race and gender		
Black female		67.0%
Black male		57.0%
White female		72.0%
White male		71.0%
Total female		70.1%
Total male		67.4%

____ 533. **Which age group had the lowest percentage of eligible voters participate in the 2000 election?**

    A. age 18-24

    B. age 25-34

    C. age 35-45

    D. age 60-64

____ 534. **Who is the chief election officer in Georgia?**

    A. governor

    B. county clerk

    C. county registrar

    D. secretary of state

SS8CG1 The student will describe the role of citizens under Georgia's constitution.
e. Explain the role of political parties in government.

ROLE OF POLITICAL PARTIES

Political parties are organized groups of people who share common ideals and who seek to influence government policies and decisions by electing members of their party to government offices. The first political parties in the country were the Federalists and the Antifederalists who fought over the powers of a central government as the U.S. Constitution was being written and ratified. These two groups evolved into two political groups known as the Federalists and the Democratic-Republicans. While these early political parties have changed over the years, we have maintained a two-party system.

Today, America has two major political parties–the Republican party and the Democratic party. Members of these groups share common beliefs about government's role in American life and the policies that government should support. People who are not members of these two major parties are usually referred to as *independents*.

There are minor political parties that do not have enough members to win major elections, but who do have an important role in the democratic process. Minor parties bring attention to specific minority ideas. As minor parties gather political support from more people, their ideas influence the thinking and the principles of party leaders in the two major political groups.

_____ 535. **What are the dominant political parties in Georgia today?**
A. Democratic and Republican
B. Republican and Independent
C. Federalist and Democratic-Republican
D. Independent, Democratic, and Republican

_____ 536. **Why are third parties important?**
A. They split the vote of the two major parties.
B. They make election campaigns more interesting.
C. They keep one party from becoming too powerful.
D. They give more people a way to express their ideas.

_____ 537. **Which statement LEAST explains the role of political parties today.**
A. Political parties give voters a choice.
B. Political parties raise funds for candidates.
C. Political parties work for the common man.
D. Political parties provide a set of issues with which individuals can relate.

S8CG2 The student will analyze the role of the legislative branch in Georgia state government.
a. Explain the qualifications, term, election, and duties of members of the General Assembly.

MEMBERS OF THE GENERAL ASSEMBLY

There are 180 members of the house of representatives and 56 members of the senate. Members of the legislature are elected by popular vote to two-year terms of office. There is no limit on the number of terms a representative or senator can serve. Each of these members is elected by voters in a house or senate district. Equally important, each house district contains about the same number of people as all of the other house districts. And each senate district contains about the same number of people as all the other senate districts.

At the time of their election, members of the senate are required by Georgia's constitution to be at least twenty-five years of age, citizens of the United States, and citizens of Georgia for at least two years. In addition, they must have been legal residents of the district from which they were elected for at least one year.

Members of the house of representatives must be at least twenty-one years of age, citizens of the United States, citizens of Georgia for at least two years, and legal residents of the district from which they were elected for at least one year.

The Georgia General Assembly meets each year for a forty-day session, beginning on the second Monday in January. Breaks and recesses do not count as part of the forty days, so the sessions usually last until the middle of March. The house of representatives and the senate operate in similar fashion except for two important differences. Only the house of representatives can write appropriations (spending) bills. Only the senate can confirm appointments the governor makes to executive offices. Either house can propose and pass bills, and all bills must be approved by both houses before being sent to the governor.

____ 538. **Which guideline is considered the MOST IMPORTANT for determining the boundaries for house and senate election districts every ten years?**
   A. incumbent members' district boundaries
   B. equal population distribution among districts
   C. keeping the dominant political party in power
   D. maintaining logical county and city boundaries

Use these requirements to answer question 539.

- must be at least 21 years old
- must be a citizen of the United States
- must be a resident of the district from which elected for one year

____ 539. **These are the requirements a candidate must meet to be elected as**
   A. governor.
   B. state senator.
   C. secretary of state.
   D. state representative.

____ 540. **What type of legislation must begin in the house of representatives?**
   A. transportation bills
   B. appropriation bills
   C. education amendments
   D. constitutional amendments

____ 541. **How long is the term of a member of the Georgia General Assembly?**
   A. 2 years
   B. 4 years
   C. 6 years
   D. 8 years

_____ **542. What unique power does the state senate have?**

    A. It confirms all executive appointments.

    B. It proposes constitutional amendments.

    C. It sends bills to the governor for a signature.

    D. It can override bills from the house of representatives.

S8CG2 **The student will analyze the role of the legislative branch in Georgia state government.**

    b. Describe the organization of the General Assembly, with emphasis on leadership and the committee system.

ORGANIZATION OF THE GENERAL ASSEMBLY

The General Assembly is bicameral; that is, it has two houses or chambers. One is the house of representatives, the second is the senate. As you read earlier, there are 180 members of the house of representatives and 56 members of the senate.

Leadership

The lieutenant governor presides over the senate. Members of the house of representatives elect a speaker as their presiding officer. The speaker, like the lieutenant governor, appoints committees and their chairpersons and assigns bills to those committees. The lieutenant governor does not have a vote in the senate, but the speaker of the house votes when it is necessary to break a tie.

A presiding officer also has the power to determine the order of business, control debate, rule out proposed amendments to bills, enforce rules of procedure for the General Assembly, control meeting times and recesses of the General Assembly, and order a roll call vote on any issue.

Committee System

Members of the Georgia house and senate are organized into committees. All bills must be reviewed by a house or senate committee before they can be brought to either the whole house or sent for a vote. The committee system makes it possible for members to study bills closely. There would not be time for such study if each bill were discussed only by the entire house or senate.

Some committees are permanent, lasting from one session to the next. These are called *standing committees*. Some of the standing committees include the Ways and Means Committee, which handles bills involving taxes; the Appropriations Committee, which works on the budget; and the Judiciary Committee, which deals with bills concerning the state's laws and court system.

Other committees are organized for a special task and last only until their work is completed. One type of special committee is an *interim committee*, one that works on assigned issues and concerns between sessions of the legislature. Another special committee is the conference committee, which is appointed when the house and senate pass different versions of a bill. The conference committee, which is made up of three senators and three representatives, takes the two versions and tries to write one bill that can be passed by both houses. A joint committee, another special committee, is made up of members from both houses and works on an assigned topic or issue.

A member of the Georgia General Assembly may serve on several committees. Committee chairpersons decide when their committees will meet. They choose the order in which assigned bills will be discussed and when the bills will be voted on.

____ **543. What are the two parts of Georgia's legislative branch?**
- A. supreme court and governor
- B. secretary of state and senate
- C. governor and General Assembly
- D. senate and house of representatives

____ **544. The presiding officer of the senate or the house of representatives does NOT**
- A. appoint committee members.
- B. assign proposed bills to committees.
- C. approve all legislation submitted to the governor.
- D. recognize speakers to discuss or debate issues on the floor.

____ **545. To which legislative committee are tax bills assigned?**
- A. Revenue Committee
- B. Income Tax Committee
- C. Appropriations Committee
- D. Ways and Means Committee

____ **546. Which is an example of a permanent legislative committee?**
- A. joint
- B. interim
- C. standing
- D. conference

____ **547. The main purpose of a legislative committee is to**
- A. decide which bills to send to the governor.
- B. propose bills to be considered by the full chamber.
- C. draft bills that have the best chance to become law.
- D. review bills before they come to the floor for discussion.

S8CG2   The student will analyze the role of the legislative branch in Georgia government.
  c. Evaluate how the legislative branch fulfills its role as the lawmaking body for the state of Georgia.

THE LEGISLATIVE BRANCH

The Georgia state constitution grants law-making power to the legislative branch. The General Assembly can pass laws on any matter not denied it by the U.S. Constitution. It can amend state laws or do away with them. The General Assembly can pass legislation on such matters as taxes, education, contracts, and real and personal property. Other subjects it deals with include inheritances, mortgages, corporations, and marriage and divorce. The legislature makes laws concerning fines, imprisonment, or death in criminal matters. It also considers public regulation, laws affecting such issues as morals, public health, business or professional regulations, or any general welfare rule that restricts personal property.

How a Bill Becomes a Law

Any citizen may suggest an idea for a law, and any senator or representative can propose a bill for consideration. All **bills** (proposed laws) that affect how the state raises or spends money must start in the house of representatives. Bills about anything else may begin in either house.

Bills in the Georgia General Assembly go through almost the same steps as those in the U.S. Congress before they become law. Let us look at a bill that starts in the state house of representatives.

1. A proposal is written in legal language and turned in to the clerk's office. There it is given a name and number. For example, the twelfth proposal turned in to the clerk of the house of representatives during a session will be "H.R. 12." After the proposal is given a number, it is called a bill.

2. Copies of the bill are made for members of the house. The bill is then assigned to a committee.

3. The committee to which the bill is assigned may hold public hearings so that interested persons may speak for or against the bill. The committee may also ask legislative staff members to gather information about the bill. The committee studies the bill and discusses its good and bad points.

4. The committee assigned to handle the bill can do several things: (a) It can hold the bill and not release it to the house; (b) It can vote the bill out of committee and recommend that it be passed; (c) It can vote the bill out of committee and recommend that it not be passed; (d) It can make changes in the bill and vote the new version out for consideration by the house; and (e) In the house only, it can vote the bill out of committee with no recommendation. If a bill is not voted out of committee, it is "killed" unless the full house votes to take the bill from the committee and assign it to another one.

5. A bill sent to the full house is discussed, debated, and perhaps amended. A majority vote is required to pass a bill.

6. When a bill is "certified" (passed) by the house, it is carried by messenger to the senate for consideration.

7. Again, the bill is assigned to a committee and studied. As before, the bill may be kept in committee, changed, or voted out without change to be handled by the entire senate.

8. If both the house and the senate pass a bill in the same form, it is signed by the presiding officers and clerks before being sent to the governor.

9. The governor can handle a bill in one of three ways. He or she can (a) sign it into law; (b) take no action, thus letting it become law automatically; or (c) veto it. If a bill is vetoed, the General Assembly can override the veto by a two-thirds vote of both houses. The bill then becomes law.

Remember that for a bill to become a law, the same version of the bill must be passed by both the house of representatives and the senate. Suppose that the senate passes a slightly different version of a bill than the one adopted by the house. When this happens, the amended bill must be sent back to the house to be reconsidered. If the two houses cannot agree to pass identical versions of a bill, the two versions are sent to a conference committee, which works out a compromise bill that both houses will accept. The compromise bill must be passed by both the senate and the house of representatives before it is sent to the governor.

____ **548. Which branch of Georgia state government has as its main responsibility the writing of state laws?**

    A. council

    B. judicial

    C. executive

    D. legislative

____ 549. **Which accurately describes the powers of the Georgia General Assembly?**
- A. It has powers specifically designated in both the U.S. and state constitutions.
- B. It has sole power over some areas and split power with the U.S. government in other areas.
- C. It has law-making power over all areas not specifically assigned to the United States Constitution.
- D. It has law-making powers over all areas of Georgia involving money, taxes, revenue, and appropriations.

____ 550. **In order for a bill to become a law in Georgia, it must**
- A. receive the signature of the president.
- B. be voted on by the people in a referendum.
- C. receive a unanimous vote in both the Senate and the House.
- D. be introduced by a legislator and receive a majority vote in both houses.

____ 551. **What happens to a bill passed by the legislature if the governor does not veto it, but does not sign it?**
- A. The bill is killed.
- B. The bill becomes law.
- C. The bill goes back to the senate.
- D. The bill goes back to the house of representatives.

____ 552. **What is the correct sequence for a bill to become a law?**
1. The bill is assigned to a committee.
2. Copies of bills are given to the legislator.
3. The governor may sign the bill.
4. The bill is sent to full chamber.
- A. 2-1-4-3
- B. 1-2-4-3
- C. 2-4-1-3
- D. 4-2-1-3

> **SS8CG3** The student will analyze the role of the executive branch in Georgia state government.
> a. Explain the qualifications, term, election, and duties of the governor and lieutenant governor.

EXECUTIVE BRANCH

The largest branch of state government is the executive branch. It is the responsibility of the executive branch to ensure that the state's laws are carried out. The executive branch is also responsible for the day-to-day management of the state.

Governor

The **governor** is the chief executive officer of the state. The governor is elected by a majority of the popular vote for a four-year term. The constitution allows governors to serve two consecutive terms, so it is possible for one person to be the state's chief executive officer for eight years. After a second term, an individual has to wait four or more years before being able to run again.

The constitution outlines the qualifications required to be elected as Georgia's chief executive. The candidate who wishes to become governor must be at least thirty years of age when taking office, a citizen of the United States for at least fifteen years, and a resident of the state for at least six years.

Formal Powers of the Governor

The Georgia constitution describes the governor's formal powers. They can be classified as executive powers, legislative powers, and judicial powers.

Executive powers include being able to appoint state officials and making sure that civil and criminal laws are enforced.

Legislative powers include sending requests and messages to the legislature, signing bills into law, and being able to veto a bill so it does not become a law. The governor may also call special sessions of the legislature.

Judicial powers include being able to pardon persons convicted of crimes and appoint state justices to fill unexpired terms.

The formal powers of the governor include:

- managing the state's budget (the plan for receiving and spending money),
- directing the attorney general to act as a representative of the state in lower court cases involving state law,
- making an annual "State of the State" address to the legislature,
- preparing budget bills for consideration by the Georgia house of representatives,
- serving as commander-in-chief of the Georgia National Guard,
- heading the state's civil defense units, and
- sending Georgia Highway Patrol officers and the Georgia Bureau of Investigation into communities in times of danger.

Informal Powers of the Governor

Georgia's governor also has many informal powers. Some are the result of tradition and custom; others are necessary to enforce the formal powers.

The informal powers of the governor include:

- communicating to the public a personal position on issues of interest to all Georgians,
- acting as honorary head of the political party that elected him or her to office,
- issuing proclamations to honor individuals, holidays, or special events and, with the legislature's approval, adding new state symbols,
- representing the state in meetings with other state officials, federal officers, or foreign dignitaries,
- meeting with business and industry leaders from other states or nations to encourage them to expand their businesses into Georgia,
- working with members of the legislature to get laws passed, and
- guiding state agencies.

Sometimes the governor's informal powers may seem more important than the formal powers. But a governor's greatest influence is through his or her power to appoint individuals to boards and executive offices.

Lieutenant Governor

The executive branch of state government also includes the office of **lieutenant governor**. The lieutenant governor is elected by popular vote at the same time the governor is elected. The lieutenant governor must meet the same qualifications for office as the govenor. However, unlike the governor, the lieutenant governor can serve an unlimited number of consecutive terms in office. For example, Zell Miller served four consecutive terms as lieutenant governor.

The lieutenant governor is the presiding officer of the state senate. In that position, he or she makes senate committee appointments, assigns senate bills to committees, and recognizes members of the senate who wish to speak. Because of these powers, the lieutenant governor may affect the passage or failure of some senate bills.

In the event of a governor's death, resignation, or impeachment, the lieutenant governor becomes the state's chief executive. The lieutenant governor also serves as the chief executive officer when the governor is out of the state.

Should both the governor and the lieutenant governor die or resign from office in the midst of a term, the speaker of the house of representatives serves as the chief executive until a new governor is elected.

____ **553. What branch of Georgia's government sees that the state's laws are implemented?**
   A. judicial
   B. executive
   C. legislative
   D. commission

____ **554. Why is the power to make appointments to boards and executive offices important to the governor of Georgia?**
   A. By appointing persons from the same political party, the governor can help one party dominate state government.
   B. Through appointments, a governor can spread his or her influence far beyond the limited powers of the governor's office.
   C. Through appointments to boards and executive offices, a governor can control the actions of all state agencies and boards.
   D. By appointing political backers and campaign contributors, the governor can repay supporters and raise money for future campaigns.

____ **555. An example of an executive power given to the governor is the power to**
   A. sign bills into laws
   B. appoint heads of agencies
   C. send messages to law makers
   D. call special sessions of the legislature

____ **556. According to Georgia's constitution, how many consecutive years can a lieutenant governor serve in that capacity?**
   A. 4 years
   B. 8 years
   C. 16 years
   D. undefined number of years

_____ **557. The lieutenant governor most effectively affects the passage or failure of legislation in the state senate by**

    A. how he or she votes on a bill.

    B. assigning senate bills to committee.

    C. being able to veto bills in committee.

    D. establishing the senate meeting schedules.

SS8CG3   The student will analyze the role of the executive branch in Georgia state government.

    b. Describe the organization of the executive branch, with emphasis on major policy areas of state programs; include education, human resources, public safety, transportation, economic development, and natural resources.

    c. Explain how the executive branch fulfills its role through state agencies that administer programs and enforce laws.

ORGANIZATION OF THE EXECUTIVE BRANCH

The governor and lieutenant governor are not the only elected members of Georgia's executive branch. Voters statewide select the following officials:

- *State attorney general*, who is the chief legal officer for the state and the head of the Department of Law.

- *Commissioner of agriculture*, who is the head of the Agriculture Department. The commissioner directs agricultural or agribusiness programs, maintains state farmers' markets, supervises services such as inspections, and expands market opportunities for Georgia agriculture.

- *Commissioner of labor*, who is the head of the Labor Department. The labor commissioner regulates the health and safety of workers, enforces state labor laws, administers unemployment insurance programs, and maintains statistical data on labor.

- *Commissioner of insurance*, who regulates insurance carriers and issues insurance licenses.

- Public service commissioners, who regulate utilities in Georgia and control the rates and services of transportation companies, telephone companies, and electric companies.

- *Secretary of state*, who maintains the state's official records, publishes laws passed by the legislature, supervises elections, appoints examining boards, grants corporate charters, and regulates securities, stocks, and bonds.

- *State school superintendent*, who is the head of the Department of Education. The superintendent directs statewide educational programs, enforces state education regulations and laws, administers state and federal education funds, certifies and licenses teachers and other educators, and approves textbooks for use in Georgia schools.

All of these officials serve four-year terms of office, except for the five members of the Public Service Commission. They serve six-year terms.

STATE AGENCIES

In addition to the officials named in the Georgia constitution, there are a large number of government officials known as *statutory officials*. Their positions are not provided for in the state's constitution, nor are they are elected officials. But their jobs are called for by statute (law). These officials are appointed either by the governor or by the head or directing boards of the department in which they serve. For example, the chief drug inspector is appointed by the commissioner of agriculture.

Another sector of Georgia's government are the boards and agencies that were created by the state constitution or by statute. There are over thirty major agencies in our government. The State Board of Pardons and Paroles, the Board of Natural Resources, and the State Personnel Board are examples of governing boards created by Georgia's constitution. The Board of Human Resources and the Board of Public Safety were created by state statute. Members of most boards are appointed by the governor. Usually, board members have staggered terms of office so that the terms of all members do not expire at the same time.

____ 558. **Which branch of Georgia's government is the largest?**
   A. local branch
   B. judicial branch
   C. executive branch
   D. legislative branch

____ 559. **Because Georgia's government is involved in many legal affairs, its officials sometime need legal advice. What state official provides this advice?**
   A. attorney general
   B. secretary of state
   C. lieutenant governor
   D. commissioner of labor

____ 560. **Which elected state official controls the administration of state and federal education funds?**
   A. governor
   B. state treasurer
   C. state school superintendent
   D. director of Department of Revenue

____ 561. **Which office maintains the state's official records and supervises elections?**
   A. Secretary of State
   B. Board of Transportation
   C. Department of Community Affairs
   D. Department of Administrative Services

SS8CG4   The student will analyze the role of the judicial branch in Georgia state government.
   a. Explain the structure of the court system in Georgia including trial and appellate procedures and how judges are selected.
   e. Evaluate how the judicial branch fulfills its role in interpreting the laws of Georgia and ensuring justice in our legal system.

JUDICIAL BRANCH

The judicial branch of government consists of the state's courts. Their role is to interpret the state constitution, protect the legal rights of citizens, and enforce the laws of the state.

Structure of Courts

The highest-ranking court in the Georgia court system is the **supreme court**. The seven supreme court justices are elected by popular vote to six-year terms. If a supreme court justice resigns or dies before the end of a term, the governor may appoint a justice to complete his or her term of office. Supreme court justices elect the chief justice from among themselves. The supreme court is an *appellate court*, which means it only reviews cases on appeal from lower-ranking courts. There are no witnesses and juries as there are in lower-ranking trial courts.

Another responsibility of the supreme court is to interpret the state constitution. It may review cases involving the constitutionality of laws, title to land, equity, wills, habeas corpus, divorce, and alimony. The supreme court automatically reviews all Georgia cases involving the death penalty. It also outlines a code of judicial conduct for the judges of the state, and regulates the admission of attorneys to practice law in Georgia. Decisions of the supreme court are binding. This means they have the final authority in matters of law at the state level.

The second highest-ranking state court is the **court of appeals**. Twelve judges serve on this court, and they elect one of their members to serve as the chief judge. The judges are elected to six-year terms. The court of appeals, like the supreme court, is an appellate court. It only hears cases appealed from lower-ranking courts.

Below the appellate courts are the **trial courts** of Georgia. The trial courts hear original cases, such as criminal cases and civil cases between private parties. The state's trial courts include 188 superior courts in 49 circuits (regions), 70 state courts, 159 probate courts, 159 juvenile courts, and 159 magistrate courts. Over 400 municipal (city) courts and special courts are also part of Georgia's judicial branch.

Interpreting Laws/Ensuring Justice

Courts enforce constitutional laws, statutory laws (those passed by the General Assembly), administrative laws (regulations of executive branch agencies), and case laws (court interpretations of written laws). The courts protect citizens from abuses by government by ensuring that each citizen has "due process of law." The U.S. Constitution says no state can deprive any citizen of life, liberty, or property without due process of law. This means that persons arrested for a crime have the right to have a lawyer present during questioning. Individuals must be given a speedy, public trial before a fair judge and jury. They may face and question witnesses, or they can remain silent so as not to incriminate (blame) themselves.

_____ 562. **Federal judges are appointed by the president of the United States. How are positions in Georgia's state courts filled?**

A. elected by Georgia voters

B. elected by Georgia's legislature

C. appointed by Georgia's governor

D. appointed by the US Supreme Court

_____ 563. **Who established the code of judicial conduct for judges of Georgia and regulates the admission of attorneys to the practice of law in the state?**

A. governor of Georgia

B. supreme court of Georgia

C. attorney general of Georgia

D. General Assembly of Georgia

____ **564. How many justices serve on the Georgia state supreme court?**

    A. 5

    B. 7

    C. 9

    D. 11

Use these items to answer question 565.

- the right to a speedy public trial
- the right to have a lawyer present during questioning
- the right to remain silent so as not to incriminate oneself

____ **565. These legal rights are part of**

    A. due process

    B. habeas corpus

    C. judicial review

    D. separation of powers

____ **566. Cases are automatically reviewed by the state supreme court when they deal with**

    A. wills.

    B. land titles.

    C. habeas corpus.

    D. the death penalty.

> **SS8CG4 The student will analyze the role of the judicial branch in Georgia state government.**
>
>   c. Describe the adult justice system, emphasizing the different jurisdictions, terminology, and steps in the criminal justice process.

ADULT JUSTICE SYSTEM

The trial courts of the state hear original cases. Each court has a special jurisdiction (the range of actions over which the court has control or influence). For example, the juvenile court handles cases involving persons under the age of seventeen. The probate court deals with the wills and estates of deceased persons. Magistrate courts can only hear civil cases involving sums under $15,000.

An important part of Georgia's court system is the concept of a jury trial, a trial before one's peers. There are two types of juries--a grand jury and a trial jury. The **grand jury** determines whether or not persons accused of crimes should be indicted (officially charged) and required to stand trial. A **trial jury** is a group of citizens who are charged with judging a person charged with a crime.

____ **567. A grand jury in Georgia decides whether or not a**

    A. due process of law was followed.

    B. person accused of a crime is guilty or innocent.

    C. law, statute, or regulation of the state has been violated or broken.

    D. person accused of a crime should be charged and stand trial for that crime.

____ 568. **Which statement BEST describes how the grand jury protects individual citizens from abuses of power by elected officials?**

    A. Citizens cannot be denied due process of law without approval of the grand jury.

    B. Citizens accused of crimes cannot be charged and tried without the approval of the grand jury.

    C. Citizens cannot receive the death penalty in Georgia without a review of their sentences by the grand jury.

    D. Citizens elected to public office cannot be accused of crimes without a review of those charges by a grand jury.

SS8CG4   The student will analyze the role of the judicial branch in Georgia state government.

    b. Explain the difference between criminal law and civil law.

CRIMINAL LAW AND CIVIL LAW

The courts protect citizens from each other by handling **civil cases** (disputes between two or more persons or groups) and **criminal cases** (cases involving violations of the law).

Civil lawsuits are personal; that is, they do not affect all of society. Civil law covers such issues as citizenship, property rights, contracts, marriage and divorce, child custody, and inheritance. The person or group who brings the legal action is called the *plaintiff*, and the person or group against whom the legal action is brought is called the *defendant*.

The state (called the *prosecution*) brings criminal charges against an individual, and a trial determines the guilt of the defendant. Crimes are divided into felonies and misdemeanors. A **felony** is a serious crime such as murder or burglary, punishable by a year or more in prison, a fine of at least $1,000, or both. A **misdemeanor** is a less serious crime punishable by less than a year in prison, a fine of less than $1,000, or both.

____ 569. **Who has the burden of proof in a criminal case?**

    A. state

    B. plaintiff

    C. accused

    D. defendant

____ 570. **Who has the burden of proof in a civil case?**

    D. state

    C. plaintiff

    A. accused

    B. defendant

____ 571. **Which is NOT a criminal charge?**

    A. rape

    B. fraud

    C. robbery

    D. murder

_____ 572. **What are the most serious criminal crimes called?**

D. torts

C. felonies

B. insurrections

A. misdemeanors

SS8CG4   The student will analyze the role of the judicial branch in Georgia state government.

d. Describe ways to avoid trouble and settle disputes peacefully.

SETTLING DISPUTES PEACEFULLY

Filing a lawsuit in a civil matter is one way to settle a dispute peacefully. There are other ways, including mediation, arbitration, compromise, negotiation, collaboration, and nonviolence.

Mediation is a way to resolve disputes in which a neutral third person meets with the two (or more) opposing sides and helps them reach an agreement. In mediation, the parties themselves determine the resolution, rather than having the resolution imposed by a third party. With arbitration, the opposing parties designate a neutral third party (called an arbitrator) and agree in advance to accept the arbitrator's solution to the disagreement. Arbitration is often used in disagreements between labor unions and management. In a compromise, each of the opposing parties gives up something in order to settle the dispute. The Missouri Compromise and the Compromise of 1850 are two well-known historical compromises. *Negotiation* is the process of discussing an issue with the intention of resolving it. Negotiation is often used to settle on the selling price of real estate. When negotiation is used in international relations, it is called *diplomacy. Collaboration* occurs when the opposing parties work together to identify common ground or objectives. Collaboration often takes place in the writing of books or songs. Finally, nonviolence is a method of seeking change that specifically rejects violence. Reverend Martin Luther King, Jr., was a proponent of the use of nonviolence in the civil rights movement.

_____ 573. **Which is NOT a method of solving conflicts peacefully?**

A. war

B. mediation

C. compromise

D. collaboration

_____ 574. **Which is NOT a good method to solve a conflict with a friend?**

A. be a good listener.

B. be confrontational.

C. argue your position.

D. have a face-to-face meeting.

_____ 575. **Which piece of advice is LEAST effective when disagreeing diplomatically?**

A. Be firm in your convictions.

B. State your position or opinion clearly.

C. Summarize your understanding of the other point of view.

D. Demonstrate the value you hold for the person with an opposite point of view.

Use this incident to answer question 576.

Tom and John are friends who go to the same school. Tom often borrows things from John, i.e., pencils, books, paper. Although John and Tom get along well, sometimes John gets irritated with his friend when Tom doesn't return the things he borrows.

One day, Tom asks to borrow John's cell phone. Because Tom has not returned borrowed items in the past, John refuses to loan him the phone. Tom becomes angry and accuses John of not being his friend. John counters that Tom is the one who is not a good friend because he never returns anything. Tom calls John a name and John lunges at him, punching him in the face. Before anything else happens, a teacher, seeing the confrontation, takes both boys to the office.

_____ 576. **How could this incident BEST be resolved without resorting to violence?**
A. allowing Tom to have the phone
B. arguing the responsibility of friendship
C. having a third party mediate the argument
D. having both boys tell their side of the story

SS8CG5   The student will analyze the role of local governments in the state of Georgia.

a. Explain the origins, functions, purposes, and differences of county and city governments in Georgia.

d. Evaluate the role of local government working with state agencies to administer state programs.

COUNTY AND CITY GOVERNMENT

Local governments are the most numerous of all governments in the United States. Georgia has 159 counties, and each of these counties has a government. In addition to the counties, there are almost six hundred cities in Georgia. Each of them has a government.

Not only are local governments the most numerous, they are also the closest to the people and the most likely to affect people directly. Local governments get their powers and their right to exist from the Georgia state constitution.

County Government

Counties are subdivisions of the state set up to carry out certain governmental functions. The state constitution sets out county powers. They include the power to tax to cover the cost of county administration; police (sheriff) and legal systems; construction and maintenance of roads and bridges; public health; medical care for people who cannot afford to pay; assistance to dependent children; parks and libraries; and public education.

The state constitution also requires that all county governments be uniform (organized the same way). However, the General Assembly may, in any county, establish commissioners of roads and revenues, consolidate the offices of tax receiver and tax collector into the office of tax commissioner, and abolish the office of treasurer. Most county governments are headed by elected **boards of commissioners**.

The commissioners are elected by the voters for four-year, staggered terms. The board of commissioners has the authority to establish county policies, adopt county ordinances (laws), establish the county budget, establish tax rates, and provide services for the citizens of the county. A county administrator, appointed by the board of commissioners, serves as the chief administrative officer.

Based on its population, each county has a different number of officials. Most counties have at least the following elected officials: commissioners, clerk of the superior court, judge of the probate court, tax commissioner, sheriff, and coroner.

Most county officials are appointed rather than elected. Examples of some appointed county officials include: county clerks, attorneys, tax assessors, emergency management services directors, fire chiefs, planning and building inspectors, registrars, roads supervisors, animal control officers, surveyors, and environmentalists.

City Goverment

A city with its own government is called a **municipality**. Georgia's first city was Savannah, and Augusta was the state's second city.

A city exists as a political unit when it receives a charter from the state legislature. To be chartered as a city, an area must meet three requirements: (1) It must have at least 200 residents; (2) It must be located at least three miles from the boundaries of the nearest city; and (3) It must have 60 percent of its land divided into tracts (parcels of land) or being used for residential, business, industrial, institutional, or government purposes.

A city government can do only what it charter authorizes it to do. For example, most city charters allow cities to provide police protection, license businesses, maintain streets and sidewalks, control traffic, and provide water and sewerage services. Other services to the citizens may be provided if they are included specifically in a city's charter. For example, Atlanta and twenty other cities in the state operate their own school systems because that power was granted by the state in their charters.

Consolidated Government

Some counties provide services outside of incorporated municipalities for things such as water, sewage, sanitation, and fire protection. As long as city and county governments provide different types of services in the same area, they do not get in each other's way. However, as a county becomes more urban, city and county governments may provide the same services to the same people.

One way to avoid this duplication is for city and county governments to form a single government. Several such mergers have taken place. For example, the city of Columbus and Muscogee County merged in 1971, and Athens and Clarke County formed a single government unit in 1991. Augusta and Richmond County merged in 1995, becoming the third consolidated government in Georgia.

_____ 577. **The main governing authority in almost all of Georgia's counties is the**
   A. mayor.
   B. judge.
   C. transit authority.
   D. board of commissioners.

_____ 578. **A Government in which a city and county government have joined to form a single government is called a(n)**
   A. city governmet.
   B. county government.
   C. municipal government.
   D. consolidated government.

_____ 579. **Which county official is elected rather than appointed?**
   A. clerk
   B. registrar
   C. commissioner
   D. road supervisor

____ **580. Which term describes a city with its own government?**

  A. town

  B. village

  C. megalopolis

  D. municipality

Use the map to answer questions 581-583.

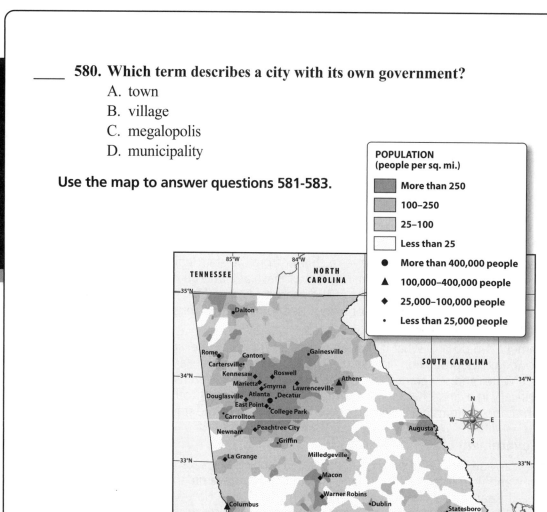

POPULATION
(people per sq. mi.)

More than 250

100–250

25–100

Less than 25

● More than 400,000 people

▲ 100,000–400,000 people

◆ 25,000–100,000 people

· Less than 25,000 people

____ **581. Which Georgia city has the largest population?**

  A. Albany

  B. Atlanta

  C. Valdosta

  D. Warner Robins

____ **582. Which city is located in an area with few people?**

  A. Augusta

  B. Valdosta

  C. Savannah

  D. East Point

_____ **583. What is the distance between Augusta and Savannah?**
   A. 50 miles
   B. 75 miles
   C. 100 miles
   D. 150 miles

> **SS8CG5   The student will analyze the role of local governments in the state of Georgia.**
>   b. Compare and contrast the weak mayor-council, the strong mayor-council, and the council-manager forms of city government.

FORMS OF CITY GOVERNMENT

The most common forms of city government are the mayor-council form, the council-manager form, and the commission form.

In the **mayor-council form** of government, the elected city council is responsible for making the laws. An elected mayor acts as the city's chief executive officer and is responsible for seeing that the laws are carried out and that city agencies do their jobs. The mayor may be either "weak" or "strong." In a *weak-mayor system*, the city council has both legislative and executive powers. The mayor has limited powers, appoints few city officials, and has little veto power. The mayor is primarily a figurehead (a person who is the head of an organization but who has no powers) who presides over council meetings and performs other ceremonial duties. Smyrna has a weak-mayor system. In the *strong-mayor system*, the mayor is a strong leader who proposes legislation, prepares the budget, appoints all department heads, and has veto power. Atlanta has a strong-mayor system.

In the **council-manager form** of government, the voters elect a city council that establishes laws and policies. There is a mayor who may be elected or named by the council. The council hires a city manager who is responsible for the day-to-day operation of the city. The city manager appoints the heads of city governments and sees that they carry out their jobs. Savannah has a council-manager form of government.

In cities with a **commission form** of government, the voters elect commissioners. Each commissioner is the head of a department within the city government, such as finance, streets, public safety, and so on. The mayor is elected by the commissioners from among themselves. Decatur has a commission form of government.

_____ **584. Why would large cities in Georgia be more likely than small cities to use an elected council and full-time manager?**
   A. Small cities in Georgia are required by the state to have a mayor and not a full-time manager.
   B. Large cities need a full-time manager to take care of the complex problems of a large population.
   C. Large cities in Georgia are required by the state to have an elected council and a full-time manager.
   D. Small cities have little reason to have a council but need a full-time manager to supervise the many complicated activities involved in running a city.

_____ **585. Which description of a council-manager form of city government is FALSE?**
   A. The council is appointed or elected.
   B. The mayor may be appointed or elected.
   C. The city council establishes laws and policies.
   D. The city manager oversees the day-to-day operation of government.

____ **586. Which is the most common type of city government in Georgia?**

    A. commission

    B. mayor-council

    C. council-manager

    D. board of commissioners-mayor

____ **587. Which statement about strong-mayor and weak-mayor forms of government is FALSE?**

    A. In a strong-mayor form of government, the mayor prepares the budget.

    B. In a weak-mayor form of government, the mayor serves as a figurehead.

    C. In a weak-mayor form of government, the council appoints department heads.

    D. In a strong-mayor form of government, the mayor only performs ceremonial duties.

SS8CG5   **The student will analyze the role of local governments in the state of Georgia.**

c. Describe the functions of special-purpose governments.

SPECIAL-PURPOSE GOVERNMENTS

There are a number of special-purpose districts in Georgia. Generally, a **special-purpose district** is created for a single job or single group of tasks. Most such districts govern themselves. A school system is one example of a special district. State law requires children to attend school, but much of the control of that school is left up to a local board of education and the school district office. Within the guidelines set by state law, local school systems can establish starting and stopping times for the school day, spell out standards of behavior and punishment, determine dress codes, and schedule students' time during the school day.

Within the metropolitan area of Atlanta, the Metropolitan Atlanta Rapid Transit Authority (MARTA) is another special-purpose district. MARTA runs a bus and rail system, determines the cost of fares, selects routes, and schedules public transportation times. The Public Housing Authority is a special-purpose district. It provides services such as determining the location of public housing, constructing and maintaining the buildings, renting the units, and drawing up tenants' rules and regulations.

Other special-purpose districts include community fire departments, parks and recreation authorities, and airport and port authorities. No matter what individual special-purpose districts are called, they all have one thing in common: they exist to provide for the public's welfare.

Use these items to answer question 588.

- county board of education
- airport authority
- port authority

____ **588. These are examples of what type of government?**

    A. state

    B. county

    C. city-municipal

    D. special-purpose

____ 589. **What is the main goal of special-purpose governments?**
    A. to consolidate services
    B. to save taxpayers money
    C. to provide for the public welfare
    D. to bring government closer to the people

> **SS8CG6**   **The student will explain how the Georgia court system treats juvenile offenders.**
> a. Explain the difference between delinquent behavior and unruly behavior and the consequences of each.

DELINQUENT BEHAVIOR AND UNRULY BEHAVIOR

Juveniles are citizens under the age of seventeen. As citizens, juveniles must follow the same local, state, and federal laws that all other citizens follow. But juveniles have special status under the law, and they must also follow some laws that do not apply to adults. For example, they must attend school until at least age sixteen. They cannot run away from home. They cannot possess alcoholic beverages or tobacco until ages twenty-one and eighteen respectively.

Two terms are important to understand juvenile laws and courts. A *delinquent* act is an act that would be considered a crime if committed by an adult. Burglary and car theft are examples of delinquent acts. A *status offense* refers to an act that would not be considered a crime if committed by an adult. Examples of status offenses include running away from home and being repeatedly truant from school.

____ 590. **Delinquent juveniles are those who**
    A. are seventeen years of age and commit serious traffic offenses.
    B. are under eighteen years of age and have been neglected or abused by parent or guardians.
    C. are under seventeen years of age and who commit acts that would be crimes if they were committed by adults.
    D. are under eighteen years of age and who commit acts that would not be considered crimes if they were committed by adults.

____ 591. **A juvenile in Georgia is one who is under the age of**
    A. 15.
    B. 16.
    C. 17.
    D. 18.

> **SS8CG6**   **The student will explain how the Georgia court system treats juvenile offenders.**
> b. Describe the rights of juveniles when taken into custody.

RIGHTS OF JUVENILES

When juveniles commit a delinquent act or a status offense and are captured by the police, they are said to be "taken into custody" rather than "under arrest."

Juveniles handled under the juvenile justice system have the same basic legal rights that other citizens have. These rights are set out in Amendments 1, 4, and 5 of the U.S. Constitution Juveniles have the right to have their cases decided quickly, just as adults have the right to a speedy trial. Juvenile cases, however, are decided by a judge, not a jury.

Juvenile court proceedings can result in the loss of liberty. As a result, juveniles have all of the rights to a fair trial: They must be notified of the charges against them; they are protected against self-incrimination; they have the right to an attorney; and they have the right to confront and to question witnesses against them. The accused juvenile has the right to present a defense, to introduce evidence, and to testify on his or her own behalf. Most importantly, the juvenile has the right to have a parent or a guardian present in all hearings. If a child's parents or guardian cannot afford a lawyer, the court must appoint an attorney to represent the child.

_____ 592. **Juveniles in Georgia are NOT guaranteed the right to**
- A. post bail
- B. a fair trial.
- C. an attorney.
- D. due process.

_____ 593. **Which protection does NOT apply to juveniles in Georgia's courts?**
- A. the right to a trial before a jury of peers
- B. the right to be represented by an attorney
- C. the right to confront and question witnesses against them
- D. the right to present a defense, and testify on one's own behalf

> **SS8CG6   The student will explain how the Georgia court system treats juvenile offenders.**
> c. Describe the juvenile justice system, emphasizing the different jurisdictions, terminology, and steps in the juvenile justice process.

JUVENILE JUSTICE SYSTEM

As citizens, juveniles must follow the same local, state, and federal laws that all other citizens follow. But juveniles have special status under the law, and they must also follow some laws that do not apply to adults. For example, they must attend school until at least age sixteen. They cannot run away from home. They cannot possess alcoholic beverages or tobacco until ages twenty-one and eighteen, respectively. In addition, juveniles may not hang around public places or wander the streets breaking local curfews, which are usually 12 midnight to 5 a.m. Juveniles cannot enter bars where alcoholic beverages are sold unless accompanied by a parent or guardian. Finally, juveniles are required to obey all of the reasonable and lawful instructions or commands of their parents or guardian.

The Juvenile Court System

In 1906, the Georgia General Assembly passed a law establishing a special court for juveniles. In 1911, Fulton County became the first county in Georgia to set up a juvenile court.

Today, every county in Georgia has one. The judges in juvenile courts are appointed to that position by superior court judges.

The juvenile courts have three main purposes: (1) to help and protect the well-being of children, (2) to make sure that any child coming under the jurisdiction of the court receives the care, guidance, and control needed, and (3) to provide care for children who have been removed from their homes.

Georgia's juvenile courts have jurisdiction over the following cases:
- Juveniles who commit traffic offenses;
- Delinquent juveniles;
- Unruly juveniles;
- Juveniles under the supervision or probation of the court;

- Deprived juveniles, children under the age of eighteen who are neglected or abused by parents or guardians or those who have no parents or legal guardians;
- Cases involving children who need mental health services; and
- Proceedings involving judicial consent for marriage, employment, or enlistment in the armed services when such consent is required by law.

Steps in the Juvenile Justice Process

When a juvenile is taken into custody, the first step is *intake*. At this time, the juvenile is turned over to a juvenile court intake officer, who investigates the case. The intake officer must decide if there is enough evidence (probable cause) to support the charges made against the juvenile. If there is not enough evidence, the intake officer must release the juvenile.

If there is enough evidence to think the juvenile may be guilty of the charges, the intake officer may (1) release the juvenile into the custody of his or her parents or legal guardian or (2) detain the juvenile. In Georgia's juvenile system, most juveniles are not detained but are released into the custody of parents or guardians. Juveniles who are detained are housed in one of the state's Regional Youth Detention Centers. In certain special circumstances, juveniles charged with serious crimes can be placed in adult jails and tried by adult superior courts rather than juvenile courts.

The second step is *detention*. If the juvenile is detained, a probable cause hearing before the juvenile judge must be held within seventy-two hours. At that point, the judge has three options: (1) dismiss the case, (2) have an *informal adjustment*, or (3) have a *formal hearing*.

Generally, an informal adjustment is held for first offenders. The juvenile and his or her parents or guardian must agree to the informal adjustment, and the young person must admit the wrongdoing. The juvenile is under the supervision of the court for at least ninety days. While under the court's supervision, the juvenile might be required to attend school regularly or participate in counseling programs. The juvenile may also be required to pay for any damages caused or to complete community service requirements.

If an informal adjustment is not held, the third step in the juvenile justice process is a *formal hearing*. First, the complaining witness files a petition outlining the wrongdoing. Once the petition is signed, a date is set for the formal hearing and a summons issued. The *summons* requires the juvenile, the parents or guardian, and those involved in the charges to attend the hearing.

The first part of a formal hearing is the *adjudicatory hearing*, which is somewhat like a trial. The juvenile judge hears the case against the juvenile and the juvenile's defense. There is no jury. After listening to all the evidence, the judge decides whether or not the child is guilty of committing a delinquent act. If found not guilty, the juvenile is released. If found guilty, the court schedules a second hearing.

The second part of the formal hearing is called the *dispositional hearing*. In this part, the judge determines the punishment for the offense. At this hearing, both the prosecutor and the defense can call witnesses and present evidence that might influence the judge's sentence.

The fourth step in the juvenile justice process is the *sentencing*. The judge may select from a number of options. The judge may: (1) Release the juvenile to the custody of parents or legal guardian with no court supervision; (2) Place the juvenile on probation; (3) Place the juvenile in a youth development center for up to ninety days; (4) Commit the juvenile to the Department of Juvenile Justice; (5) Send the juvenile to a special program such as boot camp; or (6) Assign other punishments (such as restitution and fines) and special conditions of probation (such as mandatory school attendance, community service, counseling, suspension or prohibition of driver's license)

As a final step in the process, a juvenile has the right to appeal his or her case. The court has the right to extend its custody or supervision of the juvenile for up to five years.

____ **594. Juveniles who commit specific serious and violent crimes may be placed under the jurisdiction of which state court?**
  A. superior.
  B. juvenile.
  C. supreme.
  D. magistrate.

____ **595. The first step when a juvenile is taken into custody is**
  A. a formal hearing.
  B. a dispositional hearing.
  C. an intake investigation.
  D. an adjudicatory hearing.

____ **596. Which type of juvenile hearing is similar to a trial?**
  A. a formal hearing
  B. a sentencing hearing
  C. a dispositional hearing
  D. an adjudicatory hearing

____ **597. In a dispositional hearing, the judge**
  A. determines the punishment.
  B. pronounces the punishment.
  C. advises the juvenile of his/her rights.
  D. hears the charges against the juvenile.

____ **598. If the juvenile judge determines the youth is not guilty, which is the only hearing that is held?**
  A. sentencing hearing
  B. informal adjustment
  C. adjudicatory hearing
  D. dispositional hearing

SS8CG6   The student will explain how the Georgia court system treats juvenile offenders.
  d. Explain the seven delinquent behaviors that can subject juvenile offenders to the adult criminal process, how the decision to transfer to adult court is made, and the possible consequences.

GEORGIA'S SEVEN DEADLY SINS

In 1994, the Georgia legislature addressed the issue of increasingly violent youth crimes. It passed an amendment to the Georgia Juvenile Code (SB 440) that permits youths ages 13 to 17 who are charged with certain violent crimes to be treated as though they were adults. These young offenders fall under the jurisdiction of the superior court and are treated as adult criminals.

The superior court has original jurisdiction over juveniles charged with serious crimes. The seven violent offenses, known as the "Seven Deadly Sins," are murder, rape, armed robbery (with a firearm), aggravated child molestation, aggravated sodomy, aggravated sexual battery and voluntary manslaughter. *Aggravated* describes something that makes the crime worse.

Just because a youth has been arrested for one of the Seven Deadly Sins does not mean he or she will be tried in the adult system. Before an indictment, the superior court determines in which court the case will be heard. If convicted in superior court, the juvenile serves a mandatory ten-year sentence without the possibility of parole.

____ **599. What are Georgia's "Seven Deadly Sins"?**
    A. a political version of the Ten Commandments
    B. adult crimes that can lead to seven different types of penalties
    C. violent crimes committed by adults refusing to declare a religious affiliation
    D. crimes committed by juveniles that result in the courts treating the juveniles as adults

____ **600. Which is considered one of Georgia's "Seven Deadly Sins" when committed by a 16-year-old?**
    A. murder
    B. shoplifting
    C. hijacking a bus
    D. using a fake ID

ECONOMIC UNDERSTANDINGS

> **SS8E1** The student will give examples of the kinds of goods and services produced in Georgia in different historical periods.

GOODS AND SERVICES PRODUCED IN GEORGIA

Beginning with the Native Americans that lived in Georgia, and continuing through the exploits of European explorers, the arrival of the colonists with James Oglethorpe, and onward to the present, people in Georgia have produced good and services consumed at home and broad.

When the colony was established, it was expected to produce silk, cotton dyes, and wine. Unfortunately, the soil was not good for growing grapes, and the mulberry trees were the wrong kind for producing large amounts of silk. Eventually, the colonists began growing more suitable crops, such as rice, indigo, and wheat, and making wood products. Georgia's economy flourished. Cotton was introduced in 1786, and, after the invention of the cotton gin, it came to dominate the agricultural economy. Rice, wheat, and cotton were examples of Georgia's **cash crops**, crops grown to be sold rather than simply consumed.

In the late 1800s, much of Georgia was still mainly agricultural. But Henry Grady's dream of a New South based on business and industry was, in part, coming to pass. One of the state's first industries was **textiles** (woven materials). Textile mills used raw materials, such as cotton or wool, to produce textile for clothing, bed sheets, blankets, and carpets. Once begun, Georgia's textile industry grew steadily. By 1890, Georgia's textile industry produced over $12.5 million worth of goods.

Georgia's rich forests were turned into lumber to build new factories, mills, and housing and the raw materials that wound up in a variety of products, from furniture to the **naval stores** (turpentine, rosin, tar, and pitch) used in shipbuilding to pulp and paper. Georgia's forests not only provided raw materials; they also created work in sawmills, factories, and paper mills.

The state's mineral resources also spurred new or expanded industries. Georgia's rich stores of **kaolin** (a white clay used in the manufacture of paper and other products), gold, coal, iron, and **bauxite** (a mineral used in the manufacture of aluminum) led to a growth in the mining industry.

World War II greatly stimulated both the growth and the diversification of manufacturing in the state. Ships were built at Brunswick and Savannah, and bombers were built in Marietta. Many other mills and factories switched to making war supplies, weapons, and equipment. At the close of World War II, the industrial base in Georgia was fully developed. A boom in industry and manufacturing after the war led to some of the state's most prosperous times.

Agriculture remains important, with Georgia being a major producer of, for example, peanuts. Products manufactured in the state today vary from foods and beverages, to carpet, to automobiles, to aircraft parts. **Service industries**, those involved in performing actions (services) for people rather than providing products, are the largest sector of Georgia's economy. Services include such things as medical care, banking, insurance, hair cutting, car repair, and education.

_____ 601. **What was the economic base of Georgia and the other southern colonies during the colonial period?**
   A. wheat, rye, tobacco, and rice
   B. rice, indigo, wheat, and forest products
   C. mining, manufacturing, textiles, and rice
   D. shipbuilding, naval stores, and wood furniture

602. **Which invention had the greatest effect on Georgia's economy in the early 1800s?**
  A. railroad
  B. telegraph
  C. cotton gin
  D. mechanical reaper

603. **Which BEST describes why northern businessmen invested money to build Georgia's textile industry after the Civil War?**
  A. Georgia had plenty of railroads and major seaports for transporting cotton and textile products when the Civil War started.
  B. Georgia had plenty of cotton, abundant land and water, and inexpensive labor to supply and operate textile mills.
  C. Georgia was one of the few southern states to retain capital (cash money and investments) after the Civil War.
  D. Georgia was one of the few southern states to avoid violence and terrorism after the war ended.

604. **Which is NOT an example of a product grown or manufactured in Georgia today?**
  A. poultry
  B. peaches
  C. peanuts
  D. petroleum

605. **What is an example of a service industry?**
  A. tourism
  B. chemical
  C. aerospace
  D. shipbuilding

SS8E2 The student will explain the benefits of free trade.

a. Describe how Georgians have engaged in trade in different historical time periods.

TRADE

Trade is the voluntary exchange of goods and services among people and countries. Trade and voluntary exchange occur when buyers and sellers freely and willingly engage in market transactions. When trade is voluntary and non-fraudulent, both parties benefit and are better off after the trade than they were before the trade.

At prehistoric sites throughout Georgia, archaeologists have uncovered artifacts that are not made from local materials. This has led the scientists to think that there was some trading among different groups of Indians. **Bartering** (the trading of goods and services without the use of money) was the initial economic system in the New World. When the first explorers came to the New World, they bartered with the Native Americans for items they wanted or needed.

During the colonial period, England practiced the system of **mercantilism**. English colonies were expected to produce raw materials and ship them to England. English manufacturers used those products to make finished goods, which they could then sell to the colonies and other nations.

During the late 1700s and early 1800s, transportation improved with the use of canals, railroads, steamboats, and federal roads. As transportation became more available, trade among the states also increased. Georgia's economy at the time was almost entirely agricultural. The state's cotton was shipped north or exported to Europe to make cloth and thread. At the same time, since there were so few factories, Georgians imported most manufactured goods from foreign countries. (An **import** is a product brought into a country from another country to sell. An **export** is a product a country sells to another country.) So dependent were Georgia and the South to international trade that, during the Civil War, the North set up a blockade of Confederate ports to prevent the South from selling its cotton abroad and importing needed war equipment and supplies from foreign nations.

After the Civil War, Georgia went through a long and difficult reconstruction period. Industry slowly began to grow during the late 1800s. By 1900, textiles was a major industry in the state. In 1895, Atlanta was host to 800,000 visitors during the three-month-long Cotton States and International Exposition. This exhibition was a way to showcase the economic recovery of the South (in which cotton played a large role), to highlight the region's natural resources, and to encourage trade.

Trade suffered in the early 1900s and deepened during the Great Depression. World War brought prosperity to the state as industries geared up to provide war goods. After the war, factories turned to producing consumer goods. A number of postwar governors worked to encourage trade with foreign countries, including George Busbee and Sonny Perdue.

Today, trade with many parts of the world plays an increasingly important role in Georgia's economy. For example:

- A sixth of Georgia's farm products are exported.
- There are more than 50 consulates, trade offices and bi-national chambers of commerce in Georgia.
- Germany has 245 companies operating in Georgia; Japan, 189; the United Kingdom, 118; France, 83; Canada, 74; and the Netherlands, 73.
- Japanese companies employ the most Georgians – 27,051; Germany, 14,914; Netherlands, 12,968; United Kingdom, 11,314; Canada, 9,343; France, 8,100.

Georgia's business community includes more than 2,200 internationally owned facilities from 44 countries. Foreign-based firms employ more than 125,000 Georgians and generate an estimated $15.5 billion in capital investment. Foreign investors like Georgia because it is close to markets, suppliers, and key industries, has ample air transportation, good living conditions, a mild climate, strong regional growth, and a good quality, moderately-priced labor market.

_____ **606. The trade policy of Great Britain during the period of colonization was called**
   A. free trade.
   B. trade tariffs.
   C. mercantilism.
   D. merchandising.

_____ **607. How did the colonies benefit Great Britain economically?**
   A. The colonies manufactured goods for Great Britain.
   B. The colonies imported raw materials from Great Britain.
   C. The colonies traded with one another for expensive goods and services.
   D. The colonies enabled Great Britain to manufacture goods to sell to other countries.

____ **608. How does international trade affect Georgia's economy?**
   A. It has had a declining impact for the last twenty years.
   B. It has very little effect since it is such a small part of the economy.
   C. It has strengthened the state's economy and provides thousands of jobs.
   D. It has had no effect since international trade is forbidden by the U.S. Constitution.

____ **609. When Georgia trades peanuts to China in exchange for toys,**
   A. both countries lose.
   B. both countries gain.
   C. Georgia gains, China loses.
   D. China gains, Georgia loses.

____ **610. Taxes on imported goods are known as**
   A. loans.
   B. tariffs.
   C. profits.
   D. interest.

SS8E2   The student will explain the benefits of free trade.
   b. Explain how the four transportation systems contribute to Georgia's role in world trade.

TRANSPORTATION SYSTEMS AND WORLD TRADE

World trade is on the increase in Georgia thanks to the state's two deepwater ports, Atlanta's Hartsfield-Jackson Airport, the four major interstates and thousands of miles of federal and state highways, and rail service.

Through Savannah and Brunswick, the state's two major seaports, millions of tons of soybeans, winter wheat, a clay product called kaolin, and forest products are exported each year. Ships bringing sugar, heavy equipment, and steel arrive daily at the two ports. In 1995, Savannah dredged out (dug out and deepened) its harbor so that bigger ships could unload there rather than in Charleston, South Carolina, its major rival.

Atlanta's Hartsfield-Jackson Atlanta International Airport is the busiest in the world. It is the headquarters for Delta Air Lines, and over 86 million people a year pass through the airport. There are 26 passenger airlines that operate many direct international flights to 14 countries from Hartsfield-Jackson. There are also 16 cargo airlines that operate from the airport. The cargo facilities have easy access to the interstate highways.

Hartsfield-Jackson is the largest employment center in the State of Georgia. There are approximately 55,300 airline, ground transportation, concessionaire, security, federal government, City of Atlanta, and airport tenant employees. In 2005, the total airport payroll was $2.4 billion, resulting in a direct and indirect economic impact of $5.6 billion on the local and regional economy.

In addition to Hartsfield-Jackson, there are 121 other public, 142 private, and 6 military airports in the state.

Georgia has 1,200 miles of interstate highways, 17,800 miles of state highways, 87,000 miles of paved city and county roads, and 5,400 miles of railroad track. The fantastic road system means that cargo is only 2 truckload days or less from 82 percent of the nation's industrial market and 79 percent of the country's largest consumer markets.

Products and people are also transported by rail. Rail service is provided by AMTRAK, CSX Transportation, and Norfolk Southern Corporation among others.

____ **611. Which statement BEST describes Georgia's transportation infrastructure today?**

    A. Georgia has been held back because it has less than 1,000 miles of interstate, 12,000 miles of federal and state highways, only 8 regional airports, and one seaport.

    B. Georgia has a strong transportation infrastructure including 2 deepwater ports, over 1,200 miles of interstate highways, over 5,000 miles of railroad track, and over 260 airports.

    C. Georgia has a weak transportation structure because there are limited interstate highways, federal and state highways, less than 2,500 miles of railroad track, and no modern seaports.

    D. Georgia has an outstanding transportation infrastructure involving over 10 major seaports, over 25,000 miles of state and federal highways, over 1,500 miles of interstate, and over 320 airports.

____ **612. Signs of expanding national and international markets in Georgia do NOT include**

    A. building highways.

    B. increasing foreign travel.

    C. widening runways at airports.

    D. adding container facilities at the Port of Savannah.

Use the chart to answer questions 613-614.

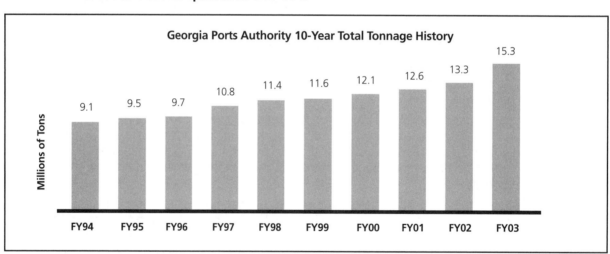

____ **613. What does the graph show?**

    A. The tonnage in Georgia ports doubled between 1994 and 2003.

    B. The tonnage in Georgia ports increased between 1994 and 2003.

    C. The tonnage in Georgia ports decreased between 1994 and 2003.

    D. The tonnage in Georgia ports stayed the same between 1994 and 2003.

____ **614. The greatest increase in tonnage in Georgia ports occurred between**

    A. 1995 and 1996.

    B. 1999 and 2000.

    C. 2001 and 2002.

    D. 2002 and 2003.

SS8E3 The student will evaluate the influence of Georgia's economic growth and development.
   a. Define profit and describe how profit is an incentive for entrepreneurs.
   b. Explain how entrepreneurs take risks to develop new goods and services to start a business.

PROFIT, RISK, AND ENTREPRENEURS

The **economy** is the system of growing, making, selling, buying, and using goods and services. In our market economy, producers and consumers determine what products are produced and what prices are paid for those products.

Georgia has had the good fortune of being home to many entrepreneurs who developed such businesses as Coca-Cola and Home Depot. **Entrepreneurs** are those people in a market economy who see a need and create goods and services to satisfy the wants of consumers. Entrepreneurs are creative, innovative thinkers and risk takers. Entrepreneurs think of new ways to combine productive resources (natural, human, capital) to produce goods and services they expect to sell for a price high enough to cover production costs. They are willing to risk their limited resources to produce these innovative goods and services in the hope they will earn a **profit**, the amount left after all production costs have been subtracted.

Because the future is not known, it is not a certainty that all entrepreneurs will earn profits. Many businesses suffer losses and eventually fail meaning the entrepreneur takes great risks. Only about 50% of small businesses are still operating three years after they begin.

____ 615. **John Pemberton, Truett Cathy, and Ted Turner are all founders of important Georgia businesses. Another name for the founder of a company is**
   A. laborer.
   B. employer.
   C. employee.
   D. entrepreneur.

____ 616. **A motivating factor for entrepreneurs is their desire to**
   A. maximize their profit and gain wealth .
   B. command the use of limited resources.
   C. risk their limited productive resources.
   D. deny consumers their ability to choose.

____ 617. **Entrepreneurs risk limited resources to produce innovative goods and services in the hope they will earn?**
   A. profit
   B. economy
   C. recognition
   D. investment

____ 618. **What factor LEAST contributes to the success of an entrepreneur?**
   A. creativity
   B. diligence
   C. hard work
   D. family money

> **SS8E3** **The student will evaluate the influence of Georgia's economic growth and development.**
>
> c. Evaluate the importance of entrepreneurs in Georgia who developed such enterprises as Coca-Cola, Delta Airlines, Georgia-Pacific, and Home Depot.

COCA-COLA

During the period of root beer, ice cream sodas, and ginger ale, two new soft drinks were added for America's taste buds. In 1898, in New Bern, North Carolina, pharmacist Caleb Bradham invented a soda called "Brad's Drink," which soon changed its name to "Pepsi." However, a few years before that, an Atlanta pharmacist, working in his own backyard, invented a soda that impacted not just Georgia, but the world.

Atlanta druggist John Pemberton mixed and sold medicines such as Globe of Flower Cough Syrup and Triplex Liver Pills. The most popular of "Doc" Pemberton's mixtures was a tonic called "French Wine Coca," a syrup that included a considerable amount of alcohol. To keep up with the demand for his "Delightful Nerve Tonic and Stimulant That Never Intoxicates," Pemberton built a small chemical plant for $160.

In 1885, the temperance movement swept across most of the country. Pemberton began looking for a way to remove the alcohol from his tonic and still have its good taste. He named his new tonic "Coca-Cola" after its two main ingredients—the coca plant and the kola nut. The tonic was put into pint beer bottles, labeled the "Intellectual Beverage and Temperance Drink," and sold for twenty-five cents in several Atlanta drugstores.

Willis Venable was the soda fountain man at Jacob's Pharmacy. One day, a customer came in with a severe headache. He bought Coca-Cola syrup and asked Venable to mix some with water so he could take it immediately. The tap water faucet was at the other end of the counter, so Venable suggested soda water instead of plain water. The customer agreed and, after drinking the mixture, said it was much better than with plain water. Within weeks, several other drugstores began mixing the medicine with soda water rather than tap water. Within a year, production had grown from 25 to 1,049 gallons.

In July 1887, Pemberton sold Venable a two-thirds interest in his company. Pemberton died in August 1888, but, before his death, a Villa Rica native and druggist named Asa Candler bought all the Coca-Cola stock for $2,300.

By 1892, the drink had become so popular that Candler sold his drugstore and formed the Coca-Cola Company. Candler became a wealthy man. In 1919, after the death of his wife, Candler sold the company to Atlanta businessman Ernest Woodruff for $25 million. At that time, it was the largest business deal ever made in the South. In 1923, Ernest Woodruff's son Robert became president. Robert Woodruff led the company into a multibillion-dollar international business.

Woodruff continued the clever marketing policies that had been begun earlier. The beverage's uniquely shaped green bottle and its wholesome advertisements were everywhere, both in this country and abroad. He built bottling plants in Europe during World War II. This gave American soldiers a little touch of home, and Europeans began to enjoy the American "pause that refreshes."

Today, Coca-Cola products are enjoyed around the world by over 470 million people each day. What was begun by "Doc" Pemberton, soda fountain man Willis Venable, and the customer with a headache has mushroomed into a giant international company with annual sales in the billions of dollars.

_____ **619. What entrepreneur is associated with Coca-Cola?**
    A. Morris Rich
    B. Bernie Marcus
    C. Alonzo Herndon
    D. John S. Pemberton

____ **620. Perhaps the GREATEST risk taken by the makers of Coca-Cola in an effort to increase their profit was a decision to change the soft drink's**

    A. price.

    B. name.

    C. bottle.

    D. advertising.

____ **621. Who was responsible for making Coca-Cola a nationally recognizable brand?**

    A. Asa Candler

    B. Arthur Blank

    C. John Pemberton

    D. Alonzo Herndon

DELTA AIRLINES

In 1924, Huff Daland Dusters was founded in Macon. This was the first commercial crop-dusting company and its target was the boll weevil that was destroying cotton crops across the South. In 1925, Huff Daland Duster moved its headquarters to Monroe, Louisiana.

In 1928, C. E. Woolman convinced a number of Monroe businessmen to buy Huff Daland Dusters. They renamed it Delta Air Service, for the Mississippi Delta region it served. The company continued its crop-dusting operations until 1966, but the company took a risk and bought five passenger planes. In 1929, Delta began its first passenger flights covering a route from Dallas, Texas, to Jackson, Mississippi, with stops in Shreveport and Monroe. In 1934, Delta won an airmail contract that brought service to Atlanta. In 1941, Delta moved its headquarters from Monroe to Atlanta.

Delta contributed to the war effort by training army pilots and mechanics, and by modifying over 1,000 aircraft for use by the military. In 1945, the company changed its name to Delta Air Lines.

In 1953, Delta merged with Chicago and Southern Airlines. It merged with Northeast Airlines in 1972 and with Western Airlines in 1987.

Delta became a leader in providing jet service. It greatly expanded its routes and in the 1990s became an international carrier.

Today, Delta Airlines' contribution to the growth of the city of Atlanta is clear. Delta offers service to more destinations--311 destinations in 52 countries--than any other global airline. Delta is adding international flights at a faster rate than any other major U.S. airline and is a leader across the Atlantic with flights to 32 trans-Atlantic destinations. In addition, Delta offers more than 600 weekly flights to 58 destinations in Latin America and the Caribbean.

____ **622. Where did the company that became Delta Airlines begin?**

    A. Macon

    B. Atlanta

    C. Monroe

    D. Savannah

____ **623. Delta Airlines is most closely associated with**

    A. the Carribbean.

    B. Monroe, Louisiana.

    C. the Mississippi Delta area.

    D. Hartsfield-Jackson Atlanta International Airport.

GEORGIA-PACIFIC

In 1927, Owen Cheatham founded the Georgia Hardwood Lumber Co. in Augusta as a wholesaler of hardwood lumber. (A wholesaler is a business that sells to other businesses.) Over the years, the company has expanded, buying land and acquiring sawmills and lumber mills. In 1956, the company changed its name to Georgia-Pacific Corp. Today, it is one of the world's leading manufacturers and marketers of tissue, pulp, paper, packaging, building products, and related chemicals. Georgia-Pacific makes a number of products that are familiar to consumers everywhere–Brawny paper towels, Dixie disposable plates and cups, Quilted Northern toilet paper.

For a time, the company had its headquarters in Portland, Oregon, but in 1982, Georgia-Pacific moved its headquarters to Atlanta. Georgia-Pacific employs some 50,000 people at more than 300 locations worldwide. Georgia facilities include Augusta, Brunswick, Madison, and Savannah. In 2005, the company was acquired as a wholly owned subsidiary of Koch Industries, Inc., a privately owned company based in Wichita, Kansas.

_____ 624. **What company, founded in Augusta in 1927, is one of the world's leading manufacturers of paper and building products?**
B. Georgia Pine
C. Georgia-Pacific
D. Atlantic Station
A. Pacific Northwest

_____ 625. **Georgia-Pacific does NOT manufacture**
A. pesticides.
B. cardboard boxes.
C. building products.
D. consumer products.

HOME DEPOT

Bernie Marcus and Arthur Blank forever changed the home improvement industry when they opened the first Home Depot stores in Atlanta on June 22, 1979. Home Depot began as a vision of warehouse stores filled from floor to ceiling with a wide assortment of products at the lowest prices. Associates were trained to give the best customer service in the industry. The original stores stocked around 25,000 products. Today, on average, The Home Depot offers 40,000 products.

Within the first five years, The Home Depot had stores in Georgia, Florida, Louisiana, Texas, and Alabama. The growth continues to this day, with more than 2,000 stores throughout the United States, Canada, Mexico, and China.

Bernie Marcus and Arthur Blank, the two entrepreneurs who founded Home Depot have retired from their jobs leading Home Depot. But they continue to be active as philanthropists in the community. Both founders provide financial support to many charities. In addition, Arthur Blank is the owner of the Atlanta Falcons and has worked to make the team a center of pride for the city. Bernie Marcus donated $200 million to build the Georgia Aquarium, the largest in the world.

_____ 626. **Who were the entrepreneurs who founded The Home Depot warehouse stores?**
A. Truett Cathy and Michael Coles
B. Bernie Marcus and Arthur Blank
C. Ted Turner and Robert Woodruff
D. John Pemberton and Asa Candler

_____ **627. Bernie Marcus and Arthur Blank became successful businessmen by**

    A. hiring Olympic athletes to work part-time.

    B. spending hundreds of thousands of dollars on advertising.

    C. providing a wide assortment of products and the best customer service.

    D. establishing a place where contractors could easily pick up the supplies they needed.

SS8E4   **The student will identify revenue sources and services provided by state and local governments.**

    a. Trace sources of state revenue such as sales taxes, federal grants, personal income taxes, and property taxes.

SOURCES OF STATE REVENUE

Georgia must work each year from a budget that outlines sources of income for the state, called **revenues**, and plans for spending those funds, called **expenditures**. State budgets must often be adjusted during the year as economic conditions change.

Georgia basically works under three types of budgets–an original budget approved for a year, an amended budget, and a supplementary budget. The original budget is the first budget approved for a **fiscal year** (a budgetary spending year). An amended budget is one in which changes are made to add, delete, or transfer monies in order to keep Georgia's budget in line with state law. (Georgia's constitution requires that the state have a balanced budget, one that matches expenditures with revenues.) A *supplementary budget* is a change made in a budget to cover new spending when additional or unspent funds are available.

Georgia's revenues come from three basic sources–state funds, federal funds, and special fees collected by agencies. Most special fees are kept by the agencies that collect them, such as the entrance fees at state parks. So Georgia's budget planners base their plans on federal and state funding sources. Those sources include income taxes, sales taxes, other taxes and fees, lottery receipts, indigent care trust funds, and tobacco settlement funds.

Federal matching funds for Medicaid is the largest source of federal revenue in the state budget. Georgia, along with several other states, receives funds from the tobacco-settlement-funds program.

However, about 90 percent of Georgia's revenue comes from taxes. Georgians pay personal income taxes on salaries they receive as well as on interest, dividends, and any profits earned on rents. Corporations operating in Georgia also pay income tax on their profits. For 2004, as an example, individual and corporate income taxes were estimated at almost $8 billion. Another large source of taxes is the state sales tax, which consumers pay on the goods and services they purchase. Estimates of sales tax revenues for the 2004 budget were $4.7 billion. Special sales taxes are collected on motor fuel, cigar and cigarette products, and alcoholic beverages. These taxes are collected even before the products are sold to consumers. For the 2004 budget, special sales taxes were estimated to be $1.1 billion.

The major source of revenue for local governments is also taxes. In 2001, Georgia's counties collected about 36 percent of their revenues from property taxes. County governments also collect sales taxes, license fees, user fees, and special user taxes such as those on alcoholic beverages. The state's municipalities collect the majority of their revenue from user fees. They also collect sales taxes, licenses and permits, property taxes, and special user fees.

_____ **628. Most of Georgia's revenue comes from which type of tax?**

    A. sales taxes

    B. income taxes

    C. property taxes

    D. motor fuel taxes

Use this figure to answer questions 629-630.

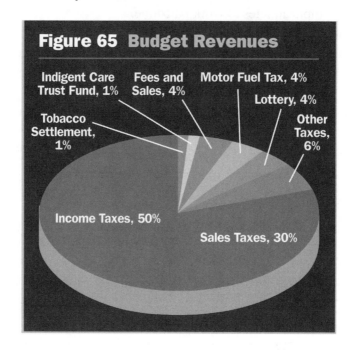

Figure 65 Budget Revenues

Indigent Care Trust Fund, 1%

Fees and Sales, 4%

Motor Fuel Tax, 4%

Lottery, 4%

Tobacco Settlement, 1%

Other Taxes, 6%

Income Taxes, 50%

Sales Taxes, 30%

____ 629. **The largest source of Georgia's revenue comes from**
  A. fees.
  B. the lottery.
  C. sales taxes.
  D. income taxes.

____ 630. **What percent of Georgia's revenue comes from sources other than income or sales taxes?**
  A. 10 percent
  B. 15 percent
  C. 20 percent
  D. 25 percent

____ 631. **Which statement about sales taxes is TRUE?**
  A. Sales taxes are only collected at the state level.
  B. Sales taxes are only collected at the county level.
  C. Sales taxes are only collected at the municipal level.
  D. Sales taxes are collected at the state, county, and municipal level.

____ 632. **What is the largest source of revenue for county governments?**
  A. user fees
  B. sales taxes
  C. property taxes
  D. licenses and permits

SS8E4 The student will identify revenue sources and services provided by state and local governments.

b. Explain the distribution of state revenue to provide services.

DISTRIBUTION OF STATE REVENUE

Georgia's government at the state, county, and municipality levels provide a variety of services for citizens. Governments pay for those services with the revenues they collect. What are those funds normally spent on?

At the state level, the largest expenditure is for education. Other expenditures include the wages and salaries of government employees, public safety, transportation, and interest on the money the state borrows. Local governments also make expenditures for education plus police and fire protection, libraries, parks, and water and sewer systems.

Use the graph to answer questions 633-635.

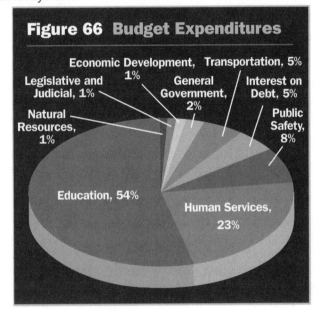

Figure 66 Budget Expenditures

____ 633. **The largest percentage of state funds is spent on**
  A. education.
  B. public safety.
  C. transportation.
  D. human services.

____ 634. **Which two expenditures total 13 percent?**
  A. public safety and transportation
  B. interest on debt and transportation
  C. natural resources and transportation
  D. economic development and public safety

____ 635. **Which statement BEST describes the data in the figure?**
  A. Human services is a high priority.
  B. Little money is spent on public safety.
  C. The same amount of money is spent on transportation and public safety.
  D. The legislature spends more than 10 percent of its funds on state government.

____ **636. Most of Georgia's revenue goes to provide**

    A. interest.

    B. new roads.

    C. services for its citizens.

    D. salaries for government employees.

> **SS8E4 The student will identify revenue sources and services provided by state and local governments.**
> c. Evaluate how choices are made given the limited revenues of state and local governments.

HOW CHOICES ARE MADE GIVEN LIMITED REVENUES

Governments at all levels, like businesses and individuals, face issues of scarcity. **Scarcity** occurs because our wants and needs are unlimited and our resources are limited.

One of the responsibilities of state and local governments is to provide essential services for the people. Examples of these services include education, environmental protection, road construction and repair, and health services. Of course, none of these services is free, and one of the ways to raise revenue to pay for the services is by levying taxes. The property tax and sales tax are two taxes used by state and local governments.

While citizens are usually willing to accept increased services, the decision to raise taxes is often met with a fair amount of resistance. Lawmakers are increasingly being forced to choose which services they can provide with limited revenues. One way to decide is to compare the costs and benefits of each service. Generally, the benefits that a community expects to receive from a particular service should outweigh the costs to provide that service. This is not as easy as it sounds; not all benefits or costs can be measured in monetary terms.

The first step in preparing a budget is for the various government departments to submit budget requests to the governor. The requests are evaluated on a cost-benefit basis. After meetings, the governor sets funding priorities and submits the budget to the legislature. In the General Assembly, the budget becomes an appropriations bill and must follow the same steps as any other bill. Once the budget is passed, state funds are allocated to the various departments to be spent as authorized. During the fiscal year, the departments and agencies must prepare quarterly reports stating exactly how they have spent the money.

Sometimes, tax collections can exceed Georgia's spending needs–creating a short-term budget **surplus**. During economic downturns, tax collections can decline–resulting in a short-term budget shortfall or **deficit** while the need for important public services continues. When expenditures exceed expected revenues, money from the surplus may be used to balance the budget.

____ **637. Georgia's stable economy during times of recessions and depressions is the result of**

    A. a required state personal and corporate income tax.

    B. the use of both a fiscal and a supplementary budget process.

    C. the foresight of legislature to save money in contingency funds.

    D. a constitutional requirement that Georgia have a balanced budget.

____ **638. What is the first step in developing Georgia's state budget?**

    A. The governor sets priorities.

    B. The counties submit their needs.

    C. Each department submits requests for funding.

    D. The General Assembly determines how much money will be available.

____ **639. What factor MOST LIKELY determines whether funding for a program is included in the state budget?**

    A. the popularity of a program

    B. the amount of revenue available

    C. the benefits and cost effectiveness of a program

    D. the inclusion of the program in the governor's platform

> **SS8E5** The student will explain personal money management choices in terms of income, spending, credit, saving, and investing.

PERSONAL MONEY MANAGEMENT CHOICES

Personal money management choices confront all of us–even you! Everyone must make choices about what to do with their **income**. Younger students may have income from an allowance, a gift, or for doing jobs at home. Older students may actually have a job and receive a paychecks.

Broadly speaking, an individual has only two choices about what to do with income: spend money now on goods and services or save it for the future. **Savings** is the income that a person has not spent after buying things he or she wants. It is an amount put aside for later. To help make decisions about using limited income, a person can develop a budget. A budget is a spending-and-savings plan, based on estimated income and expenses for an individual (or an organization), covering a specific time period.

Saving is really a form of investing. **Investing** involves putting money aside in order to receive a greater benefit in the future. Often that greater benefit is a certain amount of **interest** (a fee for the use of money) or a profit. Money can be invested in financial assets such as bank accounts, certificates of deposit, stocks, bonds, and mutual funds. All of these have different levels of liquidity, which refers to the ease with which you can access your money. In general, the less liquid, the greater the rate of interest or return. Having a good financial plan allows you to plan for both your present and your future needs.

Credit is extremely useful to the economy. Some forms of credit commonly used by consumers are car loans, home mortgage loans, and credit cards. Most people would have great difficulty in buying a house if they couldn't borrow the money. Many people also use credit to further their education. In addition, short-term credit is often used by people (through credit cards) as a simple and convenient method of paying for purchases. Keep in mind that credit always involves a finance charge or the payment of interest. It may also involve the payment of certain fees.

Businesses use credit regularly, either by borrowing from a bank or issuing corporate bonds. They might, for example, borrow money to build a new factory. Government also uses credit when it needs to borrow money to finance a budget deficit (e.g., savings bonds, treasury notes). Those who can borrow moderate or large sums of money at a reasonable rate of interest are sometimes said to have good credit, while those who cannot borrow such amounts at such rates are said to have *bad credit*.

However, excessive borrowing can be a problem for households, firms, and government. Making interest payments because you borrowed money for the house that you live in, a car that you drive, or a factory that produces goods can make good economic sense. But credit should not be used to pay for goods or consumption in the present that were completely consumed in the past. Be careful if the loan lasts longer than the item you bought with it.

_____ **640. What is an advantage of a savings account over a checking account?**
    A. Savings accounts are easier to acquire.
    B. Savings accounts pay a higher rate of interest.
    C. Savings accounts can be used to guarantee loans.
    D. Savings accounts provide more protection for your money.

_____ **641. When is the BEST time to borrow money?**
    A. when interest rates are low
    B. when a person has a poor credit rating
    C. when a person has a no job steady income
    D. when a person wants to purchase an expensive item

_____ **642. Which type of investment provides more flexibility?**
    A. savings accounts
    B. money market funds
    C. certificates of deposit
    D. stocks and mutual funds

_____ **643. When should people buy less on credit?**
    A. when they have no savings account
    B. when they have no collateral
    C. when interest rates are high
    D. when they have other debts

_____ **644. Which group of people have increased their use of credit cards the most in recent years?**
    A. teenagers
    B. college students
    C. people over age 65
    D. middle-aged people

SOCIAL STUDIES

SKILLS TEST

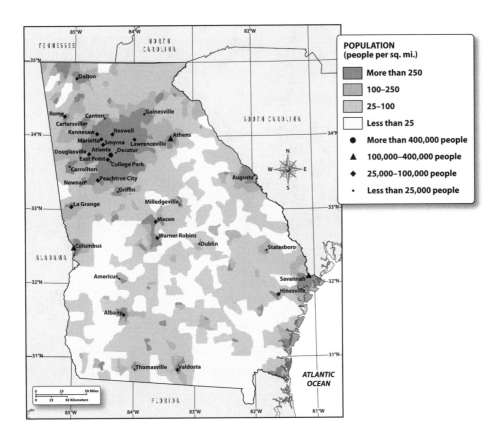

1. Which Georgia city has the largest population?

   A. Decatur

   B. Columbus

   C. Statesboro

   D. Warner Robins

2. Which city is located in an area with few people?

   A. Augusta

   B. Valdosta

   C. Savannah

   D. East Point

3. What is the distance between Augusta and Savannah?

   A. 50 miles

   B. 75 miles

   C. 100 miles

   D. 150 miles

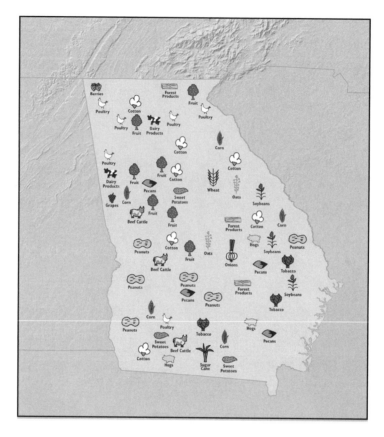

4. Which crop is grown only in west-central Georgia?

   A. cotton

   B. grapes

   C. peanuts

   D. soybeans

6. What is produced along the Savannah River?

   A. poultry

   B. soybeans

   C. forest products

   D. sweet potatoes

5. Where is the poultry industry concentrated?

   A. north Georgia

   B. south Georgia

   C. central Georgia

   D. coastal Georgia

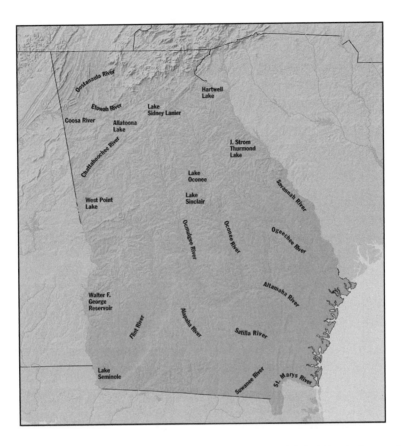

7. Which river forms part of the boundary between Georgia and Alabama?

    A. Altamaha

    B. Ogeechee

    C. Savannah

    D. Chattahoochee

8. Which river does NOT flow into the Atlantic Ocean?

    A. Flint

    B. Satilla

    C. St. Marys

    D. Ocmulgee

9. Which lake is located along the Oconee River?

    A. Lanier

    B. Sinclair

    C. Hartwell

    D. Allatoona

SOCIAL STUDIES

SKILLS TEST

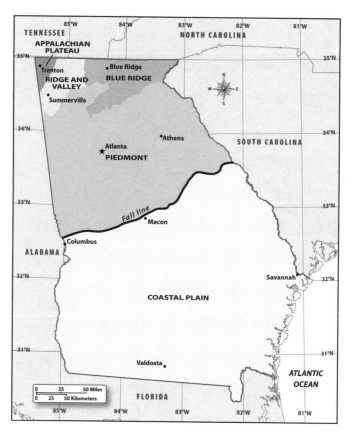

10. Which city is located on the Fall Line?

    A. Macon

    B. Atlanta

    C. Valdosta

    D. Savannah

11. Which city is located in the Piedmont?

    A. Atlanta

    B. Trenton

    C. Valdosta

    D. Blue Ridge

12. What period of history is illustrated in the drawing?

   A. Paleo

   B. Archaic

   C. Woodland

   D. Mississippian

SOCIAL STUDIES

SKILLS TEST

Early People				
	Paleo	**Archaic**	**Woodland**	**Mississippian**
Time Period	before 10,000 years ago	8000 B.C. to 1000 B.C.	1000 B.C. to 1000 A.D.	700 A.D. to 1600 A.D.
Food Sources	large animals such as bison, mammoth, ground sloth, and mastodon	small game, reptiles, fish, shellfish, berries, nuts, fruits	small game, fish, nuts and berries, some crops (squash, sunflowers)	crops (maize, beans, pumpkins, squash)
Weapons, Tools	spears	spears, choppers, drills, chipping tools, bone fish hooks, grooved axes, pipes, pottery	bow and arrow, pottery	similar to Woodland culture, stone hoes, copper headdresses
Shelter	no fixed shelter; followed herds of large animals	crude shelters, stayed in one place longer	small villages of dome-shaped huts with grass roofs, mounds	larger villages with ceremonial buildings

13. How long did the Woodland Indians live in what is now Georgia?

    A. 1,000 years

    B. 8,000 years

    C. 2,000 years

    D. 10,000 years

14. During which period was the use of pottery introduced?

    A. Paleo

    B. Archaic

    C. Woodland

    D. Mississippian

15. Which period saw the building of large villages with impressive ceremonial buildings?

    A. Paleo

    B. Archaic

    C. Woodland

    D. Mississippian

16. When were people building small, dome-shaped huts with grass roofs as their shelters?

    A. between 700 A.D. and 1600 A.D.

    B. between 1000 B.C. and 1000 A.D.

    C. between 1600 A.D. and 1900 A.D.

    D. between 10,000 B.C. and 8,000 B.C.

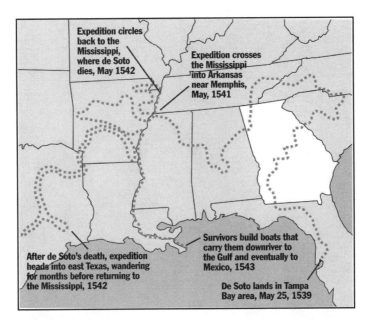

17. Hernando de Soto began his travels near present-day

   A. Atlanta, Georgia.

   C. Tampa, Florida.

   B. Memphis, Tennessee.

   D. Vicksburg, Mississippi.

18. Hernando de Soto crossed the Mississippi River for the first time near present-day

   B. Memphis, Tennessee.

   C. Natchez, Mississippi.

   A. Little Rock, Arkansas.

   D. Vicksburg, Mississippi.

19. After Hernando de Soto's death, where did his men go?

   A. Texas

   B. Alabama

   C. Arkansas

   C. Mississippi

20. What is the correct chronological order of the places de Soto visited on his travels?

   1. De Soto crossed the Mississippi near Memphis.

   2. De Soto's men went to Texas.

   3. De Soto entered Florida.

   4. De Soto died.

   A. 3-1-4-2

   B. 2-3-1-4

   C. 4-3-1-2

   D. 2-1-3-4

SKILLS TEST

Oglethorpe and Tomochichi

21. Which statement BEST describes the subject of the illustration?

    A. The Indians welcomed the British with gifts.

    B. The British took control over the Indians' land.

    C. The Indians showed distrust for the invading Englishmen.

    D. The British and the Indians had a disappointing first meeting.

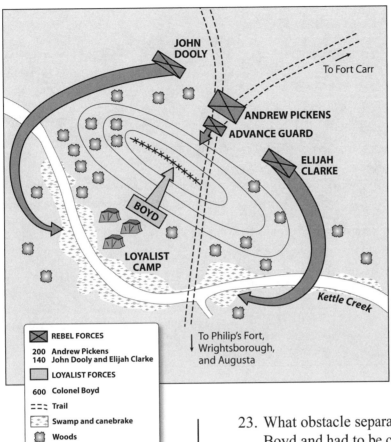

22. Which military leader commanded the most troops at the Battle of Kettle Creek?

A. John Dooly

B. Elijah Clarke

C. Colonel Boyd

D. Andrew Pickens

23. What obstacle separated Pickens and Boyd and had to be crossed for the battle to begin?

A. Fort Carr

B. Kettle Creek

C. fence and fallen trees

D. tents from the loyalist camp

24. Which military leader was loyal to King George?

A. John Dooly

B. Elijah Clarke

C. Colonel Boyd

D. Andrew Pickens

STATE of GEORGIA.

To the Honourable the *[President]* and the Members of
Council, now sitting in Augusta for the Purpose of granting
Lands in the two new Counties of Franklin and Washington

The PETITION of *[Austin Dabney]*
as a *[Refugee]* in the State aforesaid,

SHEWETH,

THAT your Petitioner is entitled to *[Two hundred and fifty]*
Acres of Land, as a Bounty for his
Services, pursuant to the Certificate hereunto annexed: That your
Petitioner is desirous of taking up the said Lands in the County of

[Washington]

May it therefore please your Honourable Board to grant your
Petitioner *[Two hundred and fifty]*
Acres of Land in the County of *[Washington]*
on the Right aforesaid, and on his complying with the
Terms mentioned in the late Land Act; and your Petiti-
oner will pray.

---

25. This document was given to Austin
    Dabney in 1821 by the State of Georgia to
    show that he had earned

    A. the title of Honourable.

    B. freedom from his master.

    C. the right to live at Mount Vernon.

    D. 50 acres of land in Washington County.

SKILLS TEST

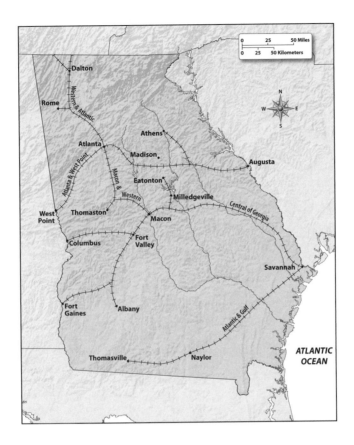

26. Which city was connected to Atlanta by the Atlanta & West Point Railroad?

    A. Augusta

    B. Madison

    C. Fort Valley

    D. Thomaston

28. The Atlantic and Gulf railroad connected Savannah and what city?

    A. Macon

    B. Atlanta

    C. Augusta

    D. Thomasville

27. Which railroad was used to travel from Dalton to Atlanta?

    A. Atlantic and Gulf

    B. Central of Georgia

    C. Macon and Western

    D. Western and Atlantic

SKILLS TEST

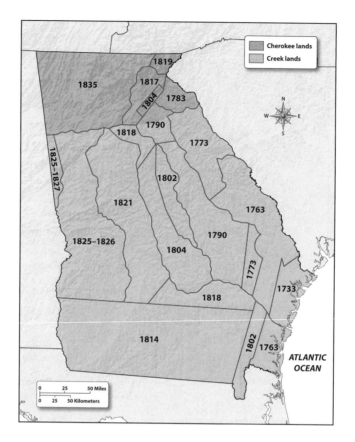

29. In what year did the Creek first cede land to the Europeans?

    A. 1733

    B. 1793

    C. 1827

    D. 1835

30. By what year had Europeans competed the removal of the Creek from Georgia?

    A. 1763

    B. 1814

    C. 1827

    D. 1835

31. The largest land cession from the Cherokee was in what year?

    A. 1763

    B. 1814

    C. 1821

    D. 1835

Panning for Gold

Choose a gravelly stream that is at least 6 inches deep.

Fill the bottom of a shallow pan about 3/4 full with gravel.

Submerge the pan in water and shake it so the heavier gold settles to the bottom. Remove all rocks larger than a pea.

Still holding the pan under water, add more water and tilt the pan away from you. Swirl it around to wash out lighter materials. Continue this step until only the heavier materials remain.

Look for gold particles among the heavier, darker minerals left in the pan.

Put any gold particles in a vial or other container.

32. What event is shown in this drawing?

   A. mining for gold in the North Georgia mountains

   B. building the railroad from Macon to Atlanta

   C. farming the rich soil of the Piedmont region

   D. picking cotton on Coastal Plain plantations

33. In what part of a stream is gold found?

   A. shallow end

   B. along the bank

   C. gravelly bottom

   D. swift-moving water

34. Which tool is needed to pan for gold?

   A. shovel

   B. pick axe

   C. shallow pan

   D. wheelbarrow

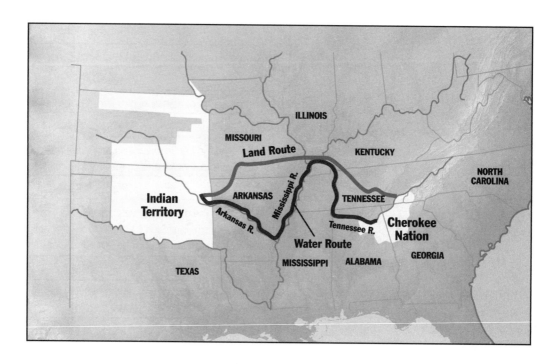

35. The Cherokee Nation was primarily located in what today is the state of

    A. Georgia.

    B. Alabama.

    C. Oklahoma.

    D. Tennessee.

36. Which river was NOT part of the water route taken by the Cherokee?

    A. Arkansas

    B. Missouri

    C. Tennessee

    D. Mississippi

37. How many routes led from the Cherokee Nation to the Indian Territory?

    A. 1

    B. 2

    C. 3

    D. 4

SOCIAL STUDIES

SKILLS TEST

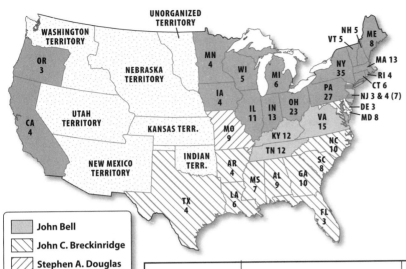

Candidate	Popular Vote Georgia	Popular Vote National	Electoral Vote
Bell	42,960	592,906	39
Breckinridge	52,176	848,356	72
Douglas	11,581	1,382,713	12
Lincoln	0	1,865,593	180
Total	106,717	4,689,568	303

38. Which candidate for president of the United States in 1860 won the electoral vote?

    A. John Bell

    B. Abraham Lincoln

    C. John Breckinridge

    D. Stephen A. Douglas

39. Which candidate won the least number of states in his bid for the presidency?

    A. John Bell

    B. Abraham Lincoln

    C. John Breckinridge

    D. Stephen A. Douglas

40. Which two candidates split the southern vote?

    A. Bell and Lincoln

    C. Lincoln and Douglas

    C. Breckinridge and Bell

    D. Douglas and Breckinridge

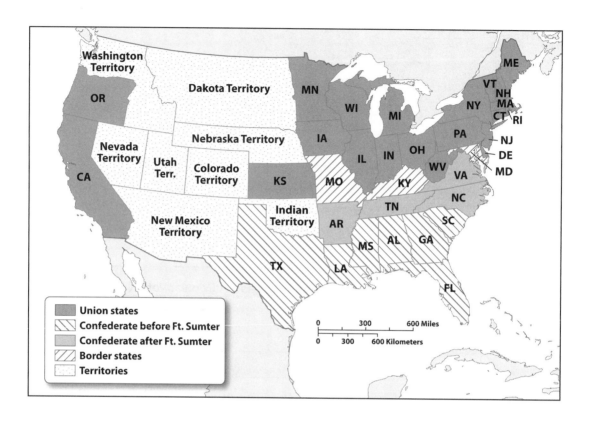

Map Legend:
- Union states
- Confederate before Ft. Sumter
- Confederate after Ft. Sumter
- Border states
- Territories

41. This map shows the United States in what year?

    A. 1776

    B. 1863

    C. 1964

    D. 1989

42. Which statement summarizes the information shown on this map?

    A. The West is unsettled territory, yet the East is organized into large states.

    B. The nation is divided evenly–north and south–into colonies and territories.

    C. The nation is evenly split–east and west–into slave states and free states.

    D. The East is overpopulated, forcing citizens to move to the western territories.

SOCIAL STUDIES

SKILLS TEST

43. What is the subject of the political cartoon?

   A. A recognition ceremony for widows of World War I

   B. Rosa Parks's meeting with a U.S. senator

   C. Rebecca Latimer Felton serving as a U.S. senator

   D. Carrie Nation's testimony before the U.S. Congress

44. Which clue helps to identify the content of the political cartoon?

   A. the gentleman's greeting

   B. the desk and table in the cartoon

   C. clothing that the two people are wearing

   D. the name of one of the people pictured

PROFESSIONAL SPORTS IN ATLANTA		
Sport	**Team**	**Facts**
Baseball	Braves	Team came to Atlanta from Milwaukee in 1966. Plays at Turner Field.
Football	Falcons	Team came to Atlanta in 1966 as a league expansion team. Plays in Georgia Dome.
Basketball	Hawks	Team came to Atlanta in 1968 from St. Louis. Plays in Phillips Arena.
Hockey	Thrashers	Team came to Atlanta in 1997 as a league expansion team. Plays in Phillips Arena.

45. What was the first expansion team to come to Atlanta?

   A. hockey

   B. football

   C. baseball

   D. basketball

46. When did the Atlanta Hawks arrive in Atlanta from St. Louis?

   A. 1966

   B. 1968

   C. 1997

   D. 2001

47. Which team plays at the Georgia Dome?

   A. Hawks

   B. Braves

   C. Falcons

   D. Thrashers

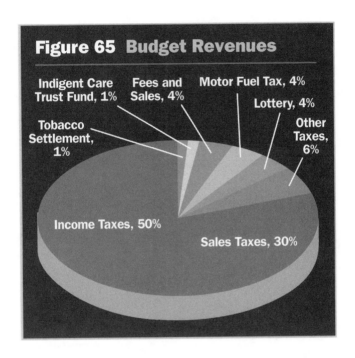

Figure 65 Budget Revenues

Indigent Care Trust Fund, 1%
Fees and Sales, 4%
Motor Fuel Tax, 4%
Lottery, 4%
Other Taxes, 6%
Tobacco Settlement, 1%
Income Taxes, 50%
Sales Taxes, 30%

48. The largest source of Georgia's revenue comes from

A. fees.

B. the lottery.

C. sales taxes.

D. state income taxes.

49. What percent of Georgia's revenue comes from sources other than income or sales taxes?

A. 10 percent

B. 15 percent

C. 20 percent

D. 25 percent

50. What historic site is located at the intersection of Oglethorpe Street and Bull Street?

    A. Cotton Exchange

    B. U.S. Customs House

    C. Tomochichi's gravesite

    D. Juliette Gordon Low's birthplace

51. Which location is located furthest north on the map?

    A. Forsyth Park

    B. Factors Walk

    C. Johnson Square

    D. Colonial Cemetery

SKILLS TEST

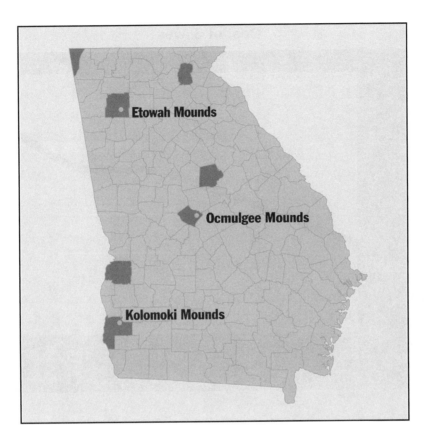

52. The information on the map indicates that the mound builders

   A. spread across Georgia.

   B. settled along the coast.

   C. believed in an afterlife.

   D. built cone-shaped mounds.

53. Mounds are located in how many Georgia counties?

   A. 5

   B. 6

   C. 7

   D. 8

SKILLS TEST

Cost of Slaves

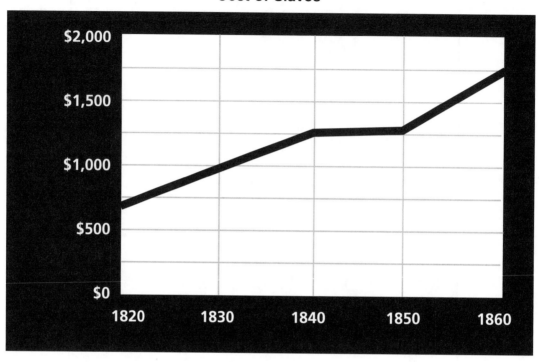

54. How much did a slave cost in 1840?

    A. $750

    B. $1,000

    C. $1,250

    D. $1,500

55. In what year did slaves cost the least?

    A. 1820

    B. 1830

    C. 1840

    D. 1850

56. During what ten-year period did the cost of slaves stay the same?

    A. 1820-1830

    B. 1830-1840

    C. 1840-1850

    D. 1850-1860

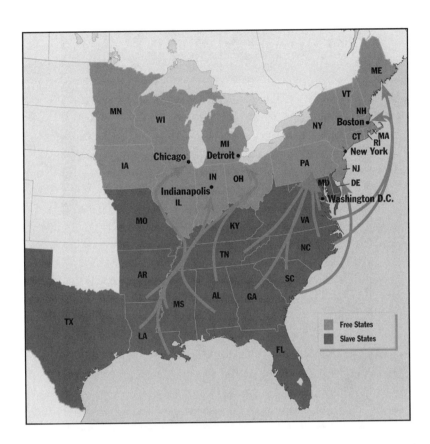

57. The Underground Railroad was a network of people helping escaped slaves leave the South for freedom in northern cities. To which city did most slaves from Georgia flee?

A. Chicago, Illinois

B. Indianapolis, Indiana

C. Boston, Massachusetts

D. Philadelphia, Pennsylvania

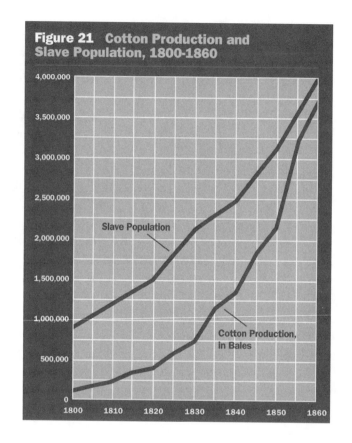

Figure 21 Cotton Production and Slave Population, 1800-1860

58. About how many bales of cotton were produced in 1830?

A. 500,000

B. 750,000

C. 1,000,000

D. 1,250,000

59. What is the main idea presented in this graph?

A. Bales of cotton went up in price as the Civil War approached.

B. The slave population increased sharply between 1800 and 1860.

C. Slavery decreased as a result of abolitionists refusing to buy cotton.

D. As the number of slaves in the U.S. increased, so did cotton production.

SKILLS TEST

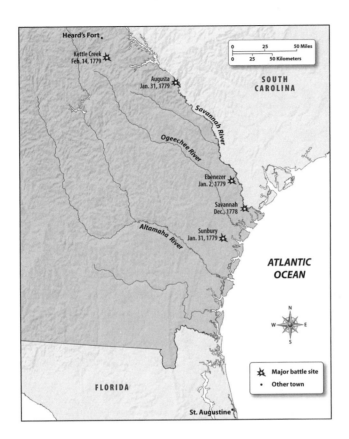

60. Where was one of the major battle sites of the Revolution in Georgia?

    A. Ebenezer

    B. Briar Creek

    C. Heard's Fort

    D. St. Augustine

PLEASE STOP! STOP!

Student Name:_____

Assignment: _____

Period:_____

Marking Instructions:

Use a No. 2 pencil (no ink or ballpoint pens)
Fill the circles in completely
Erase completely to change your answer
Make no stray marks

Student ID Number

0 0 0 0 0 0 0 0 0
1 1 1 1 1 1 1 1 1
2 2 2 2 2 2 2 2 2
3 3 3 3 3 3 3 3 3
4 4 4 4 4 4 4 4 4
5 5 5 5 5 5 5 5 5
6 6 6 6 6 6 6 6 6
7 7 7 7 7 7 7 7 7
8 8 8 8 8 8 8 8 8
9 9 9 9 9 9 9 9 9

Example:

A B C D
○ ● ○ ○

Score:

1 A B C D   ○ ○ ○ ○
2 A B C D   ○ ○ ○ ○
3 A B C D   ○ ○ ○ ○
4 A B C D   ○ ○ ○ ○
5 A B C D   ○ ○ ○ ○
6 A B C D   ○ ○ ○ ○
7 A B C D   ○ ○ ○ ○
8 A B C D   ○ ○ ○ ○
9 A B C D   ○ ○ ○ ○
10 A B C D   ○ ○ ○ ○
11 A B C D   ○ ○ ○ ○
12 A B C D   ○ ○ ○ ○
13 A B C D   ○ ○ ○ ○
14 A B C D   ○ ○ ○ ○
15 A B C D   ○ ○ ○ ○

16 A B C D   ○ ○ ○ ○
17 A B C D   ○ ○ ○ ○
18 A B C D   ○ ○ ○ ○
19 A B C D   ○ ○ ○ ○
20 A B C D   ○ ○ ○ ○
21 A B C D   ○ ○ ○ ○
22 A B C D   ○ ○ ○ ○
23 A B C D   ○ ○ ○ ○
24 A B C D   ○ ○ ○ ○
25 A B C D   ○ ○ ○ ○
26 A B C D   ○ ○ ○ ○
27 A B C D   ○ ○ ○ ○
28 A B C D   ○ ○ ○ ○
29 A B C D   ○ ○ ○ ○
30 A B C D   ○ ○ ○ ○

31 A B C D   ○ ○ ○ ○
32 A B C D   ○ ○ ○ ○
33 A B C D   ○ ○ ○ ○
34 A B C D   ○ ○ ○ ○
35 A B C D   ○ ○ ○ ○
36 A B C D   ○ ○ ○ ○
37 A B C D   ○ ○ ○ ○
38 A B C D   ○ ○ ○ ○
39 A B C D   ○ ○ ○ ○
40 A B C D   ○ ○ ○ ○
41 A B C D   ○ ○ ○ ○
42 A B C D   ○ ○ ○ ○
43 A B C D   ○ ○ ○ ○
44 A B C D   ○ ○ ○ ○
45 A B C D   ○ ○ ○ ○

46 A B C D   ○ ○ ○ ○
47 A B C D   ○ ○ ○ ○
48 A B C D   ○ ○ ○ ○
49 A B C D   ○ ○ ○ ○
50 A B C D   ○ ○ ○ ○
51 A B C D   ○ ○ ○ ○
52 A B C D   ○ ○ ○ ○
53 A B C D   ○ ○ ○ ○
54 A B C D   ○ ○ ○ ○
55 A B C D   ○ ○ ○ ○
56 A B C D   ○ ○ ○ ○
57 A B C D   ○ ○ ○ ○
58 A B C D   ○ ○ ○ ○
59 A B C D   ○ ○ ○ ○
60 A B C D   ○ ○ ○ ○

SOCIAL STUDIES UNIT TEST

GEOGRAPHY, EXPLORATION, AND NATIVE AMERICANS

1. The oldest known Native American culture in North America was the

   A. Paleo culture.

   B. Archaic culture.

   C. Woodland culture.

   D. Mississippian culture.

2. Why have few Paleo artifacts been found in any one place?

   A. People moved frequently.

   B. Artifacts disappeared over time.

   C. People did not leave any artifacts.

   D. Few people lived during that time.

3. Why did the Archaic people move frequently?

   A. to locate farmland

   B. to trade with others

   C. to find enough food

   D. to find secure shelter

4. Which factor resulted in prehistoric Indians making permanent settlements?

   A. The Indians had abundant large game.

   B. The Indians started to cultivate plants.

   C. The Indians followed herds of large animals.

   D. The Indians wanted to band together for protection.

5. The main purpose of the Spanish missions on the barrier islands was to

   A. claim land for Spain.

   B. establish trade with Spain.

   C. convert the Indians to Catholicism.

   D. provide protection for the area's European settlers.

6. Why did Hernando de Soto explore much of Georgia in 1540?

   A. He was attracted by possible gold deposits.

   B. He wanted to build forts and missions in the state.

   C. He was searching for the magical Fountain of Youth.

   D. He believed that he would find a passage to Asia through Georgia.

GEOGRAPHY, EXPLORATION, AND NATIVE AMERICANS

Use the map to answer questions 7-9.

7. Which section of the state has no mounds?

   A. northeast

   B. northwest

   C. southeast

   D. southwest

8. The information on the map indicates that the moundbuilders

   A. spread across Georgia.

   B. settled along the coast.

   C. believed in an afterlife.

   D. built cone-shaped mounds.

9. Mounds are located in how many Georgia counties?

   A. 5

   B. 6

   C. 7

   D. 8

SOCIAL STUDIES UNIT TEST

GEOGRAPHY, EXPLORATION, AND NATIVE AMERICANS

Early People			
	Paleo	**Archaic**	**Woodland**	**Mississippian**
Time Period	before 10,000 years ago	8000 B.C. to 1000 B.C.	1000 B.C. to 1000 A.D.	700 A.D. to 1600 A.D.
Food Sources	large animals such as bison, mammoths, ground sloths, and mastodons	small game, reptiles, fish, shellfish, berries, nuts, fruits	small game, fish, nuts and berries, some crops (squash, sunflowers)	crops (maize, beans, pumpkins, squash)
Weapons, Tools	spears	spears, choppers, drills, chipping tools, bone fish hooks, grooved axes, pipes, pottery	bow and arrow, pottery	similar to Woodland culture, stone hoes, copper head-dresses
Shelter	no fixed shelter; followed herds of large animals	crude shelters, stayed in one place longer	small villages of dome-shaped huts with grass roofs, mounds	larger villages with ceremonial buildings

Use the table to answer questions 10-13.

10. How long did the Woodland Indians live in what is now Georgia?

    A. 1,000 years

    B. 2,000 years

    C. 8,000 years

    D. 10,000 years

11. During which period was the use of pottery introduced?

    A. Paleo

    B. Archaic

    C. Woodland

    D. Mississippian

12. Which period saw the building of large villages with impressive ceremonial buildings?

    A. Paleo

    B. Archaic

    C. Woodland

    D. Mississippian

13. When were people building small, dome-shaped huts with grass roofs as their shelters?

    A. between 700 A.D. and 1600 A.D.

    B. between 1600 A.D. and 1900 A.D.

    C. between 1000 B.C. and 1000 A.D.

    D. between 10,000 B.C. and 8,000 B.C.

Use the map to answer questions 14-17.

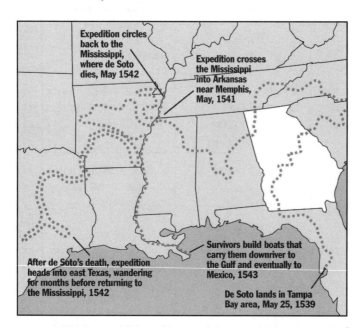

16. After Hernando de Soto's death, where did his men go?

    D. Texas

    A. Alabama

    B. Arkansas

    C. Mississippi

17. What is the correct chronological order of the places de Soto visited on his travels?

    1. De Soto crossed the Mississippi near Memphis.

    2. De Soto's men went to Texas.

    3. De Soto entered Florida.

    4. De Soto died.

    A. 3-1-4-2

    B. 2-3-1-4

    C. 4-3-1-2

    D. 2-1-3-4

14. Hernando de Soto began his travels near present-day

    C. Tampa, Florida.

    A. Atlanta, Georgia.

    B. Memphis, Tennessee.

    D. Vicksburg, Mississippi.

15. Hernando de Soto crossed the Mississippi River for the first time near present-day

    B. Memphis, Tennessee.

    C. Natchez, Mississippi.

    A. Little Rock, Arkansas.

    D. Vicksburg, Mississippi.

18. Why was de Soto's expedition considered a failure?

    A. De Soto's men died of disease.

    B. De Soto did not find any gold or riches.

    C. De Soto traveled in the wrong direction.

    D. De Soto died before the expedition was finished.

19. The first permanent English settlement in the New World was built at

    A. Jamestown.

    B. St. Augustine.

    C. Roanoke Island.

    D. Massachusetts Bay.

20. What was the name of the first British fort built in Georgia?

    A. Fort Guale

    B. Fort Frederica

    C. Fort King George

    D. Fort Santa Catalina

21. Into which hemisphere does the prime meridian place Georgia?

    A. eastern hemisphere

    B. western hemisphere

    C. northern hemisphere

    D. southern hemisphere

22. Which of the following does NOT border Georgia?

    A. Alabama.

    B. Tennessee.

    C. Pacific Ocean.

    D. Atlantic Ocean.

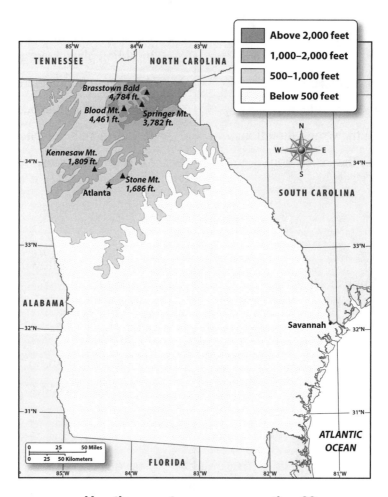

Use the map to answer question 23.

23. Which mountain rises to the highest elevation?

    A. Blood Mountain

    B. Stone Mountain

    C. Springer Mountain

    D. Kennesaw Mountain

GEOGRAPHY, EXPLORATION, AND NATIVE AMERICANS

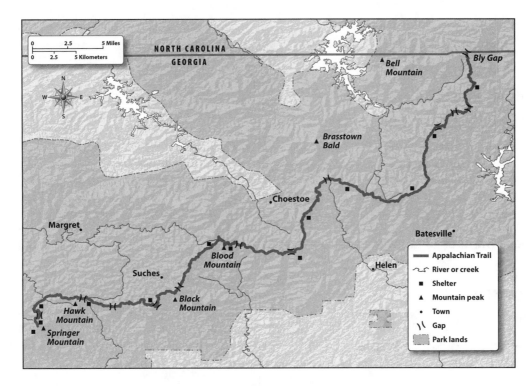

Use the map to answer questions 24–27.

24. How many gaps would a hiker pass through to get from Springer Mountain to the Hawk Mountain Shelter?

   A. 1

   B. 2

   C. 3

   D. 4

25. About how far north of the Appalachian Trail is Brasstown Bald located?

   B. 5 miles

   D. 15 miles

   A. 1 kilometer

   C. 10 kilometers

26. Where does the Appalachian Trail cross into North Carolina?

   A. Bly Gap

   B. Blood Shelter

   C. Springer Mountain

   D. Town of Batesville

27. When traveling from Black Mountain to Blood Mountain, which direction is a hiker traveling?

   A. south

   B. north

   C. northeast

   D. southwest

28. In which region are Taylor Ridge and Pigeon Mountain found?

    B. Blue Ridge

    C. Piedmont Plateau

    D. Ridge and Valley

    A. Appalachian Plateau

Use these phrases to answer question 29.

- smallest region
- source of coal deposits
- location of Lookout Mountain

29. Which Georgia region is described by these phrases?

    B. Blue Ridge

    C. Piedmont Plateau

    D. Ridge and Valley

    A. Appalachian Plateau

30. Georgia has no natural lakes, so most of the water used in this heavily populated state comes from

    A. artesian wells.

    B. reservoirs and rivers.

    C. neighboring states through irrigation pipelines.

    D. desalinization plants along the Atlantic coast.

31. Which geographical region of Georgia is characterized by red clay, gently sloping hills, and a location near the Fall Line?

    A. Piedmont

    B. Blue Ridge

    C. Coastal Plain

    D. Appalachian Plateau

SOCIAL STUDIES UNIT TEST

GEOGRAPHY, EXPLORATION, AND NATIVE AMERICANS

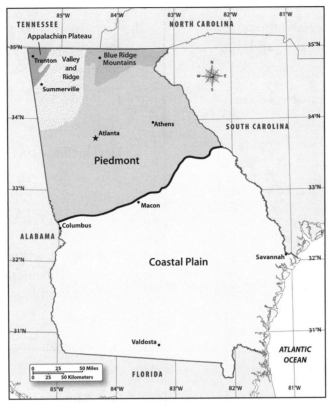

Use this map to answer questions 32-33.

32. Which city is located on the Fall Line?

    A. Atlanta

    B. Valdosta

    C. Columbus

    D. Summerville

33. Which city is located in the Piedmont?

    A. Athens

    B. Macon

    C. Trenton

    D. Savannah

34. What region is known for the production of peanuts, corn, and pecans?

    A. Piedmont

    B. Blue Ridge

    C. Coastal Plain

    D. Appalachian Plateau

35. Why have many of Georgia's cities and industries grown up along the Fall Line?

   A. Railroads were already built there.

   B. Rapidly flowing rivers were a source of energy.

   C. Ships can travel northward from there to the northeast.

   D. The land along the Fall Line was fertile and perfect for farming.

36. The border between the Georgia Piedmont and the Coastal Plain marks the point at which rivers drop in elevation creating waterfalls. This border is known as the

   A. Fall Line.

   B. Tallulah Gorge.

   C. Savannah River.

   D. Okefenokee Swamp.

37. Which is a characteristic of the Okefenokee Swamp?

   A. It is located in the Piedmont region.

   B. It has the most precipitation in the state.

   C. It is famous for its hydroelectric potential.

   D. It is the largest freshwater marsh in Georgia.

38. What river is the primary source of water for Atlanta?

   A. Flint

   B. Altamaha

   C. Savannah

   D. Chattahoochee

39. The earliest settlement of Georgia by the first English colonists was along which Georgia river?

   A. Altamaha

   B. Savannah

   C. Ocmulgee

   D. Chattahoochee

40. What is the only river that flows into Georgia from another state?

   A. Coosa

   B. Savannah

   C. Ogeechee

   D. Chattahoochee

GEOGRAPHY, EXPLORATION, AND NATIVE AMERICANS

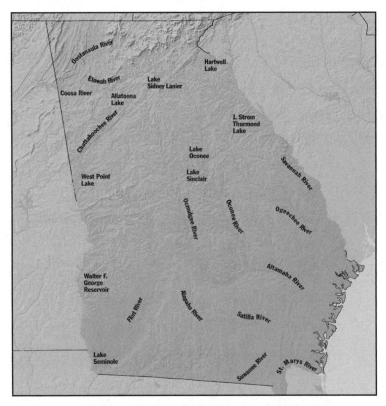

Use the map to answer questions 41-43.

41. Which river forms the boundary between Georgia and South Carolina?

    A. Altamaha

    B. Savannah

    C. Ogeechee

    D. Chattahoochee

42. Which river does NOT flow into the Atlantic Ocean?

    A. Flint

    B. Satilla

    C. Ocmulgee

    D. St. Marys

43. Which lake is located along the Oconee River?

    A. Lanier

    B. Sinclair

    C. Hartwell

    D. Allatoona

44. What is the primary function of the barrier islands?

    A. They protect the beaches from erosion.

    B. They are frequent targets of hurricanes.

    C. They protect wild horses from extinction.

    D. They serve as well-stocked hunting preserves.

45. Which city is MOST LIKELY to experience a direct hit from a hurricane?

    A. Helen

    B. Plains

    C. Athens

    D. Savannah

46. Georgia's climate attracts business and industry because the state

    A. does not have hurricanes.

    B. seldom receives much snow.

    C. rarely experiences tornadoes.

    D. has a consistently mild climate.

47. In many cases, people have to adjust to a new physical and geographic environment in order to make a living. Which person would have to make the most drastic adjustment?

    A. a Georgia cotton farmer moving to Canada

    B. a computer programmer moving from Boston to Atlanta

    C. a logger moving from the Georgia mountains to northern Maine

    D. a Georgia miner moving from the plateau region to West Virginia

SOCIAL STUDIES UNIT TEST

GEOGRAPHY, EXPLORATION, AND NATIVE AMERICANS

GEORGIA'S CLIMATE				
	January Temperatures	July Temperatures	Annual Precipitation	Length of Growing Season
North Georgia Clayton Blue Ridge	41° 40°	74° 74°	71 inches 57 inches	191 days 184 days
Central Georgia Atlanta Macon	44° 47°	79° 81°	48 inches 44 inches	231 days 240 days
Southern Georgia Savannah Brunswick	53° 54°	81° 82°	45 inches 50 inches	273 days 276 days

Use the table to answer questions 48-50.

48. The warmest areas of Georgia are in which region of the state?

    A. northern

    B. central

    C. southern

    D. cannot determine from data in this table

49. The area of Georgia that receives the most rainfall is

    A. northern Georgia.

    B. central Georgia.

    C. southern Georgia.

    D. cannot determine from data in this table

50. The area of Georgia best suited for farming is which region of the state?

    A. northern

    B. central

    C. southern

    D. cannot determine from data in this table

PLEASE STOP! STOP!

Student Name:_____

Assignment: _____

Period:_____

Marking Instructions:
- Use a No. 2 pencil (no ink or ballpoint pens)
- Fill the circles in completely
- Erase completely to change your answer
- Make no stray marks

Example: **Score:**

   A   B   C   D

1 ○ ● ○ ○

Student ID Number

0○	0○	0○	0○	0○	0○	0○	0○	0○
1○	1○	1○	1○	1○	1○	1○	1○	1○
2○	2○	2○	2○	2○	2○	2○	2○	2○
3○	3○	3○	3○	3○	3○	3○	3○	3○
4○	4○	4○	4○	4○	4○	4○	4○	4○
5○	5○	5○	5○	5○	5○	5○	5○	5○
6○	6○	6○	6○	6○	6○	6○	6○	6○
7○	7○	7○	7○	7○	7○	7○	7○	7○
8○	8○	8○	8○	8○	8○	8○	8○	8○
9○	9○	9○	9○	9○	9○	9○	9○	9○

	A	B	C	D		A	B	C	D		A	B	C	D		A	B	C	D		A	B	C	D
1	○	○	○	○	11	○	○	○	○	21	○	○	○	○	31	○	○	○	○	41	○	○	○	○
2	○	○	○	○	12	○	○	○	○	22	○	○	○	○	32	○	○	○	○	42	○	○	○	○
3	○	○	○	○	13	○	○	○	○	23	○	○	○	○	33	○	○	○	○	43	○	○	○	○
4	○	○	○	○	14	○	○	○	○	24	○	○	○	○	34	○	○	○	○	44	○	○	○	○
5	○	○	○	○	15	○	○	○	○	25	○	○	○	○	35	○	○	○	○	45	○	○	○	○
6	○	○	○	○	16	○	○	○	○	26	○	○	○	○	36	○	○	○	○	46	○	○	○	○
7	○	○	○	○	17	○	○	○	○	27	○	○	○	○	37	○	○	○	○	47	○	○	○	○
8	○	○	○	○	18	○	○	○	○	28	○	○	○	○	38	○	○	○	○	48	○	○	○	○
9	○	○	○	○	19	○	○	○	○	29	○	○	○	○	39	○	○	○	○	49	○	○	○	○
10	○	○	○	○	20	○	○	○	○	30	○	○	○	○	40	○	○	○	○	50	○	○	○	○

SOCIAL STUDIES UNIT TEST

COLONIZATION

1. One of the reasons for the colonization of Georgia was to serve as a buffer colony. This meant that Georgia was

    A. a colony for settlement by the poor.

    B. an outpost for pirates attacking Spanish galleons.

    C. a military protective zone between English and Spanish settlements.

    D. an agricultural station experimenting with new strains of cotton plants.

2. The main reason the king wanted to create the colony of Georgia was to

    A. help pay royal debts.

    B. civilize the native Indians.

    C. release debtors from prison.

    D. establish a source of raw materials.

3. Why did James Oglethorpe suggest forming a colony for the poor?

    A. England wanted to get rid of debtors permanently.

    B. Oglethorpe had a friend who died in a debtors' prison.

    C. The homeless would readily come to the New World.

    D. The poor were mostly well-educated people who had fallen on hard times.

4. What items, which Great Britain had to import from France, Russia, and Spain, did Oglethorpe promise to produce in Georgia?

    A. cotton dyes and silk

    B. wheat, rice, and wine

    C. tropical fruit and spices

    D. white potatoes, yams, and corn

5. Which term BEST describes the kind of people Oglethorpe and his associates wanted to bring to Georgia?

    A. well educated

    B. former convicts

    C. deeply religious

    D. poor but worthy

6. Georgia's charter did NOT include a provision that

    A. banned liquor in the colony.

    B. gave the king of England control of the colony.

    C. prohibited Catholics from becoming colonists.

    D. guaranteed every settler his day in court to settle differences.

COLONIZATION

7. When did King George II grant Oglethorpe and the trustees a charter for the colony of Georgia?

    A. 1492

    B. 1607

    C. 1732

    D. 1776

8. According to the charter, what religious group was NOT allowed to settle in Georgia?

    A. Baptist

    C. Jewish

    B. Catholic

    D. Methodist

9. According to Georgia's charter, which group of people was forbidden to enter Georgia?

    A. blacks

    B. soldiers

    C. lawyers

    D. preachers

10. What ship brought Oglethorpe and the first colonists to Charleston, then Savannah, during the winter of 1733?

    A. *Ann*

    B. *Maria*

    C. *Godspeed*

    D. *Mayflower*

11. The European nation that set up a colony in Georgia under the leadership of James Oglethorpe was

    A. Spain.

    B. France.

    C. Portugal.

    D. Great Britain.

12. Those who were selected to settle the colony of Georgia were required to

    A. have served time in a debtors' prison.

    B. bring their own farm tools with them.

    C. only sell their land to another Englishman.

    D. use a portion of their land to grow mulberry trees.

13. The trustees gave the first settlers in Georgia the right to

    D. own land.

    C. collect taxes.

    B. hold elections.

    A. vote for leaders.

14. What policy did the king make to ensure that the trustees did not take personal advantage of their position?

    A. The trustees could not hold office.

    B. The trustees could not serve more than one year.

    C. The trustees had to break off all ties with Great Britain.

    D. The trustees had to donate their own money to support the colonists.

Use this illustration to answer question 15.

15. Which statement BEST describes the subject of the illustration?

    A. The Indians welcomed the British with gifts.

    B. The British took control over the Indians' land.

    C. The Indians showed distrust for the invading Englishmen.

    D. The British and the Indians had a disappointing first meeting.

COLONIZATION

16. What Indians were led by Tomochichi?

    A. Creek

    B. Oconee

    C. Cherokee

    D. Yamacraw

17. Who served as the translator for Oglethorpe in his discussions with Tomochichi?

    A. Toonahowi

    B. William Bull

    C. Mary Musgrove

    D. Robert Montgomery

18. Tomochichi allowed James Oglethorpe to settle on a bluff overlooking which river?

    A. Flint River

    B. Altamaha River

    C. Savannah River

    D. St. Marys River

19. Who surveyed and helped design the city of Savannah?

    A. Noble Jones

    B. Samuel Nunez

    C. James Oglethorpe

    D. Robert Montgomery

20. Where did James Oglethorpe and the first Georgia colonists land when they arrived in Georgia?

    A. Fort Pulaski on the Savannah River

    B. Ossabaw Island on Ossabaw Sound

    C. Fort Frederica near St. Simons Island

    D. Yamacraw Bluff on the Savannah River

21. Oglethorpe's plan for the establishment of Savannah could BEST be described as

    A. heavily defended fort.

    B. a city built around open squares.

    C. a series of circular roads making travel easy.

    D. a poor design for defense against invading armies.

22. The basic pattern of Savannah was fashioned after a design by

    A. Noble Jones.

    B. William Bull.

    C. Robert Castell.

    D. James Oglethorpe.

23. Germans from Salzburg came to Georgia

    A. to receive free land.

    B. to obtain religious freedom.

    C. to be freed from debtors' prisons.

    D. to relieve the overcrowding in Germany.

24. Who was the leader of the Germans from Salzburg?

    A. John Reynolds

    B. James Oglethorpe

    C. Lachlan McIntosh

    D. John Martin Bolzius

25. Where did the Salzburgers first settle?

    A. Albany

    B. Darien

    C. Ebenezer

    D. Savannah

26. The Salzburgers moved from their original Georgia settlement because

    A. they were attacked frequently by the Indians.

    B. they had problems with the Spanish who lived nearby.

    C. the land on which they settled was marshy and not very productive.

    D. the area was plagued by harsh storms that caused extensive damage.

27. On which barrier island did the Salzburgers settle?

    A. Jekyll Island

    B. St. Simons Island

    C. Cumberland Island

    D. St. Catherines Island

28. The greatest threat to the existence of the Georgia colony came from

    D. new diseases.

    C. the area's harsh climate.

    B. Spanish soldiers in Florida.

    A. Indians who lived in the area.

29. Where did the Highland Scots settle in Georgia?

    A. Darien

    B. Augusta

    C. Savannah

    D. New Ebenezer

30. The Highland Scots opposed which policy?

    A. permitting slavery

    B. trading with the Spanish

    C. giving women the right to vote

    D. keeping close ties with Great Britain

31. Who were the malcontents of the early Georgia colony?

    A. the trustees and their families

    B. foreigners from Germany and Scotland

    C. officials who examined the contents of cargo ships

    D. people who were unhappy and constantly complaining

32. Which was NOT an area of discontent in Georgia?

    A. slavery

    B. the sale of rum

    C. unemployment

    D. ownership of land

33. With which trustee policy did the colonists disagree?

    A. hard work

    B. land allotments

    C. military training

    D. prohibition of slavery

34. What was the importance of the Battle of Bloody Marsh?

    A. It demonstrated the strength of the Spanish militia.

    B. It resulted in Georgia's gaining new lands on which to settle.

    C. It ended the threat of war from Native Americans.

    D. It was the beginning of a safe southern frontier for the British.

35. What group came to the aid of James Oglethorpe in the Battle of Bloody Marsh?

   A. Catholics

   B. Spaniards

   C. Salzburgers

   D. Highland Scots

36. The Latin motto of the trustees, *Non Sibi Sed Allis*, translates from Latin as "Not for themselves but for others." What does this mean?

   A. The king felt the colony had been a failure and the trustees had to be punished for what they had done to other people.

   B. The trustees established Georgia for the purpose of helping the poor, not for the purpose of making themselves rich.

   C. The Highland Scots and the Salzburgers were foreigners and couldn't be trusted to defend others, including the British.

   D. Religious leaders could not allow Catholics in Georgia because of protests from members of the new Methodist church.

37. What impact did the departure of Oglethorpe to England have on the colony?

   A. Great impact; the new leaders quickly turned control over to the king.

   B. Great impact; under the new leader most of the restrictive laws were changed.

   C. No impact; after he married, he quickly returned to the colony to help the poor.

   D. No impact; he was cleared of the charges against him and returned within the year.

38. In 1752, Georgia became what type of colony?

   A. royal

   B. debtor

   C. proprietary

   D. self-governing

39. Who controlled Georgia after it became a royal colony?

   A. James Oglethorpe

   B. the people of Georgia

   C. a bicameral legislature

   D. the king of Great Britain

40. What city served as Georgia's capital during its period as a royal colony?

    A. Macon

    B. Atlanta

    C. Augusta

    D. Savannah

41. When Georgia was a royal colony, how were members of the upper house of the legislature, the Governor's Council, chosen?

    A. They were elected by the voters.

    B. They were appointed by the king.

    C. They were appointed by the royal governor.

    D. They were chosen by members of the lower house of the legislature.

42. Who was the first royal governor of Georgia?

    A. Robert Castell

    B. John Reynolds

    C. James Oglethorpe

    D. Robert Montgomery

43. While John Reynolds was its royal governor, Georgia established

    A. a court system.

    B. land ownership rights.

    C. local governing bodies.

    D. a unicameral legislature.

44. Governor Reynolds disbanded the legislature because

    A. he believed the governor should have sole power.

    B. there was a conflict between the two houses in the legislature.

    C. some members of the law-making body were elected illegally.

    D. there was a disagreement over how to improve military defenses.

45. Which royal governor permitted slavery in Georgia, made farms more profitable, and increased the number of merchants selling goods?

    A. Henry Ellis

    B. James Wright

    C. John Reynolds

    D. William Stephens

COLONIZATION

46. Which person served as a royal governor of Georgia?

    A. James Wright

    B. Button Gwinnett

    C. William Stephens

    D. James Oglethorpe

47. Who was governor of Georgia when the last of the palisades were built around Savannah, Sunbury became Georgia's main port of entry, and the term *crackers* was used to refer to undesirables?

    A. Henry Ellis

    B. James Wright

    C. John Reynolds

    D. James Oglethorpe

48. How did the colonies benefit Great Britain economically?

    A. The colonies imported raw materials from Great Britain.

    B. The colonies manufactured goods for Great Britain.

    C. The colonies traded with one another for expensive goods and services.

    D. The colonies enabled Great Britain to manufacture goods to sell to other countries.

49. What goods did Great Britain import from the colonies?

    A. rye

    B. tools

    C. clothing

    D. furniture

50. Which is a reason why the vision of the trustees was never fulfilled?

    A. Georgia was a political failure.

    B. Too many Catholics settled in Georgia.

    C. Debtors were never released to come to Georgia.

    D. The Indians and Spanish caused the settlers to live in fear.

PLEASE STOP! STOP!

Student Name: _____

Assignment: _____

Period: _____

Marking Instructions:
- Use a No. 2 pencil (no ink or ballpoint pens)
- Fill the circles in completely
- Erase completely to change your answer
- Make no stray marks

Example:

	A	B	C	D
1	○	●	○	○

Score:

Student ID Number

0○	0○	0○	0○	0○	0○	0○	0○	0○
1○	1○	1○	1○	1○	1○	1○	1○	1○
2○	2○	2○	2○	2○	2○	2○	2○	2○
3○	3○	3○	3○	3○	3○	3○	3○	3○
4○	4○	4○	4○	4○	4○	4○	4○	4○
5○	5○	5○	5○	5○	5○	5○	5○	5○
6○	6○	6○	6○	6○	6○	6○	6○	6○
7○	7○	7○	7○	7○	7○	7○	7○	7○
8○	8○	8○	8○	8○	8○	8○	8○	8○
9○	9○	9○	9○	9○	9○	9○	9○	9○

	A	B	C	D			A	B	C	D			A	B	C	D			A	B	C	D			A	B	C	D
1	○	○	○	○		11	○	○	○	○		21	○	○	○	○		31	○	○	○	○		41	○	○	○	○
2	○	○	○	○		12	○	○	○	○		22	○	○	○	○		32	○	○	○	○		42	○	○	○	○
3	○	○	○	○		13	○	○	○	○		23	○	○	○	○		33	○	○	○	○		43	○	○	○	○
4	○	○	○	○		14	○	○	○	○		24	○	○	○	○		34	○	○	○	○		44	○	○	○	○
5	○	○	○	○		15	○	○	○	○		25	○	○	○	○		35	○	○	○	○		45	○	○	○	○
6	○	○	○	○		16	○	○	○	○		26	○	○	○	○		36	○	○	○	○		46	○	○	○	○
7	○	○	○	○		17	○	○	○	○		27	○	○	○	○		37	○	○	○	○		47	○	○	○	○
8	○	○	○	○		18	○	○	○	○		28	○	○	○	○		38	○	○	○	○		48	○	○	○	○
9	○	○	○	○		19	○	○	○	○		29	○	○	○	○		39	○	○	○	○		49	○	○	○	○
10	○	○	○	○		20	○	○	○	○		30	○	○	○	○		40	○	○	○	○		50	○	○	○	○

5. During the French and Indian War, why did most of the Native American tribes side with the French?

   A. The Indians had become Catholic.

   B. The Indians worked for the French as guides.

   C. The Indians negotiated treaties with the French.

   D. The Indians were trading partners with the French.

6. What two countries were involved in the negotiations that ended the French and Indian War?

   A. Spain and Portugal

   B. Spain and Great Britain

   C. France and Great Britain

   D. France and the United States

7. Which statement BEST describes Georgia's gains from the French and Indian War?

   A. Georgia gained the Creek and Cherokee Indian lands and gold mines.

   B. Georgia gained lands to the north and west, part of Florida, and waterways for travel.

   C. Georgia gained land, naval stores and timber, farm acreage, and new settlers.

   D. Georgia gained lands to the south and east, water access for shipping, and timber resources.

8. Which statement BEST describes how the French and Indian War led to America's Revolutionary War?

   A. Great Britain gained control of Canada and tried to use Canada's tax structure on the thirteen colonies.

   B. France lost the Louisiana Territory, and the colonies argued with Great Britain over claims to the newly acquired land.

   C. To get revenge, France incited rebellion in the colonies and enticed Spain to move into the territories of the British colonies.

   D. To get money to repay war debts, Great Britain taxed the colonies on the premise that the war had been necessary to protect the colonies from the French.

9. What law forbade colonists to move west of the Appalachian Mountains?

   A. Intolerable Acts

   B. Missouri Compromise

   C. Proclamation of 1763

   D. Emancipation Proclamation

10. The Proclamation of 1763 moved Georgia's southern boundary to the

    A. Flint River.

    B. St. Marys River.

    C. Suwannee River.

    D. Altamaha River.

11. Georgians who came together to oppose the Stamp Act called themselves the

    A. Liberty Boys.

    B. Sons of Liberty.

    C. Revolutionay Guards.

    D. Stamp Act Opposition.

Use these facts to answer question 13.

- Many colonists had relatives in Great Britain and did not want to put them in danger.
- The British king was still paying money to support the colonists.

12. Which was NOT a part of the Intolerable Acts?

    A. The British prohibited the Massachusetts colonists from having town meetings.

    B. The British required citizens in all the colonies to house and feed British soldiers.

    C. The British required citizens in Boston to pay additional taxes to pay for damage during the Boston Tea Party.

    D. The British closed the port of Boston until the colonists paid for the tea that was destroyed in the Boston Tea Party.

13. Because of these facts, what was the behavior of most Georgians during the Revolution?

    A. moves to Virginia

    B. riots in the streets

    C. loyalty to King George

    D. attacks on British troops

Use these actions to answer question 14.

- closing the port of Boston to trade
- prohibiting town meetings to discuss issues
- requiring citizens to house and feed British soldiers

14. These actions taken by the British were known as the

    A. Tea Act.

    B. Stamp Act.

    C. Navigation Acts.

    D. Intolerable Acts.

REVOLUTION

15. Which was the reason Georgians remained loyal to Great Britain?

    A. Georgia had poorer settlers than the other colonies, and they were more loyal to the king.

    B. Georgia was not as successful as the other colonies, and it could not afford to raise funds to fight the British.

    C. Georgia was far younger as a colony than the other colonies, and it still needed much support from Great Britain.

    D. Georgia had a much smaller population than the other colonies, and it did not have enough men to fight the British army.

16. What is the opening part of the Declaration of Independence called?

    A. Preface

    B. Objective

    C. Preamble

    D. Introduction

17. Who was the primary author of the Declaration of Independence?

    A. John Adams

    B. Thomas Paine

    C. Thomas Jefferson

    D. Benjamin Franklin

18. What is included in the middle part of the Declaration of Independence?

    A. a declaration of war

    B. a list of grievances against the king

    C. a rationale for supporting the royal family

    D. signatures of the participants at the Continental Congress

19. What is included in the third part of the Declaration of Independence?

    A. a declaration of war on Great Britain

    B. a warning to King George to change his ways

    C. a call for a meeting to establish a new government

    D. a statement about separation from Great Britain

20. Most of the fighting in Georgia during the American Revolution was between

    A. British and French soldiers.

    B. Spanish and British soldiers.

    C. Georgia Loyalists and Indians.

    D. Georgia Patriots and Loyalists.

REVOLUTION

Use these activities to answer question 21.

- Committees of Correspondence
- Boston Tea Party
- Continental Congress

21. These activities were supported by most of the

A. patriots.

B. royalists.

C. loyalists.

D. colonists.

22. Where did the first colonial victory in Georgia during the American Revolution occur?

A. Sunbury

B. Louisville

C. Savannah

D. Kettle Creek

23. Who was the leader of the militia near Washington, Georgia, and led the forces at the Battle of Kettle Creek?

A. Elijah Clarke

B. Nathaniel Greene

C. Benjamin Lincoln

D. George Washington

24. What was the importance of the Battle of Kettle Creek?

A. The Indians joined with the colonists to defeat the British.

B. The colonists took needed weapons and horses from the British.

C. The British were driven into Florida and were unable to regroup.

D. It was the last battle fought in Georgia during the Revolutionary War.

25. Who was the black soldier who was seriously wounded at the Battle of Kettle Creek?

A. Agippa Hull

B. Austin Dabney

C. Crispus Attucks

D. Frederick Douglass

REVOLUTION

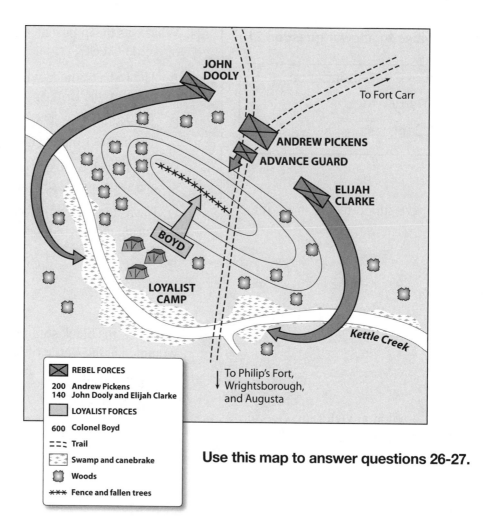

Use this map to answer questions 26-27.

26. Which military leader commanded the most troops at the Battle of Kettle Creek?

A. John Dooly

B. Elijah Clarke

C. Colonel Boyd

D. Andrew Pickens

27. What obstacle separated Pickens and Boyd and had to be crossed for the battle to begin?

A. Fort Carr

B. Kettle Creek

C. fence and fallen trees

D. tents from the loyalist camp

REVISION

REVOLUTION

STATE of GEORGIA.

To the Honourable the _____ and the Members of
Council, now fitting in Augufta for the Purpofe of granting
Lands in the two new Counties of Franklin and Wafhington.

The PETITION of _____
as a _____ in the State aforefaid,

SHEWETH,

THAT your Petitioner is entitled to _____
_____ Acres of Land, as a Bounty for his
Services, purfuant to the Certificate hereunto annexed: That your
Petitioner is defirous of taking up the faid Lands in the County of

_____

May it therefore pleafe your Honourable Board to grant your
Petitioner _____
Acres of Land in the County of _____
on the Right aforefaid, and on his complying with the
Terms mentioned in the late Land Act; and your Petiti-
oner will pray. . .

Use this document to answer question 28.

28. This document was given to Austin Dabney in 1821 by the State of Georgia to show that he had earned

    A. the title of "Honourable."

    B. freedom from his master.

    C. 50 acres of land in Washington County.

    D. the right to live at Mount Vernon George Washington.

29. Who was the female Georgia patriot famous for capturing and killing a group of Tories during the Revolution?

    A. Nancy Hart

    B. Molly Pitcher

    C. Rebecca Felton

    D. Mary Musgrove

30. Who were the three Georgians who signed the Declaration of Independence?

    A. Lyman Hall, Button Gwinnett, and James Wright

    B. Thomas Jefferson, Henry Ellis, and James Wright

    C. George Walton, Lyman Hall, and Button Gwinnett

    D. Lyman Hall, George Walton, and Noble Wimberly Jones

31. Who was the primary author of the Declaration of Independence?

    A. John Adams

    B. Thomas Painet

    C. Thomas Jefferson

    D. Benjamin Frankin

32. How could Georgia's support of the Revolutionary War effort best be described?

    A. never strong in any area

    B. strong in every area except Savannah

    C. complete in all areas from the beginning

    D. led by Savannah and the upcountry Revolutionary leaders

33. Independence from Great Britain came for Georgia and the other colonies in

    A. 1607.

    B. 1733.

    C. 1776.

    D. 1779.

34. Who was the foreign patriot who died during the siege of Savannah?

    A. Casimir Pulaski

    B. Bernardo de Galvez

    C. Marquis de Lafayette

    D. Jean Baptist Rochambeau

35. What was the MOST significant result of the siege of Savannah?

    A. The British were pushed out of Georgia.

    B. The city of Savannah remained in British hands.

    C. It was the deadliest battle of the Revolutionary War.

    D. It was the last major conflict of the Revolutionary War.

SOCIAL STUDIES UNIT TEST

REVOLUTION

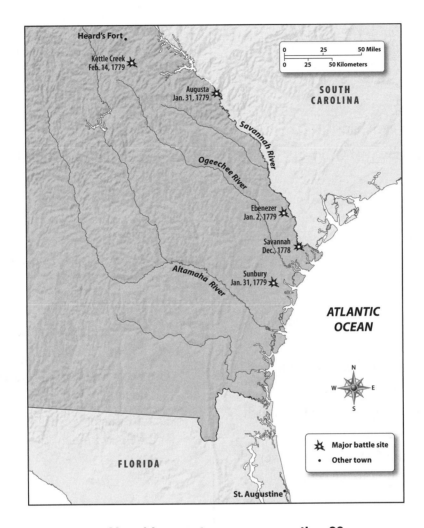

Use this map to answer question 36.

36. Where was one of the major battle sites of the Revolution in Georgia?

   A. Ebenezer

   B. Brier Creek

   C. Heard's Fort

   D. St. Augustine

37. What was the main weakness of the Georgia Constitution of 1777?

   A. It created an independent executive branch.

   B. It established two parts in the legislative branch.

   C. It gave too much power to the legislative branch.

   D. It placed too much importance on checks and balances.

REVOLUTION

38. Under Georgia's Constitution of 1777, governors were selected by

    A. the legislature.

    B. the citizens' vote.

    C. the chairman of each parish.

    D. the executive council of Georgia.

39. All of the following were reasons Georgia's first constitution limited the power of the governor except

    A. they feared the governor would become a dictator.

    B. there were no qualified candidates for governor.

    C. in the past the governor showed too much loyalty to the king.

    D. the legislature should have more power because it was closer to the people.

40. Who was elected Georgia's first governor under the Constitution of 1777?

    A. Lyman Hall

    B. John Treutlen

    C. George Walton

    D. Button Gwinnett

41. The first written plan for the government of the United States was called the

    A. American Constitution.

    B. Colonial Confederation.

    C. Articles of Confederation.

    D. Constitution of the United States.

42. The weaknesses of the Articles of Confederation led to

    A. the citizens refusing to elect a president.

    B. thirteen states not becoming a unified nation.

    C. the thirteen states refusing to sign the document.

    D. citizens paying higher taxes to support the government.

43. Under the Articles of Confederation, there was a

    A. governor.

    B. president.

    C. legislature.

    D. court system.

REVOLUTION

44. Why were government leaders hesitant to change the Articles of Confederation?

    A. They were afraid people would panic.

    B. They believed it was too soon to make changes.

    C. They did not have enough support to make changes.

    D. They were afraid foreign countries would view change as a weakness.

45. Why did the authors of the Articles of Confederation want a federal government with little power?

    A. They wanted to grow the power of the federal government slowly over time.

    B. They considered themselves thirteen separate states rather than one nation.

    C. They feared a government that gave significant power to the southern states.

    D. They had just freed themselves from the domination of a strong, powerful government in Great Britain.

46. The purpose of the Constitutional Convention, which was held in Philadelphia in 1787, was to

    A. sign the Treaty of Paris.

    B. select the nation's new president.

    C. revise the Articles of Confederation.

    D. draft a Declaration of Independence.

47. The U.S. Constitution was actually signed by only two of Georgia's four delegates. The two signers were William Few and

    A. George Walton.

    B. Button Gwinnett.

    C. Thomas Jefferson.

    D. Abraham Baldwin.

48. How many states ratified the U.S. Constitution before Georgia?

    A. 2

    B. 3

    C. 4

    D. 5

49. The initial purpose in calling the Philadelphia Convention of 1787 was to

    A. regulate trade between the states.

    B. establish a national court system.

    C. establish a stronger federal government.

    D. gain the consent of the states in order to confront the British.

50. After the U.S. Constitution was written and signed, it had to be ratified, or approved, by the states. How did Georgia respond to ratification?

   A. It was slow to approve the new Constitution.

   B. It refused to ratify until the Bill of Rights was added.

   C. It never approved it and later had to apply for admission.

   D. It approved quickly as the fourth state to enter the Union.

Student Name:_____

Assignment: _____

Period:_____

Marking Instructions:
- Use a No. 2 pencil (no ink or ballpoint pens)
- Fill the circles in completely
- Erase completely to change your answer
- Make no stray marks

Example:

A　B　C　D
1 ○ ● ○ ○

Score:

Student ID Number

0○	0○	0○	0○	0○	0○	0○	0○	0○
1○	1○	1○	1○	1○	1○	1○	1○	1○
2○	2○	2○	2○	2○	2○	2○	2○	2○
3○	3○	3○	3○	3○	3○	3○	3○	3○
4○	4○	4○	4○	4○	4○	4○	4○	4○
5○	5○	5○	5○	5○	5○	5○	5○	5○
6○	6○	6○	6○	6○	6○	6○	6○	6○
7○	7○	7○	7○	7○	7○	7○	7○	7○
8○	8○	8○	8○	8○	8○	8○	8○	8○
9○	9○	9○	9○	9○	9○	9○	9○	9○

A B C D
1 ○ ○ ○ ○　11 ○ ○ ○ ○　21 ○ ○ ○ ○　31 ○ ○ ○ ○　41 ○ ○ ○ ○
2 ○ ○ ○ ○　12 ○ ○ ○ ○　22 ○ ○ ○ ○　32 ○ ○ ○ ○　42 ○ ○ ○ ○
3 ○ ○ ○ ○　13 ○ ○ ○ ○　23 ○ ○ ○ ○　33 ○ ○ ○ ○　43 ○ ○ ○ ○
4 ○ ○ ○ ○　14 ○ ○ ○ ○　24 ○ ○ ○ ○　34 ○ ○ ○ ○　44 ○ ○ ○ ○
5 ○ ○ ○ ○　15 ○ ○ ○ ○　25 ○ ○ ○ ○　35 ○ ○ ○ ○　45 ○ ○ ○ ○
6 ○ ○ ○ ○　16 ○ ○ ○ ○　26 ○ ○ ○ ○　36 ○ ○ ○ ○　46 ○ ○ ○ ○
7 ○ ○ ○ ○　17 ○ ○ ○ ○　27 ○ ○ ○ ○　37 ○ ○ ○ ○　47 ○ ○ ○ ○
8 ○ ○ ○ ○　18 ○ ○ ○ ○　28 ○ ○ ○ ○　38 ○ ○ ○ ○　48 ○ ○ ○ ○
9 ○ ○ ○ ○　19 ○ ○ ○ ○　29 ○ ○ ○ ○　39 ○ ○ ○ ○　49 ○ ○ ○ ○
10 ○ ○ ○ ○　20 ○ ○ ○ ○　30 ○ ○ ○ ○　40 ○ ○ ○ ○　50 ○ ○ ○ ○

SOCIAL STUDIES UNIT TEST

WESTWARD EXPANSION

1. Which statement BEST describes a "land grant university" such as the University of Georgia?

   A. The land could not be used for any purpose other than a college.

   B. The land for the college was donated by the federal government.

   C. The college was a public university with free tuition to state residents.

   D. The college was established as an agricultural college to improve farming.

2. From the colonial era until Reconstruction, the capital of Georgia was moved many times in response to what factor?

   A. changing political influences in the state

   B. the changing population center of the state

   C. the changing geographic center of the state

   D. changing transportation patterns in the state

3. All the records from the Yazoo land fraud were burned in public in Georgia's then capital city of

   A. Athens.

   B. Atlanta.

   C. Savannah.

   D. Louisville.

4. By 1860, the two largest church denominations in Georgia were

   A. Baptist and Jewish.

   B. Methodist and Baptist.

   C. Episcopal and Catholic.

   D. Episcopal and Methodist.

5. Which church sent circuit riders to frontier settlements to provide monthly services?

   A. Baptist

   B. Catholic

   C. Episcopal

   D. Methodist

6. The Methodist and Baptist churches split over permitting

   A. divorce.

   B. slavery.

   C. communion for children.

   D. ordained women ministers.

WESTWARD EXPANSION

7. What was the purpose of the headright system in Georgia?

   A. It distributed Indian lands to new settlers.

   B. It administered voting and election districts.

   C. It established a method of counting population.

   D. It provided an organized system of collecting taxes.

8. What system replaced the headright system as a way of allocating land?

   A. land rush

   B. feudalism

   C. surveying

   D. land lottery

9. In the early 1800s, Georgia's policy of giving land to citizens through lotteries was meant to

   A. open the land to yeoman farmers.

   B. encourage the development of large cities.

   C. introduce new crops and farming methods.

   D. ensure peaceful relations with Native Americans.

10. With which topic was the Yazoo Fraud concerned?

    A. Indian lands in north Georgia

    B. sale of land in western Georgia territory

    C. ratification of the Constitution in Georgia

    D. creation of a national park on state property

11. What scandal took place when Georgia's governor and some legislators were bribed to sell public land to private developers at below-market prices?

    A. Yazoo land fraud

    B. Trail of Tears fraud

    C. Georgia's land lottery

    D. Mississippi land fraud

12. Why did Georgia give up land claims in present-day Mississippi and Alabama?

    A. The federal government wanted to set that land aside for the Indian population.

    B. The state did not have the millions of dollars required to purchase the land from Spain.

    C. The federal government agree to settle the Yazoo land fraud and remove the Cherokee from Georgia.

    D. The state could not claim the land because the General Assembly illegally sold it to private companies.

SOCIAL STUDIES UNIT TEST

WESTWARD EXPANSION

13. The Yazoo land fraud occurred because land companies

    A. claimed land that had been acquired illegally.

    B. bribed legislators so they could buy land cheaply.

    C. took land from the Native Americans by force.

    D. made illegal treaties with the Native Americans.

14. To whom did Georgia's governor and members of its General Assembly sell the land between the Mississippi and Yazoo rivers, resulting in the Yazoo land fraud?

    A. land companies

    B. state government

    C. federal government

    D. private land owners

15. How did Eli Whitney's invention influence the growth of slavery in the South?

    A. It made it easier for slaves to pick cotton.

    B. It increased the profits from growing cotton.

    C. It made it easier to produce cloth from cotton.

    D. It replenished the soil so that more cotton could be grown.

16. What was invented in Georgia during the 1790s that quickly changed the state's agricultural landscape and led Georgia to develop an economy based on farming?

    A. the combine

    B. the cotton gin

    C. the steam engine

    D. the spinning jenny

17. The chief cash crop in Georgia before the Civil War was

    A. apples.

    B. cotton.

    C. grapes.

    D. pecans.

18. The cotton gin was used to

    A. pick cotton.

    B. plant cotton.

    C. turn cotton fiber into thread.

    D. separate cotton seeds from cotton fiber.

WESTWARD EXPANSION

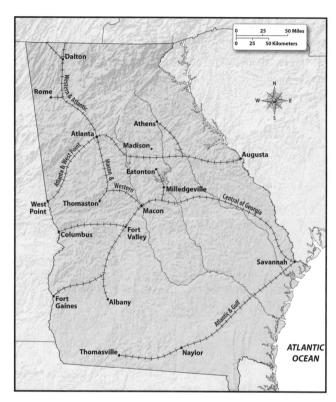

Use the map to answer questions 19-21.

19. Which city was connected to Atlanta by the Atlanta & West Point Railroad?

    A. Augusta

    B. Madison

    C. Thomaston

    D. Fort Valley

20. Which railroad was used to travel from Dalton to Atlanta?

    A. Atlantic and Gulf

    B. Central of Georgia

    C. Macon and Western

    D. Western and Atlantic

21. The Atlantic and Gulf Railroad connects Savannah and what city?

    A. Macon

    B. Atlanta

    C. Augusta

    D. Thomasville

22. Which mode of transportation was developing in Georgia just before the Civil War and that was very important to Georgia's war effort and post-war economic development?

    A. canals

    B. railroads

    C. highways

    D. riverboats

23. Which of the following was NOT a major source of transportation prior to the railroad?
    A. car

    B. ferry

    C. riverboat

    D. stagecoach

SOCIAL STUDIES UNIT TEST

WESTWARD EXPANSION

24. The two largest Indian nations living in Georgia were the

    A. Cherokee and Creek.

    B. Seminole and Cherokee.

    C. Mississippian and Creek.

    D. Cherokee and Chickasaw.

25. Who was the Creek leader in the Oconee War between the Creek and the Georgia pioneers?

    A. Sequoyah

    B. Elias Boudinot

    C. William McIntosh

    D. Alexander McGillivray

26. Why was William McIntosh, a Creek chief, murdered by his own people?

    A. He became friendly with the Cherokee.

    B. He was the cousin of Georgia Governor George Troup.

    C. He was defeated in a battle with the Georgia militia.

    D. He signed a treaty ceding the last Creek lands in Georgia.

27. Who worked out the Treaty of Indian Springs, which ceded Creek lands in Georgia to the federal government?

    A. Andrew Jackson and Chief Menawa

    B. Andrew Jackson and William McIntosh

    C. Governor George Troup and Chief Menawa

    D. Governor George Troup and William McIntosh

28. The LEAST important reason for removing the Cherokee from their land was that Georgia citizens wanted to

    A. homestead Cherokee land.

    B. trap and hunt on Cherokee land.

    C. mine gold found on Cherokee land.

    D. eliminate the possibility of Cherokee attacks.

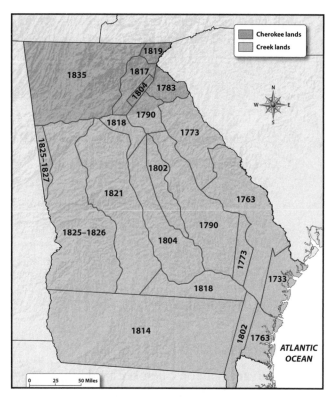

Use the map to answer questions 29-31.

29. In what year did the Creek first cede land to the Europeans?

    A. 1733

    B. 1793

    C. 1827

    D. 1835

30. By what year had Europeans completed the removal of the Creek from Georgia?

    A. 1763

    B. 1814

    C. 1827

    D. 1835

31. The largest land cession from the Cherokee was in what year?

    A. 1763

    B. 1814

    C. 1821

    D. 1835

32. What was George Gist's (Sequoyah's) major contribution to the Cherokee culture?

    A. He gained fame as a proud Cherokee hunter and trapper. .

    B. He signed the treaty giving Cherokee lands to the United States.

    C. He signed the treaty moving the Cherokee to the Indian Territory.

    D. He developed a syllabary so the Cherokee could have a written language.

SOCIAL STUDIES UNIT TEST

WESTWARD EXPANSION

Use this illustration to answer question 33.

Use this illustration to answer question 34-35.

Panning for Gold

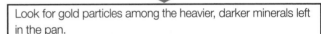

Choose a gravelly stream that is at least 6 inches deep.

Fill the bottom of a shallow pan about 3/4 full with gravel.

Submerge the pan in water and shake it so the heavier gold settles to the bottom. Remove all rocks larger than a pea.

Still holding the pan under water, add more water and tilt the pan away from you. Swirl it around to wash out lighter materials. Continue this step until only the heavier materials remain.

Look for gold particles among the heavier, darker minerals left in the pan.

Put any gold particles in a vial or other container.

33. What event is shown in this drawing?

    A. picking cotton on Coastal Plain plantations

    B. farming the rich soil of the Piedmont region

    C. building the railroad from Macon to Atlanta

    D. mining for gold in the North Georgia mountains

34. In what part of a stream is gold found?

    A. shallow end

    B. along the bank

    C. gravelly bottom

    D. swift-moving water

35. Which tool is needed to pan for gold?

    A. shovel

    B. pick axe

    C. shallow pan

    D. wheelbarrow

36. Who was the chief justice of the U.S. Supreme Court who ruled that Cherokee territory was NOT subject to state law?

    A. John Ross

    B. John Marshall

    C. John C. Calhoun

    D. Andrew Jackson

37. Who was the chief of the Cherokee who took a petition to Congress protesting the Cherokee removal from their land?

    A. Sequoyah

    B. John Ross

    C. Chief Menawa

    D. William McIntosh

38. When Andrew Jackson said "John Marshall has rendered his decision, now let him enforce it" he meant that

    A. Congress and the president agreed with and supported the decision.

    B. the president would see that troops were sent to enforce the decision.

    C. the Constitution was the supreme law of the land and could do whatever it wanted.

    D. the Supreme Court could not enforce the decision without the support of the president.

Use the map to answer questions 39-41.

39. The Cherokee Nation was primarily located in what is today the state of

    A. Georgia.

    B. Alabama.

    C. Tennessee.

    D. Oklahoma.

40. Which river was NOT part of the water route taken by the Cherokee?

    A. Missouri

    B. Arkansas

    C. Tennessee

    D. Mississippi

41. How many routes led from the Cherokee Nation to the Indian Territory?

    A. 1

    B. 2

    C. 3

    D. 4

WESTWARD EXPANSION

42. All the trails along which the Indians were taken ended in the Indian Territory, which is mainly in the present-day state of

   A. Texas.

   B. Kansas.

   C. Arkansas.

   D. Oklahoma.

43. The state of Georgia began to try to remove the Cherokee for which reason?

   A. The Cherokee were a fierce, warlike tribe whom settlers feared.

   B. Missionaries to the Cherokee said they needed to be relocated.

   C. The Cherokee tried to take land belonging to the European settlers.

   D. European settlers wanted the land on which the Cherokee lived.

44. Who disagreed with the governor of Georgia about his removal policy for the Cherokee?

   A. the military

   B. the president

   C. the gold miners

   D. the judicial branch

45. The journey of the Cherokee from Georgia to Oklahoma is called

   A. The Tragic Miles.

   B. The Trail of Tears.

   C. Our Bitter Journey.

   D. Our Voyage of Sorrow.

46. What group of North Georgia Indians was forcibly removed from its land after gold was discovered there?

   A. Seminole

   B. Cherokee

   C. Upper Creek

   D. Lower Creek

47. Which statement BEST explains why there are so few accounts written by slaves about their lives during the antebellum era?

   A. It was illegal for slaves to read and write.

   B. Only abolitionist leaders wrote books about slavery.

   C. Books about slavery were not as popular as other books.

   D. Slaves were not willing to write about the horrors of slavery.

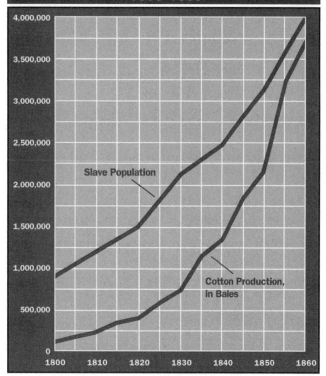

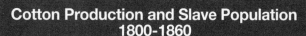

Cotton Production and Slave Population 1800-1860

Slave Population

Cotton Production, in Bales

Use the graph to answer questions 48-49.

48. About how many bales of cotton were produced in 1855?

    A. 4,000,000

    B. 3,250,000

    C. 2,000,000

    D. 1,000,000

49. What is the main idea presented in this graph?

    A. Bales of cotton went up in price as the Civil War approached.

    B. Slavery decreased as a result of abolitionists refusing to buy cotton.

    C. The slave population increased sharply between 1800 and 1860.

    D. As the number of slaves increased, so did U. S. cotton production.

50. Which region of the United States believed that the states should be able to govern themselves without interference from the national government?

    A. Southern states

    B. Northern states

    C. Great Lakes states

    D. Pacific Coast states

PLEASE STOP! STOP!

Student Name: _____

Assignment: _____

Period: _____

Marking Instructions:
- Use a No. 2 pencil (no ink or ballpoint pens)
- Fill the circles in completely
- Erase completely to change your answer
- Make no stray marks

Example:

	A	B	C	D
1	○	●	○	○

Score:

Student ID Number

0○	0○	0○	0○	0○	0○	0○	0○	0○
1○	1○	1○	1○	1○	1○	1○	1○	1○
2○	2○	2○	2○	2○	2○	2○	2○	2○
3○	3○	3○	3○	3○	3○	3○	3○	3○
4○	4○	4○	4○	4○	4○	4○	4○	4○
5○	5○	5○	5○	5○	5○	5○	5○	5○
6○	6○	6○	6○	6○	6○	6○	6○	6○
7○	7○	7○	7○	7○	7○	7○	7○	7○
8○	8○	8○	8○	8○	8○	8○	8○	8○
9○	9○	9○	9○	9○	9○	9○	9○	9○

	A	B	C	D		A	B	C	D		A	B	C	D		A	B	C	D		A	B	C	D
1	○	○	○	○	11	○	○	○	○	21	○	○	○	○	31	○	○	○	○	41	○	○	○	○
2	○	○	○	○	12	○	○	○	○	22	○	○	○	○	32	○	○	○	○	42	○	○	○	○
3	○	○	○	○	13	○	○	○	○	23	○	○	○	○	33	○	○	○	○	43	○	○	○	○
4	○	○	○	○	14	○	○	○	○	24	○	○	○	○	34	○	○	○	○	44	○	○	○	○
5	○	○	○	○	15	○	○	○	○	25	○	○	○	○	35	○	○	○	○	45	○	○	○	○
6	○	○	○	○	16	○	○	○	○	26	○	○	○	○	36	○	○	○	○	46	○	○	○	○
7	○	○	○	○	17	○	○	○	○	27	○	○	○	○	37	○	○	○	○	47	○	○	○	○
8	○	○	○	○	18	○	○	○	○	28	○	○	○	○	38	○	○	○	○	48	○	○	○	○
9	○	○	○	○	19	○	○	○	○	29	○	○	○	○	39	○	○	○	○	49	○	○	○	○
10	○	○	○	○	20	○	○	○	○	30	○	○	○	○	40	○	○	○	○	50	○	○	○	○

SOCIAL STUDIES UNIT TEST

CIVIL WAR

1. The purpose of the Missouri Compromise was to

    D. let Missouri have slavery until 1850.

    C. allow slavery in Maine but not in Missouri.

    B. maintain a balance of slave states and free states.

    A. return slaves captured in free states to their owners in slave states.

2. As a result of the Missouri Compromise,

    A. slavery was banned north of Missouri's southern border.

    B. slavery was allowed in all states east of Missouri.

    C. slavery was banned in all territories west of Missouri.

    D. slavery was allowed north of Missouri's southern border.

3. Which was a result of the Compromise of 1850?

    A. Owning slaves was forbidden in Washington, D.C.

    B. Slavery was permitted in the new state of California.

    C. Importation of slaves from Africa was declared illegal.

    D. Runaway slaves had to be returned to Southern owners.

4. The Georgia Platform was a statement supporting

    A. states' rights.

    B. popular sovereignty.

    C. the Compromise of 1850.

    D. slavery throughout the United States.

5. The purpose of the Constitutional Union party in Georgia was to

    A. preserve the Constitution.

    B. replace the Republican party in the South.

    C. get acceptance of the Compromise of 1850.

    D. illustrate the differences between the North and South.

6. The purpose of the Fugitive Slave Law was to

    A. require slaves that had run away to go back to their owners.

    B. prevent slaves from testifying against whites in court trials.

    C. require slaves to have citizenship papers in order to obtain jobs.

    D. prevent slaves from having group gatherings or meetings.

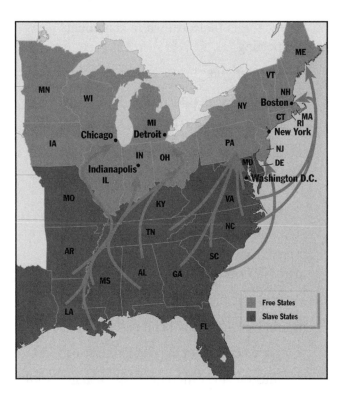

Use the map to answer question 7.

7. The Underground Railroad was a network of people helping escaped slaves leave the South for freedom in northern cities. To which city did most slaves from Georgia flee?

   A. Chicago, Illinois

   B. Indianapolis, Indiana

   C. Boston, Massachusetts

   D. Philadelphia, Pennsylvania

8. How did the Kansas-Nebraska Act change the Missouri Compromise?

   A. It made Missouri a free state.

   B. It created the territories of Kansas and Nebraska.

   C. It permitted slavery north of Missouri's southern boundary.

   D. It changed the requirements necessary for a territory to become a state.

9. Which BEST explains why the United States Supreme Court ruled against Dred Scott?

   A. because he returned to a slave state and could not be freed

   B. because Scott was a slave and was not eligible to sue in court

   C. because he did not live long enough in a free territory to be free

   D. because he was the property of his owner and could be taken anywhere

SOCIAL STUDIES UNIT TEST

CIVIL WAR

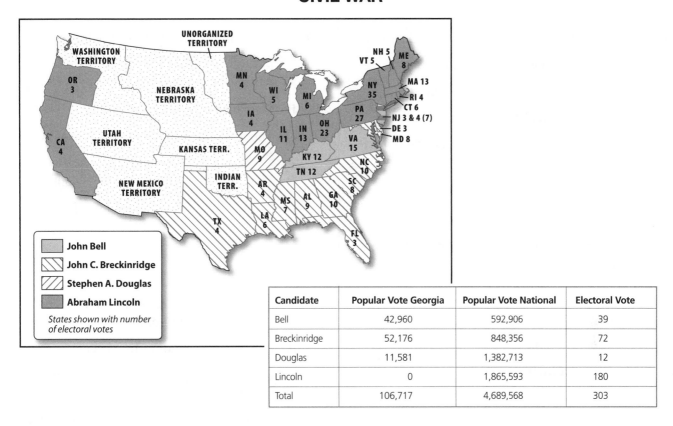

Candidate	Popular Vote Georgia	Popular Vote National	Electoral Vote
Bell	42,960	592,906	39
Breckinridge	52,176	848,356	72
Douglas	11,581	1,382,713	12
Lincoln	0	1,865,593	180
Total	106,717	4,689,568	303

Use this table and the map to answer questions 10-12.

10. Which candidate for president of the United States in 1860 won the electoral vote?

    A. John Bell

    B Abraham Lincoln

    C. John Breckinridge

    D. Stephen A. Douglas

11. Which candidate won the least number of states in his bid for the presidency?

    A. John Bell

    B. Abraham Lincoln

    C. John Breckinridge

    D. Stephen A. Douglas

12. Which two candidates split the southern vote?

    A. Bell and Lincoln

    B. Lincoln and Douglas

    C. Breckinridge and Bell

    D. Douglas and Breckinridge

13. Which Confederate official was from Georgia?

    A. Jefferson Davis, the president

    B. Lyman Hall, the secretary of state

    C. Alexander Stephens, the vice president

    D. William Sherman, the commander-in-chief

14. After Lincoln's election, which man called for Georgia to remain in the Union?

    A. Joseph Brown

    B. Thomas Cobb

    C. Robert Toombs

    D. Alexander Stephens

15. Where did the bloodiest one-day battle of the Civil War take place?

    A. Shiloh

    B. Antietam

    C. Vicksburg

    D. Gettysburg

16. After what battle was the Emancipation Proclamation issued?

    A. Bull Run

    B. Antietam

    C. Vicksburg

    D. Gettysburg

17. How was the Emancipation Proclamation a concession to the South?

    A. All slaves would be freed.

    B. Only male slaves would be freed.

    C. The South could keep their slaves if they stopped fighting.

    D. The slaves could decide if they wanted to remain on the plantations.

18. Why was Chickamauga important to the North and the South?

    A. It was near a major railroad center.

    B. It was a major recruiting center for the South.

    C. It was located halfway between two state capitals.

    D. It had a number of factories that produced war supplies.

19. What contributed to the lack of success of the Union blockade?

    A. The South had a superior navy.

    B. Blockade runners slipped through the blockade.

    C. Great Britain found other ways to trade with the South.

    D. The Union did not have enough ships to enforce the blockade.

20. Atlanta's military importance to the Confederacy was that it was the

    A. capital of the Confederacy.

    B. most populated city in the Confederacy.

    C. industrial and transportation center of the Confederacy.

    D. home to the largest number of slaves in the Confederacy.

21. During the Civil War, how would the location of the fighting in Georgia BEST be described?

    A. all in North Georgia

    B. light and almost nonexistent

    C. concentrated in the Savannah area

    D. heavy along a line from Dalton to Atlanta to Savannah

22. Who was the Confederate commander during the battle for Atlanta?

    A. John Floyd

    B. Robert E. Lee

    C. John Bell Hood

    D. William T. Sherman

23. What Union general led the northern army on its "March to the Sea" and saw to it that much of Georgia's capital resources were destroyed?

    A. Robert E. Lee

    B. Ulysses S. Grant

    C. William T. Sherman

    D. Thomas "Stonewall" Jackson

24. After the destruction caused by his march through Georgia, why did General Sherman refrain from burning Savannah?

    A. He spared the hometown of his West Point roommate.

    B. He gave Savannah to President Lincoln as a Christmas present.

    C. He protected over $28 million worth of cotton stored in Savannah.

    D. He had divided the upper and lower Confederacy and so did not need to destroy the city.

25. William T. Sherman attacked the civilian infrastructure between Atlanta and Savannah in order to

    A. retaliate for lives lost in the battle for Atlanta.

    B. force Georgia troops to return home to defend Georgia.

    C. end civilian support for the war effort and shorten the war.

    D. punish the South for seceding from the Union and forming the Confederacy.

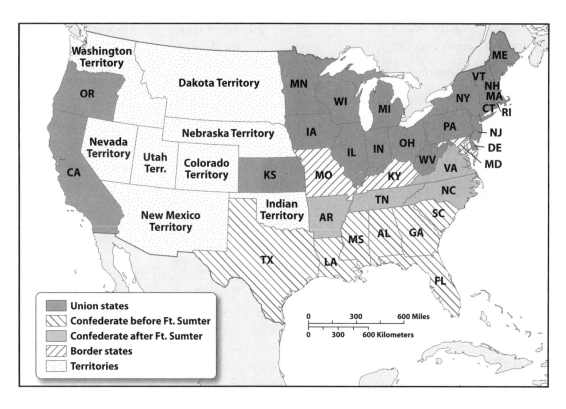

Use this map to answer questions 26-27.

26. This map shows the United States in what year?

    A. 1776

    B. 1863

    C. 1964

    D. 1989

27. Which statement summarizes the information shown on this map?

    A. The nation is evenly split–east and west– into slave states and free states.

    B. The East is overpopulated, forcing citizens to move to the western territories.

    C. The nation is divided evenly–north and south–into colonies and territories.

    D. The West is largely unsettled territory, yet the East is organized into large and states.

CIVIL WAR

28. Where was a notorious Confederate prison in Georgia?

   A. Fulton

   B. Alcatraz

   C. Belle Isle

   D. Andersonville

29. The BEST description of the Freedmen's Bureau during Reconstruction was that it

   A. registered newly freed slaves to vote.

   B. helped the newly freed slaves adjust to their freedom.

   C. provided education, training, and social services for the newly freed slaves.

   D. managed the distribution of farm land and animals to former plantation owners.

30. Which statement BEST describes the contributions of the Freedmen's Bureau in education?

   A. The bureau founded over 10,000 primary schools throughout the South for black and white children.

   B. The bureau established six major colleges in the South, all of which are located in the metropolitan Atlanta area.

   C. The bureau opened government agencies, including schools, colleges, and universities for poor blacks and whites in the South.

   D. The bureau set up thousands of primary schools, industrial or vocational schools, and teacher-training centers for African Americans in the South.

31. After the Civil War, what system was developed to provide labor to work the former plantations?

   A. Convict Lease

   B. Sharecropping

   C. Knights of Labor

   D. Farmers' Alliance

CIVIL WAR

32. How were tenant farmers different from sharecroppers?

    A. Tenant farmers owned all their equipment.

    B. Tenant farmers usually made a small profit.

    C. Tenant farmers bought their seed from the owner.

    D. Tenant farmers usually didn't pay rent for their house.

33. Which BEST describes the differences between sharecropping and tenant farming?

    A. Tenant farmers earned equity or an interest in the land they worked from year to year so that eventually they would own their own property.

    B. Sharecroppers owned nothing but their labor, while tenant farmers owned farm animals and equipment to use in working other people's lands.

    C. Tenant farmers received a cash salary or wage for their farm work, while sharecroppers received only a portion of the crops they raised.

    D. Sharecroppers received a percentage of the crops produced and could set aside cash money to purchase their own land, while tenant farmers had difficulty saving cash.

34. What was President Abraham Lincoln's plan for Reconstruction called?

    A. 10-Percent Plan

    B. 100-Percent Plan

    C. Congressional Plan

    D. Radical Republican Plan

35. According to Lincoln's Reconstruction plan, which group of southerners would be pardoned after taking an oath of allegiance?

    A. government officials

    B. Confederate generals

    C. former soldiers and prisoners of war

    D. high-ranking civil and military leaders

36. To be pardoned, former Confederates had to agree to

    A. lay down their arms.

    B. pay their fair share of taxes.

    C. defend the U.S. Constitution.

    D. not purchase additional slaves.

CIVIL WAR

37. To whom did President Johnson's Reconstruction plan deny a general pardon?

   A. Southerners who owned more than 25 slaves

   B. Southerners who owned more than 50 slaves

   C. Southerners who owned more than $20,000 worth of land

   D. Southerners who owned more than $50,000 worth of land

38. Why was President Lincoln's Reconstruction plan NOT enacted?

   A. The plan was too easy on the South.

   B. The plan did not pass with a majority vote.

   C. The plan did not have the support of the states.

   D. The plan did not become effective before Lincoln was assassinated.

39. Which provision was NOT part of President Andrew Johnson's Reconstruction plan?

   A. Southern states had to pay higher taxes.

   B. Southern states had to nullify their ordinances of secession.

   C. Southern states had to approve the Thirteenth Amendment.

   D. Southern states had to promise not to repay those who helped finance the Confederacy.

40. Why did President Johnson appoint James Johnson as provisional governor of Georgia in 1865?

   A. He had opposed succession as a congressman.

   B. He was extremely popular with the people of Georgia.

   C. He had supported Johnson when he ran for vice president.

   D. He denounced the Congressional Reconstruction plan.

41. Which statement accurately describes the difference between Lincoln's and the Radical Republicans' plans for Reconstruction?

   A. Lincoln's plan consisted of many complicated steps; the Radical Republicans' was simpler.

   B. Lincoln's plan sought to punish the south for the Civil War; the Radical Republicans' plan was aimed at rehabilitation.

   C. Lincoln's plan called for the quick return of Southern states to the Union; the Radical Republicans' sought to delay their return.

   D. Lincoln's plan called for the abolition of slavery throughout the South; the Radical Republicans' plan would have allowed slavery to continue.

42. What did the Thirteenth Amendment to the U.S. Constitution do that brought about many changes in Georgia's society and economic structure after the Civil War?

    A. It freed the slaves.

    B. It changed who owned land.

    C. It gave blacks the right to vote.

    D. It make blacks United States citizens.

43. Under the terms of the Radical Republican plan of Reconstruction, what amendment did a southern state have to ratify before it could rejoin the Union?

    A. Thirteenth

    B. Fourteenth

    C. Fifteenth

    D. Sixteenth

44. What did the Fourteenth Amendment to the U.S. Constitution do?

    A. It gave slaves freedom.

    B. It gave blacks citizenship.

    C. It gave blacks the right to vote.

    D. It gave blacks the right to own property.

45. What did the Fifteenth Amendment to the U.S. Constitution do?

    A. It gave blacks citizenship.

    B. It gave the slaves freedom.

    C. It gave blacks the right to vote.

    D. It gave blacks the right to own property.

46. The Fourteenth Amendment to the U.S. Constitution was passed in response to the

    A. adoption of laws known as Black Codes by the southern states.

    B. refusal of southern political leaders to call for an end to slavery.

    C. rising violence from terrorist organizations such as the Ku Klux Klan.

    D. objections of white southerners about providing freedmen with land and farm animals.

47. Henry McNeal Turner was expelled from his seat in the Georgia state legislature on the grounds that he did not

    A. win the election fairly and honestly.

    B. have the knowledge to be a legislator.

    C. have the right to vote or hold political office.

    D. live in the district from which he was elected.

CIVIL WAR

48. Beginning soon after the end of the Civil War, what secret organization used force and violence to influence Georgia's society?

A. Ku Klux Klan

B. Freedmen's Bureau

C. Free and Accepted Masons

D. United Confederate Veterans

49. The main goal of the Ku Klux Klan was to

A. return land to former Confederates.

B. attract members from all social classes.

C. force the carpetbaggers to move back north.

D. to prevent the freedmen from exercising their rights.

50. Sharecroppers paid their landowners by

A. paying a monthly rental or lease fee.

B. allowing landowners to use their equipment.

C. providing labor and a large percentage of the crop.

D. agreeing to work without pay for five to seven years.

Student Name:_____

Assignment:_____

Period:_____

Marking Instructions:

- Use a No. 2 pencil (no ink or ballpoint pens)
- Fill the circles in completely
- Erase completely to change your answer
- Make no stray marks

Example:

  A B C D
1 ○ ● ○ ○

Score:

Student ID Number

0○	0○	0○	0○	0○	0○	0○	0○	0○
1○	1○	1○	1○	1○	1○	1○	1○	1○
2○	2○	2○	2○	2○	2○	2○	2○	2○
3○	3○	3○	3○	3○	3○	3○	3○	3○
4○	4○	4○	4○	4○	4○	4○	4○	4○
5○	5○	5○	5○	5○	5○	5○	5○	5○
6○	6○	6○	6○	6○	6○	6○	6○	6○
7○	7○	7○	7○	7○	7○	7○	7○	7○
8○	8○	8○	8○	8○	8○	8○	8○	8○
9○	9○	9○	9○	9○	9○	9○	9○	9○

	A B C D		A B C D		A B C D		A B C D		A B C D
1	○ ○ ○ ○	11	○ ○ ○ ○	21	○ ○ ○ ○	31	○ ○ ○ ○	41	○ ○ ○ ○
2	○ ○ ○ ○	12	○ ○ ○ ○	22	○ ○ ○ ○	32	○ ○ ○ ○	42	○ ○ ○ ○
3	○ ○ ○ ○	13	○ ○ ○ ○	23	○ ○ ○ ○	33	○ ○ ○ ○	43	○ ○ ○ ○
4	○ ○ ○ ○	14	○ ○ ○ ○	24	○ ○ ○ ○	34	○ ○ ○ ○	44	○ ○ ○ ○
5	○ ○ ○ ○	15	○ ○ ○ ○	25	○ ○ ○ ○	35	○ ○ ○ ○	45	○ ○ ○ ○
6	○ ○ ○ ○	16	○ ○ ○ ○	26	○ ○ ○ ○	36	○ ○ ○ ○	46	○ ○ ○ ○
7	○ ○ ○ ○	17	○ ○ ○ ○	27	○ ○ ○ ○	37	○ ○ ○ ○	47	○ ○ ○ ○
8	○ ○ ○ ○	18	○ ○ ○ ○	28	○ ○ ○ ○	38	○ ○ ○ ○	48	○ ○ ○ ○
9	○ ○ ○ ○	19	○ ○ ○ ○	29	○ ○ ○ ○	39	○ ○ ○ ○	49	○ ○ ○ ○
10	○ ○ ○ ○	20	○ ○ ○ ○	30	○ ○ ○ ○	40	○ ○ ○ ○	50	○ ○ ○ ○

SOCIAL STUDIES

RECONSTRUCTION, THE NEW SOUTH, WORLD WAR I

1. What was the Georgia Act of 1869?

   A. federal legislation returning Georgia to military control because of KKK terrorism against freedmen

   B. federal legislation refusing to admit Georgia to the Union until it ratified the Thirteenth Amendment

   C. state legislation allowing freedmen the right to vote and the right to hold public office

   D. state legislation ending Reconstruction in Georgia thanks to its demonstrated success

2. Which of the following men was NOT a member of the Bourbon Triumvirate?

   A. Henry Grady

   B. John Gordon

   C. Joseph Brown

   D. Alfred Colquitt.

3. Joseph Brown, a member of the Bourbon Triumvirate, did NOT support

   A. states' rights.

   B. increased agricultural development.

   C. creating stronger economic ties to the North.

   D. increasing the number of industries in the South.

4. The Bourbon Triumvirate believed in

   A. improving working conditions.

   B. increased industrial investment.

   C. economic assistance for the poor.

   D. expansion of educational opportunities.

5. Which of the following best describes the Bourbon Triumvirate's goals during Redemption period?

   A. A time for social, economic, and political reforms to ease the suffering caused by the war

   B. A New South Progressive era when farms had to be replaced by business and industry in order for the South to prosper

   C. A blending of the new and the old, keeping old southern traditions while building new traditions around industries to rival the North

   D. A time for black and white southerners to come together and work in harmony to rebuild the state's economic, social and political systems

6. As the leader of the New South movement, what was Henry Grady supporting?

   A. blacks leaving the South to work in the North

   B. northern investment in southern industry

   C. southern investment in northern factories

   D. southerners growing more cotton for export

7. Which Georgian and his achievement are matched correctly?

   A. Tom Watson—civil rights leader

   B. Hoke Smith—inventor of the steam engine

   C. Henry Grady—editor of *The Atlanta Constitution*

   D. Robert Toombs—mayor of Atlanta after the Civil War

8. The New South, envisioned by Henry W. Grady, would

   A. promote tourism.

   B. maintain its southern heritage.

   C. rival the North economically.

   D. provide separate facilities for different races.

9. The main purpose of the International Cotton Exposition that was held in Atlanta was to

   C. showcase the cotton gin.

   D. bring visitors to Georgia.

   B. get ideas from foreign countries.

   A. showcase the industries of the New South.

10. What Georgia Populist leader called on black farmers and white farmers to unite in an effort to gain fair treatment from the state and national governments?

    A. Hoke Smith

    B. Tom Watson

    C. Henry Grady

    D. Joseph E. Brown

11. The Populist party in Georgia was the party of the

    A. wealthy.

    B. abolitionists.

    C. small farmers.

    D. federal bureaucrats.

12. What group was supported by Tom Watson, a Georgia populist?

    A. miners

    B. farmers

    C. mill workers

    D. railroad workers

13. What was Tom Watson's greatest accomplishment?

    A. a bill allowing women to vote

    B. a bill to provide meat inspections

    C. a bill requiring rural mail delivery

    D. a bill to increase the minimum wage

RECONSTRUCTION, THE NEW SOUTH, WORLD WAR I

Use the political cartoon to answer questions 14-17.

14. When Rebecca Latimer Felton wrote for the *Atlanta Journal*, she focused on the need for reforms in

    A. voting laws.

    B. race relations.

    C. the prison system.

    D. working conditions.

15. Rebecca Latimer Felton did NOT support the

    A. suffrage movement.

    B. temperance movement.

    C. convict lease movement.

    D. educational reform movement.

16. What is the subject of the political cartoon?

    A. a woman meeting with a U. S. senator

    B. a recognition ceremony for widows of World War I

    C. Rebecca Latimer Felton serving as a U.S. senator

    D. Carrie Nation's testimony before the U.S. Congress

17. Which clue helps to identify the content of the political cartoon?

    A. the gentleman's greeting

    B. the desk and table in the cartoon

    C. the name of one of the people pictured

    D. the clothing that the two people are wearing

SOCIAL STUDIES

RECONSTRUCTION, THE NEW SOUTH, WORLD WAR I

18. The immediate cause of the riot that occurred in Atlanta in 1906 was

    A. the killing of a black family.

    B. blacks being denied the right to vote.

    C. the election of Hoke Smith as governor.

    D. newspaper stories of black violence against whites.

19. Which was NOT a result of the Atlanta riot of 1906?

    A. The major resigned.

    B. Martial law was declared.

    C. Eighteen blacks were killed.

    D. Hundreds of people were injured.

20. The murder of Leo Frank resulted in a(n)

    A. mistrial.

    B. hung jury.

    C. acquittal.

    D. death sentence.

21. What happened to Leo Frank after his trial?

    A. He was sentenced and put to death.

    B. He was taken from jail and lynched.

    C. He spent the rest of his life in prison.

    D. He was found guilty, but was later freed.

22. The county unit system affected voting and politics in Georgia by

    A. giving the rural areas more power.

    B. helping blacks get more voting power.

    C. focusing power inside the Atlanta area.

    D. favoring cities where most people lived.

23. Who benefitted from the county unit system?

    A. cities

    B. rural areas

    C. urban areas

    D. metropolitan regions

24. What was a positive aspect of the county unit system?

    A. It made buying votes easier for elected officials..

    B. It made the administration of elections easier..

    C. It allowed people to be elected without a majority of the popular vote.

    D. It gave less-populated areas the same political power as highly populated areas.

25. Which piece of legislation allowed less populated counties in Georgia to have the same or greater power and influence in the General Assembly as the more populated counties?

    A. Populist Party

    B. Watson's RFD

    C. Voting Rights Act

    D. Neill Primary Act

26. What was the purpose of the "Jim Crow" or segregation laws passed by Georgia's government at the turn of the century?

    A. to make alcohol illegal

    B. to continue white control

    C. to promote industry in Georgia

    D. to provide equality for black Georgians

27. What did the U.S. Supreme Court rule in *Plessy v. Ferguson*?

    A. Schools must be integrated.

    B. Blacks and whites were equal.

    C. Segregated facilities must be equal.

    D. Blacks could be denied the right to vote.

28. What became legal under *Plessy v. Ferguson*?

    A. slavery

    B. integration

    C. segregation

    D. black codes

29. *Plessy v. Ferguson* gave states the right to promote

    A. integration.

    B. segregation.

    C. equal rights.

    D. voting rights for blacks.

30. According to *Plessy v. Ferguson*, what Constitutional amendment was NOT violated by establishing "separate-but-equal" facilities?

    A. Thirteenth Amendment

    B. Fourteenth Amendment

    C. Fifteenth Amendment

    D. Sixteenth Amendment

31. Homer Plessy sat in the "Whites Only" car on a train because he wanted

    A. the only seat available.

    B. the comfortable seats there.

    C. to sit with his traveling companions.

    D. to test the legality of a law requiring separate-but-equal facilities.

32. What Georgia case tested the decision in *Plessy v. Ferguson*?

    A. *Roe v. Wade*

    B. *Worcester v. Georgia*

    C. *Brown v. Board of Education*

    D. *Cummings v. Richmond County Board of Education*

33. The purpose of the grandfather clause of 1908 was to

    A. take the right to vote away from blacks.

    B. give grandfathers opportunities to get better jobs.

    C. make everyone trace their family background.

    D. ask every family to guarantee living quarters for the elderly.

34. Why did Georgia's political leaders adopt such policies as Jim Crow, the grandfather clause, and the white primary during the early 1900s?

    A. to allow women to vote

    B. to stop blacks from voting

    C. to segregate Georgia's schools

    D. to create the county unit system

35. In 1920, the Nineteenth Amendment to the U.S. Constitution was ratified. How did this amendment change the make-up of those who could vote in Georgia?

    A. It allowed blacks to vote.

    B. It allowed women to vote.

    C. It stopped blacks from voting.

    D. It stopped women from voting.

36. Which voter qualification was designed to prevent African Americans from voting?

    A. literacy test

    B. party affiliation

    C. identification number

    D. residency requirement

37. What belief would Booker T. Washington NOT support?

   A. Vocational education was essential for African Americans who sought equality.

   B. Truth and knowledge would cause different races to understand and accept each other.

   C. Economic equality was much more important than social equality for African Americans.

   D. Political and social equality for African Americans would come from economic independence.

38. Booker T. Washington is BEST known for his ideas on

   A. integration.

   B. segregation.

   C. social equality.

   D. economic independence.

39. With what racial issue, promoted by Booker T. Washington, did W. E. B. DuBois disagree?

   A. the idea that education was important

   B. the idea that all black Americans should have social equality.

   C. the idea that economic independence alone would lead to social equality

   D. the idea that a "Talented Tenth: of black Americans would lead social change

40. Who was the first black president of Atlanta Baptist College?

   A. John Hope

   B. W. E. B. DuBois

   C. Frederick Douglass

   D. Booker T. Washington

41. To what did Atlanta Baptist College change its name?

   A. Spelman

   B. Morehouse

   C. Morris Brown

   D. Atlanta University

42. What organization was founded by Lugenia Burns Hope?

   A. Y.W.C.A.

   B. D.E.C.C.A.

   C. Girl Scouts

   D. Neighborhood Union

43. All of the following services were offered by the organization founded by Lugenia Burns Hope EXCEPT

    A. vocational classes

    B. clubs for boys and girls

    C. financial aid for the needy

    D. remedial education classes

44. What business made Alonzo Herndon a successful businessman?

    A. Coca-Cola

    B. Georgia Pacific

    C. Western and Atlantic Railroad

    D. Atlanta Mutual Insurance Company

45. Alonzo Herndon became a successful businessman by

    A. becoming the sole employee of his new business.

    B. hiring college graduates to run his company.

    C. spending hundreds of thousands of dollars on advertising.

    D. moving his company to a larger metropolitan area.

46. What countries were allies in World War I?

    A. Germany, Japan, and Russia

    B. Germany, Russia, and Austria-Hungary

    C. Great Britain, France, United States, and Russia

    D. United States, France, Austria-Hungary, and Great Britain

47. What was the "final blow" that led President Woodrow Wilson to ask Congress to declare war against the Central Powers in World War I?

    A. Zimmermann telegram

    B. sinking of the *Lusitania*

    C. attacks on American merchant ships

    D. anti-German propaganda in the United States

48. At which Georgia military installation did infantry train in World War I?

    A. Camp Gordon

    B. Camp Augusta

    C. Camp Benning

    D. Camp McPherson

49. What event is celebrated on the 11th hour of the 11th day of the 11th month of the year?

    A. sinking of the *Titanic*

    B. sinking of the *Lusitania*

    C. armistice that ended World War I

    D. the founding of the state of Georgia

50. The information used by the Allied nations to promote their cause and entice the United States to enter World War I was called

    A. libel.

    B. slander.

    C. propaganda.

    D. yellow journalism.

PLEASE STOP! STOP!

Student Name:_____

Assignment: _____

Period:_____

Marking Instructions:
- Use a No. 2 pencil (no ink or ballpoint pens)
- Fill the circles in completely
- Erase completely to change your answer
- Make no stray marks

Example:

    A   B   C   D
1 ○ ● ○ ○

Score:

Student ID Number

0○	0○	0○	0○	0○	0○	0○	0○	0○
1○	1○	1○	1○	1○	1○	1○	1○	1○
2○	2○	2○	2○	2○	2○	2○	2○	2○
3○	3○	3○	3○	3○	3○	3○	3○	3○
4○	4○	4○	4○	4○	4○	4○	4○	4○
5○	5○	5○	5○	5○	5○	5○	5○	5○
6○	6○	6○	6○	6○	6○	6○	6○	6○
7○	7○	7○	7○	7○	7○	7○	7○	7○
8○	8○	8○	8○	8○	8○	8○	8○	8○
9○	9○	9○	9○	9○	9○	9○	9○	9○

Answer grid (A B C D for each):

1 ○○○○   11 ○○○○   21 ○○○○   31 ○○○○   41 ○○○○
2 ○○○○   12 ○○○○   22 ○○○○   32 ○○○○   42 ○○○○
3 ○○○○   13 ○○○○   23 ○○○○   33 ○○○○   43 ○○○○
4 ○○○○   14 ○○○○   24 ○○○○   34 ○○○○   44 ○○○○
5 ○○○○   15 ○○○○   25 ○○○○   35 ○○○○   45 ○○○○
6 ○○○○   16 ○○○○   26 ○○○○   36 ○○○○   46 ○○○○
7 ○○○○   17 ○○○○   27 ○○○○   37 ○○○○   47 ○○○○
8 ○○○○   18 ○○○○   28 ○○○○   38 ○○○○   48 ○○○○
9 ○○○○   19 ○○○○   29 ○○○○   39 ○○○○   49 ○○○○
10 ○○○○   20 ○○○○   30 ○○○○   40 ○○○○   50 ○○○○

SOCIAL STUDIES UNIT TEST

THE GREAT DEPRESSION AND WORLD WAR II

1. What two events caused Georgia and the rest of the South's economies to be weakened long before the beginning of the Great Depression?

   A. prohibition and disenfranchisement

   B. the boll weevil and the drop in cotton prices

   C. adoption of child labor laws and the county unit system

   D. election of Woodrow Wilson and the beginning of World War I

2. The boll weevil larvae feed on the

   A. white, fluffy cotton.

   B. leaves of the cotton plant.

   C. yellow flowers on the cotton plant.

   D. insects that are found on the cotton stalk.

3. In addition to the boll weevil, Georgia cotton farmers in the 1920s were hurt by

   A. fires.

   B. frosts.

   C. droughts.

   D. tornadoes.

4. What positive impact did the 1924 drought make on Georgia?

   A. It decreased tourism at state parks.

   B. It created a good climate to attract industry.

   C. It slowed down the destruction by the boll weevil.

   D. It contributed to the end of the Great Depression.

Use these events to answer question 5.

- borrowing more money than could be repaid
- speculating in the stock market
- overproducing farm products

5. These events led to

   A. World War II.

   B. the Great Society.

   C. Hoover's reelection.

   D. the Great Depression.

SOCIAL STUDIES UNIT TEST

THE GREAT DEPRESSION AND WORLD WAR II

Use this material to answer question 6.

In Franklin D. Roosevelt's 1933 inaugural address, he said, "We are stricken by no plague of locust. Compared with the perils which our forefathers conquered because they believed and were not afraid, we have still much to be thankful for. Nature still offers her bounty and human efforts have multiplied it. Plenty is at our doorstep. . . ."

6. This statement was meant to give the American people hope to overcome

   A. World War I.

   B. World War II.

   C. the Great Depression.

   D. the nationwide drought.

7. What United States president's policies are blamed for the Great Depression?

   A. Harry Truman

   B. Herbert Hoover

   C. Dwight Eisenhower

   D. Franklin D. Roosevelt

8. Laissez-faire policies of the U.S. government helped bring about the depression by

   A. overextending trade agreements.

   B. giving businesses too many loans.

   C. encouraging people to invest in the stock market.

   D. not doing anything to help solve the country's economic problems.

9. Georgians did not feel the impact of the stock market crash because

   A. the state was already in a depression.

   B. banks were protected by state insurance.

   C. citizens had little money invested in the stock market.

   D. the state constitution prohibited investing tax dollars in the stock market.

10. What Georgia governor served during the Great Depression and spent a great deal of his time speaking out against the New Deal, blacks, and the metropolitan areas?

    A. Ellis Arnall

    B. Eurith Rivers

    C. Richard Russell

    D. Eugene Talmadge

THE GREAT DEPRESSION AND WORLD WAR II

11. Which policy did Governor Eugene Talmadge support?

    A. public welfare

    B. reduced property taxes

    C. voting rights for blacks

    D. federal assistance programs

12. How many times was Eugene Talmadge elected governor?

    A. 1

    B. 2

    C. 3

    D. 4

13. From what group of voters did Talmadge receive his greatest support?

    A. rural voters

    B. black voters

    C. women voters

    D. wealthy voters

14. Which issue did Eugene Talmadge support?

    A. integration

    B. higher taxes

    C. states' rights

    D. white supremacy

15. What action by Eugene Talmadge resulted in the loss of accreditation of ten Georgia public colleges and universities, including the University of Georgia?

    A. He withheld federal funds from Georgia's colleges and universities.

    B. He ordered the Confederate flag to be flown at all colleges in Georgia.

    C. He fired two University System administrators who supported integration.

    D. He approved the admission of several black students at two all-white colleges.

16. In what industry did Eugene Talmadge put down a strike?

    A. mining

    B. textiles

    C. transportation

    D. auto manufacturing

17. For what office did Eugene Talmadge run in 1936 in which he was defeated?

    A. governors

    B. U.S. senator

    C. attorney general

    D. U.S. representative

18. Besides himself and God, who did Eugene Talmadge call the friend of rural voters?

    A. Sears Roebuck

    B. William Hartsfield

    C. Montgomery Ward

    D. Franklin D. Roosevelt

19. What was NOT a purpose of the New Deal?

    A. to provide loans to students

    B. to improve lifestyles for Americans

    C. to reform the defects in the economy

    D. to relieve the suffering of the unemployed

20. Which New Deal program was responsible for such projects in Georgia as developing Roosevelt State Park in Pine Mountain, building Tybee Island's seawall, constructing Augusta's Savannah River Levee, and building Macon's airport?

    A. CCC

    B. NYA

    C. TVA

    D. WPA

21. Why did the Agricultural Adjustment Act fail to benefit African Americans in Georgia?

    A. Only whites were hired by the Works Progress Administration.

    B. Subsidies were paid to property owners, not the tenant farmers.

    C. Only whites qualified for Social Security and Medicare benefits.

    D. Young blacks were not hired under the National Youth Administration.

22. Which group of Georgians failed to benefit from the Agricultural Adjustment Act?

    A. wealthy

    B. alcoholics

    C. tenant farmers

    D. property owners

23. Which group of Georgians benefited most from the Agricultural Adjustment Act?

    A. blacks

    B. renters

    C. tenant farmers

    D. property owners

THE GREAT DEPRESSION AND WORLD WAR II

36. What were Liberty ships?

    A. battleships

    B. cargo ships

    C. submarines

    D. landing craft

37. Where in Georgia were Liberty ships built during World War II?

    A. Atlanta and Augusta

    B. Brunswick and Savannah

    C. Brunswick and Jekyll Island

    D. St. Simons Island and Augusta

38. What was the impact of Richard Russell's service in the U.S. Senate from 1932 to 1971?

    A. It declined because he lacked wealth or a strong military record.

    B. It was not significant because Russell had no political opposition.

    C. It gave Georgia leadership in the Senate as a result of his length of service.

    D. It showed that a Republican could be repeatedly elected from Georgia.

39. Because of Senator Richard Russell's sponsorship of a program for school children, what nickname did he earn?

    A. father of the graded school

    B. father of the unified curriculum

    C. father of the county school system

    D. father of the school lunch program

Use these actions to answer question 40.

- consolidating state offices
- running state government like a successful business
- establishing the Board of Regents of the University System of Georgia

40. Which Depression-era governor implemented these changes?

    A. Carl Vinson

    B. Walter George

    C. Richard Russell

    D. Eugene Talmadge

41. The youngest governor in Georgia history was

    A. Carl Vinson

    B. Walter George

    C. Richard Russell

    D. Eugene Talmadge

Use these remarks to answer question 42.

> "I devoutly hope that the casting of every gun and the building of every ship will be done with a prayer for the peace of America. I have at heart no sectional nor political interest, but only the Republic's safety."

42. Which statement best describes the meaning of Carl Vinson's remarks?

 A. War is better than peace.

 B. War is needed in order to protect our country.

 C. A strong military is needed in case we need to defend ourselves in war.

 D. The United States needs to build a large navy to keep up with other nations.

43. What Georgian is known as the "father of the two-ocean navy"?

 A. Ben Epps

 B. Carl Vinson

 C. Walter F. George

 D. Richard B. Russell, Jr.

44. Which legislation, supported by Carl Vinson, most directly benefited Georgia?

 A. law to increase the military readiness of the United States

 B. law to expand the naval aviation system to 10,000 planes

 C. law to provide military supplies to our World War II allies

 D. law to ease labor restrictions in the shipbuilding industry

45. Who was the world leader who instigated the Holocaust?

 A. Adolf Hitler

 B. Joseph Stalin

 C. Benito Mussolini

 D. Emperor Hirohito

46. The Holocaust was the name given to the actions used by Hitler and the Nazis for

 A. eliminating enemy prisoners of war.

 B. murdering 6 million Jews and other people.

 C. frightening those who opposed Adolph Hitler.

 D. getting rid of the bodies of those who died or were killed in World War II.

SOCIAL STUDIES UNIT TEST

THE GREAT DEPRESSION AND WORLD WAR II

Use these terms to answer question 47.

- Auschwitz
- Dachau
- Treblinka

47. What do these terms associated with World War II have in common?

   A. concentration camps

   B. Allied Forces generals

   C. Axis Power capital cities

   D. major battlefields of Europe

48. How did the NIRA affect Georgia?

   A. It outlawed unions in the textile industry.

   B. It was responsible for a strike in the textile industry.

   C. It allowed enabled factory owners to hire more workers.

   D. It created better working conditions in the textile industry.

49. Why did Franklin Roosevelt spend so much time in Georgia?

   A. Roosevelt had originally been a farmer and he loved farm life.

   B. Roosevelt's wife was a native of Calhoun and visited relatives.

   C. Roosevelt used the warm mineral waters of Warm Springs to ease his polio.

   D. Roosevelt was a native of Augusta and traveled widely across the state.

50. Where did President Franklin Roosevelt die while sitting for a portrait?

   A. Washington, D. C.

   B. Hyde Park, New York

   C. Warm Springs, Georgia

   D. Camp David, Maryland

PLEASE STOP! STOP!

Student Name: _____

Assignment: _____

Period: _____

Marking Instructions:

- Use a No. 2 pencil (no ink or ballpoint pens)
- Fill the circles in completely
- Erase completely to change your answer
- Make no stray marks

Example:

	A	B	C	D
1	○	●	○	○

Score: _____

Student ID Number

0○	0○	0○	0○	0○	0○	0○	0○	0○
1○	1○	1○	1○	1○	1○	1○	1○	1○
2○	2○	2○	2○	2○	2○	2○	2○	2○
3○	3○	3○	3○	3○	3○	3○	3○	3○
4○	4○	4○	4○	4○	4○	4○	4○	4○
5○	5○	5○	5○	5○	5○	5○	5○	5○
6○	6○	6○	6○	6○	6○	6○	6○	6○
7○	7○	7○	7○	7○	7○	7○	7○	7○
8○	8○	8○	8○	8○	8○	8○	8○	8○
9○	9○	9○	9○	9○	9○	9○	9○	9○

#	A	B	C	D		#	A	B	C	D		#	A	B	C	D		#	A	B	C	D		#	A	B	C	D
1	○	○	○	○		11	○	○	○	○		21	○	○	○	○		31	○	○	○	○		41	○	○	○	○
2	○	○	○	○		12	○	○	○	○		22	○	○	○	○		32	○	○	○	○		42	○	○	○	○
3	○	○	○	○		13	○	○	○	○		23	○	○	○	○		33	○	○	○	○		43	○	○	○	○
4	○	○	○	○		14	○	○	○	○		24	○	○	○	○		34	○	○	○	○		44	○	○	○	○
5	○	○	○	○		15	○	○	○	○		25	○	○	○	○		35	○	○	○	○		45	○	○	○	○
6	○	○	○	○		16	○	○	○	○		26	○	○	○	○		36	○	○	○	○		46	○	○	○	○
7	○	○	○	○		17	○	○	○	○		27	○	○	○	○		37	○	○	○	○		47	○	○	○	○
8	○	○	○	○		18	○	○	○	○		28	○	○	○	○		38	○	○	○	○		48	○	○	○	○
9	○	○	○	○		19	○	○	○	○		29	○	○	○	○		39	○	○	○	○		49	○	○	○	○
10	○	○	○	○		20	○	○	○	○		30	○	○	○	○		40	○	○	○	○		50	○	○	○	○

MODERN GEORGIA

1. What factor MOST DIRECTLY determines which crops can be grown in a certain part of Georgia?

   A. market

   B. terrain

   C. climate

   D. labor supply

Use the map to answer questions 2-4.

2. Which crop is grown only in northwest Georgia?

   A. cotton

   B. berries

   C. peanuts

   D. soybeans

3. Where is the poultry industry concentrated?

   A. south Georgia

   B. north Georgia

   C. coastal Georgia

   D. central Georgia

4. What is produced along the Savannah River?

   A. pecans

   B. soybeans

   C. beef cattle

   D. sugar cane

5. What was the issue for which William Hartsfield is best remembered?

   A. aviation

   B. business

   C. education

   D. tax reform

MODERN GEORGIA

Use these accomplishments to answer question 6.

- integrating city government and fire departments
- reducing restrictions on African American police officers
- removing "Colored" and "White" signs in Atlanta's City Hall

6. These accomplishments were implemented by which mayor?

   A. Ivan Allen

   B. Sam Massell

   C. Andrew Young

   D. William Hartsfield

7. Who was the mayor of Atlanta responsible for bringing professional athletic teams to the city?

   A. Ivan Allen

   B. Lester Maddox

   C. Maynard Jackson

   D. William Hartsfield

8. Which member of the Atlanta Braves broke Babe Ruth's career home run record?

   A. Phil Niekro

   B. Hank Aaron

   C. John Smoltz

   D. Chipper Jones

9. Why did Atlanta business and civic leaders of the 1960s decide to bring professional sports teams to Atlanta?

   A. to give outstanding athletes opportunities to play sports

   B. to improve Atlanta's image as a major American city

   C. to give the people something to do for entertainment

   D. to boost the ratings of ESPN and other television sports shows

PROFESSIONAL SPORTS IN ATLANTA		
Sport	Team	Facts
Baseball	Braves	Team came to Atlanta from Milwaukee in 1966. Plays at Turner Field.
Football	Falcons	Team came to Atlanta in 1966 as a league expansion team. Plays in Georgia Dome.
Basketball	Hawks	Team came to Atlanta in 1968 from St. Louis. Plays in Phillips Arena.
Hockey	Thrashers	Team came to Atlanta in 1997 as a league expansion team. Plays in Phillips Arena.

Use the table to answer questions 10-12.

10. What was the first expansion team to come to Atlanta?

   A. hockey

   B. football

   C. baseball

   D. basketball

11. When did the Atlanta Hawks arrive in Atlanta from St. Louis?

   A. 1966

   B. 1968

   C. 1997

   D. 2001

12. Which team plays at the Georgia Dome?

   A. Hawks

   B. Braves

   C. Falcons

   D. Thrashers

13. Which state agency was removed from the control of the governor's office under the administration of Ellis Arnall?

   A. Board of Regents

   B. Board of Public Safety

   C. Department of Revenue

   D. Department of Natural Resources

14. Which of the following is NOT true of former governor Ellis Arnall?

    A. He established the board of corrections.

    B. He was the first to serve a four-year term.

    C. He fought to prevent integration of Georgia's schools.

    D. He regained the accreditation for Georgia's universities.

15. What factor enabled Herman Talmadge to be elected governor of Georgia in 1950?

    A. his campaign style and popularity

    B. his victory in the 1948 special election

    C. his support from wealthy businessmen

    D. his position on segregation and voting rights

16. In what area did Herman Talmadge make his greatest contributions as governor?

    A. education

    B. tax reform

    C. voting rights

    D. attracting new business

17. Herman Talmadge's 3 percent sales tax was passed primarily to fund

    A. the creation of county health departments.

    B. the purchase of Jekyll Island as a state park.

    C. Georgia's part in the Interstate Highway System.

    D. a lengthened school year and school improvements.

18. What political office did Benjamin Mays hold?

    A. state legislator

    B. secretary of state

    C. mayor of Atlanta

    D. governor of Georgia

19. The famous controversy surrounding the 1946 election for governor came about because

    A. Ellis Arnall was impeached and removed from office.

    B. Herman Talmadge and Eugene Talmadge were on the same ballot.

    C. Eugene Talmadge died before taking office and two men claimed the office.

    D. Carmichael got more popular votes and Talmadge got more county unit votes.

20. The purpose of the "white primary" was to

    A. prevent blacks from voting for governor.

    B. help blacks get elected to statewide public office.

    C. keep blacks from having input into the party nominees.

    D. allow blacks to have more influence in the general election.

21. What was the ruling of the U.S. Supreme Court in *Brown v. Board of Education*?

    A. Schools would be segregated and kept separate.

    B. The separate-but-equal policy was unconstitutional.

    C. Black schools would get more money for books and teachers.

    D. Blacks could only attend white schools if there was space available.

22. Dr. Martin Luther King, Jr., favored bringing about social change through

    A. unity.

    B. democracy.

    C. compromise.

    D. nonviolence.

23. What was one reason for keeping the Georgia state flag of 1956?

    A. It was easy for school children to draw.

    B. It was a memorial to the Confederate dead.

    C. It was supported by a majority of Georgians.

    D. It was similar to the flags of other southern states.

24. What organization was founded two months after the 1960 sit-in at the Woolworth's lunch counter in Greensboro, North Carolina?

    A. CORE

    B. SCLC

    C. SNCC

    D. NAACP

25. During the civil rights movement of the 1960s, the Sibley Commission recommended

    A. integrating Georgia's public transportation system.

    B. making proposals to the legislature to address racial issues.

    C. establishing a quota system to ensure the hiring of black workers.

    D. allowing local school systems to decide if they wanted integration.

MODERN GEORGIA

26. Who was the governor of Georgia when the first black students were admitted to the University of Georgia?

A. Ed Rivers

B. Lester Maddox

C. Ernest Vandiver

D. Herman Talmadge

27. The focus of the Albany Movement in Georgia was to

A. end segregation of public schools in Albany.

B. integrate interstate bus station waiting rooms in Albany.

C. implement a "first-come, first-served" policy on Albany buses.

D. force the hiring of African American bus drivers for Albany's bus station.

28. Dr. Martin Luther King, Jr.'s, "I Have a Dream" speech is associated with the

A. Montgomery bus boycott.

B. "remembrance of his father."

C. March on Washington, D.C.

D. eulogy delivered at his funeral.

29. The Civil Rights Act of 1964 did NOT integrate

A. hotels.

B churches.

C. restaurants.

D. public facilities.

30. Which method of influencing political decision making led to the Civil Rights Act of 1964?

A. the ballot

B. freedom fighters

C. special interest groups

D. the power of public opinion

Use these actions to answer question 31.

- He increased programs for the arts.
- He addressed the need to expand the airport.
- He led an effort to have the Olympics held in Atlanta.

31. Which mayor of Atlanta promoted these improvements for the city?

A. Ivan Allen

B. Sam Massell

C. Andrew Young

D. Maynard Jackson

20. The purpose of the "white primary" was to

    A. prevent blacks from voting for governor.

    B. help blacks get elected to statewide public office.

    C. keep blacks from having input into the party nominees.

    D. allow blacks to have more influence in the general election.

21. What was the ruling of the U.S. Supreme Court in *Brown v. Board of Education*?

    A. Schools would be segregated and kept separate.

    B. The separate-but-equal policy was unconstitutional.

    C. Black schools would get more money for books and teachers.

    D. Blacks could only attend white schools if there was space available.

22. Dr. Martin Luther King, Jr., favored bringing about social change through

    A. unity.

    B. democracy.

    C. compromise.

    D. nonviolence.

23. What was one reason for keeping the Georgia state flag of 1956?

    A. It was easy for school children to draw.

    B. It was a memorial to the Confederate dead.

    C. It was supported by a majority of Georgians.

    D. It was similar to the flags of other southern states.

24. What organization was founded two months after the 1960 sit-in at the Woolworth's lunch counter in Greensboro, North Carolina?

    A. CORE

    B. SCLC

    C. SNCC

    D. NAACP

25. During the civil rights movement of the 1960s, the Sibley Commission recommended

    A. integrating Georgia's public transportation system.

    B. making proposals to the legislature to address racial issues.

    C. establishing a quota system to ensure the hiring of black workers.

    D. allowing local school systems to decide if they wanted integration.

26. Who was the governor of Georgia when the first black students were admitted to the University of Georgia?

    A. Ed Rivers

    B. Lester Maddox

    C. Ernest Vandiver

    D. Herman Talmadge

27. The focus of the Albany Movement in Georgia was to

    A. end segregation of public schools in Albany.

    B. integrate interstate bus station waiting rooms in Albany.

    C. implement a "first-come, first-served" policy on Albany buses.

    D. force the hiring of African American bus drivers for Albany's bus station.

28. Dr. Martin Luther King, Jr.'s, "I Have a Dream" speech is associated with the

    A. Montgomery bus boycott.

    B. "remembrance of his father."

    C. March on Washington, D.C.

    D. eulogy delivered at his funeral.

29. The Civil Rights Act of 1964 did NOT integrate

    A. hotels.

    B churches.

    C. restaurants.

    D. public facilities.

30. Which method of influencing political decision making led to the Civil Rights Act of 1964?

    A. the ballot

    B. freedom fighters

    C. special interest groups

    D. the power of public opinion

Use these actions to answer question 31.

- He increased programs for the arts.
- He addressed the need to expand the airport.
- He led an effort to have the Olympics held in Atlanta.

31. Which mayor of Atlanta promoted these improvements for the city?

    A. Ivan Allen

    B. Sam Massell

    C. Andrew Young

    D. Maynard Jackson

32. What did Lester Maddox accomplish as governor?

    A. He decreased funding to public schools and the arts.

    B. He appointed many African Americans to state boards.

    C. He started the lottery and HOPE scholarships.

    D. He changed the state flag to remove the Confederate symbols.

33. How did Lester Maddox get input from the voters?

    A. suggestion boxes

    B. statewide caravans

    C. monthly luncheons

    D. meeting with citizens

34. Which governor won office by being chosen by the General Assembly rather than the people?

    A. Zell Miller

    B. Ellis Arnall

    C. Roy Barnes

    D. Lester Maddox

35. Andrew Young helped establish "citizenship schools," which taught

    A. young blacks their citizenship rights.

    B. nonviolent organizing strategies to potential leaders.

    C. the art of campaigning to potential black political leaders.

    D. the basic principles found in the U.S. Constitution to high school students.

36. To what position did President Jimmy Carter appoint Andrew Young?

    A. secretary of the interior

    B. president of South Africa

    C. ambassador to the United Nations

    D. secretary of housing and urban development

37. What change did NOT occur in Georgia as a result of the end of the county unit system?

    A. More political power went to the more heavily populated areas.

    B. More women were elected to state office in the executive branch.

    C. More African Americans were elected to office in the state legislature.

    D. More members of the General Assembly were elected from the urban areas.

38. Which amendment to the U.S. Constitution did the county unit system violate?

    A. Thirteenth Amendment

    B. Fourteenth Amendment

    C. Fifteenth Amendment

    D. Sixteenth Amendment

39. From what area did most of the members of Georgia's house of representatives come after the end of the county unit system?

    A. Atlanta

    B. rural areas

    C. large areas

    D. coastal areas

40. How did the end of the county unit system change the focus of campaigning in Georgia?

    A. Candidates rallies were held less often.

    B. Candidates used television more often.

    C. Candidates had to appeal to voters statewide.

    D. Candidates concentrated on heavily populated areas.

41. What was the greatest problem with the county unit system?

    A. Candidates could be elected on popularity, not issues.

    B. It created a great deal of corruption in the government.

    C. Most often the least-qualified candidate won the election.

    D. A candidate could be elected without receiving a majority of the popular vote.

42. When the U.S. Supreme Court ordered Georgia to reapportion its Congressional districts in 1964, it meant that

    A. Georgia had too many districts to satisfy the Constitution.

    B. Georgia's growing population required more districts.

    C. all Georgia Congressional districts should have equal population.

    D. all the rural areas needed more Congressional representation.

43. The 1963 court decision calling for the Georgia General Assembly to redraw voting districts to guarantee equal representation was the first time which phrase was used?

    A. "Equality for all"

    B. "One-person, one-vote"

    C. "I have not yet begun to fight"

    D. "Taxation without representation"

SOCIAL STUDIES UNIT TEST

FOUNDATIONS OF GOVERNMENT, POLITICAL PARTIES, AND THE ECONOMY

1. How did the "Solid Democratic South" affect local and state political races?

   A. The races were much more expensive than races held before this period.

   B. Local political races became more important than state races in most areas.

   C. It was highly likely that a Democratic candidate would win any political race.

   D. It became more likely that the best and most qualified candidate would be elected.

2. During Reconstruction, the nation's government was controlled by which fairly new political party, which most white Georgians did not like?

   A. Whig

   B. Democratic

   C. Republican

   D. American Independent

3. Which factor signaled the beginning of a two-party political system in Georgia in the 2002 elections?

   A. Republican George W. Bush was elected president of the United States.

   B. Democrats and Republicans split the seats on the Georgia supreme court.

   C. There was a full slate of candidates for statewide offices from both the Democratic and Republican parties.

   D. Democrats controlled the Georgia General Assembly, but Republicans were elected to the U.S. Senate and House from Georgia.

4. Since Reconstruction, most political figures in Georgia have been members of which political party?

   A. Unitarian

   B. Libertarian

   C. Republican

   D. Democratic

5. The first Republican governor in Georgia since Reconstruction was
   A. Zell Miller.

   B. Sonny Perdue.

   C. James Earl Carter.

   D. Joe Frank Harris.

FOUNDATIONS OF GOVERNMENT, POLITICAL PARTIES, AND THE ECONOMY

6. Which statement BEST describes the role of political parties in Georgia over the last hundred years?

   A. Three political parties have played a major role in Georgia politics.

   B. Georgia has gradually changed from a two-party to a one-party system.

   C. Minority parties have been less important than the two major political parties.

   D. Since the end of Reconstruction, Georgia was dominated by one political party.

7. Which is a result of a one-party system of government?

   A. Laws are created along nonpartisan lines.

   B. The opposition party struggles to be heard

   C. There can be debates focusing on real issues.

   D. Politicians have to appeal to a broader range of voters.

8. The purpose of the Georgia constitution is to

   A. clarify the meaning of vague laws.

   B. protect and benefit all the people of Georgia.

   C. administer the rights assigned to the states by the U.S. Constitution.

   D. make laws, enforce laws, and collect revenue for Georgia's citizens.

9. According to the system of checks and balances, the judicial branch has the power to

   A. appoint state judges.

   B. impeach the governor.

   C. declare a law unconstitutional.

   D. confirm appointments to the judicial branch.

10. The term *separation of powers* refers to the division of specific powers to

    A. the nations' citizens.

    B. state and municipal government.

    C. each of the three branches of the government.

    D. the federal government and certain powers to the state government.

SOCIAL STUDIES UNIT TEST

FOUNDATIONS OF GOVERNMENT, POLITICAL PARTIES, AND THE ECONOMY

11. According to the system of checks and balances, the executive branch checks the legislative branch

    A. by interpreting laws.

    B. through impeachment.

    C. through the use of the veto.

    D. by proposing constitutional changes.

12. One criticism of the system of checks and balances is that it

    A. is costly, ineffective, and doesn't help.

    B. is difficult to understand and implement.

    C. takes power away from elected officials.

    D. creates ill feelings among elected officials.

13. What explanation BEST justifies the inclusion of the separation of powers doctrine in the constitution?

    A. It streamlines government.

    B. It makes government run more smoothly.

    C. It makes a distinction among the branches of government.

    D. It keeps one branch of government from becoming too powerful.

14. Which right is NOT given to United States citizens in the U.S. Constitution?

    A. freedom of religion

    B. freedom of the press

    C. the right to a fair trial

    D. the right to an education

15. The process by which a person from another country becomes an American citizen is called

    A. emigration.

    B. immigration.

    C. naturalization.

    D. nationalization.

16. What financial responsibility does a citizen have toward the government?

    A. paying taxes

    B. paying debts

    C. buying on credit

    D. political contributions

17. How old must a person be to vote in Georgia today?

  A. 16

  B. 18

  C. 21

  D. 25

18. Low voter turnout during state elections results in

  A. less effective bureaucrats.

  B. more efficient politicians.

  C. higher costs for government.

  D. influential special interest groups.

Use the table to answer questions 19-21.

VOTING STATISTICS FOR GEORGIA GENERAL ELECTIO		
Voting Category	**1996 Election**	**2(**
Statewide turnout of voters	61.5%	69
Percent of votes cast by white voters	78.8%	76
Percent of votes cast by African Americans	21.2%	23
Percent of votes cast by 18-24 year olds	5.6%	6.8
Turnout among registered white voters		71
Turnout among registered African American voters		62
Percent of total ballots cast by women		55.
Percent of total ballots cast by men		44.
Selected turnout of voters by age		
Age 18-24		44.
Age 25-34		59.
Age 35-45		70.
Age 46-59		75.
Age 60-64		81.
Selected turnout of voters by race and gender		
Black female		
Black male		67.
White female		57.
White male		72.
Total female		71.
Total male		70.
		67.

19. Which age group had the highest voter turnout in general elections in Georgia?

   A. age 18-24

   B. age 35-45

   C. age 45-49

   D. age 60-64

21. Which age grou|
   eligible voters pa|

   A. age 18-24

   B. age 25-34

   C. age 35-45

   D. age 60-64

20. Which group by race and gender had the highest participation in the 2000 election in Georgia?

   A. black males

   B. white males

   C. black females

   D. white females

22. Whc

   A. g

   B. c

   C. c

   D. s

23. Whi
   in G

   A. a
      v

   B. a

   C. |

   D. a

24. Wha
   Geo

   A. |

   B. |

   C. |

   D. |

is the chief election officer in Georgia?

overnor

ounty clerk

ounty registrar

cretary of state

25. Which two businesses and industries have contributed the most to Atlanta's economic growth over the past twenty years?

  A. computer software and tourism

  B. railroads and the movie industry

  C. transportation and communications

  D. aircraft production and food processing

h requirement is NOT necessary to vote orgia?

resident of Georgia and the county in hich you are voting

registered member of a political party

years of age before the election

citizen of the United States

26. What entrepreneur is associated with Coca-Cola?

  A. Morris Rich

  B. Bernie Marcus

  C. John Pemberton

  D. Alonzo Herndon

are the dominant political parties in gia today?

emocratic and Republican

epublican and Independent

ederalist and Democratic-Republican

dependent, Democratic, and Republican

27. Who was responsible for making Coca-Cola a nationally recognizable brand?

  A. Asa Candler

  B. Arthur Blank

  C. John Pemberton

  D. Alonzo Herndon

28. Where did the company that became Delta Airlines begin?

   A. Macon

   B. Atlanta

   C. Monroe

   D. Savannah

29. What company, founded in Augusta in 1927, is the world's leading manufacturer of paper and building products?

   A. Georgia Pine

   B. Georgia-Pacific

   C. Atlantic Station

   D. Pacific Northwest

30. As founders of important Georgia businesses, John Pemberton, Truett Cathy, and Ted Turner are called

   A. workers.

   B. laborers.

   C. immigrants.

   D. entrepreneurs.

31. A motivating factor for entrepreneurs is their desire to

   A. maximize their profit and gain wealth.

   B. risk their limited productive resources.

   C. command the use of limited resources.

   D. deny consumers their ability to choose.

32. Who were the entrepreneurs who founded the Home Depot warehouse stores?

   A. Truett Cathy and Michael Coles

   B. Bernie Marcus and Arthur Blank

   C. Ted Turner and Robert Woodruff

   D. John Pemberton and Asa Candler

33. When growing their crops, farmers face the greatest risk of losing their productive resources from

   A. climate change and drought.

   B. nearby nuclear power plants.

   C. revitalization of the inner city.

   D. decline of the size of the family farm.

34. Which natural resource from Georgia is used to produce textiles?

    A. profit

    B. slave

    C. cotton

    D. tractor

35. Most of Georgia's revenue comes from which type of tax?

    A. sales taxes

    B. lottery sales

    C. property taxes

    D. motor fuel taxes

36. Which statement about sales taxes is TRUE?

    A. Sales taxes are only collected at the state level.

    B. Sales taxes are only collected at the county level.

    C. Sales taxes are only collected at the municipal level.

    D. Sales taxes are collected at the state, county, and municipal level.

37. Most of Georgia's revenue goes to provide

    A. interest.

    B. new roads.

    C. services for its citizens.

    D. salaries for government employees.

38. Most of Georgia's budget is spent on

    A. health care.

    B. public roads.

    C. public schools.

    D. police and fire.

FOUNDATIONS OF GOVERNMENT, POLITICAL PARTIES, AND THE ECONOMY

Use the graph to answer questions 39-41.

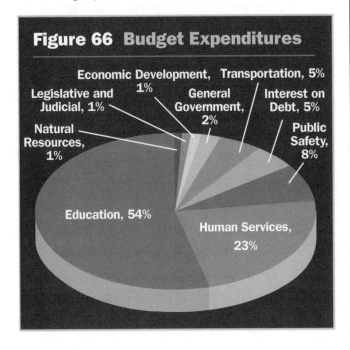

Figure 66 Budget Expenditures

Economic Development, 1%
Transportation, 5%
Legislative and Judicial, 1%
General Government, 2%
Interest on Debt, 5%
Natural Resources, 1%
Public Safety, 8%
Education, 54%
Human Services, 23%

39. The largest percentage of state funds is spent on

  A. education

  B. public safety

  C. transportation

  D. human services

40. What portion of Georgia's budget is spent on roads and highways?

  A. 1 percent

  B. 2 percent

  C. 5 percent

  D. 8 percent

41. Which statement is supported by the data in the graph?

  A. Human services is a low priority.

  B. Little money is spent to preserve natural resources.

  C. The same amount of money is spent on transportation and public safety.

  D. The legislature spends more than 10 percent of its funds on state government.

42. Georgia's stable economy during national times of recessions and depressions is the result of

  A. a required state personal and corporate income tax.

  B. the foresight of legislature to save money from the lottery.

  C. the use of both a fiscal and a supplementary budget process.

  D. a constitutional requirement that Georgia have a balanced budget.

43. What is the first step in developing Georgia's state budget?

  A. The governor sets priorities.

  B. The counties submit their needs.

  C. Each department submits requests for funding.

  D. The General Assembly determines how much money will be available.

44. What factor MOST LIKELY determines whether funding for a program is included in the state budget?

   A. the popularity of a program

   B. the amount of revenue available

   C. the benefits and cost effectiveness of a program

   D. the inclusion of the program in the governor's platform

45. Which method of transportation moves the largest amount of freight in Georgia?

   A. trucks

   B. airlines

   C. railroads

   D. shipping

46. Where is the largest single container facility on the East Coast located?

   A. Savannah

   B. Columbus

   C. Brunswick

   D. Jekyll Island

47. Perhaps the MOST IMPORTANT reason to invest in expanding infrastructure is to

   A. help the economy grow.

   B. attract new airlines to Georgia.

   C. keep abreast of new developments.

   D. ensure that traffic congestion is minimized.

48. When Georgia trades peanuts to China in exchange for toys,

   A. both countries lose.

   B. both countries gain.

   C. Georgia gains and China loses.

   D. China gains and Georgia loses.

49. Taxes on imported goods are known as

   A. loans.

   B. tariffs.

   C. profits.

   D. interest.

50. Which statement about sales taxes is TRUE?

   A. Sales taxes are only collected at the state level.

   B. Sales taxes are only collected at the county level.

   C. Sales taxes are only collected at the municipal level.

   D. Sales taxes are collected at the state, county, and municipal level.

Student Name: _____

Assignment: _____

Period: _____

Marking Instructions:
- Use a No. 2 pencil (no ink or ballpoint pens)
- Fill the circles in completely
- Erase completely to change your answer
- Make no stray marks

Student ID Number

0○	0○	0○	0○	0○	0○	0○	0○
1○	1○	1○	1○	1○	1○	1○	1○
2○	2○	2○	2○	2○	2○	2○	2○
3○	3○	3○	3○	3○	3○	3○	3○
4○	4○	4○	4○	4○	4○	4○	4○
5○	5○	5○	5○	5○	5○	5○	5○
6○	6○	6○	6○	6○	6○	6○	6○
7○	7○	7○	7○	7○	7○	7○	7○
8○	8○	8○	8○	8○	8○	8○	8○
9○	9○	9○	9○	9○	9○	9○	9○

Example: **Score:**

```
   A   B   C   D
1  ○   ●   ○   ○
```

	A	B	C	D			A	B	C	D			A	B	C	D			A	B	C	D			A	B
1	○	○	○	○		11	○	○	○	○		21	○	○	○	○		31	○	○	○	○		41	○	○
2	○	○	○	○		12	○	○	○	○		22	○	○	○	○		32	○	○	○	○		42	○	○
3	○	○	○	○		13	○	○	○	○		23	○	○	○	○		33	○	○	○	○		43	○	○
4	○	○	○	○		14	○	○	○	○		24	○	○	○	○		34	○	○	○	○		44	○	○
5	○	○	○	○		15	○	○	○	○		25	○	○	○	○		35	○	○	○	○		45	○	○
6	○	○	○	○		16	○	○	○	○		26	○	○	○	○		36	○	○	○	○		46	○	○
7	○	○	○	○		17	○	○	○	○		27	○	○	○	○		37	○	○	○	○		47	○	○
8	○	○	○	○		18	○	○	○	○		28	○	○	○	○		38	○	○	○	○		48	○	○
9	○	○	○	○		19	○	○	○	○		29	○	○	○	○		39	○	○	○	○		49	○	○
10	○	○	○	○		20	○	○	○	○		30	○	○	○	○		40	○	○	○	○		50	○	○

11

SOCIAL STUDIES UNIT TEST

STATE GOVERNMENT

1. How long is a regular session of the Georgia General Assembly?

   A. 30 days

   B. 35 days

   C. 40 days

   D. 45 days

Use these requirements to answer question 2.

> - must be at least 21 years old
> - must be a citizen of the United States
> - must be a resident of the district from which elected for one year

2. These are the requirements a candidate must meet to be elected as

   A. governor

   B. state senator

   C. secretary of state

   D. state representative

3. What type of legislation must begin in the house of representatives?

   A. education bills

   B. constitutional bills

   C. transportation bills

   D. appropriations bills

4. How long is the term of a member of the Georgia General Assembly?

   A. 2 years

   B. 4 years

   C. 6 years

   D. 8 years

5. What unique power does the state senate have?

   A. It confirms all executive appointments.

   B. It proposes constitutional amendments.

   C. It sends bills to the governor for a signature.

   D. It can override bills from the house of representatives.

6. Which branch of Georgia state government has as its main responsibility the writing of state laws?

   A. council

   B. judicial

   C. executive

   D. legislative

7. What are the two parts of Georgia's legislative branch?

    A. secretary of state and senate

    B. supreme court and governor

    C. governor and General Assembly

    D. senate and house of representatives

8. To which legislative committee are tax bills assigned?

    A. Revenue Committee

    B. Income Tax Committee

    C. Appropriations Committee

    D. Ways and Means Committee

9. Which statement accurately describes the powers of the Georgia General Assembly?

    A. It has powers specifically designated in both the U.S. and state constitutions.

    B. It has sole power over some areas and split power with the U.S. government in other areas.

    C. It has law-making power over all areas not specifically assigned to the United States Congress.

    D. It only has law-making powers related to money, taxes, revenue, and appropriations in Georgia.

10. How many people serve in Georgia's house of representatives?

    A. 100

    B. 145

    C. 180

    D. 200

11. How many people serve in the Georgia's state senate?

    A. 56

    B. 60

    C. 65

    D. 70

12. Which is an example of a permanent legislative committee?

    A. conference

    B. interim

    C. joint

    D. standing

STATE GOVERNMENT

13. The main purpose of a legislative committee is to

    A. decide which bills to send to the governor.

    B. propose bills to be considered by the full chamber.

    C. review bills before they come to the floor for discussion.

    D. draft bills that have the best chance to become law.

14. Who presides over the Georgia state senate?

    A. governor

    B. senate pro tempore

    C. lieutenant governor

    D. speaker of the house

15. Who presides over the Georgia house of representatives?

    A. lieutenant governor

    B. speaker of the house

    C. most senior member of the House

    D. leader of the majority political party

16. The leader of the house of representatives is chosen by

    A. district.

    B. seniority.

    C. the governor.

    D. house members.

17. In order for a bill to become a law in Georgia, it must

    A. receive the signature of the president.

    B. be voted on by the people in a referendum.

    C. receive a unanimous vote in both the senate and the house.

    D. be introduced by a legislator and receive a majority vote in both houses.

18. How can a Georgia governor stop a bill from becoming a law after it has been approved by the legislature?

    A. veto the bill

    B. advise the press

    C. appeal to the courts

    D. dismiss the legislature

19. What happens when the house and the senate versions of a bill differ after being passed by their respective bodies?

    A. The bill is referred to the governor to sign or veto.

    B. The bill is referred to a standing committee to rewrite.

    C. The bill is considered to be dead and cannot become law.

    D. The bill is referred to a conference committee for compromise.

20. What happens to a bill passed by the legislature if the governor does not veto it, but does not sign it?

    A. The bill is killed.

    B. The bill becomes law.

    C. The bill goes back to the senate.

    D. The bill goes back to the house of representatives.

21. What is the correct sequence for a bill to become a law?

    1. The bill is sent to full chamber.

    2. The governor may sign the bill.

    3. The bill is assigned to a committee.

    4. Copies of bills are given to the legislator.

    A. 4-3-1-2

    B. 1-2-4-3

    C. 2-4-1-3

    D. 4-2-1-3

22. If the governor vetoes a bill, the legislature can override the veto by a

    A. two-thirds vote of one house.

    B. majority vote of both houses.

    C. two-thirds vote of both houses.

    D. three-fourths vote of both houses.

23. What branch of Georgia's government sees that the state's laws are implemented?

    A. judicial

    B. executive

    C. legislative

    D. commission

24. What is the maximum number of consecutive years that a Georgia governor may serve as the state's chief executive officer?

    A. 4

    B. 6

    C. 8

    D. 10

25. Which is an informal power of Georgia's governor?

    A. signing bills from the legislature into law

    B. serving as commander-in-chief of the Georgia National Guard

    C. preparing an annual budget for consideration by the General Assembly

    D. representing Georgia in meetings with federal officials or other state's governors

26. Who becomes Georgia's governor in the event both the governor and lieutenant governor are unable to serve?

    A. attorney general

    B. secretary of state

    C. president pro tempore of the senate

    D. speaker of the house of representatives

27. Why is the power to make appointments to boards and executive offices important to the governor of Georgia?

    A. By appointing persons from the same political party, the governor can help one party dominate state government.

    B. Through appointments, a governor can spread his or her influence far beyond the limited powers of the governor's office.

    C. Through appointments to boards and executive offices, a governor can control the actions of all state agencies and boards.

    D. By appointing political backers and campaign contributors, the governor can repay supporters and raise money for future campaigns.

28. Which qualification is NOT a requirement to be elected governor of Georgia?

    A. A governor must be a citizen of the U.S. for at least 15 years.

    B. A governor must be a college graduate or have an advanced degree.

    C. A governor must be at least 30 years old before taking office in Georgia.

    D. A governor must be a resident of Georgia for at least 6 years prior to taking office.

29. The lieutenant governor most effectively affects the passage or failure of legislation in the state senate by

    A. how he or she votes on a bill.

    B. assigning senate bills to committee.

    C. being able to veto bills in committee.

    D. establishing the senate meeting schedules.

30. An example of an executive power given to the governor is the power to

    A. sign bills.

    B. appoint heads of agencies.

    C. send messages to lawmakers.

    D. call special sessions of the legislature.

31. A judicial power given to the governor is the power to

    A. enforce laws.

    B. impeach judges.

    C. pardon criminals.

    D. call special sessions.

32. Which branch of Georgia's government is the largest?

    A. local branch

    B. judicial branch

    C. executive branch

    D. legislative branch

33. Because Georgia's government is involved in many legal affairs, its officials sometime need legal advice. What state official provides this advice?

    A. secretary of state

    B. attorney general

    C. lieutenant governor

    D. commissioner of labor

34. What state official is given the responsibility to oversee elections?

    A. attorney general

    B. secretary of state

    C. lieutenant governor

    D. speaker of the house

STATE GOVERNMENT

35. Which official is elected, not appointed?

    A. food and drug inspector

    B. commissioner of insurance

    C. State Board of Education member

    D. a member of the State Board of Regents

36. The chief legal officer of the state of Georgia is the

    A. governor.

    B. chief justice.

    C. attorney general.

    D. chief magistrate.

37. Which office maintains the state's official records and supervises elections?

    A. secretary of state

    B. secretary of defense

    C. Board of Transportation

    D. Department of Administrative Services

38. Who established the code of judicial conduct for judges of Georgia and regulates the admission of attorneys to the practice of law in the state?

    A. governor of Georgia

    B. Supreme Court of Georgia

    C. attorney general of Georgia

    D. General Assembly of Georgia

39. Which statement BEST describes how the grand jury protects individual citizens from abuses of power by elected officials?

    A. Citizens cannot be denied due process of law without approval of the grand jury.

    B. Citizens accused of certain crimes cannot be charged and tried without the approval of the grand jury.

    C. Citizens cannot receive the death penalty in Georgia without a review of their sentences by the grand jury.

    D. Citizens elected to public office cannot be accused of crimes without a review of those charges by a grand jury.

40. How long is the term of a member of the Georgia state supreme court?

    A. 2 years

    B. 4 years

    C. 6 years

    D. 8 years

STATE GOVERNMENT

41. How many justices serve on the Georgia state supreme court?

   A. 5

   B. 7

   C. 9

   D. 11

Use this information to answer question 42.

- the right to a speedy public trial
- the right to have a lawyer present during questioning
- the right to remain silent so as not to incriminate oneself

42. These legal rights are part of

   A. due process.

   B. habeas corpus.

   C. judicial review.

   D. separation of powers.

43. Cases are automatically reviewed by the state supreme court when they deal with

   A. wills.

   B. land titles.

   C. habeas corpus.

   D. the death penalty.

44. How are members of the state supreme court chosen?

   A. They are elected by magistrates.

   B. They are elected by popular vote.

   C. They are appointed by the governor.

   D. They are appointed by the legislature.

45. Who has the burden of proof in a criminal case?

   D. state

   C. defense

   A. accused

   B. plaintiff

46. Who has the burden of proof in a civil case?

   A. state

   B. defense

   C. accused

   D. plaintiff

47. What are the most serious criminal crimes called?

   A. torts

   B. felonies

   C. insurrections

   D. misdemeanors

48. Which sentencing option is NOT an example of "community service" that could be assigned by a juvenile judge?

   A. running errands for a local hospice

   B. suspending a student's license to drive

   C. working at a kitchen in a homeless shelter

   D. volunteering in work programs at schools and libraries

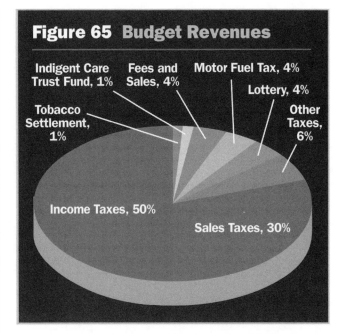

Use the graph to answer questions 49-50.

49. The largest source of Georgia's revenue comes from

   A. user fees.

   B. the lottery.

   C. sales taxes.

   D. income taxes.

50. What percent of Georgia's revenue comes from sources other than income or sales taxes?

   A. 10 percent

   B. 15 percent

   C. 20 percent

   D. 25 percent

PLEASE STOP!

Student Name:_____

Assignment: _____

Period:_____

Marking Instructions:
Use a No. 2 pencil (no ink or ballpoint pens)
Fill the circles in completely
Erase completely to change your answer
Make no stray marks

Example:

A B C D
○ ● ○ ○

Score:

Student ID Number

0○ 0○ 0○ 0○ 0○ 0○ 0○ 0○ 0○
1○ 1○ 1○ 1○ 1○ 1○ 1○ 1○ 1○
2○ 2○ 2○ 2○ 2○ 2○ 2○ 2○ 2○
3○ 3○ 3○ 3○ 3○ 3○ 3○ 3○ 3○
4○ 4○ 4○ 4○ 4○ 4○ 4○ 4○ 4○
5○ 5○ 5○ 5○ 5○ 5○ 5○ 5○ 5○
6○ 6○ 6○ 6○ 6○ 6○ 6○ 6○ 6○
7○ 7○ 7○ 7○ 7○ 7○ 7○ 7○ 7○
8○ 8○ 8○ 8○ 8○ 8○ 8○ 8○ 8○
9○ 9○ 9○ 9○ 9○ 9○ 9○ 9○ 9○

	A	B	C	D			A	B	C	D			A	B	C	D			A	B	C	D			A	B	C	D
1	○	○	○	○		11	○	○	○	○		21	○	○	○	○		31	○	○	○	○		41	○	○	○	○
2	○	○	○	○		12	○	○	○	○		22	○	○	○	○		32	○	○	○	○		42	○	○	○	○
3	○	○	○	○		13	○	○	○	○		23	○	○	○	○		33	○	○	○	○		43	○	○	○	○
4	○	○	○	○		14	○	○	○	○		24	○	○	○	○		34	○	○	○	○		44	○	○	○	○
5	○	○	○	○		15	○	○	○	○		25	○	○	○	○		35	○	○	○	○		45	○	○	○	○
6	○	○	○	○		16	○	○	○	○		26	○	○	○	○		36	○	○	○	○		46	○	○	○	○
7	○	○	○	○		17	○	○	○	○		27	○	○	○	○		37	○	○	○	○		47	○	○	○	○
8	○	○	○	○		18	○	○	○	○		28	○	○	○	○		38	○	○	○	○		48	○	○	○	○
9	○	○	○	○		19	○	○	○	○		29	○	○	○	○		39	○	○	○	○		49	○	○	○	○
10	○	○	○	○		20	○	○	○	○		30	○	○	○	○		40	○	○	○	○		50	○	○	○	○

SOCIAL STUDIES UNIT TEST

LOCAL GOVERNMENT AND PERSONAL FINANCE

1. The main governing authority in almost all of Georgia's counties is the

   C. mayor

   D. judge

   B. transit authority

   A. board of commissioners

2. Georgia's first counties were established by the

   A. Constitution of 1732.

   B. Constitution of 1777.

   C. Constitution of 1867.

   D. Constitution of 1956.

3. How many counties does Georgia have today?

   A. 50

   B. 109

   C. 159

   D. 219

4. A government in which a city and county government have joined to form a single government is called a(n)

   A. city government.

   B. county government.

   C. municipal government.

   D. consolidated government.

5. Which county official is elected rather than appointed?

   A. clerk

   B. registrar

   C. commissioner

   D. road supervisor

6. Which position is appointed rather than elected?

   A. county attorney

   B. probate court judge

   C. county commissioner

   D. county tax commissioner

7. Which term describes a city with its own government?

   A. town

   B. village

   C. megalopolis

   D. municipality

8. What is the name of Georgia's oldest city?

   A. Augusta

   B. Sunbury

   C. Savannah

   D. Oglethorpe

SOCIAL STUDIES UNIT TEST

LOCAL GOVERNMENT AND PERSONAL FINANCE

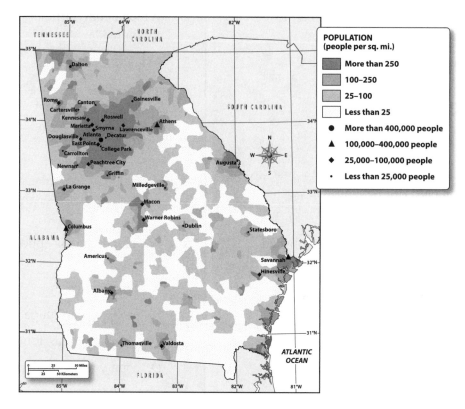

Use the map to answer questions 9-11.

9. Which Georgia city has the largest population?

   A. Decatur

   B. Columbus

   C. Statesboro

   D. Warner Robins

10. Which city is located in an area with few people?

    A. Augusta

    B. Valdosta

    C. Savannah

    D. East Point

11. What is the distance between Augusta and Savannah?

    A. 50 miles

    B. 75 miles

    C. 100 miles

    D. 150 miles

SOCIAL STUDIES UNIT TEST

LOCAL GOVERNMENT AND PERSONAL FINANCE

12. Which requirement is NOT necessary in order to obtain a city charter from the state legislature?

    A. The city must divide at least 60 percent of the land area into tracts.

    B. The city must have at least 200 residents and have voted to incorporate.

    C. The city must be three or more miles from the boundaries of next nearest city.

    D. The city must provide police, fire, ambulance, 911, water, and sewage services.

13. Why would large cities in Georgia be more likely than small cities to use an elected council and a full-time manager?

    A. Small cities in Georgia are required by the state to have a mayor, not a full-time manager.

    B. Large cities need a full-time manager to take care of the complex problems of a large population.

    C. Large cities in Georgia are required by the state to have an elected council and a full-time manager.

    D. Small cities have little reason to have a council but need a full-time manager to supervise the many complicated activities involved in running a city.

14. A county administrator or county manager does NOT typically

    A. proclaim or pass county ordinances.

    B. manage the day-to-day operations of county government.

    C. carry out policies established by the County Commissioners.

    D. appoint or supervise many department heads within the county.

15. Which form of city government is uncommon in Georgia?

    A. commissioner

    B. mayor-council

    C. council-manager

    D. commissioners-mayor

16. Which statement describing a commission form of city government is TRUE?

    A. Commissioners are county and city officials.

    B. The mayor is selected from the commissioners.

    C. The mayor is elected along with the commissioners.

    D. Commissioners hire the heads of government agencies or departments.

17. Which description of a council-manager form of city government is FALSE?

   A. The council is appointed or elected.

   B. The mayor may be appointed or elected.

   C. The city council establishes laws and policies.

   D. The city manager oversees the day-to-day operation of government.

18. What type of government would MOST LIKELY be used by large cities?

   A. commission

   B. mayor-council

   C. council-manager

   D. board of commissioners-mayor

19. Which is the most common type of city government in Georgia?

   A. commission

   B. mayor-council

   C. council-manager

   D. board of commissioners-mayor

20. Which statement about strong-mayor and weak-mayor forms of government is FALSE?

   A. In a strong-mayor form of government, the mayor prepares the budget.

   B. In a weak-mayor form of government, the mayor serves as a figurehead.

   C. In a weak-mayor form of government, the council appoints department heads.

   D. In a strong-mayor form of government, the mayor only performs ceremonial duties.

Use this information to answer question 21.

- county board of education
- airport authority
- port authority

21. These are examples of what type of government?

   A. city

   B. state

   C. county

   D. special-purpose

22. What is the main goal of special-purpose governments?

   A. to consolidate services

   B. to save taxpayers money

   C. to provide for the public welfare

   D. to bring government closer to the people

23. What is the largest source of revenue for county governments?

    A. user fees

    B. sales taxes

    C. property taxes

    D. licenses and permits

24. What is the largest source of revenue for municipal governments?

    A. user fees

    B. sales taxes

    C. property taxes

    D. licenses and permits

25. Which guideline is considered the MOST IMPORTANT for determining the boundaries for house and senate election districts every ten years?

    A. equal population splits among districts

    B. incumbent members' district boundaries

    C. keeping the dominant political party in power

    D. maintaining logical county and city boundaries intact

26. Juvenile courts judge those who

    A. commit extreme and violent traffic offenses.

    B. are neglected or abused by parents or guardians.

    C. are under seventeen years of age and who commit acts that would be crimes if they were committed by adults.

    D. are under eighteen years of age and who commit acts that would not be considered crimes if they were committed by adults.

27. A juvenile in Georgia is one who is under the age of

    A. 15.

    B. 16.

    C. 17.

    D. 18.

28. Juveniles in Georgia are NOT guaranteed the right to

    A. post bail.

    B. a fair trial.

    C. an attorney.

    D. due process.

29. Which protection does NOT apply to juveniles in Georgia's courts?

    A. the right to a trial before a jury of peers

    B. the right to be represented by an attorney

    C. the right to confront and question witnesses against them

    D. the right to present a defense, introduce evidence, and testify on one's own behalf

30. Which of the following is NOT an option available to a juvenile court judge at a probable cause hearing?.
    A. dismiss the case

    B. have a fromal hearing

    C. sentence the juvenile

    D. have an informal adjustment

31. How are juvenile court judges selected?

    A. They are elected by the people.

    B. They are appointed by the governor.

    C. They are appointed by the legislature.

    D. They are appointed by superior court judges.

32. Juveniles who commit specific serious and violent crimes may be placed under the jurisdiction of which state court?

    A. juvenile

    B. superior

    C. supreme

    D. magistrate

33. Which sentencing option is NOT an example of "community service" that could be assigned by a juvenile judge?

    A. running errands for Hospice

    B. suspending a student's license to drive

    C. working at a kitchen in a homeless shelter

    D. volunteering in work programs at schools and libraries

34. The first step when a juvenile is taken into custody is

    A. a formal hearing.

    B. a dispositional hearing.

    C. an intake investigation.

    D. an adjudicatory hearing.

LOCAL GOVERNMENT AND PERSONAL FINANCE

35. Which type of juvenile hearing is similar to a trial?

    A. formal hearing

    B. sentencing hearing

    C. dispositional hearing

    D. adjudicatory hearing

36. In a dispositional hearing, the judge

    A. determines the punishment.

    B. pronounces the punishment.

    C. advises the juvenile of his/her rights.

    D. hears the charges against the juvenile.

37. If the juvenile judge determines the youth is not guilty, which is the only hearing that is held?

    A. sentencing hearing

    B. informal adjustment

    C. adjudicatory hearing

    D. dispositional hearing

38. What are Georgia's "Seven Deadly Sins"?

    A. a political version of the Ten Commandments

    B. adult crimes that can lead to seven different types of penalties

    C. crimes committed by juveniles that result in the courts treating them as adults

    D. violent crimes committed by adults who refuse to declare a religious affiliation

39. What is an advantage of a savings account over a checking account?

    A. Savings accounts are easier to acquire.

    B. Savings accounts can be used to guarantee loans.

    C. Savings accounts pay a higher rate of interest.

    D. Savings accounts provide more protection for your money.

40. Why do periods of low interest rates create jobs?

    A. People save more money.

    B. People borrow money to buy more goods.

    C. People are willing to work for less money.

    D. Savings accounts pay a lower rate of interest.

41. When is the BEST time to borrow money?

    A. when interest rates are low

    B. when a person has a poor credit rating

    C. when a person has no job or steady income

    D. when a person wants to purchase an expensive item

42. Which type of investment provides more flexibility?

    A. money market

    B. savings accounts

    C. certificates of deposit

    D. stocks and mutual funds

43. How has technology NOT changed banking?

    A. It has provided personal bankers.

    B. It has made debit cards a choice over credit cards.

    C. It has made direct deposit through an ATM possible.

    D. It has permitted easy transfer of funds from one account to another.

44. When should people buy less on credit?

    A. when interest rates are low

    B. when they have other debts

    C. when they have no collateral

    D. when they have no savings account

45. Which group of people have increased their use of credit cards the most in recent years?

    A. teenagers

    B. college students

    C. people over age 65

    D. middle-aged people

46. Which is a method of saving money?

    A. purchasing bonds

    B. purchasing stocks

    C. purchasing mutual funds

    D. purchasing certificates of deposit

47. Compared to other workers, entrepreneurs

    A. take more federal aid.

    B. work better in groups.

    C. work fewer hours per day.

    D. are more creative thinkers.

48. Which is the most diversified investment?

    A. municipal bond

    B. stock in Coca-Cola

    C. bank savings account

    D. Vanguard mutual fund

49. Which allows people to increase their income?

    A. arguing with the boss

    B. attending a training class

    C. applying for a credit card

    D. opening a checking account

50. Which form of payment is the most expensive for the buyer?

    A. cash

    B. check

    C. debit card

    D. credit card

PLEASE STOP! STOP!

Student Name:_____

Assignment: _____

Period:_____

Marking Instructions:
Use a No. 2 pencil (no ink or ballpoint pens)
Fill the circles in completely
Erase completely to change your answer
Make no stray marks

Example:

A B C D
○ ● ○ ○

Score:

Student ID Number

0	0	0	0	0	0	0	0	0
1	1	1	1	1	1	1	1	1
2	2	2	2	2	2	2	2	2
3	3	3	3	3	3	3	3	3
4	4	4	4	4	4	4	4	4
5	5	5	5	5	5	5	5	5
6	6	6	6	6	6	6	6	6
7	7	7	7	7	7	7	7	7
8	8	8	8	8	8	8	8	8
9	9	9	9	9	9	9	9	9

	A B C D		A B C D		A B C D		A B C D		A B C D
1	○ ○ ○ ○	11	○ ○ ○ ○	21	○ ○ ○ ○	31	○ ○ ○ ○	41	○ ○ ○ ○
2	○ ○ ○ ○	12	○ ○ ○ ○	22	○ ○ ○ ○	32	○ ○ ○ ○	42	○ ○ ○ ○
3	○ ○ ○ ○	13	○ ○ ○ ○	23	○ ○ ○ ○	33	○ ○ ○ ○	43	○ ○ ○ ○
4	○ ○ ○ ○	14	○ ○ ○ ○	24	○ ○ ○ ○	34	○ ○ ○ ○	44	○ ○ ○ ○
5	○ ○ ○ ○	15	○ ○ ○ ○	25	○ ○ ○ ○	35	○ ○ ○ ○	45	○ ○ ○ ○
6	○ ○ ○ ○	16	○ ○ ○ ○	26	○ ○ ○ ○	36	○ ○ ○ ○	46	○ ○ ○ ○
7	○ ○ ○ ○	17	○ ○ ○ ○	27	○ ○ ○ ○	37	○ ○ ○ ○	47	○ ○ ○ ○
8	○ ○ ○ ○	18	○ ○ ○ ○	28	○ ○ ○ ○	38	○ ○ ○ ○	48	○ ○ ○ ○
9	○ ○ ○ ○	19	○ ○ ○ ○	29	○ ○ ○ ○	39	○ ○ ○ ○	49	○ ○ ○ ○
10	○ ○ ○ ○	20	○ ○ ○ ○	30	○ ○ ○ ○	40	○ ○ ○ ○	50	○ ○ ○ ○

SOCIAL STUDIES UNIT TEST

CRCT PRACTICE TEST

Early People			
	Paleo	**Archaic**	**Woodland**	**Mississippian**
Time Period	before 10,000 years ago	8000 B.C. to 1000 B.C.	1000 B.C. to 1000 A.D.	700 A.D. to 1600 A.D.
Food Sources	large animals such as bison, mammoth, ground sloth, and mastodon	small game, reptiles, fish, shellfish, berries, nuts, fruits	small game, fish, nuts and ber- ries, some crops (squash, sunflowers)	crops (maize, beans, pumpkins, squash)
Weapons, Tools	spears	spears, choppers, drills, chipping tools, bone fish hooks, grooved axes, pipes, pottery	bow and arrow, pottery	similar to Woodland culture, stone hoes, copper head- dresses
Shelter	no fixed shelter; followed herds of large animals	crude shelters, stayed in one place longer	small villages of dome-shaped huts with grass roofs, mounds	larger villages with ceremonial buildings

Use the table to answer questions 1-3.

1. How long did the Woodland Indians live in what is now Georgia?

   A. 1,000 years

   B. 2,000 years

   C. 8,000 years

   D. 10,000 years

2. During which period was the use of pottery introduced?

   A. Paleo

   B. Archaic

   C. Woodland

   D. Mississippian

3. Which period saw the building of large villages with impressive ceremonial buildings?

   A. Paleo

   B. Archaic

   C. Woodland

   D. Mississippian

4. Why did Hernando de Soto explore much of Georgia in 1540?

   A. He wanted to build forts and missions in the area.

   B. He was attracted by possible large gold deposits.

   C. He was searching for the magical Fountain of Youth.

   D. He believed that he would find a passage to Asia through Georgia.

Use this information to answer question 5.

- smallest region
- source of coal deposits
- location of Lookout Mountain

5. Which Georgia region is described by these phrases?

   A. Blue Ridge

   B. Ridge and Valley

   C. Piedmont Plateau

   D. Appalachian Plateau

6. Why have many of Georgia's cities and industries grown up along the fall line?

   A. Railroads were already built there.

   B. Rapidly flowing rivers were a source of energy.

   C. Ships can travel northward from there to the northeast.

   D. The land along the fall line was fertile and perfect for farming.

7. In many cases, people have to adjust to a new physical and geographic environment in order to make a living. Which person would have to make the most drastic adjustment?

   A. a Georgia cotton farmer moving to Canada

   B. a computer programmer moving from Boston to Atlanta

   C. a logger moving from the Georgia mountains to northern Maine

   D. a Georgia miner moving from the plateau region to West Virginia

8. One of the reasons for the colonization of Georgia was to serve as a buffer colony. This meant that Georgia was

    A. a colony for settlement by the poor.

    B. an outpost for pirates attacking Spanish galleons.

    C. a military protective zone between British and Spanish settlements.

    D. an agricultural station experimenting with new strains of cotton plants.

9. The Latin motto of the trustees, *Non Sibi Sed Allis*, translates from Latin as "Not for themselves but for others." What does this mean?

    A. The king felt the colony had been a failure and the trustees had to be punished for what they had done to other people.

    B. The trustees established Georgia for the purpose of helping the poor, not for the purpose of making themselves rich.

    C. The Highland Scots and the Salzburgers were foreigners and couldn't be trusted to defend others, including the British.

    D. Religious leaders could not allow Catholics in Georgia because of protests from members of the new Methodist church.

10. How did the colonies benefit Great Britain economically?

    A. The colonies manufactured goods for Great Britain.

    B. The colonies imported raw materials from Great Britain.

    C. The colonies traded with one another for expensive goods and services.

    D. The colonies enabled Great Britain to manufacture goods to sell to other countries.

Use these facts to answer question 11.

- Many colonists had relatives in Great Britain and did not want to put them in danger.
- The British king was still paying money to support the colonists.

11. Because of these facts, what was the behavior of most Georgians during the Revolution?

    A. They moved to Virginia.

    B. They rioted in the streets.

    C. They attacked British troops.

    D. They were loyal to King George.

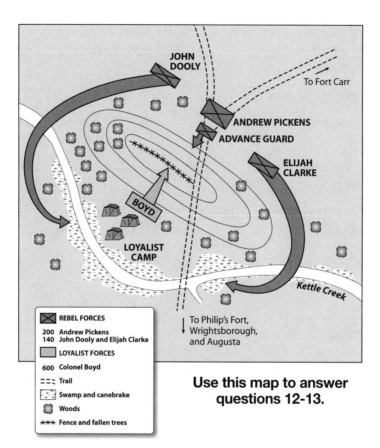

Use this map to answer questions 12-13.

12. Which military leader commanded the most troops at the Battle of Kettle Creek?

    A. John Dooly

    B. Elijah Clarke

    C. Colonel Boyd

    D. Andrew Pickens

13. What obstacle separated Pickens and Boyd and had to be crossed for the battle to begin?

    A. Fort Carr

    B. Kettle Creek

    C. fence and fallen trees

    D. tents from the loyalist camp

14. What was the main weakness of the Georgia Constitution of 1777?

    A. It created an independent executive branch.

    B. It gave too much power to the legislative branch.

    C. It established two parts in the legislative branch.

    D. It placed too much importance on checks and balances.

15. From the colonial era until Reconstruction, the capital of Georgia was moved many times in response to what factor?

    A. changing population center of the state

    B. changing geographic center of the state

    C. changing political influences in the state

    D. changing transportation patterns in the state

16. How did Eli Whitney's invention of the cotton gin influence the growth of slavery in the South?

    A. It made it easier for slaves to pick cotton.

    B. It increased the profits from growing cotton.

    C. It made it easier to produce cloth from cotton.

    D. It replenished the soil so that more cotton could be grown.

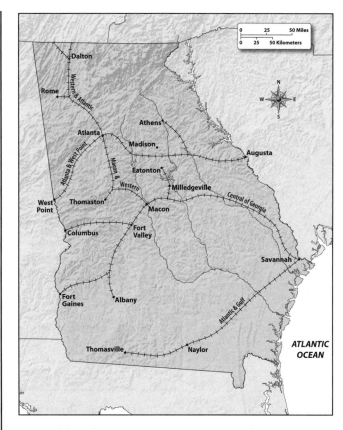

Use the map to answer question 17.

17. The Atlantic and Gulf railroad connects Savannah and what city?

    A. Macon

    B. Atlanta

    C. Augusta

    D. Thomasville

Use this illustration to answer question 18.

18. What event is shown in this drawing?

 A. picking cotton on Coastal Plain plantations

 B. farming the rich soil of the Piedmont region

 C. building the railroad from Macon to Atlanta

 D. mining for gold in the North Georgia mountains

19. When Andrew Jackson said "John Marshall has rendered his decision, now let him enforce it," he meant that

 A. Congress and the president agreed with and supported the decision.

 B. the Congress would see that troops were sent to enforce the decision.

 C. the Supreme Court was the supreme law of the land and could do whatever it wanted.

 D. the Supreme Court could not enforce the decision without the support of the president.

SOCIAL STUDIES UNIT TEST

CRCT PRACTICE TEST

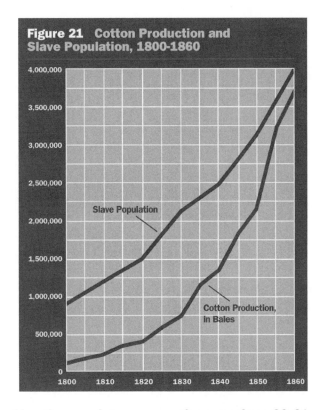

Figure 21 Cotton Production and Slave Population, 1800-1860

Slave Population

Cotton Production, in Bales

Use the graph to answer the questions 20-21.

20. How many bales of cotton were produced in 1830?

    A. 500,000

    B. 750,000

    C. 1,000,000

    D. 1,250,000

21. What is the main idea presented in this graph?

    A. Bales of cotton went up in price as the Civil War approached.

    B. The slave population increased sharply between 1800 and 1860.

    C. Slavery decreased as a result of abolitionists refusing to buy cotton.

    D. As the number of slaves in the United States increased, so did cotton production.

22. Which region of the United States believed that the states should be able to govern themselves without interference from the national government?

    A. Northern states

    B. Southern states

    C. Great Lakes states

    D. Pacific Coast states

23. The "Georgia Platform" was a statement supporting

    A. states' rights.

    B. popular sovereignty.

    C. the Compromise of 1850.

    D. slavery throughout the United States.

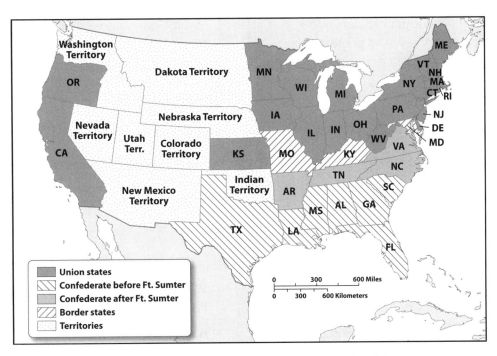

Use this map to answer questions 24-25.

24. This map shows the United States in what year?

  A. 1776

  B. 1863

  C. 1964

  D. 1989

25. Which statement summarizes the information shown on this map?

  A. The nation is evenly split–east and west– into slave states and free states.

  B. The East is overpopulated, forcing citizens to move to the western territories.

  C. The nation is divided evenly–north and south–into colonies and territories.

  D. The West is largest unsettled territory, yet the East is organized into large states.

26. Beginning soon after the end of the Civil War, what secret organization used force and violence to influence Georgia's society in an attempt to return control of the southern state governments to the Democrats?

  A. Ku Klux Klan

  B. Freedmen's Bureau

  C. Free and Accepted Masons

  D. United Confederate Veterans

27. The main purpose of the International Cotton Exposition that was held in Atlanta was to

  A. bring tourists to Atlanta.

  B. showcase the cotton gin.

  C. get ideas from foreign countries.

  D. showcase the industries of the New South.

28. Why did Georgia's political leaders adopt such policies as Jim Crow, the grandfather clause, and the white primary during the early 1900s?

    A. to allow women to vote

    B. to stop blacks from voting

    C. to segregate Georgia's schools

    D. to create the county unit system

29. With what racial issue, promoted by Booker T. Washington, did W. E. B. DuBois disagree?

    A. the idea that education was important

    B. the idea that all black Americans should have social equality

    C. the idea that economic independence alone would lead to social equality

    D. the idea that a "Talented Tenth" of black Americans would lead social change

30. What two factors caused the economies of Georgia and the rest of the South to be depressed before the beginning of the Great Depression?

    A. Prohibition and disfranchisement

    B. the boll weevil and the drop in cotton prices

    C. adoption of child labor laws and the county unit system

    D. election of Woodrow Wilson and the beginning of World War I

31. What Georgia governor served during the Great Depression and spent a great deal of his time speaking out against the New Deal, blacks, and the metropolitan areas?

    A. Ellis Arnall

    B. Eurith Rivers

    C. Richard Russell

    D. Eugene Talmadge

32. What famous statement refers to the attack on Pearl Harbor?

    A. "the British are coming"

    B. "day that will live in infamy"

    C. "we have only begun to fight"

    D. "shot heard around the world"

Use this information to answer question 33.

- consolidating state offices
- running state government like a successful business
- establishing the Board of Regents of the University System of Georgia

33. Which Depression-era governor implemented these changes?

    A. Carl Vinson

    B. Walter George

    C. Richard Russell

    D. Eugene Talmadge

Use this statement to answer question 34.

> "I devoutly hope that the casting of every gun and the building of every ship will be done with a prayer for the peace of America. I have at heart no sectional nor political interest, but only the Republic's safety."

34. Which statement best describes the meaning of Carl Vinson's remarks?

A. War is better than peace.

B. War is needed in order to protect our country.

C. A strong military is needed in case we need to defend ourselves in war.

D. The United States needs to build a large navy to keep up with other nations.

35. Why did Franklin Roosevelt spend so much time in Georgia?

A. Roosevelt used the warm mineral waters of Warm Springs to ease his polio.

B. Roosevelt was a native of Augusta and traveled widely across the state.

C. Roosevelt's wife was a native of Calhoun and visited relatives.

D. Roosevelt had originally been a farmer and he loved farm life.

Use the map to answer questions 36-37.

36. Which crop is grown only in southern Georgia?

A. corn

B. cotton

C. berries

D. tobacco

37. Where is the poultry industry concentrated?

A. south Georgia

B. north Georgia

C. central Georgia

D. coastal Georgia

Use this information to answer question 38.

- integrating city government and fire departments
- reducing restrictions on African American police officers
- removing "Colored" and "White" signs in Atlanta's City Hall

38. These accomplishments were implemented by which mayor?

A. Ivan Allen

B. Sam Massell

C. Andrew Young

D. William Hartsfield

39. The famous controversy surrounding the 1946 election for governor came about because

A. Ellis Arnall was impeached and removed from office.

B. Herman Talmadge and Eugene Talmadge were on the same ballot.

C. Eugene Talmadge died before taking office and two men claimed the office.

D. Carmichael got more popular votes and Talmadge got more county unit votes.

40. The purpose of the "white primary" was to

A. help blacks get elected to statewide public office.

B. keep blacks from having input into the party nominees.

C. allow blacks to have more influence in the general election.

D. promote voting by blacks in the early stages of the electoral process.

41. Dr. Martin Luther King, Jr.'s "I Have a Dream" speech is associated with the

A. Montgomery bus boycott.

B. eulogy given at his funeral.

C. "remembrance of his father."

D. March on Washington, D.C.

SOCIAL STUDIES UNIT TEST

CRCT PRACTICE TEST

Use this information to answer question 42.

- He increased programs for the arts.
- He addressed the need to expand the airport.
- He led an effort to have the Olympics held in Atlanta.

42. Which mayor of Atlanta promoted these improvements for the city?

   A. Ivan Allen

   B. Sam Massell

   C. Andrew Young

   D. Maynard Jackson

43. The 1963 court action calling for the Georgia General Assembly to redraw voting districts to guarantee equal representation was the first time which phrase was used?

   A. "Equality for all."

   B. "One-person, one-vote."

   C. "I have not yet begun to fight."

   D. "Taxation without representation."

44. What was the centerpiece of Jimmy Carter's foreign policy?

   A. isolationism

   B. human rights

   C. international free trade

   D. containing communism

Use this information to answer question 45.

- received the Nobel Peace Prize
- worked with Habitat for Humanity
- published many best-selling books

45. Which Georgian received all of these honors?

   A. Carl Vinson

   B. Jimmy Carter

   C. Richard B. Russell

   D. Martin Luther King, Jr.

46. Which of the following is NOT an impact immigrant populations have on Georgia's communities?

   A. new laws and voting requirements are passed

   B. new restaurants, churches and businessess are founded

   C. school populations swell as immigrant families move into new areas

   D. seasonal jobs are filled with immigrant workers seeking employment

47. What explanation BEST justifies the inclusion of the separation of powers doctrine in the constitution?

   A. It streamlines government.

   B. It makes government run more smoothly.

   C. It makes a distinction among the branches of government.

   D. It keeps one branch of government from becoming too powerful.

48. Where is the largest single-container facility on the East Coast located?

   A. Savannah

   B. Brunswick

   C. Columbus

   D. Jekyll Island

49. As founders of important Georgia businesses, John Pemberton, Truett Cathy, and Ted Turner are called

   A. laborers.

   B. employees.

   C. immigrants.

   D. entrepreneurs.

50. The main purpose of a legislative committee is to

   A. decide which bills to send to the governor.

   B. propose bills to be considered by the full chamber.

   C. draft bills that have the best chance to become law.

   D. review bills to decide which will go to the floor for discussion.

51. In order for a bill to become a law in Georgia, it must

   A. receive the signature of the president.

   B. be voted on by the people in a referendum.

   C. receive a unanimous vote in both the Senate and the House.

   D. be introduced by a legislator and receive a majority vote in both houses.

52. Which branch of Georgia's government is the largest?

   A. local branch

   B. judicial branch

   C. executive branch

   D. legislative branch

53. What are the most serious criminal crimes called?

   A. torts

   B. felonies

   C. insurrections

   D. misdemeanors

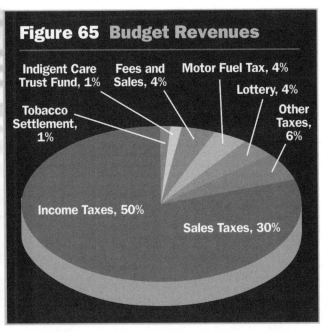

Figure 65 Budget Revenues

Indigent Care Trust Fund, 1%
Fees and Sales, 4%
Motor Fuel Tax, 4%
Lottery, 4%
Tobacco Settlement, 1%
Other Taxes, 6%
Income Taxes, 50%
Sales Taxes, 30%

Use the graph to answer questions 54-55.

54. The largest source of Georgia's revenue comes from

   A. fees.

   B. the lottery.

   C. sales taxes.

   D. state income taxes.

55. What percent of Georgia's revenue comes from sources other than income or sales taxes?

   A. 10 percent

   B. 15 percent

   C. 20 percent

   D. 25 percent

56. Juvenile courts judge those who

   A. commit extreme and violent traffic offenses.

   B. are neglected or abused by parents or guardians.

   C. are under seventeen years of age and who commit acts that would be crimes if they were committed by adults.

   D. are under eighteen years of age and who commit acts that would not be considered crimes if they were committed by adults.

57. What are Georgia's "Seven Deadly Sins"?

   A. a political version of the Ten Commandments

   B. adult crimes that can lead to seven different types of penalties

   C. crimes committed by juveniles that result in the courts treating them as adults

   D. violent crimes committed by adults who refuse to declare a religious affiliation

58. Which type of investment provides more flexibility?

    A. money market

    B. savings accounts

    C. certificates of deposit

    D. stocks and mutual funds

59. When should people buy less on credit?

    A. when interest rates are low

    B. when they have other debts

    C. when they have no collateral

    D. when they have no savings account

60. Which is a method of saving money?

    A. purchasing stocks

    B. purchasing bonds

    C. purchasing mutual funds

    D. purchasing certificates of deposit

Student Name:_____

Assignment: _____

Period:_____

Marking Instructions:
Use a No. 2 pencil (no ink or ballpoint pens)
Fill the circles in completely
Erase completely to change your answer
Make no stray marks

Student ID Number

0○ 0○ 0○ 0○ 0○ 0○ 0○ 0○ 0○
1○ 1○ 1○ 1○ 1○ 1○ 1○ 1○ 1○
2○ 2○ 2○ 2○ 2○ 2○ 2○ 2○ 2○
3○ 3○ 3○ 3○ 3○ 3○ 3○ 3○ 3○
4○ 4○ 4○ 4○ 4○ 4○ 4○ 4○ 4○
5○ 5○ 5○ 5○ 5○ 5○ 5○ 5○ 5○
6○ 6○ 6○ 6○ 6○ 6○ 6○ 6○ 6○
7○ 7○ 7○ 7○ 7○ 7○ 7○ 7○ 7○
8○ 8○ 8○ 8○ 8○ 8○ 8○ 8○ 8○
9○ 9○ 9○ 9○ 9○ 9○ 9○ 9○ 9○

Sample:

A B C D
○ ● ○ ○

Score:

1 A○ B○ C○ D○	16 A○ B○ C○ D○	31 A○ B○ C○ D○	46 A○ B○ C○ D○
2 A○ B○ C○ D○	17 A○ B○ C○ D○	32 A○ B○ C○ D○	47 A○ B○ C○ D○
3 A○ B○ C○ D○	18 A○ B○ C○ D○	33 A○ B○ C○ D○	48 A○ B○ C○ D○
4 A○ B○ C○ D○	19 A○ B○ C○ D○	34 A○ B○ C○ D○	49 A○ B○ C○ D○
5 A○ B○ C○ D○	20 A○ B○ C○ D○	35 A○ B○ C○ D○	50 A○ B○ C○ D○
6 A○ B○ C○ D○	21 A○ B○ C○ D○	36 A○ B○ C○ D○	51 A○ B○ C○ D○
7 A○ B○ C○ D○	22 A○ B○ C○ D○	37 A○ B○ C○ D○	52 A○ B○ C○ D○
8 A○ B○ C○ D○	23 A○ B○ C○ D○	38 A○ B○ C○ D○	53 A○ B○ C○ D○
9 A○ B○ C○ D○	24 A○ B○ C○ D○	39 A○ B○ C○ D○	54 A○ B○ C○ D○
10 A○ B○ C○ D○	25 A○ B○ C○ D○	40 A○ B○ C○ D○	55 A○ B○ C○ D○
11 A○ B○ C○ D○	26 A○ B○ C○ D○	41 A○ B○ C○ D○	56 A○ B○ C○ D○
12 A○ B○ C○ D○	27 A○ B○ C○ D○	42 A○ B○ C○ D○	57 A○ B○ C○ D○
13 A○ B○ C○ D○	28 A○ B○ C○ D○	43 A○ B○ C○ D○	58 A○ B○ C○ D○
14 A○ B○ C○ D○	29 A○ B○ C○ D○	44 A○ B○ C○ D○	59 A○ B○ C○ D○
15 A○ B○ C○ D○	30 A○ B○ C○ D○	45 A○ B○ C○ D○	60 A○ B○ C○ D○

GLOSSARY

A

absolute location identifies a precise position on Earth's surface; often stated in longitude and latitude

annex to add on, such as adding territory to an existing town, city, or state

antebellum the period before the Civil War

Appalachian Plateau region a physiographic region of Georgia in the far northwestern corner of the state

armistice an agreement to stop fighting

Articles of Confederation the first constitution of the United States; ratified in 1781, it created a weak federal government and was eventually replaced

B

barter economy an economy based on the ability to trade or exchange goods or services without the use of money

bill a proposed law

Black Code a set of laws passed by Georgia, and most southern states, after the Civil War to restrict the rights of the freedmen

blockade to obstruct or prevent access to

Blue Ridge region a physiographic region of Georgia located in the northeastern part of the state

board of commissioners the elected governing body for most Georgia counties

boll weevil a small, grayish, long-snouted beetle that attacked the cotton plant

Brown v. Board of Education a U.S. Supreme Court case in which the Court declared that the separate-but-equal schools were unconstitutional

budget a plan for receiving and spending money

C

carpetbagger a northerner who moved to the South after the Civil War

cash crop crops like wheat or cotton that were grown to be sold

charter a legal document that grants special rights and privileges

checks and balances the system that provides to each branch of government some power that controls or prevents some actions of the other two branches

climate the type of weather a region experiences over a long period of time

Coastal Plain region a physiographic region of Georgia that runs from the coast to the Piedmont Plateau

colony a group of people who settle in a new land but who keep their ties to their homeland

commission form a form of municipal government in which voters elect comissioners, each of whom is the head of a department with city government

Compromise of 1850 legislation passed by Congress by which California entered the Union as a free state, slave trading was ended in the District of Columbia, Texas gave up its claims to New Mexico in exchange for money, residents of the territories of New Mexico and Utah would be able to determine whether they wanted slavery, and a stronger Fugitive Slave Act was enacted

council-manager form a form of municipal government in which voters elect a city council, which hires a city manager responsible for the day-to-day operations of the city

county unit system a procedure for political primaries that gave the more populous counties more unit votes; established by the Neill Primary Act

court of appeals the second highest ranking court in the Georgia court system; an appellate court

crackers a group of what plantation owners called "undesirable people" who moved from Virginia and the Carolinas to the middle and western parts of the colony

credit the ability to buy something now and pay for it later or over a period of time

D

discrimination unfair treatment of a person or group because of prejudice

disfranchise to take the right to vote away from someone or some group

drought a lack of precipitation over a period of time that results in water shortages

E

economy the system of growing, making, selling, buying, and using goods and services

Emancipation Proclamation a document issued by President Abraham Lincoln in 1862 that freed the slaves in the Confederacy

expenditure money spent or paid out

F

Fall Line the point at which hilly or mountainous lands meet the coastal plain

federalism a system in which the national and state governments share authority over the same territory and the same people

felony a serious crime such as murder or burglary punishable by a year or more in prison, a fine of at least $1,000, or both

Fifteenth Amendment an amendment to the U.S. Constitution, ratified in 1870, that extended the right to vote to all males

fiscal year a budgetary spending year; Georgia's fiscal year begins July 1 and ends June 30

Fourteenth Amendment an amendment to the U.S. Constitution, ratified in 1868, that granted citizenship to the former slaves and forbade the states from denying anyone the "equal protection of the law"

freedmen the former slaves

Freedmen's Bureau a federal government organization established in 1865 that helped the newly freed slaves after the Civil War

free state a state that did not allow slavery

G

Georgia Act legislation passed by Congress in 1869 that returned Georgia to military rule and required the state to ratify the Fifteenth Amendment

gerrymander to draw up an election district in such a way that it benefits a certain group

governor the head of the executive branch of the state government

grandfather clause a clause inserted in the Georgia constitution in 1908 that stated only those men whose fathers or grandfathers had been eligible to vote in 1867 were eligible to vote; the clause disfranchised most of Georgia's African Americans

grand jury a group of citizens who determine whether or not a person accused of a crime should be indicted and required to stand trial

H

headright system a system of distributing land by which each white male as the "head" of a family had the "right" to receive up to 1,000 acres

Holocaust the name given to the systematic extermination of 6 million Jews and other "undesirables" during World War II

horticulture the science of cultivating plants and trees

I

infrastructure basic facilities such as roads, bridges, and ports

injunction a court order stating that something must or must not be done

integrate to open something to members of all races and ethnic groups

J

Jim Crow laws laws passed in the South to establish "separate-but-equal" facilities for whites and for blacks

juvenile a citizen under the age of seventeen

K

Ku Klux Klan a secret racist organization, formed in 1865, that worked to keep the freedmen from voting after the Civil War

L

laissez-faire the doctrine that the government should not interfere in the private sector of the economy

lieutenant governor an elected official who serves as a deputy to the governor

lynching an illegal hanging, usually by a mob

M

martial law the use of military forces to maintain order because civilian forces will not or cannot maintain order

mayor-council form a form of municipal government where voters elect a mayor and a city council; mayors may be either "weak" or "strong"

militia a citizen army

minimum wage the least amount an employer can pay an employee for a certain number of hours worked

misdemeanor a less serious crime punishable by less than a year in prison, a fine of less than $1,000, or both

Missouri Compromise legislation passed by Congress in 1820 by which Maine entered the Union as a free state, Missouri entered the Union as a slave state, and slavery was prohibited north of the southern border of Missouri

municipality a city with its own government

N

National Association for the Advancement of Colored People (NAACP) an organization formed in 1909 by white liberals and members of the Niagara Movement to work for the rights of African Americans

neutral to not take sides in a disagreement

New South a term coined by Henry W. Grady and used to describe the southern states after Reconstruction

Nineteenth Amendment an amendment to the U.S. Constitution that gave women the right to vote

nullify to declare invalid

O

one-person, one-vote concept the policy that every citizen's vote should be equal to every other citizen's vote no matter where the person lives

P

palisades fences made of sharpened stakes

political party an organized group of people who share common ideals and who seek to influence government policies and decisions by electing members of their party to government office

poll tax a tax paid to be able to vote

popular sovereignty the ability of the residents of an area to decide upon an issue, such as whether they would allow slavery

precipitation rain, hail, sleet, or snow

profit the amount left after all production costs have been subtracted

propaganda information that is spread for the purpose of promoting some cause

proprietary colony a colony directed by those to whom a charter was given

R

reapportion to redraw voting districts to ensure districts of equal population sizes

Reconstruction the period immediately after the Civil War when the South rebuilt and the southern states returned to the Union

relative location describes where a place is compared with other places

revenue a source of income

Ridge and Valley region a physiographic region of Georgia that lies between the Blue Ridge Mountains and the Appalachian Mountains

royal colony a colony directly governed by the king

S

secession   the act of pulling out of the Union

segregate   to separate by race

separation of powers   a division of responsibilities for government among the three branches (legislative, executive, judicial)

service industry   an industry involved in providing services to people rather than products

sharecropping   an agricultural system common after the Civil War where landless farmers worked the land of a landowner who also supplied a house, farming tools and animals, seed, and fertilizer in return for a share of the harvest

siege   a military action that occurs when forces try to capture a fortified fort or town by surrounding it and preventing any supplies from reaching it

sit-in   a type of demonstration where people enter a public building and refuse to leave until they are served or their demands are met

slave state   a state that allowed slavery

Southern Christian Leadership Conference (SCLC)   an organization founded by Dr. Martin Luther King, Jr., to work for civil rights for African Americans

sovereignty   the idea of supreme power or source of authority

special-purpose district   a form of local government created for a single job or single group of tasks

states' rights   the belief that a state's interests should take precedence over the interests of the national government

stretch out   a textile mill practice requiring workers to tend more machines

strike   a work stoppage in protest over some grievance

Student Nonviolent Coordinating Committee (SNCC)   an organization founded in 1960 to coordinate and publicize sit-ins

subsidy   a grant of money from the government

suburbs   residential areas around cities

suffrage   the right to vote

supreme court   the highest-ranking court in the Georgia court system

syllabary   a group of symbols that stand for whole syllables

T

tariff   a tax on imported goods

temperance   the antialcohol movement

Thirteenth Amendment   an amendment to the U.S. Constitution, ratified in 1865, that made slavery illegal

trade   the voluntary exchange of goods and services among people and countries

trial court   the court that has original jurisdiction in the Georgia court system; includes superior courts, state courts, probate courts, juvenile courts, and magistrate courts

trial jury   a group of citizens who are charged with judging a person charged with a crime

tribe   a group of people who share a common ancestry, name, and way of living

trustee   a person who holds responsibility on behalf of others

V

vertical climate   climate that is influenced by elevation; the higher the elevation, the cooler the temperature

W

weather   the day-to-day conditions and changes in the atmosphere

wetland   a low-lying land area where water lies close to the surface creating sloughs, swamps, bogs, ponds, and freshwater marshes; a lowland that is influenced by tidal water flows

white supremacy   the belief that the white race is superior to any other race

INDEX

INDEX

Order Form
CRCT Test Prep

Clairmont Press

Phone: 1-800-874-8638   Fax: 1-800-874-9190   E-mail: gacrct@clairmontpress.com
1494 Bellflower Court   Lilburn, Georgia 30047

Ship to:

Name _____ Position

School/District

Street Address   (not PO Box)

City _____ State _____ Zip Code

Telephone

E-mail Address

Bill to:

Name _____ Position

School/District

Street Address or PO Box

City _____ State _____ Zip Code

Purchase Order Number

Item #	Quantity	Title/Description	Price	Total
978-1-56733-099-1		**6th Grade** CRCT Test Prep TEACHING THE GEORGIA PERFORMANCE STANDARDS		
978-1-56733-098-4		**7th Grade** CRCT Test Prep TEACHING THE GEORGIA PERFORMANCE STANDARDS		
978-1-56733-097-7		**8th Grade** CRCT Test Prep TEACHING THE GEORGIA PERFORMANCE STANDARDS		

* Shipping and handling charges:
• For orders of less than $500.00, add 10% for standard shipping and $5.95 for handling.
• For orders of $500.00 or more, add 10% for standard shipping and handling.

Subtotal	
Shipping and Handling*	
TOTAL	

You may charge this order to your VISA® or MasterCard®

Card type (please check one): ☐ MasterCard   ☐ VISA   Signature _____

Credit Card Number: ☐☐☐☐ ☐☐☐☐ ☐☐☐☐ ☐☐☐☐   Expiration Date: ☐☐/☐☐   CVV code on back of card ☐☐☐
                                                                M   M   Y   Y

Credit Card Billing Address: _____
Street   City   State   Zip

100+ Copies	$ 8.00 each
30-99 Copies	$ 9.00 each
20-29 Copies	$10.00 each
10-19 Copies	$11.00 each
5-9 Copies	$12.00 each

Minimum Order is 5 books. Above pricing applies to total number of books ordered (a combination of all grade levels) with a minimum of five (5) books.

TEACHERS: The answers to all questions and tests can be found at **www.clairmontpress.com**

Click on GA CRCT Test Prep and complete **registration** for the password. Passwords are e-mailed after approval.

080110

Order Form
CRCT Test Prep

Clairmont Press

Phone: 1-800-874-8638   Fax: 1-800-874-9190   E-mail: gacrct@clairmontpress.com
1494 Bellflower Court   Lilburn, Georgia 30047

Ship to:

Name _____ Position

School/District

Street Address   (not PO Box)

City _____ State _____ Zip Code

Telephone

E-mail Address

Bill to:

Name _____ Position

School/District

Street Address or PO Box

City _____ State _____ Zip Code

Purchase Order Number

Item #	Quantity	Title/Description	Price	Total
978-1-56733-099-1		**6th Grade** CRCT Test Prep TEACHING THE GEORGIA PERFORMANCE STANDARDS		
978-1-56733-098-4		**7th Grade** CRCT Test Prep TEACHING THE GEORGIA PERFORMANCE STANDARDS		
978-1-56733-097-7		**8th Grade** CRCT Test Prep TEACHING THE GEORGIA PERFORMANCE STANDARDS		
			Subtotal	
			Shipping and Handling*	
			TOTAL	

* Shipping and handling charges:
• For orders of less than $500.00, add 10% for standard shipping and $5.95 for handling.
• For orders of $500.00 or more, add 10% for standard shipping and handling.

You may charge this order to your VISA® or MasterCard®

Card type (please check one): ☐ MasterCard   ☐ VISA   Signature _____

Credit Card Number: ☐☐☐☐ ☐☐☐☐ ☐☐☐☐ ☐☐☐☐   Expiration Date: ☐☐/☐☐   CVV code on back of card ☐☐☐
M M Y Y

Credit Card Billing Address: _____
Street   City   State   Zip

100+ Copies	$ 8.00 each
30-99 Copies	$ 9.00 each
20-29 Copies	$10.00 each
10-19 Copies	$11.00 each
5-9 Copies	$12.00 each

Minimum Order is 5 books. Above pricing applies to total number of books ordered (a combination of all grade levels) with a minimum of five (5) books.

TEACHERS: The answers to all questions and tests can be found at **www.clairmontpress.com**

Click on GA CRCT Test Prep and complete **registration** for the password. Passwords are e-mailed after approval.

080110